UNDERSTANDING
PUBLIC POLICY

UNDERSTANDING PUBLIC POLICY

seventh edition

Thomas R. Dye
*McKenzie Professor of Government
and Public Policy
Florida State University*

Prentice Hall, Englewood Cliffs, New Jersey 07632

Library of Congress Cataloging-in-Publication Data

DYE, THOMAS R.

   Understanding public policy / Thomas R. Dye.—7th ed.
     p. cm.
   Includes bibliographical references and index.
     ISBN 0-13-933607-9
     1. United States—Social policy. 2. United States—Social
conditions—1960-1980. 3. United States—Politics and
government—20th century. I. Title.
HN65.D9 1992
361.6'1'0973—dc20   90-25132
                                        CIP

Acquisitions editor: Karen Horton
Editorial/production supervision
  and interior design: Mary Anne Shahidi
Photo research: Page Poore
Cover design: Bruce Kenselaar
Prepress buyer: Debra Kesar
Manufacturing buyer: Mary Ann Gloriande

Printed in the United States of America
10 9 8 7 6 5 4 3

ISBN 0-13-933607-9

Prentice-Hall International (UK) Limited, *London*
Prentice-Hall of Australia Pty. Limited, *Sydney*
Prentice-Hall Canada Inc., *Toronto*
Prentice-Hall Hispanoamericana, S.A., *Mexico*
Prentice-Hall of India Private Limited, *New Delhi*
Prentice-Hall of Japan, Inc., *Tokyo*
Simon & Schuster Asia Pte. Ltd., *Singapore*
Editora Prentice-Hall do Brasil, Ltda., *Rio de Janeiro*

CONTENTS

2

MODELS OF POLITICS
some help in thinking
about public policy   19

3

CIVIL RIGHTS
elite and mass interaction   47

4

CRIMINAL JUSTICE
rationality and irrationality
in public policy   81

5

HEALTH AND WELFARE
the search for a rational strategy   114

6

EDUCATION
the group struggle   161

7

ENVIRONMENTAL POLICY
externalities and interests   187

8

DEFENSE POLICY
strategies for serious games   209

9

PRIORITIES AND PRICE TAGS
incrementalism at work   241

10

TAX POLICY
battling the special interests   268

11

AMERICAN FEDERALISM
institutional arrangements
and public policy   293

12

INPUTS, OUTPUTS, AND BLACK BOXES
a systems analysis of state policies   312

13

THE POLICY-MAKING PROCESS
getting inside the system   327

14

POLICY EVALUATION
finding out what happens
after a law is passed   352

PREFACE

Policy analysis is concerned with "who gets what" in politics and, more importantly, "why" and "what difference it makes." We are concerned not only with *what* policies governments pursue but also *why* governments pursue the policies they do, and *what* the consequences of these policies are.

Political science, like other scientific disciplines, has developed a number of concepts and models to help describe and explain political life. These models are not really competitive in the sense that any one could be judged "best." Each focuses on separate elements of politics and each helps us to understand different things about political life.

We begin with a brief description of nine analytic models in political science and the potential contribution of each of them to the study of public policy. They are:

an institutional model	an incremental model
a process model	a game theory model
a group model	a public choice model
an elite model	a systems model
a rational model	

We then attempt to desribe and explain public policy by the use of these various analytic models. Readers are not only informed about public policy in a variety of key domestic policy areas but, more importantly, they are encouraged to utilize these conceptual models in political science to explain the causes and consequences of public policies in these areas. The policy areas studied are:

civil rights	budgeting and spending
criminal justice	taxation
health and welfare	national defense
education	state and local spending and services
environment	

Most public policies are a combination of rational planning, incrementalism, competition among groups, elite preferences, systemic forces, public choice, political processes, and institutional influences. Throughout this volume we employ these models, both singly and in combination, to describe and explain public policy. However, certain chapters rely more on one model than another.

Any of these policy areas might be studied by employing more than one model. Frequently our selection of a particular analytic model to study a specific policy area was based as much upon pedagogical considerations as anything else. We simply wanted to demonstrate how political scientists employ analytic models. Once readers are familiar with the nature and uses of analytic models in political science, they may find it interesting to explore the utility of models other than the ones selected by the author in the explanation of particular policy outcomes. For example, we use an elitist model to discuss civil rights policy, but the reader may wish to view civil rights policy from the perspective of group theory. We employ the language of game theory to discuss national defense policy, but the reader might enjoy reinterpreting defense policy in a systems model.

Each chapter concludes with a series of propositions, which are derived from one or more analytic models, and which attempt to summarize the policies discussed. The purpose of these summaries is to suggest the kinds of policy explanations that can be derived from analytic models and to tie the policy material back to one or another of our models.

In short, this volume is not only an introduction to the study of public policy but also an introduction to the models political scientists use to describe and explain political life.

I would like to thank the following reviewers for their helpful comments: Martin Kyre, Texas Tech University; Michael Mumper, Ohio University; and Dale Krane, University of Nebraska at Omaha.

THOMAS R. DYE
Florida State University

UNDERSTANDING PUBLIC POLICY

1

POLICY ANALYSIS

what governments do,
why they do it,
and what difference it makes

George Bush takes the oath of office as president of the United States. (AP/Wide World Photos)

POLICY ANALYSIS IN POLITICAL SCIENCE

This book is about public policy. It is concerned with what governments do, why they do it, and what difference it makes. It is also about political science and the ability of this academic discipline to describe, analyze, and explain public policy.

Definition.   Public policy is whatever governments choose to do or not to do.[1] Governments do many things. They regulate conflict within society; they organize society to carry on conflict with other societies; they distribute a great variety of symbolic rewards and material services to members of the society; and they extract money from society, most often in the form of taxes. Thus, public policies may regulate behavior, organize bureaucracies, distribute benefits, or extract taxes—or all these things at once.

Scope.   Governments in the United States directly allocate about 35 percent of the Gross National Product, the sum of all of the goods and services produced in the nation each year. About two-thirds of the governmental sector of the GNP is accounted for by the federal government itself; the remaining one-third is attributable to eighty thousand state, city, county, township, school district, and special district governments combined. Overall government employment in the United States comprises 16 percent of the nation's workforce.

Public policies may deal with a wide variety of substantive areas—defense, energy, environment, foreign affairs, education, welfare, police, highways, taxation, housing, social security, health, economic opportunity, urban development, inflation and recession, and so on. They may range from the vital to the trivial—from the allocation of tens of billions of dollars for a mobile missile system to the designation of an official national bird.

Political Science.   Public policy is not a new concern of political science: the earliest writings of political philosophers reveal an interest in the policies pursued by governments, the forces shaping these policies, and the impact of these policies on society. Yet the major focus of attention of political science has never really been on policies themselves, but rather on the institutions and structures of government and on the political behaviors and processes associated with policy making.

"Traditional" political science focused its attention primarily on the institutional structure and philosophical justification of government. This involved the study of constitutional arrangements, such as federalism, separation of power, and judicial review; powers and duties of official bodies such as Congress, president, and courts; intergovernmental relations; and

---

[1]See insert, "Defining Public Policy: Playing Word Games."

the organization and operation of legislative, executive, and judicial agencies. Traditional studies described the *institutions* in which public policy was formulated. But unfortunately the linkages between important institutional arrangements and the content of public policy were largely unexplored.

Modern "behavioral" political science focused its attention primarily on the processes and behaviors associated with government. This involved the study of the sociological and psychological bases of individual and group behavior; the determinants of voting and other political activities; the functioning of interest groups and political parties; and the description of various processes and behaviors in the legislative, executive, and judicial arenas. Although this approach described the *processes* by which public policy was determined, it did not deal directly with the linkages between various processes and behaviors and the content of public policy.

Policy Studies.   Today many political scientists have shifted their focus to *public policy*—to the *description and explanation of the causes and consequences of government activity.* This focus involves a description of the content of public policy; an analysis of the impact of social, economic, and political forces on the content of public policy; an inquiry into the effect of various institutional arrangements and political processes on public policy; and an evaluation of the consequences of public policies on society, in terms of both expected and unexpected consequences.

DEFINING PUBLIC POLICY: PLAYING WORD GAMES

This book discourages elaborate academic discussions of the definition of public policy—we say simply that public policy is whatever governments choose to do or not to do. Books, essays, and discussions of a "proper" definition of public policy have proven futile, even exasperating, and they often divert attention from the study of public policy itself. Moreover, even the most elaborate definitions of public policy, upon close examination, seem to boil down to the same thing. For example, political scientist David Easton defines public policy as "the authoritative allocation of values for the whole society"—but it turns out that only the government can "authoritatively" act on the "whole" society, and everything the government chooses to do or not to do results in the "allocation of values."

Political scientist Harold Lasswell and philosopher Abraham Kaplan define policy as "a projected program of goals, values, and practices," and political scientist Carl Friedrick says, "It is essential for the policy concept that there be a goal, objective, or purpose." These definitions imply a difference between specific governmental actions and an overall program of action toward a given goal. But the problem raised in insisting that government actions must have goals in order to be labeled "policy" is that we can never be sure whether or not a particular action has a goal, or if it does, what that goal is. Some people may assume that if a government chooses to do something there must be a goal, objective, or purpose, but all we can really observe is what governments choose to do or not to do. Realistically, our notion of public policy must include *all actions* of government, and not what governments or officials say they are going to do. We may wish that governments act in a "purposeful goal-oriented" fashion, but we know that all too frequently they do not.

Still another approach to defining public policy is to break down this general notion into various component parts. Political scientist Charles O. Jones asks that we consider the distinction among various proposals (specified means for achieving goals); programs (authorized means for achieving goals); decisions (specific actions taken to implement programs); and effects (the measurable impacts of programs). But again we have the problem of assuming that decisions, programs, goals, and effects are linked. Certainly in many policy areas we will see that the decisions of government have little to do with announced "programs," and neither are connected with national "goals." It may be unfortunate that our government does not function neatly to link goals, programs, decisions, and effects, but as a matter of fact, it does not.

Political scientists Heinz Eulau and Kenneth Prewitt supply still another definition of public policy: "Policy is defined as a 'standing decision' characterized by behavioral consistency and repetitiveness on the part of both those who make it and those who abide by it." Now certainly it would be a wonderful thing if government activities were characterized by "consistency and repetitiveness"; but it is doubtful that we would ever find "public policy" in government if we insist on these criteria. Much of what government does is inconsistent and nonrepetitive.

So we shall stick with our simple definition: *public policy is whatever governments choose to do or not to do.* Note that we are focusing not only on government action, but also on government inaction, that is, what government chooses *not* to do. We contend that government *in*action can have just as great an impact on society as government action.

See David Easton, *The Political System* (New York: Knopf, 1953), p. 129; Harold D. Lasswell and Abraham Kaplan, *Power and Society* (New Haven: Yale University Press, 1970), p. 71; Carl J. Friedrich, *Man and His Government* (New York: McGraw-Hill, 1963), p. 70; Charles O. Jones, *An Introduction to the Study of Public Policy* (Boston: Duxbury, 1977), p. 4; Heinz Eulau and Kenneth Prewitt, *Labyrinths of Democracy* (Indianapolis: Bobbs-Merrill, 1973), p. 465; and Hugh Heclo, "Policy Analysis," *British Journal of Political Science*, 2 (January 1972), p. 85.

WHY STUDY PUBLIC POLICY?

Why should political scientists devote greater attention to the study of public policy?

Scientific Understanding.   First of all, public policy can be studied for purely *scientific reasons:* understanding the causes and consequences of policy decisions improves our knowledge of society. Public policy can be viewed as a dependent variable, and we can ask what socioeconomic forces and political system characteristics operate to shape the content of policy. Alternatively, public policy can be viewed as an independent variable, and we can ask what impact public policy has on society and its political system. By asking such questions we can improve our understanding of the linkages between socioeconomic forces, political processes, and public policy. An understanding of these linkages contributes to the breadth, significance, reliability, and theoretical development of social science.

Problem Solving.   Public policy can also be studied for *professional reasons:* understanding the causes and consequences of public policy permits us to apply social science knowledge to the solution of practical problems. Factual knowledge is a prerequisite to prescribing for the ills of society. If certain ends are desired, then the question of what policies would best implement these ends is a factual question requiring scientific study. In other words, policy studies can produce professional advice, in terms of "if . . . then . . ." statements, about how to achieve desired goals.

Policy Recommendations.   Finally, public policy can be studied for *political purposes:* to ensure that the nation adopts the "right" policies to achieve the "right" goals. It is frequently argued that policial science should not be silent or impotent in the face of great social and political crises, and that political scientists have a moral obligatioɩ to advance specific public policies. An exclusive focus on institutions, processes, or behaviors is frequently looked upon as "dry," "irrelevant," and "amoral," because it does not direct attention to the really important policy questions facing American society. Policy studies can be undertaken not only for scientific and professional purposes but also to inform political discussion, advance the level of political awareness, and improve the quality of public policy. Of course, these are very subjective purposes—Americans do not always agree on what constitutes the "right" policies or the "right" goals—but we will assume that knowledge is preferable to ignorance, even in politics.

QUESTIONS IN POLICY ANALYSIS

What can we learn about public policy?

Description.   First of all, we can *describe* public policy—we can learn what government is doing (and not doing) in welfare, defense, education, civil rights, health, the environment, taxation, and so on. A factual basis of information about national policy is really an indispensable part of everyone's education. What does the Civil Rights Act of 1964 actually say about discrimination in employment? What did the Supreme Court rule in the *Bakke* case about affirmative action programs? What is the condition of the nation's social security program? What do the Medicaid and Medicare programs promise for the poor and the aged? What is the purpose of the MX missile, the B-2 bomber, or the Trident submarine? How much are we really spending on national defense and on social welfare? How much money are we paying in taxes? How much money does the federal government spend each year? These are examples of descriptive questions.

Causes.   Second, we can inquire about the *causes*, or determinants, of public policy. Why is public policy what it is? Why do governments do what they do? We might inquire about the effects of political institutions, processes, and behaviors on public policies. For example: Does it make any difference in tax and spending levels whether Democrats or Republicans control the presidency and Congress? What is the impact of interest group conflict on federal aid to education? What is the impact of lobbying by the special interests on efforts to reform the federal tax system? We can also inquire about the effects of social, economic, and cultural forces in shaping public policy. For example: What are the effects of changing public attitudes about race on civil rights policy? What are the effects of wars and recessions on government spending? What is the effect of an increasingly older population on the social security and Medicare programs? In scientific terms, when we study the *causes* of public policy, policies become the *dependent* variables, and their various political, social, economic, and cultural determinants become the *independent* variables.

Consequences.   Third, we can inquire about the *consequences*, or impacts, of public policy. What difference, if any, does public policy make in people's lives? For example: Does capital punishment help to deter crime? Are welfare programs a disincentive to work? Is busing an effective means of ending racial inequalities in education? Do liberal welfare benefits result in larger numbers of poor people? Does increased educational spending produce higher student achievement scores? In scientific terms, when we study the *consequences* of public policy, policies become the *independent* variables, and their political, social, economic, and cultural impacts on society become the *dependent variables.*

POLICY ANALYSIS AND POLICY ADVOCACY

It is important to distinguish *policy analysis* from *policy advocacy. Explaining* the causes and consequences of various policies is not equivalent to *prescribing* what policies governments ought to pursue. Learning *why* governments do what they do and what the consequences of their actions are is not the same as saying *what* governments ought to do or bringing about changes in what they do. Policy advocacy requires the skills of rhetoric, persuasion, organization, and activism. Policy analysis encourages scholars and students to attack critical policy issues with the tools of systematic inquiry. There is an implied assumption in policy analysis that developing scientific knowledge about the forces shaping public policy and the consequences of public policy is itself a socially relevant activity, and that such analysis is a prerequisite to prescription, advocacy, and activism.

Specifically, *public analysis* involves:

1. A *primary concern with explanation rather than prescription.* Policy recommendations—if they are made at all—are subordinate to description and explanation. There is an implicit judgment that understanding is a prerequisite to prescription, and that understanding is best achieved through careful analysis rather than rhetoric or polemics.

2. A *rigorous search for the causes and consequences of public policies.* This search involves the use of scientific standards of inference. Sophisticated quantitative techniques may be helpful in establishing valid inferences about causes and consequences, but they are not really essential.

3. An *effort to develop and test general propositions about the causes and consequences of public policy and to accumulate reliable research findings of general relevance.* The object is to develop general theories about public policy that are reliable and that apply to different governmental agencies and different policy areas. Policy analysts clearly prefer to develop explanations that fit more than one policy decision or case study—explanations that stand up over time in a variety of settings.

POLICY ANALYSIS IN ACTION: ACHIEVING EDUCATIONAL OPPORTUNITY

One of the more interesting examples of policy analysis over the years has been the social science research on equal educational opportunity and how to achieve it. "Educational opportunity" has been one of the most controversial topics in American politics, and social science has played an important role in policy making in this area. However, as we shall see, the more controversial the policy area, the more difficult it is to conduct policy research.

Early Research—the Coleman Report

The early landmark research on educational opportunity in America was sociologist James S. Coleman's *Equality of Educational Opportunity,* frequently referred to as the "Coleman Report."[2] The Coleman Report dealt primarily with the *consequences* of educational policy—specifically, the impact of schools on the aspiration and achievement levels of pupils. Although

---

[2]James S. Coleman, *Equality of Educational Opportunity* (Washington, D.C.: Government Printing Office, 1966).

Coleman's study was not without its critics,[3] it was nonetheless the first comprehensive analysis of the American public school system and included data on 600,000 children, 60,000 teachers, and 4,000 schools.

The results of Coleman's study undermined much of the conventional wisdom about the impact of public educational policies on student learning and achievement. Prior to the study, legislators, teachers, school administrators, school board members, and the general public assumed that factors such as the number of pupils in the classroom, the amount of money spent on each pupil, library and laboratory facilities, teachers' salaries, the quality of the curriculum, and other characteristics of the school affected the quality of education and educational opportunity. But systematic analysis revealed that these factors had *no* significant effect on student learning or achievement. Even the size of the class was found to be unrelated to learning, although educators had asserted the importance of this factor for decades. In short, the things that "everybody knew" about education turned out not to be so!

The only factors that were found to affect a student's learning to any significant degree were (1) family background and (2) the family background of classmates. Family background affected the child's verbal abilities and attitudes toward education, and these factors correlated very closely with scholastic achievement. Of secondary but considerable significance were the verbal abilities and attitudes toward education of the child's classmates. Peer-group influence had its greatest impact on children from lower-class families. Teaching excellence mattered very little to children from upper- and middle-class backgrounds; they learned well despite mediocre or poor teaching. Children from lower-class families were slightly more affected by teacher quality.

Reanalyzing Coleman's data for the U.S. Commission on Civil Rights, Thomas F. Pettigrew and others found that black students attending predominantly black schools had lower achievement scores and lower levels of aspiration than black students *with comparable family backgrounds* who attended predominantly white schools.[4] When black students attending predominantly white schools were compared with black students attending predominantly black schools, the average difference in levels of achievement amounted to

---

[3]For reviews of the Coleman Report, see Robert A. Dentler, "Equality of Educational Opportunity: A Special Review," *The Urban Review* (December 1966); Christopher Jenks, "Education: The Racial Gap," *The New Republic* (October 1, 1966); James K. Kent, "The Coleman Report: Opening Pandora's Box," *Phi Delta Kappan* (January 1968); James S. Coleman, "Educational Dilemmas: Equal Schools or Equal Students," *The Public Interest* (Summer 1966); James S. Coleman, "Toward Open Schools," *The Public Interest* (Fall 1967); and a special issue devoted to educational opportunity of *Harvard Educational Review,* vol. 38 (Winter 1968).

[4]U.S. Commission on Civil Rights, *Racial Isolation in the Public Schools,* 2 vols. (Washington, D.C.: Government Printing Office, 1967).

more than *two grade levels*. On the other hand, achievement levels of white students in classes nearly half-black in composition were *not* any lower than those of white students in all-white schools. Finally, special programs to raise achievement levels in predominantly black schools were found to have no lasting effect.

Policy Implications

The Coleman Report made no policy recommendations. But, like a great deal of policy research, policy recommendations were inferred from its conclusions. First of all, if the Coleman Report was correct, it seemed pointless to simply pour more money into the existing system of public education—raising per pupil expenditures, increasing teachers' salaries, lowering the number of pupils per classroom, providing better libraries and laboratories, adding educational frills, or adopting any specific curricular innovations. These policies were found to have no significant impact on learning.

The findings of the Coleman Report undermined the logic of Title I of the Elementary and Secondary Education Act of 1965 (see Chapter 7). This piece of congressional legislation authorized large amounts of federal assistance each year for "poverty impacted" schools. The purpose of this program was to remedy learning problems of disadvantaged children by increasing spending for special remedial programs. But the Coleman Report implied that compensatory programs have little educational value. They may have symbolic value for ghetto residents, or political value for officeholders who seek to establish an image of concern for the underprivileged, but they are of little educational value for children.

The reaction of professional educators was largely one of silence. Perhaps they hoped the Coleman Report would disappear into history without significantly affecting the longstanding assumptions about the importance of money, facilities, classroom size, teacher training, and curricula. Perhaps they hoped that subsequent research would refute Coleman's findings. Daniel Moynihan writes:

> The whole rationale of American public education came very near to crashing down, and would have done so had there not been a seemingly general agreement to act as if the report had not occurred. But it had, and public education will not now be the same. The relations between resource input and educational output, which all school systems, all legislatures, all executives have accepted as given, appear not to be given at all. At very least what has heretofore been taken for granted must henceforth be proved.[5]

[5]Daniel P. Moynihan, *Maximum Feasible Misunderstanding* (New York: Free Press, 1969), p. 195.

The U.S. Commission on Civil Rights used the Coleman Report to buttress its policy proposals to end racial imbalance in public schools. Inasmuch as money, facilities, and compensatory programs have little effect on student learning, and inasmuch as the socioeconomic background of the student's *classmates* does affect his or her learning, it seemed reasonable to argue that the assignment of lower-class black students to predominantly middle-class white schools would be the only way to improve educational opportunities for ghetto children. Moreover, because the findings indicated that the achievement levels of middle-class white students were unaffected by blacks in the classroom (as long as blacks were less than a majority), the commission concluded that assigning ghetto blacks to predominantly white schools would not adversely affect the learning of white pupils. Hence, the Commission called for an end to neighborhood schools and for the *busing* of black and white children to racially balanced schools.

Research on Busing

However, in 1972, Harvard sociologist David Armor reviewed the available evidence of the effect of busing on achievement levels of black students.[6] His conclusions: busing black students out of their neighborhoods to predominantly white schools did *not* improve their performance relative to that of white students, even after three or four years of integrated education. His interpretation of the impact of busing on the achievement levels of black students indicated that black students were not being helped "in any significant way" by busing, and he urged consideration of the question of whether psychological harm was being done to black students by placing them in a situation where the achievement gap was so great. Note that Armor was not contradicting the Coleman Report. Coleman was observing black children who were attending predominantly white schools not as a result of deliberate government action, but rather within the previously existing pattern of "neighborhood schools." In contrast, Armor was observing black children who had been deliberately reassigned to integrated schools by government action.

The policy implications of Armor's work appeared to support opponents of government-mandated racial balancing. Other social scientists disputed Armor's review of the relevant research findings, including Thomas F. Pettigrew, who originally used the Coleman data in support of busing.[7] They argued that Armor's work undermined progress toward an integrated society and reinforced racism. But Armor replied that social science findings

[6] David J. Armor, "The Evidence on Busing," *The Public Interest*, no. 28 (Summer 1972), 90–126.

[7] Thomas F. Pettigrew et al., "Busing: A Review of 'The Evidence,'" *The Public Interest*, no. 31 (Spring 1973), 88–113.

cannot be used only when they fit the political beliefs of social scientists and ignored when their policy implications are painful.[8]

Busing and "White Flight"

Coleman himself reentered the fray in 1975 with the publication of a new report, *Trends in School Desegregation.*[9] This "Second Coleman Report" appeared to counter earlier implications about busing as a means to achieve equality of educational opportunity. In examining changes in segregation over time in twenty-two large cities and forty-six medium-sized cities, Coleman found that an increase in desegregation was associated with a loss of white pupils—"white flight." This white response to desegregation was greatest in large cities with large proportions of black school pupils, which were surrounded by predominantly white, independent, suburban school districts. Coleman predicted that the long-run effect of white-pupil loss in these cities would offset government efforts to desegregate public schools and contribute to *greater* rather than less racial isolation. As Coleman explained:

> There are numerous examples of government policy in which the result of the interaction between policy and response is precisely the opposite of the result intended by those who initiated the policy. It is especially important in the case of school desegregation to examine this interaction, because many of the actions taken by individuals, and some of those taken by their local government bodies, have precisely the opposite effect to that intended by the federal government. The most obvious such individual action, of course, is a move of residences to flee school integration.[10]

Coleman had not lost his earlier belief in the achievement benefits of school integration. But he believed that large-scale busing had so many

---

[8]David J. Armor, "The Double Double Standard," *The Public Interest*, no. 31 (Spring 1973), 119–31. Still another reaction to the Coleman Report is found in the work of Harvard educator Christopher Jenks, *Inequality: A Reassessment of the Effect of Family and Schooling in America* (New York: Basic Books, 1972). Jenks reanalyzed Coleman's data and conducted additional research on the impact of schooling on economic success. He found that school quality has little effect on an individual's subsequent success in earning income. He concluded, therefore, that no amount of educational reform would ever bring about economic equality. Jenks assumed that *absolute equality* of income is the goal of society, not merely *equality of opportunity* to achieve economic success. Because the schools cannot ensure that everyone ends up with the same income, Jenks concludes that nothing short of a radical redistribution of income (steeply progressive taxes and laws preventing individuals from earning more than others) will bring about true equality in America. Attempts to improve the educational system, therefore, are a waste of time and effort. Thus, the Coleman findings have been used to buttress *radical* arguments about the ineffectiveness of *liberal* reforms.

[9]James S. Coleman et al., *Trends in School Desegregation 1968–1973* (Washington, D.C.: Urban Institute, 1975).

[10]Ibid., p. 2.

negative consequences, including white flight from the cities, that busing was self-defeating as a means of achieving equal educational opportunity.

Critics of the notion of "white flight" argue that there are many reasons besides desegregation which encourage white migration out of central cities.[11] Many before and after studies of black students bused to majority-white middle-class schools report significant gains by the black students in verbal and mathematical skills over several years. And almost all researchers report that desegregation has little, if any, effect on the achievement levels of white students.[12] There is very little racial interaction in desegregated schools except in supervised activities such as sports, band, and cheerleading.

Educational Reform: What Works?

Early educational policy analysis, especially Coleman's research in the 1960s and 1970s, documented the *in*effectiveness of many policy alternatives. Spending more money on the existing educational system was unproductive: as federal aid to education increased during the 1970s, student achievement test scores declined. Racial imbalances in many large city school systems increased despite busing, and the achievement scores of inner city black pupils failed to improve. But social science can take little comfort from predicting what does *not* work. Social science has a societal responsibility to search for policies that do work.

In recent years, spurred on by evidence that American students perform poorly in comparison with students of other advanced industrial nations,[13] social scientists as well as policy makers throughout the United States sought to identify policy alternatives that could improve the educational achievement levels of pupils (see Chapter 7). Again, sociologist James S. Coleman and his associates produced the most influential analysis of school factors that affected achievement levels.

While Coleman's early research indicated that nearly all differences in student achievement levels are attributable to home and peer group influences and very little to differences in public schools, Coleman remained puzzled by the consistently higher achievement scores of pupils in Catholic schools. Indeed, Coleman documented the fact that overall differences in verbal and mathematical achievement levels between tenth-grade students in Catholic schools and public schools was over two full grade levels.[14] But

[11]See Edward J. Hayes, *Busing and Desegregation: The Real Truth* (Springfield, Mass.: Charles C. Thomas, 1981).

[12]See Nicolaus Mills, ed., *The Great School Bus Controversy* (New York: Teachers College Press, 1973); and Gary Orfield, *Must We Bus?* (Washington, D.C.: Brookings Institution, 1978).

[13]National Commission on Excellence in Education, *A Nation at Risk* (Washington, D.C.: Government Printing Office, 1983).

[14]James S. Coleman, Thomas Hoffer, and Sally Kilgore, *High School Achievement* (New York: Basic Books, 1982).

the question remained whether this difference was a product of different educational policies and practices in Catholic and public schools, or differences in the types of pupils and families who chose to send their children to Catholic schools. Coleman was able to control statistically for differences in race, religion, socioeconomic status, family type, and other student background characteristics, by comparing achievement levels of Catholic and public school students with the same backgrounds. It turned out that students who attended Catholic schools scored over one full grade level higher than public school students *from comparable family backgrounds*. In short, while family background is most important, schools can and do make a difference in educational achievement. Yet the "Catholic school effect" was *not* a result of smaller classrooms, or higher teachers' salaries, or better facilities; on the contrary, Catholic schools scored poorly on these traditional educational policy measures.

Many public school educators were angered by the implication that Catholic schools produced better results than public schools. Some fell back on the old argument of "progressive" education that verbal and mathematic achievement scores are not really good measures of educational outcomes. Others argued that Catholic schools were "creaming" off the better students and leaving poorer students in the public schools. Still others repeated the myth that Catholic schools expelled problem children that public schools had to accept. (Actually Catholic schools receive many problem and delinquent pupils from families who send them there because "they need discipline.")

Catholic school students not only performed better on achievement tests than students from comparable backgrounds in public schools, Catholic school students also learned more over time. Coleman and his associates followed up on their earlier study of tenth graders by testing these same pupils in the twelfth grade. Catholic school students *raised* their scores significantly more than public school students over these two years. The greatest gains in achievement in Catholic schools occurred among students from disadvantaged backgrounds: blacks, Hispanics, and children of parents with low education levels. Moreover, the dropout rate for public school students in Coleman's study for this two-year period was 14.3 percent; in Catholic schools it was only 3.4 percent. And the lower dropout rate for Catholic schools occurred among students of all family backgrounds.

Why do Catholic schools work better than public schools? Coleman himself attributed the different results of Catholic and public schools to "social capital"—strong relationships within the family and between the family and the school. The families of Catholic school pupils deliberately *chose* to send their children to Catholic schools. When the school is perceived by the student as an extension of the family, or in cases where no strong family ties exist and the school is a substitute for the family, students perform well.

Agreement among family, pupil, classmates, and teacher on values and norms produces a high expectation for achievement and an orderly and disciplined learning environment. These factors help explain why students from comparable family backgrounds perform better in Catholic schools than in public schools.

Reforming Public Schools

Thus, social science research indicates that children's educational performance improves when the school is perceived as an extension or substitute for the family. The family act of *choosing* a school for the child, rather than having the child assigned to a school by government authorities, helps to establish the linkage between family and school.

What are the implications of this research for public policy? The research provides a rationale for reforming education to encourage parental choice of schools. Some reformers use the research to support the use of educational vouchers given to parents to spend at any school they choose, public or private. The state would redeem the vouchers submitted by each school in amounts equivalent to the costs of educating each child. Schools would be encouraged to compete for students since educational funds would flow to schools on the basis of enrollment. Competition would encourage magnet schools to allow freedom for principals and teachers to determine goals, curriculum, discipline, and structure within their schools, and to develop programs that appeal to parents, their "customers." The "best" schools would have excess demand and might have to turn pupils away; other schools would have to improve themselves or close.

Alternatively, a parental choice system might be limited to public schools. This would be a less radical reform, but it would still encourage parental involvement in education and competition among schools. Several states and school districts have already experimented with choice plans: parents choose a public school for their children and state educational funds flow to the schools on the basis of enrollment. (See Chapter 7.)

However, not many in the public educational establishment—school district administrators, state education officials, colleges of education, teachers' unions—are prepared to support these reforms. Parental choice threatens the traditional power of educators to assign pupils, determine curricula, establish goals, and monitor student progress, with only minimal parental involvement.

Policy Analysis and Political Conflict

The point of this brief discussion is that policy analysis sometimes produces unexpected and even embarrassing findings, that public policies do not always work as intended, and that different political interests will interpret their findings of policy research differently—accepting, rejecting, or using these findings as they fit their own purposes.

POLICY ANALYSIS AND THE QUEST
FOR "SOLUTIONS" TO AMERICA'S PROBLEMS

It is questionable that policy analysis can ever provide "solutions" to America's problems. War, ignorance, crime, poor health, poverty, racial cleavage, inequality, poor housing, pollution, congestion, and unhappy lives have afflicted people and societies for a long time. Of course, this is no excuse for failing to work toward a society free of these maladies. But our striving for a better society should be tempered with the realization that "solutions" to these problems may be very difficult to find. There are many reasons for tempering our enthusiasm for policy analysis, some of which are illustrated in the battle over educational policy.

Limits on Government Power. First of all, it is easy to exaggerate the importance, both for good and for ill, of the policies of governments. It is not clear that government policies, however ingenious, could cure all or even most of society's ills. Governments are constrained by many powerful environmental forces—wealth, technology, patterns of family life, class structure, child-rearing practices, religious beliefs, and so on. These forces are not easily managed by governments, nor could they be controlled even if it seemed desirable to do so. In the final chapter of this volume we will examine policy impacts, but it is safe to say here that some of society's problems are very intractable. For example, it may be that the *only* way to ensure equality of opportunity is to remove children from disadvantaged family backgrounds at a very early age, perhaps before they are six months old. The weight of social science evidence suggests that the potential for achievement may be determined at a very young age. However, a policy of removing children from their family environment at such an early age runs contrary to our deepest feelings about family attachments. The forcible removal of children from their mothers is "unthinkable" as a governmental policy. So it may turn out that we never really provide equality of opportunity because cultural forces prevent us from pursuing an effective policy.

Disagreement Over the "Problem." Second, policy analysis cannot offer "solutions" to problems when there is no general agreement on what the problems are. Coleman's research assumed that raising achievement levels (measures of verbal and quantitative abilities) and raising aspiration levels (the desire to achieve by society's standards) were the "problems" to which our efforts should be directed. But others argue that racial segregation in the schools is constitutionally impermissible, whether or not integration improves the achievement levels of students. In other words, there is no real agreement on what societal values should be implemented in educational policy. Policy analysis is not capable of resolving value conflicts. At best it can advise on how to achieve certain outcomes, after these outcomes have been agreed upon as valuable; it cannot determine what is truly valuable for society.

Subjectivity in Interpretation.   Third, policy analysis deals with very subjective topics and must rely upon interpretation of results. Professional researchers frequently interpret the results of their analyses differently. Social science research cannot be "value-free." Even the selection of the topic for research is affected by one's values about what is important in society and worthy of attention. Years ago, sociologist Louis Wirth observed:

> Since every assertion of a "fact" and the social world touches the interests of some individual or group, one cannot even call attention to the existence of certain "facts" without courting the objections of those whose very *raison d'être* in society rests upon a divergent interpretation of the "factual" situation.[15]

Limitations on Design of Human Research.   Another set of problems in systematic policy analysis centers around inherent limitations in the design of social science research. It is not really possible to conduct some forms of controlled experiments on human beings. For example, researchers cannot order middle-class white children to go to ghetto schools for several years just to see if it has an adverse impact on their achievement levels. Instead, social researchers must find situations in which educational deprivation has been produced "naturally" in order to make the necessary observations about the causes of such deprivation. Because we cannot control all the factors that go into a real-world situation, it is difficult to pinpoint precisely what it is that causes educational achievement or nonachievement. Moreover, even where some experimentation is permitted, human beings frequently modify their behavior simply because they know they are being observed in an experimental situation. For example, in educational research it frequently turns out that children perform well under *any* new teaching method or curricular innovation. It is difficult to know whether the improvements observed are a product of the new teaching method or curricular improvement or merely a product of the experimental situation. Finally, it should be noted that the people doing policy research are frequently program administrators who are interested in proving the positive results of their programs. It is important to separate research from policy implementation, but this is a difficult thing to do.

---

[15]Louis Wirth, Preface to Karl Mannheim, *Ideology and Utopia: An Introduction to the Sociology of Knowledge* (New York: Harcourt Brace Jovanovich, 1936).

Complexity of Human Behavior. Perhaps the most serious reservation about policy analysis is the fact that social problems are so complex that social scientists are unable to make accurate predictions about the impact of proposed policies. *Social scientists simply do not know enough about individual and group behavior to be able to give reliable advice to policy makers.* Occasionally policy makers turn to social scientists for "solutions," but social scientists do not have any "solutions." Most of society's problems are shaped by so many variables that a simple explanation of them, or remedy for them, is rarely possible. A detailed understanding of such a complex system as human society is beyond our present capabilities. The fact that social scientists give so many contradictory recommendations is an indication of the absence of reliable scientific knowledge about social problems. Although some scholars argue that no advice is better than contradictory or inaccurate advice, policy makers still must make decisions, and it is probably better that they act in the light of whatever little knowledge social science can provide than that they act in the absence of any knowledge at all. Even if social scientists cannot predict the impact of future policies, they can at least attempt to measure the impact of current and past public policies and make this knowledge available to decision makers.

POLICY ANALYSIS AS ART AND CRAFT

Understanding public policy is both an art and a craft. It is an art because it requires insight, creativity, and imagination in identifying societal problems and describing them, in devising public policies that might alleviate them, and then, in finding out whether these policies end up making things better or worse. It is a craft because these tasks usually require some knowledge of economics, political science, public administration, sociology, law, and statistics. Policy analysis is really an applied subfield of all these traditional academic disciplines.

We doubt that there is any "model of choice" in policy analysis—that is, a single model or method that is preferable to all others and that consistently renders the best solutions to public problems.

Instead we are in agreement with political scientist Aaron Wildavsky, who wrote:

> Policy analysis is one activity for which there can be no fixed program, for policy analysis is synonymous with creativity, which may be stimulated by theory and sharpened by practice, which can be learned but not taught.[16]

Wildavsky goes on to warn students that "solutions" to great public questions are not to be expected.

[16]Aaron Wildavsky, *Speaking Truth to Power* (New York: John Wiley, 1979), p. 3.

In large part, it must be admitted, knowledge is negative. It tells us what we cannot do, where we cannot go, wherein we have been wrong, but not necessarily how to correct these errors. After all, if current efforts were judged wholly satisfactory, there would be little need for analysis and less for analysts.[17]

There is no one model of choice to be found in this book, but if anyone wants to begin a debate about different ways of understanding public policy, this book is a good place to begin.

BIBLIOGRAPHY

ANDERSON, JAMES E., DAVID W. BRADY, and CHARLES BULLOCK. *Public Policy and Politics in America.* Boston: Duxbury, 1978.

COCHRAN, CLARKE E., et al. *American Public Policy: An Introduction.* 3rd ed. New York: St. Martin's, 1990.

DYE, THOMAS R. *Policy Analysis: What Governments Do, Why They Do It, What Difference It Makes.* University, Ala.: University of Alabama Press, 1976.

LERNER, DANIEL, and HAROLD D. LASSWELL, eds. *The Policy Sciences.* Stanford, Calif.: Stanford University Press, 1960.

STOKEY, EDITH and RICHARD ZECKHAUSER. *A Primer for Policy Analysis.* New York: Norton, 1978.

WILDAVSKY, AARON. *Speaking Truth to Power.* New York: John Wiley, 1979.

[17]Ibid., p. 401.

2

MODELS OF POLITICS
some help in thinking
about public policy

Public policy is authoritatively determined, implemented, and enforced by government institutions. (AP/Wide World Photos)

MODELS FOR POLICY ANALYSIS

A model is a simplified representation of some aspect of the real world. It may be an actual physical representation—a model airplane, for example, or the table-top buildings that urban planners use to show how things will look when proposed projects are completed. Or a model may be a diagram—a road map, for example, or a flow chart that political scientists use to show how a bill becomes a law.

Uses of Models. The models we shall use in studying policy are *conceptual models*. These are word models that try to:

1. simplify and clarify our thinking about politics and public policy;
2. identify important aspects of policy problems;
3. help us to communicate with each other by focusing on essential features of political life;
4. direct our efforts to understand public policy better by suggesting what is important and what is unimportant; and
5. suggest explanations for public policy and predict its consequences.

Selected Policy Models. Over the years, political science, like other scientific disciplines, has developed a number of models to help us understand political life. Throughout this volume we will try to see whether these models have any utility in the study of public policy. Specifically we want to examine public policy from the perspective of the following models:

> institutional model
> process model
> group model
> elite model
> rational model
> incremental model
> game theory model
> public choice model
> systems model

Each of these terms identifies a major conceptual model that can be found in the literature of political science. None of these models was derived especially to study public policy, yet each offers a separate way of thinking about policy and even suggests some of the general causes and consequences of public policy.

These models are not competitive in the sense that any one of them could be judged "best." Each one provides a separate focus on political life, and each can help us to understand different things about public policy.

Although some policies appear at first glance to lend themselves to explanation by one particular model, most policies are a combination of rational planning, incrementalism, interest group activity, elite preferences, systemic forces, game-playing, public choice, political processes, and institutional influences. In later chapters these models will be employed, singularly and in combination, to describe and explain specific policies. Following is a brief description of each model, with particular attention to the separate ways in which public policy can be viewed.

INSTITUTIONALISM: POLICY AS INSTITUTIONAL OUTPUT

Governmental institutions have long been a central focus of political science. Traditionally, political science has been defined as the study of governmental institutions. Political activities generally center around particular government institutions—Congress, the presidency, courts, states, municipalities, political parties, and so on. Public policy is authoritatively determined, implemented, and enforced by these institutions.

The relationship between public policy and governmental institutions is very close. Strictly speaking, a policy does not becomes a *public* policy until it is adopted, implemented, and enforced by some governmental institution. Governmental institutions give public policy three distinctive characteristics. First of all, government lends *legitimacy* to policies. Governmental policies are generally regarded as legal obligations that command the loyalty of citizens. People may regard the policies of other groups and associations in society—corporations, churches, professional organizations, civic associations, and so forth—as important and even binding. But only government policies involve legal obligations. Second, government policies involve *universality*. Only government policies extend to all people in a society; the policies of other groups or organizations only reach a part of the society. Finally, government monopolizes *coercion* in society—only government can legitimately imprison violators of its policies. The sanctions that can be imposed by other groups or organizations in society are more limited. It is precisely this ability of government to command the loyalty of all its citizens, to enact policies governing the whole society, and to monopolize the legitimate use of force that encourages individuals and groups to work for enactment of their preferences into policy.

Traditionally, the institutional approach in political science did *not* devote much attention to the linkages between the structure of governmental institutions and the content of public policy. Instead, institutional studies usually described specific governmental institutions—their structures, organization, duties, and functions—without systematically inquiring about the impact of institutional characteristics on policy outputs. Constitutional and legal arrangements were described in detail, as were the myriad govern-

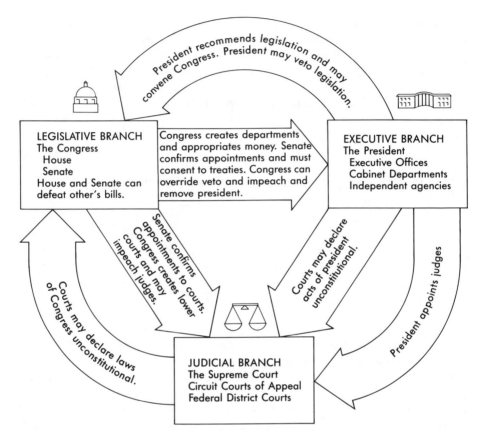

FIGURE 2-1   An Institutional Model: Constitutional Checks and Balances.

ment offices and agencies at the federal, state, and local level. (See Figure 2–1 for an organizational description of the federal government.) However, the linkage between institutional arrangements and policy remained largely unexamined.

Despite the narrow focus of early institutional studies in political science, the institutional approach is not necessarily an unproductive one. Governmental institutions are really structured patterns of behavior of individuals and groups. By "structured" we mean that these patterns of behavior tend to persist over time. These stable patterns of individual and group behavior may affect the content of public policy. Institutions may be so structured as to facilitate certain policy outcomes and to obstruct other policy outcomes. They may give advantage to certain interests in society and withhold advantage from other interests. Certain individuals and groups may enjoy greater access to government power under one set of structural characteristics than under another set. In short, the structure of governmental institutions may have important policy consequences.

INSTITUTIONALISM: APPLYING THE MODEL

Governmental institutions and organizations are mentioned throughout this book. But in Chapter 11, "American Federalism: Institutional Arrangements and Public Policy," we shall examine some of the problems of American federalism—the distribution of money and power between federal, state, and local governments.

The institutional approach need not be narrow or descriptive. We can ask what relationships exist between institutional arrangements and the content of public policy, and we can investigate these relationships in a comparative, systematic fashion. For example, in the area of urban affairs we can ask: Are the policies of the federal government more responsive to popular preferences than the policies of state or local governments? How does the division of responsibility among federal, state, and local governments affect the content of public policy? These questions can be dealt with systematically and involve a focus on institutional arrangements.

It is important to remember that the impact of institutional arrangements on public policy is an empirical question that deserves investigation. Too frequently, enthusiastic reformers have asserted that a particular change in institutional structure would bring about changes in public policy without investigating the true relationship between structure and policy. They have fallen into the trap of *assuming* that institutional changes will bring about policy changes. We must be cautious in our assessment of the impact of structure on policy. We may discover that *both* structure and policy are largely determined by social or economic forces, and that tinkering with institutional arrangements will have little independent impact on public policy if underlying forces remain constant.

PROCESS: POLICY AS POLITICAL ACTIVITY

Political processes and behaviors have been a central focus of political science for several decades. Modern "behavioral" political science since World War II has studied the activities of voters, interest groups, legislators, presidents, bureaucrats, judges, and other political actors. One of the main purposes has been to discover identifiable patterns of activities—or "processes." Recently some political scientists have tried to group various activities according to their relationship with public policy. The result is a set of *policy processes* which usually follow this general outline:

Identifying Problems	Demands are expressed for government action.
Formulating Policy Proposals	Agenda is set for public discussion. Development of program proposals to resolve problem.

Legitimating Policies	Selecting a proposal.
	Building political support for it.
	Enacting it as a law.
Implementing Policies	Organizing bureaucracies.
	Providing payments or services.
	Levying taxes.
Evaluating Policies	Studying programs.
	Reporting "outputs" of government programs.
	Evaluating "impacts" of programs on target and nontarget groups in society.
	Suggesting changes and adjustments.

In short, one can view the policy process as a series of political activities—problem identification, formulation, legitimation, implementation, and evaluation. A popular example of the process approach is shown in Table 2–1.

It has been argued that *political scientists* must limit their studies of public policy to these processes, and only these processes. According to political scientist Charles O. Jones:

> I maintain that the special purview of the political scientist is the political process and how it works. His or her interest in the substance of problems and policies, therefore, is in how it interacts with process, not necessarily in the substance itself. . . . this also suggests that my remedies for the social system tend to be of the process variety—more access for more interest, providing for criticism and opposition, publicizing decisions, and how they are made.[1]

This argument allows students of political science to study *how* decisions are made, and perhaps even how they *should* be made. But it does not permit students of political science to comment on the substance of public policy—who gets what and why. Books organized around the process theme have sections on identifying problems, formulating proposals, legitimating policies, and so on. It is not the *content* of public policy that is to be studied, but rather the *processes* by which public policy is developed, implemented, and changed.

Despite the narrow focus of the process model, it is still useful in helping us to understand the various activities involved in policy making. We want to keep in mind that *policy making* involves agenda setting (capturing the attention of policy makers); formulating proposals (devising and selecting policy options); legitimating policy (developing political support, winning congressional, presidential, or court approval); implementing policy (creating bureaucracies, spending money, enforcing laws); and evaluating policy (finding out whether policies work, whether they are popular).

Indeed, it may even be the case that the way policies are made affects

---

[1]Charles O. Jones, *An Introduction to the Study of Public Policy,* 2nd ed. (Boston: Duxbury, 1978), p. 6.

TABLE 2-1   The Policy Process—A Framework for Analysis

FUNCTIONAL ACTIVITIES	CATEGORIZED IN GOVERNMENT	AND AS SYSTEMS	WITH OUTPUT
Perception Definition Aggregation Organization Representation	Problems to Government	Problem Identification	Problem to Demand
Formulation Legitimation Appropriation	Action in Government	Program Development	Proposal to Budgeted Program
Organization Interpretation Application	Government to Problem	Program Implementation	Varies (service, payments, facilities, controls, etc.)
Specification Measurement Analysis	Program to Government	Program Evaluation	Varies (justification, recommendation, etc.)
Resolution/ Termination	Problem Resolution or Change	Program Termination	Solution or Change

Source: Charles O. Jones. *An Introduction to the Study of Public Policy,* 2nd ed. (Boston: Duxbury, 1978) p. 12. Copyright © 1977 by Wadsworth Publishing Co., Inc. Reprinted by permission of the publisher, Brooks/Cole Publishing Co., Pacific Grove, CA 93950.

the content of public policy and vice versa. At least this is a question that deserves attention. But again, just as we warned readers in our discussion of the institutional model: we do not want to fall into the trap of *assuming* that a change in the process of policy making will always bring about changes in the content of policy. It may turn out that social, economic, or technological constraints on policy makers are so great that it makes little or no difference in the content of policy whether the process of policy making is open or closed, competitive or noncompetitive, pluralist or elitist, or whatever. Political scientists are fond of discussing how a bill becomes a law, and even how various interests succeed in winning battles over policy questions. But changing either the formal or informal processes of decision making may or may not change the content of public policy.

We all may prefer to live in a political system where everyone has an equal voice in policy making, where many separate interests put forward solutions to public problems, where discussion, debate, and decision are open and accessible to all, where policy choices are made democratically, where implementation is reasonable, fair, and compassionate. But merely because we prefer such a political system does not necessarily mean that such a system would produce significantly different policies in national defense, education, welfare, health, or criminal justice. The linkages between *process* and *content* must still be investigated.

PROCESSES: APPLYING THE MODEL

Political processes and behaviors are considered in each of the policy areas studied in this book. Additional commentary on the impact of political activity on public policy is found in Chapter 13, "The Policy-Making Process: Getting Inside the System."

GROUP THEORY: POLICY AS GROUP EQUILIBRIUM

Group theory begins with the proposition that interaction among groups is the central fact of politics.[2] Individuals with common interests band together formally or informally to press their demands upon government. According to political scientist David Truman, an interest group is "a shared-attitude group that makes certain claims upon other groups in the society"; such a group becomes political "if and when it makes a claim through or upon any of the institutions of government."[3] Individuals are important in politics only when they act as part of, or on behalf of, group interests. The group becomes the essential bridge between the individual and the government. Politics is really the struggle among groups to influence public policy. The task of the political system is to *manage group conflict* by (1) establishing rules of the game in the group struggle, (2) arranging compromises and balancing interests, (3) enacting compromises in the form of public policy, and (4) enforcing these compromises.

According to group theorists, public policy at any given time is the equilibrium reached in the group struggle (see Figure 2–2). This equilibrium is determined by the relative influence of interest groups. Changes in the relative influence of any interest groups can be expected to result in changes in public policy; policy will move in the direction desired by the groups gaining in influence and away from the desires of groups losing influence. Political scientist Earl Latham described public policy from the group theory viewpoint as follows:

> What may be called public policy is actually the equilibrium reached in the group struggle at any given moment, and it represents a balance which the contending factions or groups constantly strive to tip in their favor. . . . The legislature referees the group struggle, ratifies the victories of the successful coalition, and records the terms of the surrenders, compromises, and conquests in the form of statutes.[4]

[2]The classic statement on group theory is David B. Truman, *The Governmental Process* (New York: Knopf, 1951).

[3]Ibid., p. 37.

[4]Earl Latham, "The Group Basis of Politics," in *Political Behavior*, ed. Heinz Eulau, Samuel J. Eldersveld, and Morris Janowitz (New York: Free Press, 1956), p. 239.

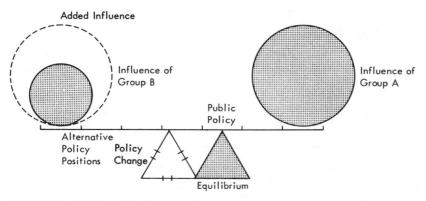

FIGURE 2-2 The Group Model.

The influence of groups is determined by their numbers, wealth, organizational strength, leadership, access to decision makers, and internal cohesion.

Group theory purports to describe all meaningful political activity in terms of the group struggle. Policy makers are viewed as constantly responding to group pressures—bargaining, negotiating, and compromising among competing demands of influential groups. Politicians attempt to form a majority coalition of groups. In so doing, they have some latitude in determining what groups are to be included in the majority coalition. The larger the constituency of the politician, the greater the number of diverse interests and the greater his or her latitude in selecting the groups to form a majority coalition. Thus, members of the House have less flexibility than senators, who have larger and generally more diverse constituencies; and the president has more flexibility than members of Congress and senators. Executive agencies are also understood in terms of their group constituencies.

Parties are viewed as coalitions of groups. The Democratic party coalition from the Roosevelt era until recently was composed of labor, central-city dwellers, ethnic groups, Catholics, the poor, liberal intellectuals, blacks, and Southerners. The difficulties of the Democratic party today can be traced largely to the weakening of this group coalition—the disaffection of the South and the group conflict between white labor and ethnic groups and blacks. The Republican coalition has consisted of rural and small-town residents, the middle class, whites, Protestants, white-collar workers, and suburbanites.

The whole interest group system—the political system itself—is held together in equilibrium by several forces. First of all, there is a large, nearly universal, *latent group* in American society that supports the constitutional system and prevailing "rules of the game." This group is not always visible but can be activated to administer overwhelming rebuke to any group that attacks the system and threatens to destroy the equilibrium.

Second, *overlapping group membership* helps to maintain the equilibrium by preventing any one group from moving too far from prevailing values.

GROUP THEORY: APPLYING THE MODEL

Throughout this volume we will describe struggles over public policy. In Chapter 6, "Education: The Group Struggle," we will examine group conflict over public policy in our discussions of education and school issues. In Chapter 10, "Tax Policy: Battling the Special Interests," we will observe the power of interest groups in obtaining special treatments in the tax code and obstructing efforts to reform the nation's tax laws.

Individuals who belong to any one group also belong to other groups, and this fact moderates the demands of groups who must avoid offending their members who have other group affiliations.

Finally, the *checking and balancing resulting from group competition* also helps to maintain equilibrium in the system. No single group constitutes a majority in American society. The power of each group is checked by the power of competing groups. "Countervailing" centers of power function to check the influence of any single group and protect the individual from exploitation.

ELITE THEORY: POLICY AS ELITE PREFERENCE

Public policy may also be viewed as the preferences and values of a governing elite.[5] Although we often assert that public policy reflects the demands of "the people," this may express the myth rather than the reality of American democracy. Elite theory suggests that "the people" are apathetic and ill-informed about public policy, that elites actually shape mass opinion on policy questions more than masses shape elite opinion. Thus, public policy really turns out to be the preferences of elites. Public officials and administrators merely carry out the policies decided upon by the elite. Policies flow "downward" from elites to masses; they do not arise from mass demands (see Figure 2–3).

Elite theory can be summarized briefly as follows:

1. Society is divided into the few who have power and the many who do not. Only a small number of persons allocate values for society; the masses do not decide public policy.
2. The few who govern are not typical of the masses who are governed. Elites are drawn disproportionately from the upper socioeconomic strata of society.
3. The movement of nonelites to elite positions must be slow and continuous to maintain stability and avoid revolution. Only nonelites who have accepted the basic elite consensus can be admitted to governing circles.

[5]Elite theory is explained at length in Thomas R. Dye and Harmon Zeigler, *The Irony of Democracy*, 8th ed. (Monterey, Calif.: Brooks/Cole, 1990).

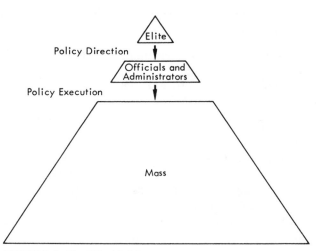

FIGURE 2-3   The Elite Model.

4. Elites share consensus in behalf of the basic values of the social system and the preservation of the system. In America, the bases of elite consensus are the sanctity of private property, limited government, and individual liberty.

5. Public policy does not reflect demands of masses but rather the prevailing values of the elite. Changes in public policy will be incremental rather than revolutionary.

6. Active elites are subject to relatively little direct influence from apathetic masses. Elites influence masses more than masses influence elites.

What are the implications of elite theory for policy analysis? First of all, elitism implies that public policy does not reflect demands of "the people" so much as it does the interests and values of elites. Therefore, change and innovations in public policy come about as a result of redefinitions by elites of their own values. Because of the general conservatism of elites— that is, their interest in preserving the system—change in public policy will be incremental rather than revolutionary. Public policies are frequently modified but seldom replaced. Changes in the nature of the political system occur when events threaten the system, and elites, acting on the basis of enlightened self-interest, institute reforms to preserve the system and their place in it. The values of elites may be very "public-regarding." A sense of *noblesse oblige* may permeate elite values, and the welfare of the masses may be an important element in elite decision-making. Elitism does not mean that public policy will be against mass welfare, but only that the responsibility for mass welfare rests upon the shoulders of elites, not masses.

Second, elitism views the masses as largely passive, apathetic, and ill-informed; mass sentiments are more often manipulated by elites, rather than elite values being influenced by the sentiments of masses; and for the most part, communication between elites and masses flows downward. Therefore,

---

ELITE THEORY: APPLYING THE MODEL

In Chapter 3, "Civil Rights: Elite and Mass Interaction," we will portray the civil rights movement as an effort by established national elites to extend equality of opportunity to blacks. Opposition to civil rights policies is centered among white masses in the states.

---

popular elections and party competition do not enable the masses to govern. Policy questions are seldom decided by the people through elections or through the presentation of policy alternatives by political parties. For the most part these "democratic" institutions—elections and parties—are important only for their symbolic value. They help tie the masses to the political system by giving them a role to play on election day and a political party with which they can identify. Elitism contends that the masses have at best only an indirect influence over the decision-making behavior of elites.

Elitism also asserts that elites share in a consensus about fundamental norms underlying the social system, that elites agree on the basic "rules of the game," as well as the continuation of the social system itself. The stability of the system, and even its survival, depends upon elite consensus in behalf of the fundamental values of the system, and only policy alternatives that fall within the shared consensus will be given serious consideration. Of course, elitism does not mean that elite members never disagree or never compete with each other for preeminence. It is unlikely that there ever was a society in which there was no competition among elites. But elitism implies that competition centers around a very narrow range of issues and that elites agree on more matters than they disagree.

In the United States, topics of elite consensus include constitutional government, democratic procedures, majority rule, freedom of speech and press, freedom to form opposition parties and run for public office, equality of opportunity in all segments of life, sanctity of private property, the importance of individual initiative and reward, and the legitimacy of the free enterprise, capitalist economic system. Masses may give superficial support to democratic symbols, but they are not as consistent or reliable in their support for these values as elites.

RATIONALISM: POLICY AS MAXIMUM SOCIAL GAIN

A rational policy is one that achieves maximum social gain. By "maximum social gain" we mean

> Governments should choose policies resulting in gains to society that exceed costs by the greatest amount, and governments should refrain from policies if costs are not exceeded by gains.

Note that there are really two important guidelines included in this definition of maximum social gain. First of all, no policy should be adopted if its costs exceed its benefits. Second, among policy alternatives, decision makers should choose the policy that produces the greatest benefit over cost.[6]

In other words, a policy is rational when the difference between the values it achieves and the values it sacrifices is positive and greater than any other policy alternative. One should *not* view rationalism in a narrow dollars-and-cents framework, in which basic social values are sacrificed for dollar savings. Rationalism involves the calculation of *all* social, political, and economic values sacrificed or achieved by a public policy, not just those that can be measured in dollars.

To select a rational policy, policymakers must (1) know all the society's value preferences and their relative weights, (2) know all the policy alter-natives available, (3) know all the consequences of each policy alternative, (4) calculate the ratio of benefits to costs for each policy alternative, and (5) select the most efficient policy alternative.[7] This rationality assumes that the value preferences of *society as a whole* can be known and weighted. It is not enough to know and weight the values of *some* groups and not others. There must be a complete understanding of *societal* values. Rational policy making also requires *information* about alternative policies, the *predictive capacity* to foresee accurately the consequences of alternate policies, and the *intelligence* to calculate correctly the ratio of costs to benefits. Finally, rational policy making requires a *decision-making system* that facilitates rationality in policy formation. A diagram of such a system is shown in Figure 2–4.

This model of maximum social gain is often used to think about the optimal size of government programs. Government budgets should increase until maximum net gain is achieved and then no more should be spent. The model of maximum social gain is applied to public policy making in benefit-cost analysis. The first applications were developed in the 1930s by the U.S. Corps of Engineers in programs for dams and river basin development. Today it is applied to virtually all government policies and programs. It is the principal analytic framework used to evaluate public spending decisions.

However, there are many barriers to rational decision making.[8] In fact, there are so many barriers to rational decision making that it rarely takes place at all in government. Yet the model remains important for analytic purposes because it helps to identify barriers to rationality. It assists in pos-ing the question: Why is policy making not a more rational process? At the

[6]See Robert Henry Haveman, *The Economics of the Public Sector* (New York: John Wiley, 1970).

[7]See Yehezdel Dror, *Public Policy-Making Re-examined,* Part IV, "An Optional Model of Public Policy-Making" (San Francisco: Chandler, 1968).

[8]See Charles E. Lindblom, "The Science of Muddling Through," *Public Administration Re-view,* 19 (Spring 1959), 79–88; David Braybrooke and Charles E. Lindblom, *A Strategy of Decision* (New York: Free Press, 1963); Aaron Wildavsky, *The Politics of the Budgetary Process* (Boston: Little, Brown, 1964).

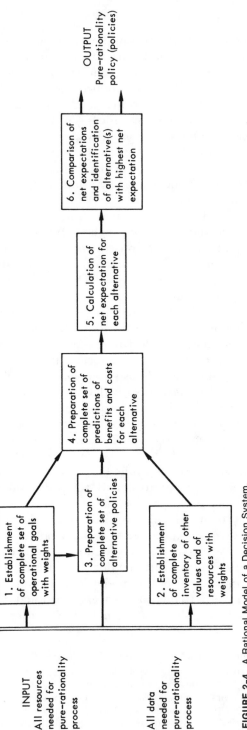

FIGURE 2-4 A Rational Model of a Decision System.

outset we can hypothesize several important obstacles to rational policy making:

1. There are no *societal* benefits that are usually agreed upon, but only benefits to specific groups and individuals, many of which are conflicting.
2. The many conflicting benefits and costs cannot be compared or weighted; for example, it is impossible to compare or weigh the value of individual dignity against a tax increase.
3. Policy makers are not motivated to make decisions on the basis of societal goals, but instead try to maximize their own rewards—power, status, reelection, money, and so forth.
4. Policy makers are not motivated to *maximize* net social gain, but merely to *satisfy* demands for progress; they do not search until they find "the one best way"; instead they halt their search when they find an alternative that "will work."
5. Large investments in existing programs and policies ("sunk costs") prevent policy makers from reconsidering alternatives foreclosed by previous decisions.
6. There are innumerable barriers to collecting all the information required to know all possible policy alternatives and the consequences of each alternative, including the cost of information gathering, the availability of the information, and the time involved in its collection.
7. Neither the predictive capacities of the social and behavioral sciences nor the predictive capacities of the physical and biological sciences are sufficiently advanced to enable policy makers to understand the full benefits or costs of each policy alternative.
8. Policy makers, even with the most advanced computerized analytical techniques, do not have sufficient intelligence to calculate accurately costs and benefits when a large number of diverse political, social, economic, and cultural values are at stake.
9. Uncertainty about the consequences of various policy alternatives compels policy makers to stick as closely as possible to previous policies to reduce the likelihood of disturbing, unanticipated consequences.
10. The segmentalized nature of policy making in large bureaucracies makes it difficult to coordinate decision making so that the input of all the various specialists is brought to bear at the point of decision.

RATIONALISM: APPLYING THE MODEL

In Chapter 4, "Criminal Justice: Rationality and Irrationality in Public Policy," we will show that rational policies to deter crime—policies ensuring certainty, swiftness, and severity of punishment—have seldom been implemented, and that the nation's high crime rate is partly a product of this irrationality. The problems of achieving rationality in public policy are also discussed in Chapter 5, "Health and Welfare: The Search for a Rational Strategy." We will describe the general design of alternative strategies in dealing with poverty, health, and welfare. We will observe how these strategies are implemented in public policy, and we will analyze some of the obstacles to the achievement of rationality in public policy.

INCREMENTALISM: POLICY AS VARIATIONS ON THE PAST

Incrementalism views public policy as a continuation of past government activities with only incremental modifications. Political scientist Charles E. Lindblom first presented the incremental model in the course of a critique of the traditional rational model of decision making.[9] According to Lindblom, decision makers do *not* annually review the whole range of existing and proposed policies, identify societal goals, research the benefits and costs of alternative policies in achieving these goals, rank order of preferences for each policy alternative in terms of the maximum net benefits, and then make a selection on the basis of all relevant information. On the contrary, constraints of time, information, and cost prevent policy makers from identifying the full range of policy alternatives and their consequences. Constraints of politics prevent the establishment of clear-cut societal goals and the accurate calculation of costs and benefits. The incremental model recognizes the impractical nature of "rational-comprehensive" policy making, and describes a more conservative process of decision making.

Incrementalism is conservative in that existing programs, policies, and expenditures are considered as a base, and attention is concentrated on new programs and policies and on increases, decreases, or modifications of current programs. (For example, budgetary policy for any government activity or program for 1993 might be viewed incrementally, as shown in Figure 2–5.) Policy makers generally accept the legitimacy of established programs and tacitly agree to continue previous policies.

They do this, first of all, because they do not have the time, information, or money to investigate all the alternatives to existing policy. The cost of collecting all this information is too great. Policy makers do not have sufficient predictive capacities, even in the age of computers, to know what all the consequences of each alternative will be. Nor are they able to calculate cost-benefit ratios for alternative policies when many diverse political, social, economic, and cultural values are at stake. Thus completely "rational" policy may turn out to be "inefficient" (despite the contradiction in terms) if the time and cost of developing a rational policy are excessive.

Second, policy makers accept the legitimacy of previous policies because of the uncertainty about the consequences of completely new or different policies. It is safer to stick with known programs when the consequences of new programs cannot be predicted. Under conditions of uncertainty, policy makers continue past policies or programs whether or not they have proven effective.

Third, there may be heavy investments in existing programs ("sunk costs" again) which preclude any really radical change. These investments may be in money, buildings, or other hard items, or they may be in psy-

---

[9]Lindblom, "The Science of Muddling Through," 79–88.

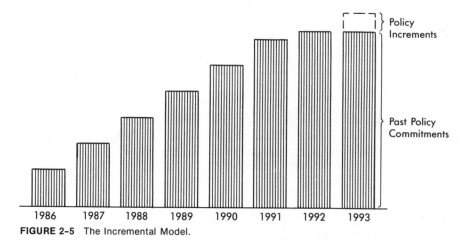

FIGURE 2-5 The Incremental Model.

chological dispositions, administrative practices, or organizational structure. It is accepted wisdom, for example, that organizations tend to persist over time regardless of their utility, that they develop routines that are difficult to alter, and that individuals develop a personal stake in the continuation of organizations and practices, all of which makes radical change very difficult. Hence, not all policy alternatives can be seriously considered, but only those which cause little physical, economic, organizational, and administrative dislocation.

Fourth, incrementalism is politically expedient. Agreement comes easier in policy making when the items in dispute are only increases or decreases in budgets, or modifications to existing programs. Conflict is heightened when decision making focuses on major policy shifts involving great gains or losses, or "all-or-nothing," "yes-or-no" policy decisions. Because the political tension involved in getting new programs or policies passed *every* year would be very great, past policy victories are continued into future years unless there is a substantial political realignment. Thus incrementalism is important in reducing conflict, maintaining stability, and preserving the political system itself.

The characteristics of policy makers themselves also recommend the incremental model. Rarely do human beings act to maximize all their values; more often they act to satisfy particular demands. People are pragmatic; they seldom search for the "one best way" but instead end their search when they find "a way that will work." This search usually begins with the familiar— that is, with policy alternatives close to current policies. Only if these alternatives appear to be unsatisfactory will the policy maker venture out toward more radical policy innovation. In most cases modification of existing programs will satisfy particular demands, and the major policy shifts required to maximize values will be overlooked.

INCREMENTALISM: APPLYING THE MODEL

We will give special attention to incrementalism in our discussion of government budgeting in Chapter 9, "Priorities and Price Tags: Incrementalism at Work."

Finally, in the absence of any agreed-upon societal goals or values, it is easier for the government of a pluralist society to continue existing programs rather than to engage in overall policy planning toward specific societal goals.

GAME THEORY: POLICY AS RATIONAL CHOICE IN COMPETITIVE SITUATIONS

Game theory is the study of rational decisions in situations in which two or more participants have choices to make and the outcome depends on the choices made by each of them. It is applied to areas in policy making in which there is no *independently* "best" choice that one can make—in which the "best" outcomes depend upon what others do.

The idea of a "game" is that decision makers are involved in choices that are interdependent. "Players" must adjust their conduct to reflect not only their own desires and abilities but also their expectations about what others will do. Perhaps the connotation of a "game" is unfortunate, suggesting that game theory is not really appropriate for *serious* conflict situations. But just the opposite is true: game theory can be applied to decisions about war and peace, the use of nuclear weapons, international diplomacy, bargaining and coalition building in Congress or the United Nations, and to a variety of other important political situations. A "player" may be an individual, a group, or a national government—indeed, anybody with well-defined goals that is capable of rational action.

Game theory is an abstract and deductive model of policy making. It does not describe how people actually make decisions, but rather how they would go about making decisions in competitive situations if they were completely rational. Thus, game theory is a form of rationalism, but it is applied in *competitive* situations where the outcome depends on what two or more participants do.

The *rules of the game* describe the choices that are available to all the players. The choices are frequently portrayed in a "matrix"—a diagram that presents the alternative choices of each player and all the possible outcomes of the game. A two-by-two matrix is the simplest; there are only two players and each player has only two alternatives to choose from:

		PLAYER A	
		ALTERNATIVE A₁	ALTERNATIVE A₂
	Alternative B₁	outcome	outcome
Player B			
	Alternative B₂	outcome	outcome

There are four possible outcomes to this simple game, each represented by a cell in a matrix. The actual outcome depends upon the choices of both Player *A* and Player *B*.

In game theory, *payoff* refers to the values that each player receives as a result of his or her choices and those of the opponent. Payoffs are frequently represented by numerical values placed on each outcome; these numerical values are placed inside each cell of the matrix and presumably correspond to the values each player places on each outcome. Because players value different outcomes differently, there are two numerical values inside each cell—one for each player.

Consider the game of "chicken." Two adolescents drive their cars toward each other at high speed, each with one set of wheels on the center line of the highway. If neither veers off-course they will crash. Whoever veers is "chicken." Both drivers prefer to avoid death but they also want to avoid the "dishonor" of being "chicken." The outcome depends on what both drivers do, and each driver must try to predict how the other will behave. This form of "brinkmanship" is common in international relations (see Figure 2–6).

Inspection of the payoff matrix suggests that it would be better for both drivers to veer in order to minimize the possibility of a great loss (-10).

		DRIVER A	
		STAY ON COURSE	VEER
	Stay on Course	A: -10 B: -10	A: -5 B: $+5$
Driver B			
	Veer	A: $+5$ B: -5	A: -1 B: -1

FIGURE 2-6 A Game-Theoretic Matrix for the Game of "Chicken." The game theorist him- or herself supplies the numerical values to the payoffs. If Driver *A* chooses to stay on course and Driver *B* chooses to stay on course also, the result might be scored as -10 for both players who wreck their cars. But if Driver *A* chooses to stay on course and Driver *B* veers, then Driver *A* might get $+5$ ("courage") and Driver *B* -5 ("dishonor"). If Driver *A* veers but Driver *B* stays on course, the results would be reversed. If both veer, each is dishonored slightly (-1) but not as much as when one or the other stayed on course.

But the matrix is too simple. One or both players may place a different value on the outcomes than is suggested by the numbers. For example, one player may prefer death to dishonor in the game. Each player must try to calculate the values of the other and neither has complete information about the values of the opponent. Moreover, bluffing or the deliberate misrepresentation of one's values or resources to an opponent is always a possibility. For example, a possible strategy in the game of chicken is to allow your opponent to see you drink heavily before the game, stumble drunkenly toward your car, and mumble something about having lived long enough in this rotten world. The effect of this communication on your opponent may increase his estimate of your likelihood of staying on course, and hence provide incentive for him to veer and allow you to win.

A key concept in game theory is *strategy*. Strategy refers to rational decision making in which a set of moves is designed to achieve optimum payoff even after consideration of all of the opponent's possible moves. Game theorists employ the term "minimax" to refer to the rational strategy that either *minimizes the maximum loss or maximizes the minimum gain* for a player, regardless of what the opponent does. The minimax strategy is designed to protect a player against the opponent's best play. It might be viewed as a conservative strategy in that it is designed to reduce losses and insure minimum gains rather than to seek maximum gains at the risk of great losses. But most game theorists view minimax as the best rational strategy. (The rational player in the game of chicken will veer, because this choice minimizes the player's maximum loss.)

It should be clear from this discussion that game theory embraces both very complex and very simple ideas. The crucial question is whether any of these game theory ideas is really useful in studying public policy.

Game theory is more frequently proposed as an *analytic* tool by social scientists than as a practical guide to policy making by government officials. The conditions of game theory are seldom approximated in real life. Seldom do policy alternatives present themselves neatly in a matrix. More importantly, seldom can policy makers know the real payoff values for themselves or their opponents of various policy alternatives. Finally, as we have already indicated, there are many obstacles to rational policy making by governments.

Yet game theory provides an interesting way of thinking clearly about policy choices in conflict situations. Perhaps the real utility of game theory

---

GAME THEORY: APPLYING THE MODEL

Game theory is frequently applied in international conflict situations. We will explore the utility of game theory in our own efforts to describe and explain in Chapter 8, "Defense Policy: Strategies for Serious Games."

in policy analysis at the present time is in suggesting interesting questions and providing a vocabulary to deal with policy making in conflict situations.

PUBLIC CHOICE THEORY: POLICY AS COLLECTIVE DECISION MAKING BY SELF-INTERESTED INDIVIDUALS

Public choice is the economic study of nonmarket decision making, especially the application of economic analyses to public policy making. Traditionally, economics studied behavior in the marketplace and assumed that individuals pursued their private interests; political science studied behavior in the public arena and assumed that individuals pursued their own notion of the public interest. Thus, separate versions of human motivation developed in economics and political science: *homo economicus* assumed a self-interested actor seeking to maximize personal benefits; *homo politicus* assumed a public-spirited actor seeking to maximize societal welfare. But public choice theory challenges the notion that individuals act differently in politics than they do in the marketplace. Public choice theory assumes that all political actors— voters, taxpayers, candidates, legislators, bureaucrats, interest groups, parties, bureaucracies, and governments—seek to maximize their personal benefits in politics as well as in the marketplace. James Buchanan, the Nobel-Prize-winning economist and leading scholar in modern public choice theory, argues that individuals come together in politics for their own mutual benefit, just as they come together in the marketplace; and by agreement (contract) among themselves they can enhance their own well-being, in the same way they can by trading in the marketplace.[10] In short, people pursue their self-interest in both politics and the marketplace, but even with selfish motives they can mutually benefit through collective decision making.

Government itself arises from a social contract among individuals who agree for their mutual benefit to obey laws and support the government in exchange for protection of their own lives, liberties, and property. Thus, public choice theorists claim to be intellectual heirs to the English political philosopher John Locke, as well as to Thomas Jefferson, who incorporated this social contract notion into the American Declaration of Independence. Enlightened self-interest leads individuals to a constitutional contract establishing a government to protect life, liberty, and property.

Public choice theory recognizes that government must perform certain functions that the marketplace is unable to handle, that is, it must remedy certain "market failures". First, government must provide *public goods*—goods and services that must be supplied to everyone if they are supplied to anyone.

---

[10]James M. Buchanan and Gordon Tullock, *The Calculus of Consent* (Ann Arbor: University of Michigan Press, 1962).

The market cannot provide public goods because their costs exceed their value to any single buyer, and a single buyer would not be in a position to keep nonbuyers from using it. National defense is the most common example: protection from foreign invasion is too expensive for a single person to buy, and once it is provided no one can be excluded from its benefits. So people must act collectively through government to provide for the common defense. Second, *externalities* are another recognized market failure and justification for government intervention. An externality occurs when an activity of one individual or firm or local government imposes uncompensated costs on others. The most common examples are air and water pollution: the discharge of air and water pollutants imposes costs on others. Governments respond by either regulating the activities that produce externalities, or alternatively impose penalties (fines) on these activities in order to compensate for their costs to society.

Public choice theory helps to explain why political parties and candidates generally fail to offer clear policy alternatives in election campaigns. Parties and candidates are not interested in advancing principles but rather in winning elections. They formate their policy positions in order to win elections; they do not win elections in order to formulate policy. Thus each party and candidate seeks out policy positions that will attract the greatest number of voters.[11] Given a unimodal distribution of opinion on any policy question (see Figure 2–7), parties and candidates will move toward the center to maximize votes. Only "ideologues" (irrational, ideologically-motivated people) ignore the vote-maximizing centrist strategy.

But public choice theory has developed its own critique of the simple median-voter model by recognizing the separate interests of politicians and bureaucrats in contrast to the interest of voters. The interests of politicians and bureaucrats are to win reelection, garner generous campaign contributions, expand agency budgets, gain greater authority and prestige, and expand the power of government. The constitutional rules for governmental decision making do not always ensure that the interests of politicians and bureaucrats coincide with those of the median voter. Even a totally selfless, altruistic public official who tries diligently to implement the preferences of his or her constituents—the median voters—may find many obstacles. Government officials do not have continuous information to assess changing preferences of consumer-taxpayers. Unlike marketplace consumers, voter consumers do not engage in continuous voting. When politicians find out what the voters really want, it may be too late, for the election will be won or lost. Even after the contest, elected officials can only guess at what they did right or wrong. Voting outcomes are not always policy informative.

In the absence of good information about citizen preferences, the "natural tendencies" of politicians and bureaucrats to expand their power

[11]Anthony Downs, *An Economic Theory of Democracy* (New York: Harper & Row, 1957).

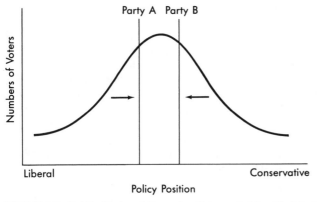

FIGURE 2-7   Public Choice: A Downsian Vote-maximizing Model of Party Competition.

in society are unchecked. They exaggerate the benefits of government spending programs and understate their costs. Various "fiscal illusions"—hidden taxes, payroll deductions, and deficit financing—contribute further to the citizens' underestimation of the costs of government. These "political failures" all contribute to the government's oversupplying of public goods and services and to its overtaxing the citizens.

Public choice theory also contributes to our understanding of interest groups and their effects on public policy. Most government programs provide "quasi-public goods"—services that benefit some groups in society more than others. It is rational for individuals seeking specific benefits, subsidies, privileges, or protections to organize themselves to pressure for government action. The costs of these specific benefits can be dispersed to all taxpayers, none of whom individually bears enough of the cost to merit spending time, energy, or money to organize in opposition to the expenditure. This concentration of benefits to the few and dispersal of costs to the many results in an interest-group system that favors small, well-organized, homogenous interests seeking expansion of government activity at the expense of larger but less organized groups of citizen-taxpayers. Over long periods of time, the activities of many special interest groups, each seeking concentrated benefits to themselves and dispersed costs to others, results in an overproduction of government regulations, programs, and services. Indeed, the cumulative effect of interest group activity on society is "organizational sclerosis"—a political economy so encrusted with subsidies, benefits, regulations, protections, and special treatments for organized interest groups, that work, productivity, and investment are discouraged.

To attract members and contributions, interest groups must dramatize and publicize their cause. Interest groups leaders must compete for members and money by exaggerating the dangers to society of ignoring their demands. Even when governments meet their original demands, interest groups must generate new demands with new warnings of danger if they are to remain

---

PUBLIC CHOICE: APPLYING THE MODEL

The public choice theory is employed in Chapter 7, "Environmental Policy: Externalities and Interests" to aid in recognizing environmental pollution as a problem in the control of externalities in human activity. Public choice theory also helps us to understand the behavior of environmental interest groups in dramatizing and publicizing their cause.

---

in business. In short, interest groups, like other political actors, pursue their self-interest in the political marketplace.

SYSTEMS THEORY: POLICY AS SYSTEM OUTPUT

Another way to conceive of public policy is to think of it as a response of a political system to forces brought to bear upon it from the environment.[12] Forces generated in the environment that affect the political system are viewed as *inputs*. The *environment* is any condition or circumstance defined as external to the boundaries of the political system. The *political system* is that group of interrelated structures and processes which functions authoritatively to allocate values for a society. *Outputs* of the political system are authoritative value allocations of the system, and these allocations constitute *public policy*.

This conceptualization of political activity and public policy can be diagramed as in Figure 2–8. This diagram is a simplified version of the idea of the political system described at great length by political scientist David Easton. The notion of a political system has been employed, either implicitly or explicitly, by many scholars who have sought to analyze the causes and consequences of public policy.

Systems theory portrays public policy as an output of the political system. The concept of *system* implies an identifiable set of institutions and activities in society that function to transform demands into authoritative decisions requiring the support of the whole society. The concept of *system* also implies that elements of the system are interrelated, that the system can respond to forces in its environment, and that it will do so in order to preserve itself. Inputs are received into the political system in the form of both demands and support. Demands occur when individuals or groups, in response to real or perceived environmental conditions, act to affect public policy. Support is rendered when individuals or groups accept the outcome of elections, obey the laws, pay their taxes, and generally conform to policy

[12]This conceptualization is based upon David Easton, *A Framework for Political Analysis* (Englewood Cliffs, N.J.: Prentice Hall, 1965).

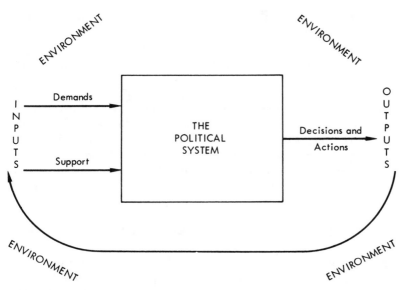

FIGURE 2-8 The Systems Model.

decisions. Any system absorbs a variety of demands, some of which conflict with each other. In order to transform these demands into output (public policies), it must arrange settlements and enforce these settlements upon the parties concerned. It is recognized that outputs (public policies) may have a modifying effect on the environment and the demands arising from it, and may also have an effect upon the character of the political system. The system preserves itself by (1) producing reasonably satisfying outputs, (2) relying upon deeply rooted attachments to the system itself, and (3) using, or threatening to use, force.

SYSTEMS THEORY: APPLYING THE MODEL

The systems model is particularly helpful in Chapter 12, "Inputs, Outputs, and Black Boxes: A Systems Analysis of State Policies, in examining public policies in the American states. By *comparing* states, we will assess the impact of various environmental conditions—particularly income—on levels of spending, benefits, and services in education, welfare, highways, police, corrections, and finance. We will see how federal policy sometimes tries to offset the impact of environmental variables on domestic policy in the states. We will examine the impact of political system characteristics—particularly party competition and voter participation—on levels of taxing, spending, benefits, and service, and attempt to compare the impact of these system characteristics on public policy with the impact of environmental conditions.

The value of the systems model to policy analysis lies in the questions that it poses:

1. What are the significant dimensions of the environment that generate demands upon the political system?
2. What are the significant characteristics of the political system that enable it to transform demands into public policy and to preserve itself over time?
3. How do environmental inputs affect the character of the political system?
4. How do characteristics of the political system affect the content of public policy?
5. How do environmental inputs affect the content of public policy?
6. How does public policy affect, through feedback, the environment and the character of the political system?

MODELS: HOW TO TELL IF THEY ARE HELPING OR NOT

A model is merely an abstraction or representation of political life. When we think of political "systems" or "elites" or "groups" or "rational decision making" or "incrementalism" or "games" we are abstracting from the real world in an attempt to simplify, clarify, and understand what is really important about politics. Before we begin our study of public policy, let us set forth some general criteria for evaluating the usefulness of concepts and models.

Order and Simplify Reality.   Certainly the utility of a model lies in its ability to *order and simplify* political life so that we can think about it more clearly and understand the relationships we find in the real world. Yet too much simplification can lead to inaccuracies in our thinking about reality. If a concept is too narrow or identifies only superficial phenomena, we may not be able to use it to explain public policy. On the other hand, if a concept is too broad, and suggests overly complex relationships, it may become so complicated and unmanageable that it is not really an aid to understanding. In other words, some theories of politics may be too complex to be helpful, while others may be too simplistic.

Identify What Is Significant.   A model should also *identify* the really significant aspects of public policy. It should direct attention away from irrelevant variables or circumstances, and focus upon the "real" causes and "significant" consequences of public policy. Of course, what is "real," "relevant," or "significant" is to some extent a function of an individual's personal values. But we can all agree that the utility of a concept is related to its ability to identify what it is that is really important about politics.

Congruent with Reality.   Generally, a model should be *congruent with reality*—that is, it ought to have real empirical referents. We would expect to have difficulty with a concept that identifies a process that does not really occur, or symbolizes phenomena that do not exist in the real world. On the other hand, we must not be too quick to dismiss "unrealistic" concepts *if* they succeed in directing our attention to why they are unrealistic. For example, no one contends that government decision making is completely rational—public officials do not always act to maximize societal values and minimize societal costs. Yet the concept of "rational decision making" may be still useful, albeit "unrealistic," if it makes us realize how irrational government decision making really is and prompts us to inquire about why it is irrational.

Meaningful Communication. A concept or model should also *communicate* something meaningful. If too many people disagree over the meaning of a concept, its utility in communication is diminished. For example, if no one really agrees on what constitutes an *elite,* then the concept of an *elite* does not mean the same thing to everyone. If one defines an *elite* as a group of democratically elected public officials who are representative of the general public, then one is communicating a different idea in using the term than one who defines an *elite* as an unrepresentative minority that makes decisions for society based on its own interests.

Direct Inquiry and Research. A model should help to *direct inquiry and research* into public policy. A concept should be operational—that is, it should refer directly to real-world phenomena that can be observed, measured, and verified. A concept, or a series of interrelated concepts (which we refer to as a *model*), should suggest relationships in the real world that can be tested and verified. If there is no way to prove or disprove the ideas suggested by a concept, then the concept is not really useful in developing a science of politics.

Suggest Explanations. Finally, a model approach should *suggest an explanation* of public policy. It should suggest hypotheses about the causes and consequences of public policy—hypotheses that can be tested against real-world data. A concept that merely *describes* public policy is not as useful as a concept that *explains* public policy, or at least suggests some possible explanations.

BIBLIOGRAPHY

BUCHANAN, JAMES M., and GORDON TULLOCK. *The Calculus of Consent.* Ann Arbor: University of Michigan Press, 1962.
DOWNS, ANTHONY. *An Economic Theory of Democracy.* New York: Harper & Row, 1957.
DYE, THOMAS R., and HARMON ZEIGLER. *The Irony of Democracy.* 8th ed. Monterey, Calif.: Brooks/Cole, 1990.

EASTON, DAVID. *A Framework for Political Analysis.* Englewood Cliffs, N.J.: Prentice Hall, 1965.
HAVEMAN, ROBERT HENRY. *The Economics of the Public Sector.* New York: John Wiley, 1970.
LINDBLOM, CHARLES E. *The Policy-Making Process.* Englewood Cliffs, N.J.: Prentice Hall, 1968.
TRUMAN, DAVID B. *The Government Process.* New York: Knopf, 1954.
WILDAVSKY, AARON. *The Politics of the Budgetary Process.* 4th ed. Boston: Little, Brown, 1984.

3

CIVIL RIGHTS
elite and mass interaction

Martin Luther King, Jr., is shown here giving his "I Have a Dream. . ." speech. (UPI/Bettman News-photos)

ELITE AND MASS ATTITUDES AND RACE

The central domestic issue of American politics over the long history of the nation has been the place of blacks in American society. In describing this issue we have relied heavily on the elite model—because elite and mass attitudes toward civil rights differ a great deal, and public policy appears to reflect the attitudes of elites rather than masses. Civil rights policy is a response of a national elite to conditions affecting a minority of Americans, rather than a response of national leaders to majority sentiments. Policies of the national elite in civil rights have met with varying degrees of resistance from states and communities. We will contend that national policy has shaped mass opinion more than mass opinion has shaped national policy.

The attitudes of white masses toward blacks in America are ambivalent. Today most whites believe that there is very little discrimination toward blacks in jobs, housing, or education, and that any differences between whites and blacks in society is a result of lack of motivation among blacks (see Table 3–1). Blacks disagree. Most blacks believe that they are not treated equally in employment, housing, or education, and that differences between blacks and whites in standards of living are "mainly due to discrimination." Whites constitute a large majority of the nation's population—over 87 percent. If public policy reflected the views of this majority, there would be very little civil rights legislation. This strongly suggests that civil rights policy is *not* a response of government to the demands of the white majority.

Opinion Lags Behind Policy.   White majority opinion has *followed* civil rights policy rather than inspired it. Public policy has shaped white opinion rather than white opinion shaping public policy. Consider the changes in opinion among whites toward school integration over the years. Between 1942 and 1982 samples of white Americans were asked the question, "Do you think white and black students should go to the same schools or separate schools?" (see Table 3–2). In 1942 not one white American in three approved of integrated schools. In 1956, two years after the historic *Brown* v. *Topeka* court decision, white attitudes had shifted markedly. By 1963, two out of every three whites supported integrated schools. In recent years, there has been a continuation of the upward trend in the proportion of white Americans who favor school integration. Additional survey information suggests that whites are becoming increasingly accommodating toward equal rights for blacks over time in other areas as well. But it should be noted that white opinion generally *follows* public policy, rather than leads it.

Elite-Mass Opinion Differences.   There is a wide gap between the attitudes of masses and elites on the subject of black rights. The least favorable attitudes toward blacks are found among the less-privileged, less-educated whites. Lower socioeconomic-status whites are much less willing to have con-

TABLE 3-1 White and Black Attitudes toward Discrimination

	PERCENT AGREE WHITES	BLACKS
Do you feel that, compared to whites, blacks . . .		
get equal pay for equal work?	72%	31%
are treated equally by the justice system?	51%	17%
On the average blacks have worse jobs, income, and housing than white people. Do you think these differences are . . .		
because most blacks have less inborn ability to learn?	21%	16%
because most blacks do not have the motivation or willpower to pull themselves out of poverty?	62%	36%
because most blacks don't have the education that it takes to rise out of poverty?	52%	68%
Most people agree that on the average, blacks have worse jobs, income, and housing than whites. Do you think the differences are . . .		
mainly due to discrimination?	7%	70%

Source: Derived from data reported in *The American Enterprise* January/February 1990, pp. 96–103.

tact with blacks than higher socioeconomic-status whites, whether it is a matter of using the same public restrooms, going to a movie or restaurant, or living next door. It is the affluent, well-educated white who is most concerned with discrimination and who is most willing to have contact with blacks. The political implication of this finding is obvious: opposition to civil rights legislation and to black advancement in education, jobs, income, housing, and so on, is likely to be strongest among less-educated and less-affluent whites. Within the white community support for civil rights will continue to come from the educated and affluent.

Mass Opposition to Affirmative Action.   In general whites are willing to support laws eliminating direct discrimination. But what about compensatory

TABLE 3-2 White Attitudes toward School Integration

Question: Do you think white students and black students should go to the same school or to separate schools?

	SAME SCHOOLS						
	1942	1956	1963	1966	1973	1980	1982
Total whites	30	49	62	67	82	88	91

Source: Paul B. Sheatsley, "White Attitudes Toward the Negro," *Daedalus*, 95, no. 1 (Winter 1966). Reprinted by permission of *Daedalus*, Journal of the American Academy of Arts and Sciences, Boston, Mass., Winter 1966. *The Negro American-2.* Updating from *Gallup Opinion Index* (October 1973), and *Public Opinion* (April/May 1981), and (October/November 1982).

TABLE 3-3   Attitudes toward Affirmative Action

Question: Some people say that to make up for past discrimination, women and members of minority groups should be given preferential treatment in getting jobs and places in colleges. Others say that ability, as determined by test scores, should be the main consideration. Which point of view comes closest to how you feel in this matter?

	GIVE PREFERENCE	ABILITY MAIN CONSIDERATION	NO OPINION
Total	11%	83%	7%
Male	9	85	6
Female	11	82	7
White	7	87	6
Nonwhite	29	57	14

Source: *Public Opinion,* April/May, 1981.

efforts to overcome the effects of past discrimination and uplift the black community? Here the evidence is that most whites are not prepared to make any special effort to change the conditions of blacks. The overwhelming majority of white Americans and a majority of black Americans *oppose* affirmative action programs (see Table 3–3). As we shall observe in this chapter, public policy in affirmative action, busing, and civil rights is not determined by public opinion but rather by the actions of elites—Congress, the president, the bureaucracy, and especially the U.S. Supreme Court.

THE DEVELOPMENT OF CIVIL RIGHTS POLICY

The initial goal in the struggle for equality in America was the elimination of discrimination and segregation practiced by governments, particularly in voting and public education. Later, discrimination in both public and private life—in transportation, theaters, parks, stores, restaurants, businesses, employment, and housing—came under legal attack.

The Fourteenth Amendment.   The Fourteenth Amendment, passed by Congress after the Civil War and ratified in 1868, declares:

> All persons born or naturalized in the United States, and subject to the Jurisdiction thereof, are citizens of the United States and of the State wherein they reside. No State shall make or enforce any law which shall abridge the privileges or immunities of citizens of the United States; nor shall any State deprive any person of life, liberty, or property, without due process of law; nor deny to any person within its jurisdiction the equal protection of the laws.

The language of the Fourteenth Amendment and its historical context leave little doubt that its original purpose was to achieve the full measure of citizenship and equality for black Americans. During Reconstruction and the military occupation of the Southern states, some radical Republicans were prepared to carry out in Southern society the revolution this amendment implied. But by 1877, Reconstruction had been abandoned; the national government was not prepared to carry out the long, difficult, and disagreeable task of really reconstructing society in the eleven states of the former Confederacy. In the Compromise of 1877, the national government agreed to end military occupation of the South, gave up its efforts to rearrange Southern society, and lent tacit approval to white supremacy in that region. In return, the Southern states pledged their support of the Union, accepted national supremacy, and, of course, agreed to permit the Republican candidate, Rutherford B. Hayes, to assume the presidency, even though his Democratic opponent, Samuel J. Tilden, had won more popular votes in the disputed election of 1876.

Segregation. The Supreme Court agreed to the terms of the compromise. The result was a complete inversion of the meaning of the Fourteenth Amendment so that it became a bulwark of segregation. State laws segregating the races were upheld. The constitutional argument on behalf of segregation under the Fourteenth Amendment was that the phrase "equal protection of the laws" did not prevent state-enforced separation of the races. Schools and other public facilities that were "separate but equal" won constitutional approval. This separate-but-equal doctrine became the Supreme Court's interpretation of the Equal Protection Clause of the Fourteenth Amendment in *Plessy* v. *Ferguson:*

> The object of the [14th] Amendment was undoubtedly to enforce the absolute equality of the two races before the law, but in the nature of things it could not have been intended to abolish distinctions based upon color, or to enforce social, as distinguished from political, equality, or a commingling of the two races upon terms unsatisfactory to either. Laws permitting, and even requiring, their separation in places where they are liable to be brought into contact do not necessarily imply the inferiority of either race to the other, and have been generally, if not universally, recognized as within the competency of the state legislatures in the exercise of their police power. The most common instance of this is connected with the establishment of separate schools for white and colored children, which has been held to be a valid exercise of the legislative power. . . . [1]

However, segregated facilities, including public schools, were seldom if ever equal, even with respect to physical conditions. In practice, the doc-

[1] *Plessy* v. *Ferguson,* 163 U.S. 537 (1896).

trine of segregation was "separate and *un*equal." The Supreme Court began to take notice of this after World War II. Although it declined to overrule the segregationist interpretation of the Fourteenth Amendment, it began to order the admission of individual blacks to white public universities where evidence indicated that separate black institutions were inferior or nonexistent.[2]

NAACP. Leaders of the newly emerging civil rights movement in the 1940s and 1950s were not satisfied with court decisions that examined the circumstances in each case to determine if separate school facilities were really equal. Led by Roy Wilkins, executive director of the National Association for the Advancement of Colored People, and Thurgood Marshall, chief counsel for the NAACP, the civil rights movement pressed for a court decision that segregation itself meant inequality within the meaning of the Fourteenth Amendment, whether or not facilities were equal in all tangible respects. In short, they wanted a complete reversal of the "separate-but-equal" interpretation of the Fourteenth Amendment and a ruling that laws *separating* the races were unconstitutional.

The civil rights groups chose to bring suit for desegregation to Topeka, Kansas, where segregated black and white schools were equal with respect to buildings, curricula, qualifications and salaries of teachers, and other tangible factors. The object was to prevent the Court from ordering the admission of blacks because *tangible* facilities were not equal, and to force the Court to review the doctrine of segregation itself.

Brown* v. *Topeka. The Court rendered its historic decision in *Brown* v. *Board of Education of Topeka, Kansas,* on May 17, 1954:

> Segregation of white and colored children in public schools has a detrimental effect upon the colored children. The impact is greater when it has the sanction of law, for the policy of separating the races is usually interpreted as denoting the inferiority of the Negro group. A form of inferiority affects the motivation of a child to learn. Segregation with the sanction of law, therefore, has a tendency to retard the educational and mental development of Negro children and to deprive them of some of the benefits they would receive in a racially integrated school system.[3]

The original *Brown* v. *Topeka* decision was symbolically very important. Although it would be many years before any significant number of black children would attend formerly segregated white schools, the decision by the nation's highest court undoubtedly stimulated black hopes and expectations. Black sociologist Kenneth Clark writes:

[2]*Sweatt* v. *Painter,* 339 U.S. 629 (1950).
[3]*Brown* v. *Board of Education of Topeka, Kansas,* 347 U.S. 483 (1954).

This [civil rights] movement would probably not have existed at all were it not for the 1954 Supreme Court school desegregation decision which provided a tremendous boost to the morale of Negroes by its *clear* affirmation that color is irrelevant to the rights of American citizens. Until this time the Southern Negro generally had accommodated to the separation of the black from the white society.[4]

Note that this first great step toward racial justice in the twentieth century was taken by the *nonelective* branch of the federal government. Nine men, secure in their positions with lifetime appointments, responded to the legal arguments of highly educated black leaders, one of whom—Thurgood Marshall—would later become a Supreme Court justice himself. The decision was made by a judicial elite, not by "the people" or their elected representatives.

MASS RESISTANCE TO CIVIL RIGHTS POLICY

Although the Supreme Court had spoken forcefully in the *Brown* case in declaring segregation unconstitutional, from a *political* viewpoint the battle over segregation was just beginning. Segregation would remain a part of American life, regardless of its constitutionality, until effective elite power was brought to bear to end it. The Supreme Court, by virtue of the American system of federalism and separation of powers, has little formal power at its disposal. Congress, the president, state governors and legislatures, and the people have more power at their disposal than the federal judiciary. The Supreme Court must rely largely on the other branches of the federal government, on the states, and on private individuals and organizations to effectuate the law of the land.

Segregationist States. Yet in 1954 the practice of segregation was widespread and deeply ingrained in American life. Seventeen states *required* the segregation of the races in public schools:

Alabama	Texas
Arkansas	Virginia
Florida	Delaware
Georgia	Kentucky
Louisiana	Maryland
Mississippi	Missouri
North Carolina	Oklahoma
South Carolina	West Virginia
Tennessee	

[4]Kenneth B. Clark, *Dark Ghetto* (New York: Harper & Row, 1965), pp. 77–78.

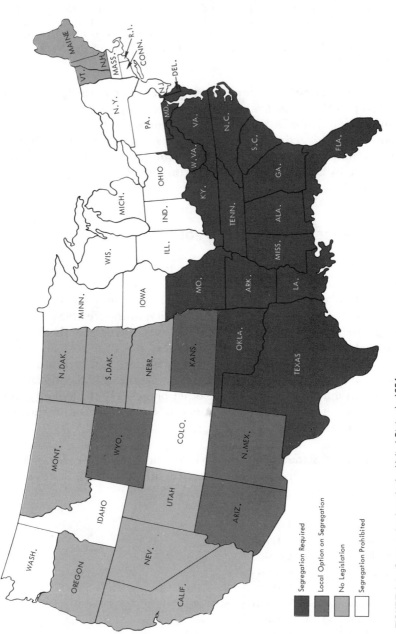

FIGURE 3-1 Segregation laws in the United States in 1954

Segregation Required

Local Option on Segregation

No Legislation

Segregation Prohibited

The Congress of the United States *required* the segregation of the races in the public schools of the District of Columbia. Four additional states—Arizona, Kansas, New Mexico, and Wyoming—*authorized* segregation upon the option of local school boards.

Thus, in deciding *Brown* v. *Topeka,* the Supreme Court struck down the laws of twenty-one states and the District of Columbia in a single opinion. Such a far-reaching decision was bound to meet with difficulties in implementation. In an opinion delivered the following year, the Supreme Court declined to order immediate nationwide desegregation, but instead turned over the responsibility for desegregation to state and local authorities under the supervision of federal district courts. The way was open for extensive litigation, obstruction, and delay by states that chose to resist desegregation.

The six border states with segregated school systems—Delaware, Kentucky, Maryland, Missouri, Oklahoma, West Virginia—together with the school districts in Kansas, Arizona, and New Mexico that had operated segregated schools, chose not to resist desegregation formally. The District of Columbia also desegregated its public schools the year following the Supreme Court's decision.

Resistance.   However, resistance to school integration was the policy choice of the eleven states of the Old Confederacy. Refusal of a school district to desegregate until it was faced with a federal court injunction was the most common form of delay. Segregationists also pressed for state laws that would create an endless chain of litigation in each of the nearly 3,000 school districts in the South in the hope that these integration efforts would drown in a sea of protracted court controversy. State laws that were obviously designed to evade constitutional responsibilities to end segregation were struck down in federal courts; but court suits and delays slowed progress toward integration. On the whole, those states that chose to resist desegregation were quite successful in doing so from 1954 to 1964. In late 1964, ten years after the *Brown* decision, only about 2 percent of the black schoolchildren in the eleven Southern states were attending integrated schools!

Denial of Federal Funds.   Finally Congress entered the civil rights field in support of court efforts to achieve desegregation. The Civil Rights Act of 1964, Title VI, provided that every federal department and agency must take action to end segregation in all programs or activities receiving federal financial assistance. It was specified that this action was to include termination of financial assistance if states and communities receiving federal funds refused to comply with federal desegregation orders. Thus, in addition to *court orders* requiring desegregation, states and communities faced *administrative orders* or "guidelines" from federal executive agencies threatening loss of federal funds for noncompliance. Acting under the authority of Title VI, the U.S. Office of Education (now the Department of Education) required all school districts in the seventeen formerly segregated states to submit desegregation plans as a condition of federal assistance. "Guidelines" governing the acceptability of these plans were frequently unclear, often contradictory, and always changing, yet progress toward desegregation was speeded up.

Unitary Schools.   The last legal excuse for delay in implementing school desegregation collapsed in 1969 when the Supreme Court rejected a request by Mississippi school officials for a delay in implementing school desegregation in that state. School officials contended that immediate desegregation in several southern Mississippi counties would encounter "administrative and legislative difficulties." The Supreme Court stated that no delay could be granted. The Court declared that every school district was obligated to end dual school systems "at once" and "now and hereafter" to operate only unitary schools.[5] The effect of the decision, fifteen years after the original *Brown* case, was to eliminate any further legal justification for the continuation of segregation in public schools.

DE FACTO SCHOOL SEGREGATION AND BUSING

In *Brown* v. *Board of Education of Topeka,* the Supreme Court quoted approvingly the view that segregation had "a tendency to retard the educational and mental development of Negro children and to deprive them of some of the benefits they would receive in a racially integrated school system." The U.S. Commission on Civil Rights reported in 1966 that even when the segregation was *de facto*—that is, the product of segregated housing patterns and neighborhood schools rather than direct discrimination—the adverse effects on black students were still significant.[6] Black students attending predominantly black schools had lower achievement scores and lower levels of aspiration than blacks with comparable socioeconomic backgrounds who attended predominantly white schools. When a group of black students attending school with a majority of advantaged whites was compared to a group of blacks attending school with a majority of disadvantaged blacks, the average difference in levels of achievement amounted to more than two grade levels. On the other hand, the commission found that the achievement levels of white students in classes roughly half-white in composition were not substantially different from those of white students in all-white schools. This early finding became a strong argument for ending *de facto* segregation in both Northern and Southern school districts.

[5]*Alexander* v. *Holmes County Board of Education,* 396 U.S. 19 (1969).

[6]U.S. Commission on Civil Rights, *Racial Isolation in the Public School* (Washington, D.C.: Government Printing Office, 1966).

Racial Balance.   Ending racial isolation in the public schools frequently involves busing schoolchildren into and out of segregated neighborhoods. The objective is to achieve a racial "balance" in each public school, so that each has roughly the same percentage of blacks and whites as are found in the total population of the entire school district. Indeed, in some large cities where blacks comprise the overwhelming majority of public school students, desegregation may require city students to be bused to the suburbs and suburban students to be bused to the core city.

White Flight.   However, social science research suggests that busing is not accomplishing its intended effects. Black students who are *bused* out of their neighborhoods to predominantly white schools do not improve their educational performance relative to white students. (See "Policy Analysis in Action: Achieving Educational Opportunity" in Chapter 1.) Moreover, in some cities where extensive busing is employed, "white flight" from the public schools is so widespread that the schools end up more segregated than before busing was imposed.

Busing in Boston.   The Boston experience with busing indicated the extent of mass resistance to busing and how white flight defeated the original policy objective. In 1974 U.S. Federal District Court Judge W. Arthur Garrity found that Boston school authorities had knowingly endeavored to keep their schools racially segregated. He ordered massive busing throughout the city. When the Boston School Committee refused to cooperate, he took over the governance of the school system himself. Serious racial conflict accompanied early attempts to bus students to and from high schools in working-class white neighborhoods. But Judge Garrity stuck to his plans: "No amount of public or parental opposition will excuse avoidance by school officials, of constitutionally imposed obligations."[7]

Prior to Judge Garrity's busing orders in 1973, Boston had 94,000 public school students, 57 percent of whom were white. When Judge Garrity finally removed himself from the case in 1985 and returned control of the schools to elected city officials, only 57,000 students remained in Boston's schools, and only 27 percent of them were white.[8] There was no creditable evidence that black students had improved their performance on standard test scores. Most white students in the Boston area attended either suburban schools or private schools (Judge Garrity lived in suburban Wellesley). Yet over time racial conflict in Boston subsided. The most vocal anti-busing politicians were eventually voted out of office.

[7]George M. Metcalf, *From Little Rock To Boston: The History of School Desegregation* (Westport, Conn.: Greenwood Press, 1983), p. 202.

[8]*The New York Times,* 15 September 1985.

The greatest opposition to busing comes when white middle-class children are ordered to attend predominantly black schools. Opposition is greatly reduced when black children are ordered to attend predominantly white middle-class schools. Most whites do not believe in sending youngsters from a good school to a bad school in order to achieve racial integration. Proponents of busing argue that it brings children of different cultures together and teaches them to live, work, and play with others who are different from themselves. But racial balancing does not always result in genuine integration; as one Pennsylvania high-school student remarked after a city-wide busing program: "I thought the purpose of busing was to integrate the schools, but in the long run, the white kids sit in one part of the bus and the black kids in another part."[9]

BUSING: THE CONSTITUTIONAL QUESTION

The question of equality in public education, however, is a constitutional question to be resolved by federal courts rather than public opinion. The Fourteenth Amendment guarantees "equal protection of the laws." If the Supreme Court requires busing and racial balancing in public schools in order to fulfill the constitutional mandate of the Fourteenth Amendment, then only another amendment to the Constitution specifically prohibiting busing and racial balancing could overturn that decision.

Overcoming Discrimination. Where racial imbalance and *de facto* segregation are a product of past or present discriminatory practices by states or school districts, the Supreme Court has held that school officials have a duty to eliminate all vestiges of segregation, and this responsibility may entail busing and deliberate racial balancing to achieve integration in education. In the important case of *Swann* v. *Charlotte-Mecklenburg Board of Education* (1971),[10] the Supreme Court held that the racial composition of the school in a Southern district that had previously been segregated by law could be used as evidence of violation of constitutional rights, and busing to achieve racial balance could be imposed as a means of ending all traces of dualism in the schools. The Supreme Court was careful to say, however, that racial imbalance in school is not itself grounds for ordering busing unless it is also shown that some present or past government action has contributed to that imbalance. Thus, the impact of the Swann decision falls largely on *Southern* schools.

Cross-District Busing. The constitutional question in *Northern* cities is somewhat different from that in Southern cities. In *Milliken* v. *Bradley* (1974),

---

[9]*Time*, 15 November 1971. p. 63.

[10]*Swann* v. *Charlotte-Mecklenburg Board of Education*, 402 U.S. 1 (1971).

the Supreme Court decided by a 5-to-4 vote that the Fourteenth Amendment does *not* require busing across city-suburban school district boundaries to achieve integration.[11] Where central-city schools are predominantly black, and suburban schools are predominantly white, *cross-district* busing is not required, unless it is shown that some official action brought about this segregation. The Supreme Court threw out a lower federal court order for massive busing of students between Detroit and fifty-two suburban school districts. Although Detroit city schools were 70 percent black, none of the Detroit area school districts segregated students within their own boundaries.

Chief Justice Burger, writing for the majority, said:

> The constitutional right of the Negro respondents residing in Detroit is to attend a unitary school system in that district. Unless petitioners drew the district lines in a discriminatory fashion, or arranged for the white students residing in the Detroit district to attend schools in Oakland or Macomb counties, they were under no constitutional duty to make provisions for Negro students to do so.

In a strong dissent, Justice Thurgood Marshall wrote:

> In the short run it may seem to be the easiest course to allow our great metropolitan areas to be divided up each into cities—one white, the other black—but it is a course, I predict, our people will ultimately regret.

This important decision means that largely black central cities, surrounded by largely white suburbs, will remain *de facto* segregated because there are not enough white students living within the city to achieve integration.

Note that this decision applies only to city-surburban cross-district busing. If a federal district court judge in any city, North or South, finds that any actions by governments or school officials have contributed to racial imbalances (for example, drawing school district attendance lines), the judge may still order busing within the city to overcome any racial imbalances produced by official action. In recent years, an increasing number of Northern cities have come under federal district court orders to improve racial balances in their schools through busing.

THE CIVIL RIGHTS MOVEMENT

The first goal of the civil rights movement in America was to prevent discrimination and segregation by governments, particularly states, municipalities, and school districts. But even while important victories for the civil rights movement were being recorded in the prevention of

[11]*Milliken* v. *Bradley*, 418 U.S. 717 (1974).

discrimination by governments, particularly in the *Brown* case, the movement began to broaden its objectives to include the elimination of discrimination in *all* segments of American life, private as well as public. Governments should not only cease discriminatory practices of their own, they should also act to halt discrimination by private organizations and individuals.

The goal of eliminating discrimination in private life creates a positive obligation of government to act forcefully in public accommodations, employment, housing, and many other sectors of society. When the civil rights movement turned to combating private discrimination, it had to carry its fight into the legislative branch of government. The federal courts could help restrict discrimination by state and local governments and school authorities, but only Congress, state legislatures, and city councils could restrict discrimination practiced by private owners of restaurants, hotels and motels, private employers, and other individuals who were not government officials.

The Montgomery Bus Boycott.   The leadership in the struggle to eliminate discrimination and segregation from private life was provided by a young black minister, Martin Luther King, Jr. His father was the pastor of one of the South's largest and most influential congregations, the Ebenezer Baptist Church in Atlanta, Georgia. Martin Luther King, Jr., received his doctorate from Boston University and began his ministry in Montgomery, Alabama. In 1955 the black community of Montgomery began a year-long boycott with frequent demonstrations against the Montgomery city buses over segregated seating practices. The dramatic appeal and the eventual success of the boycott in Montgomery brought nationwide attention to its leader, and led to the creation in 1957 of the Southern Christian Leadership Conference.

Nonviolent Direct Action.   Under King's leadership the civil rights movement developed and refined political techniques for minorities in American politics, including *nonviolent direct action.* Nonviolent direct action is a form of protest which involves breaking "unjust" laws in an open, "loving," nonviolent fashion. The general notion of civil disobedience is not new; it has played an important role in American history from the Boston Tea Party to the abolitionists who illegally hid runaway slaves, to the suffragettes who demonstrated for women's voting rights, to the labor organizers who formed the nation's major industrial unions, to the civil rights workers of the early 1960s who deliberately violated segregation laws. The purpose of nonviolent direct action is to call attention, or to "bear witness," to the existence of injustice. In the words of Martin Luther King, Jr., civil disobedience "seeks to dramatize the issue so that it can no longer be ignored."[12]

---

[12]For an inspiring essay on nonviolent direct action and civil disobedience in a modern context, read Martin Luther King, Jr., "Letter from Birmingham City Jail," April 16, 1963, reprinted in Thomas R. Dye and Brett W. Hawkins, eds., *Politics in the Metropolis* (Columbus: Charles E. Merrill, 1967).

There should be no violence in true civil disobedience, and only "unjust" laws are broken. Moreover, the law is broken "openly, lovingly" and with a willingness to accept the penalty. Punishment is actively sought rather than avoided, since punishment will help to emphasize the injustice of the law. The object is to stir the conscience of an elite, and win support for measures that will eliminate the injustices. By willingly accepting punishment for the violation of an unjust law, one demonstrates the strength of one's convictions. The dramatization of injustice makes news; the public's sympathy is won when injustices are spotlighted; and the willingness of demonstrators to accept punishment is visible evidence of their sincerity. Cruelty or violence directed against the demonstrators by police or others plays into the hands of the protesters by further emphasizing the injustices they are experiencing.

Martin Luther King, Jr. In 1963 a group of Alabama clergymen petitioned Martin Luther King, Jr., to call off mass demonstrations in Birmingham. King, who had been arrested in the demonstrations, replied in his famous "Letter from Birmingham City Jail":

> In no sense do I advocate evading or defying the law as the rabid segregationist would do. This would lead to anarchy. One who breaks an unjust law must do it *openly, lovingly* (not hatefully as the white mothers did in New Orleans when they were seen on television screaming "nigger, nigger, nigger") and with a willingness to accept the penalty. I submit that an individual who breaks a law that conscience tells him is unjust, and willingly accepts the penalty by staying in jail to arouse the conscience of the community over its injustice, is in reality expressing the very highest respect for law.

It is important to note that King's tactics relied primarily on an appeal to the conscience of white elites. The purpose of demonstrations was to call attention to injustice and stimulate established elites to remedy the injustice by lawful means. The purpose of civil disobedience was to dramatize injustice; only *unjust* laws were to be broken "openly and lovingly," and punishment was accepted to demonstrate sincerity. King did *not* urge black masses to remedy injustice themselves by any means necessary; and he did *not* urge the overthrow of established elites.

In 1964, Martin Luther King, Jr., received the Nobel Peace Prize in recognition of his unique contributions to the development of nonviolent methods of social change.

Birmingham, 1963. Perhaps the most dramatic confrontation between the civil rights movement and the Southern segregationists occurred in Birmingham, Alabama, in the spring of 1963. In support of a request for desegregation of downtown eating places and the formation of a biracial committee to work out the integration of public schools, Martin Luther King,

Reverend Martin Luther King, Jr., won the Nobel Prize
for his leadership in the American civil rights movement. (The Bergen Evening Record Corporation,
Hackensack, N.J.)

Jr., led several thousand Birmingham blacks in a series of orderly street
marches. The demonstrators were met with strong police action, including
fire hoses, police dogs, and electric cattle prods. Newspaper pictures of blacks
being attacked by police and bitten by dogs were flashed all over the world.
More than 25,000 demonstrators, including Dr. King, were jailed.

The year 1963 was probably the most important for nonviolent direct
action. The Birmingham action set off demonstrations in many parts of the
country; the theme remained one of nonviolence, and it was usually whites
rather than blacks who resorted to violence in these demonstrations. Responsible black elites remained in control of the movement and won widespread
support from the white liberal community.

"I Have a Dream."   The culmination of the nonviolent philosophy was
a giant, yet orderly march on Washington, held on August 28, 1963. More
than 200,000 blacks and whites participated in the march, which was endorsed

by many labor leaders, religious groups, and political figures. The march ended at the Lincoln Memorial where Martin Luther King, Jr., delivered his most eloquent appeal, entitled "I Have a Dream."

> I have a dream. It is a dream deeply rooted in the American dream. I have a dream that one day this nation will rise up and live up and live out the true meaning of its creed: 'We hold these truths to be self-evident, that all men are created equal.'

In response President Kennedy sent a strong civil rights bill to Congress which was passed after his death—the famous Civil Rights Act of 1964.

The Civil Rights Act of 1964.   The Civil Rights Act of 1964 passed both houses of Congress by better than a two-thirds favorable vote; it won the overwhelming support of both Republican and Democratic members of Congress. It was signed into law on July 4, 1964. It ranks with the Emancipation Proclamation, the Fourteenth Amendment, and *Brown* v. *Topeka* as one of the most important steps toward full equality for blacks in America.

The Civil Rights Act of 1964 provides that:

1. It is unlawful to apply unequal standards in voter registration procedures, or to deny registration for irrelevant errors or omissions on records or applications.
2. It is unlawful to discriminate or segregate persons on the grounds of race, color, religion, or national origin in any public accommodation, including hotels, motels, restaurants, movies, theaters, sports arenas, entertainment houses, and other places that offer to serve the public. This prohibition extends to all establishments whose operations affect interstate commerce or whose discriminatory practices are supported by state action.
3. The attorney general shall undertake civil action on behalf of any person denied equal access to a public accommodation to obtain a federal district court order to secure compliance with the act. If the owner or manager of a public accommodation should continue to discriminate, he would be in contempt of court and subject to peremptory fines and imprisonment without trial by jury. [This mode of enforcement gave establishments a chance to mend their ways without punishment, and it also avoided the possibility that Southern juries would refuse to convict persons for violations of the act.]
4. The attorney general shall undertake civil actions on behalf of persons attempting orderly desegregation of public schools.
5. The Commission on Civil Rights, first established in the Civil Rights Act of 1957, shall be empowered to investigate deprivations of the right to vote, study, and collect information regarding the discrimination in America, and make reports to the president and Congress.
6. Each federal department and agency shall take action to end discrimination in all programs or activities receiving federal financial assistance in any form. This action shall include termination of financial assistance.
7. It shall be unlawful for any employer or labor union to discriminate against any individual in any fashion in employment, because of his race, color, religion, sex, or national origin, and that an Equal Employment Opportunity Commis-

sion shall be established to enforce this provision by investigation, conference, conciliation, persuasion, and if need be, civil action in federal court.

The Civil Rights Act of 1968.   For many years "fair housing" had been considered the most sensitive area of civil rights legislation. Discrimination in the sale and rental of housing was the last major civil rights problem on which Congress took action. Discrimination in housing had not been mentioned in any previous legislation—not even in the comprehensive Civil Rights Act of 1964. Prohibiting discrimination in the sale or rental of housing affected the constituencies of Northern members of Congress more than any of the earlier Southern-oriented legislation.

The prospects for a fair housing law were not very good at the beginning of 1968. However, when Martin Luther King, Jr., was assassinated on April 4 the mood of Congress and the nation changed dramatically. Congress passed a fair housing law as tribute to the slain civil rights leader.

The Civil Rights Act of 1968 prohibited the following forms of discrimination:

> Refusal to sell or rent a dwelling to any person because of his race, color, religion, or national origin.
>
> Discrimination against a person in the terms, conditions, or privileges of the sale or rental of a dwelling.
>
> Advertising the sale or rental of a dwelling indicating a preference or discrimination based on race, color, religion, or national origin.
>
> Inducing persons to sell or rent a dwelling by referring to the entry into the neighborhood of persons of a particular race, religion, or national origin (the "blockbusting" technique of real estate selling).

But despite "fair housing" legislation, America is becoming *more* segregated over time, as black populations of large, central cities increase and white populations flee to surrounding suburbs. Black majorities are found in many of the nation's large cities: Washington, Atlanta, Newark, Detroit, Baltimore, New Orleans, Oakland, Cleveland, Gary. This suggests a developing pattern of predominantly black core cities, surrounded by nearly all-white suburbs. Even if direct discrimination is ended by "fair housing" laws, blacks and whites will continue to live in separate neighborhoods.

PUBLIC POLICY AND AFFIRMATIVE ACTION

Although the gains of the civil rights movement were immensely important, it must be recognized that they were *symbolic* rather than *actual* changes in the conditions under which most blacks live in America. Racial politics today center around the actual inequalities between blacks and whites in incomes, jobs, housing, health, education, and other conditions of life.

Continuing Inequalities. The problem of inequality is usually posed as differences in the "life chances" of blacks and whites. Figures can reveal only the bare outline of the black's "life chances" in American society (see Table 3-4). The average income of a black family is less than 60 percent of the average white family's income. Nearly 32 percent of all black families are below the recognized poverty line, while less than 11 percent of white families live in poverty. The black unemployment rate is over twice as high as the white unemployment rate. Blacks are less likely to hold prestigious white-collar jobs in professional, managerial, clerical, or sales work. They do not hold many skilled craft jobs in industry, but are concentrated in operative, service, and laboring positions. The civil rights movement opened up new opportunities for black Americans. But equality of *opportunity* is not the same as *absolute* equality.

Policy Choices. What public policies should be pursued to achieve equality in America? Is it sufficient that government eliminate discrimination, guarantee "equality of opportunity," and apply "colorblind" standards to both blacks and whites? Or should government take "affirmative action" to

TABLE 3-4 Minority Life Chances

MEDIAN INCOME OF FAMILIES			
	1975	1980	1985	1988
White	14,268	21,904	29,152	33,915
Black	8,779	12,674	16,786	19,329
Hispanic	9,551	14,716	19,027	21,769

% PERSONS BELOW POVERTY LEVEL			
White	9.7	10.2	11.4	10.1
Black	31.3	32.5	31.3	31.6
Hispanic	26.9	25.7	29.0	26.8

EDUCATION: PERCENT PERSONS OVER 25 COMPLETING (1988):	
	HIGH SCHOOL	COLLEGE
White	78	21
Black	64	11
Hispanic	51	10

UNEMPLOYMENT RATE		
	1980	1985	1988
White	6.3	6.2	4.7
Black	14.3	15.1	11.7
Hispanic	10.1	10.5	8.2

Source: *Statistical Abstract of the United States 1990.*

overcome the results of past unequal treatment of blacks—preferential or compensatory treatment that will favor black applications for university admissions and scholarships, job hiring and promotion, and other opportunities for advancement in life?

Opportunity versus Results.   Most Americans are concerned more with *equality of opportunity* than equality of results. Equality of opportunity refers to the ability to make of oneself what one can, to develop one's talents and abilities, and to be rewarded for work, initiative, and achievement. Equality of opportunity means that everyone comes to the same starting line with the same chance of success, that whatever differences develop over time do so as a result of abilities, talents, initiative, hard work, and perhaps good luck. *Equality of results* refers to the equal sharing of income, jobs, contracts, and material rewards regardless of one's condition in life. Equality of results means that everyone starts *and finishes* the race together, regardless of ability, talent, initiative, or work.

Insofar as affirmative action programs seek to ensure equality of opportunity, to help everyone make the best of their lives, to insure that minorities are sought out and given a fair shot at jobs, educations, and promotions, to bring everyone up to the same starting line, then there is widespread support for these programs.[13] But when affirmative action programs seek to provide equality of results, to distribute jobs, education, or promotions according to racial quotas, to put race ahead of ability, talent, experience, or hard work, then affirmative action loses support among both blacks and whites (see Table 3–3).

Equal Employment Opportunity.   The earlier emphasis of government policy, of course, was nondiscrimination, or *equal employment opportunity.* Equal employment opportunity ". . . was not a program to offer special privilege to any one group of persons because of their particular race, religion, sex, or national origin."[14] This appeared to conform to the original nondiscrimination approach, beginning with President Harry Truman's decision to desegregate the armed forces in 1946, and carrying through Title VI and Title VII of the Civil Rights Act of 1964 to eliminate discrimination in federally aided projects and private employment.

Gradually, however, the goal of the civil rights movement shifted from the traditional aim of equality of opportunity through nondiscrimination alone, to affirmative action to establish "goals and timetables" to achieve

[13]Sidney Verba and Gary R. Owen, *Equality in America* (Cambridge, Mass.: Harvard University Press, 1985).

[14]See David H. Rosenbloom, "The Civil Service Commission's Decision to Authorize the Use of Goals and Timetables in Federal Equal Employment Opportunity Programs," *Western Political Quarterly,* 26 (June 1973), 236–51.

absolute equality between blacks and whites. While avoiding the term *quota*, the notion of affirmative action tests the success of equal employment opportunity by observing whether blacks achieve admissions, jobs, and promotions in proportion to their numbers in the population.

Affirmative Action.   Affirmative action programs are products of the federal bureaucracy. These programs were not initiated by Congress. Instead, these programs were developed by the federal executive agencies that were authorized by the Civil Rights Act of 1964 to develop "rules and regulations" for desegregating activities receiving federal funds (Title VI) and private employment (Title VII). President Lyndon B. Johnson gave impetus to affirmative action with Executive Order No. 11246 in 1965, covering employment and promotion in federal agencies and businesses contracting with the federal government. In 1972 the U.S. Office of Education issued guidelines that mandated "goals" for university admissions and faculty hiring of blacks and women. The Equal Employment Opportunity Commission, established by the Civil Rights Act of 1964 (Title VII) to eliminate discrimination in private employment, has carried the notion of affirmative action beyond federal contractors and recipients of federal aid into all sectors of private employment.

Federal officials generally measure "progress" in "affirmative action" in terms of the number of blacks admitted, employed, or promoted. The pressure to show "progress" and retain federal financial support can result in preferential treatment of blacks. It also puts pressure on traditional measures of qualifications—test scores and educational achievement. Blacks argue that these are not good predictors of performance on the job or in school and that these measures are biased in favor of white culture. State and local governments, schools, colleges and universities, and private employers are under pressure to drop these standards. But how far can any school, agency, or employer go in dropping traditional standards? It is not difficult to drop educational requirements for sanitation workers, but what about for physicians, surgeons, attorneys, pilots, and others whose skills directly affect health and safety?

The question becomes even more complex if we try to weigh the costs of some "reverse discrimination" against the value of achieving greater representation of blacks in all echelons of society. Perhaps it is better for society as a whole to make some sacrifices to bring black Americans into the mainstream of economic life—to give them a "stake in society," and hence to sew up the worn fabric of the social system. But who must make these sacrifices? It is not the established white upper classes, but the sons and daughters of white middle- and working-class families who are in direct competition with upwardly mobile blacks. Must the price of past discrimination against blacks now fall on these young whites? Does preferential treatment imply that blacks cannot "make it" without such treatment? Clearly there are sensitive moral and ethical questions surrounding this area of public policy, as well as the constitutional question of equal protection of the laws.

AFFIRMATIVE ACTION IN THE COURTS

The constitutional question posed by "affirmative action" programs is whether or not they discriminate against whites in violation of the Equal Protection Clause of the Fourteenth Amendment. A related question is whether or not affirmative action programs discriminate against whites in violation of the Civil Rights Act of 1964, which prohibits discrimination "on account of race," not just discrimination against blacks. Clearly, these are questions for the Supreme Court to resolve, but unfortunately the Court has failed to develop clear-cut answers.

The Bakke Case. In *Regents of the University of California* v. *Bakke* (1978), the Supreme Court struck down a special admissions program for minorities at a state medical school on the grounds that it excluded a white applicant because of his race and violated his rights under the Equal Protection Clause.[15] Allan Bakke applied to the University of California Davis Medical School two consecutive years and was rejected; in both years black applicants with significantly lower grade point averages and medical aptitude test scores were accepted through a special admissions program that reserved sixteen minority places in a class of one hundred.[16] The University of California did not deny that its admissions decisions were based on race. Instead, it argued that its racial classification was "benign," that is, designed to assist minorities, not to hinder them. The special admissions program was designed (1) to "reduce the historical deficit of traditionally disfavored minorities in medical schools and the medical profession," (2) to "counter the effects of societal discrimination," (3) to "increase the number of physicians who will practice in communities currently underserved," and (4) to "obtain the educational benefits that flow from an ethnically diverse student body."

The Court held that these objectives were legitimate and that race and ethnic origin *may* be considered in reviewing applications to a state school without violating the Equal Protection Clause. However, the Court also held that a *separate* admissions program for minorities with a specified quota of openings which were unavailable to white applicants violated the Equal Protection Clause. "The guarantee of equal protection cannot mean one thing when applied to one individual and something else when applied to another. If both are not accorded the same protection, then it is not equal."

---

[15]*Regents of the University of California* v. *Bakke,* 438 U.S. 265 (1978).

[16]Bakke's grade point average was 3.51; his MCAT scores were: verbal-96, quantitative-94, science-97, general information-72. The average for the special admissions students were: grade point average-2.62, MCAT verbal-34, quantitative-30, science-37, general information-18.

The Court ordered Bakke admitted to medical school and the elimination of the special admissions program. It recommended that California consider an admissions program developed at Harvard that considered disadvantaged racial or ethnic background as a "plus" in an overall evaluation of an application, but did not set numerical quotas or exclude any persons from competing for all positions.

Reaction to the decision was predictable: supporters of affirmative action, particularly government officials from affirmative action programs, emphasized the Supreme Court's willingness to allow minority status to be considered a positive factor; opponents emphasized the Supreme Court's unwillingness to allow quotas which excluded whites from competing for a certain number of positions. Since Bakke had "won" the case, most observers felt that the Supreme Court was not going to permit discriminatory quota systems.

Cases Upholding Affirmative Action. However, in *United Steelworkers of America* v. *Weber* (1979), the Supreme Court approved a plan developed by a private employer and a union to reserve 50 percent of higher paying, skilled jobs for minorities. Kaiser Aluminum Corporation and the United Steelworkers Union, under federal government pressure, had established a program to get more blacks into skilled technical jobs; only 2 percent of the skilled jobs were held by blacks in the plant where Weber worked, while 39 percent of the local workforce was black. When Weber was excluded from the training program, and blacks with less seniority and fewer qualifications were accepted, Weber filed suit in federal court claiming that he had been discriminated against because of his race in violation of Title VII of the Civil Rights Act of 1964. (Weber could not claim that his rights under the Fourteenth Amendment's Equal Protection Clause had been violated, because this clause applies only to the "state," that is, governmental discrimination, and not to private employers.) Title VII prevents *all* discrimination in employment on the basis of race; it does not specify only discrimination against blacks or minorities.

The Supreme Court held that Title VII of the Civil Rights Act of 1964 "left employers and unions in the private sector free to take such race-conscious steps to eliminate manifest racial imbalances in traditionally segregated job categories. We hold that Title VII does not prohibit such . . . affirmative action plans." Weber's reliance on the clear language of Title VII was "misplaced." According to the Court, it would be "ironic indeed" if the Civil Rights Act were used to prohibit voluntary private race-conscious efforts to overcome the past effects of discrimination.[17]

The Weber ruling was applauded by the U.S. Equal Employment Opportunity Commission, as well as by various civil rights organizations, who

---

[17]*United Steelworkers* v. *Weber*, 443 U.S. 193 (1979).

hoped to use the decision to step up affirmative action plans in industry and government. The decision does not directly affect women, but it may be used as a precedent to strengthen affirmative action programs for them.

Cases Questioning Affirmative Action. Yet the Supreme Court has continued to express concern about whites who are directly and adversely affected by government action solely because of their race. In *Firefighters Local Union* v. *Stotts* (1984) the Court ruled that a city could not lay off white firefighters in favor of black firefighters with less seniority.[18] In *Richmond* v. *Crosen* (1989) the Supreme Court held that a minority set-aside program in Richmond, Virginia, which mandated that 30 percent of all city construction contracts must go to "blacks, Spanish-speaking, Orientals, Indians, Eskimoes, or Aleuts," violated the Equal Protection clause of the Fourteenth Amendment.[19] The U.S. Justice Department under President Reagan argued that any affirmative action plan that granted preference to one race over another was unconstitutional. But the Supreme Court has not yet adopted a completely "colorblind" standard.

How can these decisions be reconciled into a coherent policy on affirmative action? They probably *cannot* be reconciled. Rather than search for consistency in the law, perhaps we should resign ourselves to some uncertainties about how far affirmative action programs can go without becoming "reverse discrimination." Perhaps each program will have to be judged separately, and no clear-cut national policy will emerge.

SEXUAL EQUALITY AND PUBLIC POLICY

The earliest active feminist organizations grew out of the pre-Civil War antislavery movement. The first generation of feminists included Lucretia Mott, Elizabeth Cady Stanton, Lucy Stone, and Susan B. Anthony. They learned to organize, hold public meetings, and conduct petition campaigns as abolitionists. After the Civil War, women were successful in changing many state laws which abridged the property rights of married women and otherwise treated them as "chattel" (property) of their husbands. Women were also prominent in the Anti-Saloon League, which succeeded in outlawing prostitution and gambling in every state (except Nevada) and provided a major source of support for the Eighteenth Amendment (Prohibition). In the early twentieth century the feminist movement concentrated on women's suffrage—the drive to guarantee women the right to vote. The early suffragettes employed mass demonstrations, parades, picketing, and occasional disruption and civil disobedience—tactics similar to those of the civil rights movement of the 1960s.

---

[18]*Firefighters Local Union* v. *Stotts,* 467 U.S. 561 (1984).
[19]*Richmond* v. *Crosen,* 109 S. Ct. 706 (1989).

Nineteenth Amendment.   The culmination of the early feminist move-ment was the passage in 1920 of the Nineteenth Amendment to the Con-stitution: "The right of citizens of the United States to vote shall not be denied or abridged by the United States or by any state on account of sex." The more moderate wing of the American suffrage movement became the League of Women Voters; in addition to women's right to vote, they sought protec-tion of women in industry, child welfare laws, and honest election practices.

Renewed interest in feminist politics came after the civil rights move-ment of the 1960s. The feminist movement of recent years worked in the states and in Congress on behalf of a wide range of causes—the Equal Rights Amendment to the Constitution, equal employment opportunities for women, reform of divorce and child support laws, more convictions in sex-ual assault cases, and opposition to laws regulating abortion. New organiza-tions sprung up to compete with the conventional activities of the League of Women Voters by presenting a more militant and activist stance toward women's liberation. The largest of these newer organizations is the National Organization of Women (NOW) founded in 1966, which promised to change "the false image of women now prevalent in the mass media and in the texts, ceremonies, laws and practices of our major social institutions" that "perpetuate contempt for women by society and by women for themselves."[20]

Employment.   The federal Civil Rights Act of 1964, Title VII, prevents sexual (as well as racial) discrimination in hiring, pay, and promotions. The Equal Employment Opportunity Commission (EEOC), which is the federal agency charged with eliminating discrimination in employment, has established guidelines barring stereotyped classifications of "men's jobs" and "women's jobs." State laws and employer practices which differentiate be-tween men and women in hours, pay, retirement age, and so forth, have been struck down. Under active lobbying from feminist organizations, federal agencies, including the U.S. Office of Education and the Office of Federal Contract Compliance, have established affirmative action guidelines for government agencies, universities, and private businesses doing work for the government; these guidelines set goals and timetables for employers to alter their workforce to achieve higher female percentages at all levels.

Credit.   The Federal Equal Credit Opportunity Act of 1974 prohibits sex discrimination in *credit* transactions. Most states now have similar laws. Both federal and state laws prevent banks, credit unions, savings and loan associations, retail stores, and credit card companies from denying credit because of sex or marital status. However, these businesses may still deny credit for a poor or nonexistent credit rating, and some women who have

---

[20]Congressional Quarterly, *The Women's Movement* (Washington, D.C.: Congressional Quarterly Inc., 1973), p. 14.

always maintained accounts in their husband's name may still face credit problems if they apply in their own name.

Education.   Title IX of the federal Education Amendment of 1972 deals with sex discrimination in *education*. This federal law bars discrimination in admissions, housing, rules, financial aid, faculty and staff recruitment and pay, and—most troublesome of all—athletics. The latter problem has proven very difficult because men's football and basketball programs have traditionally brought in the money to finance all other sports, and men's football and basketball have received the largest share of school athletic budgets.

Sexual Equality.   To date, the Supreme Court has *not* held that the Equal Protection Clause of the U.S. Constitution bans all sexual differences in state or federal law. However, the Court has decreed that sexual classification in the law "must be reasonable and not arbitrary, and must rest on some ground of difference having fair and substantial relation to the object of the legislation."[21] For example, a state can no longer set different ages for men and women to become legal adults[22] or purchase alcoholic beverages;[23] women cannot be barred from police or firefighting jobs by arbitrary height and weight requirements;[24] insurance and retirement plans for women must pay the same monthly benefits even though women on the average live longer;[25] and schools must pay coaches in girls' sports the same as coaches in boys' sports.[26] However, all-male and all-female schools are still permitted;[27] and Congress may draft men for military service without drafting women.[28] Moreover, Congress bars women from combat roles in the military services.

WOMEN AND JOBS

Sexual differences in the workplace have generated very important policy debates as more and more women have joined the nation's work force. Today 65 percent of the adult female population works outside of the home, compared to only 32 percent a generation earlier (1960).

Earnings Gap.   Women's earnings are substantially less than men's earnings. In 1987 the median earnings for all men was $26,008 compared

[21]*Reed* v. *Reed*, 404 U.S. 71 (1971).
[22]*Stanton* v. *Stanton*, 421 U.S. 7 (1975).
[23]*Craig* v. *Boren*, 429 U.S. 191 (1976).
[24]*Dothand* v. *Raulinson*, 433 U.S. 321 (1977).
[25]*Arizona* v. *Norvis*, 103 S. Ct. 3492 (1983).
[26]*E.E.O.C.* v. *Madison Community School District*, 55 U.S.L.W. 2644 (1987)
[27]*Vorcheheimer* v. *Philadelphia School District*, 430 U.S. 703 (1977).
[28]*Rostker* v. *Goldberg*, 453 U.S. 57 (1981).

to $16,909 for women, indicating that women on the average earned only about 65 percent of what men did.[29] This earnings gap is not so much a product of direct discrimination, that is, women in the same job with the same skills, qualifications, experience, and work record being paid less than men. This form of direct discrimination has been illegal since the Civil Rights Act of 1964. Rather, the earnings gap is primarily a product of a division in the labor market between traditionally male and female jobs, with lower salaries paid in traditionally female occupations.

The initial efforts of the women's movement were directed toward ensuring that women enjoyed equal access to traditionally male "white collar" occupations, for example, those of physician, lawyer, and engineer. Success in these efforts would automatically narrow the wage gap. And indeed, women have been very successful over the last several decades in increasing their representation in prestigious white collar occupations (see Table 3–5), although most of these occupational fields continue to be dominated by men.

"Dual" Labor Market.   Nonetheless, evidence of a "dual" labor market, with male-dominated "blue collar" jobs distinguishable from female-dominated "pink collar" jobs, continues to be a major obstacle to economic equality between men and women. A study sponsored by the National Academy of Sciences concluded that most of the differences in men's and women's earnings could be attributed to sex segregation in occupations.[30] These occupational differences were attributed to cultural stereotyping, social conditioning, and premarket training and education which narrow the choices available to women. While significant progress has been made in recent years in reducing occupational sex segregation, nonetheless many observers doubt that sexually differentiated occupations will be eliminated in the foreseeable future.

"Comparable Worth."   As a result of a growing recognition that the wage gap is more a result of occupational differentiation than direct discrimination, some feminist organizations have turned to a new approach—the demand that pay levels in various occupations be determined by "comparable worth" rather than by the labor market. "Comparable worth" means *more* than paying men and women equally for the same work; it means paying the same wages for jobs of comparable value to the employer. "Comparable worth" means that traditionally male and female jobs would be evaluated by government agencies or courts to determine their "worth" to the employer, perhaps by considering responsibilities, effort, knowledge, and skill requirements. Jobs adjudged to be "comparable" would be paid equal wages.

[29]*Statistical Abstract of the United States 1989,* p. 408.

[30]National Research Council, National Academy of Sciences, *Women's Work, Men's Work* (Washington D.C.: National Academy Press, 1985).

TABLE 3-5   Percentage of Women at Work

"WHITE COLLAR"			

Women are increasingly entering white collar occupation fields traditionally dominated by men.

	1960	1983	1987
Architects	3	13	13
Computer analysts	11	28	34
College and university teachers	28	36	34
Engineers	1	6	7
Lawyers and judges	4	16	20
Physicians	10	16	20

"PINK COLLAR"			

Women continue to be concentrated in occupational fields traditionally dominated by women.

	1970	1980	1987
Secretaries	98	99	98
Cashiers	84	84	83
Waitresses and waiters	91	88	85
Nurses	97	96	95
Office clerks	75	82	83

"BLUE COLLAR"			

Women continue to be largely excluded from blue collar occupational fields traditionally dominated by men.

	1970	1980	1987
Truck drivers	1	2	4
Carpenters	1	2	1
Laborers	17	19	18
Auto mechanics	1	1	1
Bartenders	21	44	50

Sources: U.S. Department of Labor, *Employment in Perspective: Working Women* (Washington D.C.: Government Printing Office, 1983); National Research Council, National Academy of Sciences, *Women's Work, Men's Work* (Washington D.C.: National Academy Press, 1985); *Statistical Abstract of the United States 1989.*

Government agencies or the courts would replace the free labor market in the determination of wage rates.

But comparable worth raises problems of implementation: Who would decide what wages should be for various jobs? What standards would be used to decide? If government agencies set wage rates by law instead of the free market, would an illegal black market for labor arise? What penalties would be imposed on employers who paid wages different than those set by government? The U.S. Equal Employment Opportunity Commission has rejected the notion of comparable worth and declined to recommend wages for traditionally male and female jobs. And so far the federal courts have refused to declare that different wages in traditionally male and female occupations is evidence of sexual discrimination in violation of federal law. However, some state governments and private employers have undertaken to review their own pay scales to determine if traditionally female occupations are underpaid.

ERA

At the center of feminist activity in the 1970s was the Equal Rights Amendment to the Constitution. The amendment stated simply: "Equality of rights under the law shall not be denied or abridged by the United States or by any state on account of sex." The ERA passed the Congress easily in 1972 and was sent to the states for the necessary ratification by three-fourths (thirty-eight) of them. The amendment won quick ratification by half the states, but a developing "Stop ERA" movement slowed progress and eventually defeated the amendment itself. In 1979, the original seven-year time period for ratification—the period customarily set by Congress for ratification of constitutional amendments—expired. Proponents of the ERA persuaded Congress to extend the ratification period for three more years, to 1982. But despite heavy lobbying efforts in the states and public opinion polls showing national majorities favoring the ERA, the amendment failed to win ratification by the necessary thirty-eight states.[31]

Proponents of the ERA argued in the state legislatures that most of the progress women have made toward equality in marriage, property, employment, credit, education, and so on, depends upon state and federal *law*. The guarantee of equality of the sexes would be much more secure if this guarantee were made part of the U.S. Constitution. Moreover, the ERA would eliminate the need to pass separate laws in a wide variety of fields to ensure sexual equality. The ERA, as a permanent part of the U.S. Constitution, would provide a sweeping guarantee of equality, directly enforceable by court action. Finally, the ERA has taken on a great deal of symbolic meaning; even if federal and state laws prohibit sexual discrimination now, it is nonetheless important to many to see the ERA as part of the U.S. Constitution—"the supreme law of the land."

Opponents of the ERA charged that it would eliminate many legal protections for women, such as financial support by husbands, an interest in the husband's property, exemption from military service, and so forth. In addition to these specific objectives, opponents of "women's liberation" in

[31]By 1982, thirty-four states had ratified the ERA. Three of them—Idaho, Nebraska, and Tennessee—subsequently voted to "rescind" their ratification; but the U.S. Constitution does not mention "rescinding" votes. The states which had not ratified by 1982 were Nevada, Utah, Arizona, Oklahoma, Illinois, Indiana, Missouri, Arkansas, Louisiana, Mississippi, Alabama, Georgia, Florida, North Carolina, South Carolina, and Virginia.

general charged that the movement weakens the family institution and demoralizes women who wish to devote their lives to their families, husbands, and children.

ABORTION AND THE RIGHT TO LIFE

Abortion is a highly sensitive issue. It is not an issue that can easily be compromised. The arguments touch on fundamental moral and religious principles. Proponents of abortion, who often refer to themselves as "pro choice," argue that a woman should be permitted to control her own body and should not be forced by law to have unwanted children. They cite the heavy toll in lives lost in criminal abortions and the psychological and emotional pain of an unwanted pregnancy. Opponents of abortion, who often refer to themselves as "pro life," generally base their belief on the sanctity of life, including the life of the unborn child, which they believe deserves the protection of law—"the right to life." Many believe that the killing of an unborn child for any reason other than the preservation of the life of the mother is murder.

Early State Laws. Historically, abortions for any purpose other than saving the life of the mother were criminal offenses under state law. About a dozen states acted in the late 1960s to permit abortions in cases of rape or incest, or to protect the physical health of the mother, and in some cases her mental health as well. Relatively few abortions were performed under these laws, however, because of the red tape involved—review of each case by several concurring physicians, approval of a hospital board, and so forth. Then in 1970, New York, Alaska, Hawaii, and Washington enacted laws that in effect permitted abortion at the request of the woman involved and the concurrence of her physician.

Roe v. *Wade.* The U.S. Supreme Court's 1973 decision in *Roe* v. *Wade* was one of the most important and far-reaching in the court's history.[32] The Supreme Court ruled that the constitutional guarantee of "liberty" in the Fifth and Fourteenth Amendments included a woman's decision to bear or not to bear a child. The Supreme Court ruled that the word *person* in the Constitution did not include the unborn child. Therefore, the Fifth and Fourteenth Amendments to the Constitution, guaranteeing "life, liberty and property," did not protect the "life" of the fetus. The Court also ruled that a state's power to protect the health and safety of the mother could not justify *any* restriction on abortion in the first three months of pregnancy. Between the third and sixth months of pregnancy, a state could set standards for abor-

[32]*Roe* v. *Wade*, 410 U.S. 113 (1973).

tion procedures in order to protect the health of women, but a state could not prohibit abortions. Only in the final three months could a state prohibit or regulate abortion to protect the unborn.

Government Funding of Abortions.   The Supreme Court's decision did not end the controversy over abortion. Congress defeated efforts to pass a constitutional amendment restricting abortion or declaring that the guarantee of life begins at conception. However, Congress banned the use of federal funds under Medicaid (medical care for the poor) for abortions except to protect the life of a woman. The Supreme Court upheld the constitutionality of federal and state laws denying tax funds for abortions. While women retained the right to an abortion, the Court held that there was no constitutional obligation for governments to pay for abortions;[33] the decision about whether to pay for abortion from tax revenues was left to Congress and the states.

Efforts by the states to restrict abortion ran into Supreme Court opposition. The Court held that states and cities may *not* interfere with, or try to influence, a woman's decision to terminate a pregnancy. Specifically, the Supreme Court held that states may not require all abortions be performed in hospitals; require parental consent for all minors; require that physicians inform women of particular risks associated with abortion or provide information about fetal development; require a twenty-four hour waiting period between authorizing and performing an abortion.[34]

Abortions in the U.S.   About 1.5 million abortions are performed each year in the United States. This is about 43 percent of the number of live births. About 85 percent of all abortions are performed at abortion clinics; others are performed in physicians' offices or in hospitals, where the cost is significantly higher. Most of these abortions are performed in the first three months; about 10 percent are performed after the third month.

The Webster Case.   Opponents of abortion won a victory in *Webster* v. *Reproductive Health Services* (1989), when the Supreme Court upheld a Missouri law sharply restricting abortions.[35] The right to abortion under *Roe* v. *Wade* was not overturned, but it was narrowed in application. The effect of the decision was to return the question of abortion restrictions to the states for decision.

The Court held that Missouri could deny public funds for abortions that were not necessary for the life of the women, and could deny the use

[33]*Harris* v. *McRae,* 448 U.S. 297 (1980).

[34]*Planned Parenthood of Missouri* v. *Danforth,* 428 U.S. 52 (1976); Bellotti v. Baird, 443 U.S. 622 (1979); *Akron* v. *Akron Center for Reproductive Health,* 103 S. Ct. 2481 (1983).

[35]*Webster* v. *Reproductive Health Services,* 492 U.S. 111 (1989).

TABLE 3-6   Abortion Opinion

General

Should abortion be legal as it is now, or legal only in such cases as rape, incest or to save the life of the mother, or should it not be permitted at all?

Legal as it is now	49%
Legal only in certain cases	39
Not permitted at all	9

Specific Reasons

Please tell me whether or not you think it should be possible for a pregnant woman to obtain a legal abortion:

	YES	NO
if the woman's health is seriously endangered?	87%	7%
if there is a strong chance of serious defect in the baby?	69	21
if the family has a very low income and cannot afford any more children?	43	49
if she is not married and does not want to marry the man?	42	50
if the pregnancy interfered with work or education?	26	65

Restrictions

Would you support or oppose the following restrictions on abortion that may come before state legislatures?

	SUPPORT	OPPOSE
Medical tests must show fetus unable to survive outside womb.	54%	33%
Teenagers must have parent's permission.	75	22
Women seeking abortions must be counseled on the dangers and on alternatives to abortion.	88	9
No public funds for abortion except to save a woman's life.	61	34
No abortions in public facilities, except to save a woman's life.	54	41
Public employees may not perform, assist in, or advise abortion.	40	50

Sources: New York Times/CBS Poll, April, 1989 reported in *New York Times*, 26 April 1989; Newsweek Poll reported in *Newsweek*, 17 July 1989.

of public facilities or employees in performing or assisting in abortions. More importantly, the Court upheld the requirement for a test of "viability" after twenty weeks and a prohibition on abortions of a viable fetus except to save a woman's life. The Court recognized the state's "interest in the protection of human life when viability is possible." The Court did not specifically overrule *Roe* v. *Wade*'s assertion that abortion was a personal liberty of women protected by the U.S. Constitution. However, several justices appeared to believe that no such right could be found in the text of the Constitution. The minority dissent in this 5–4 decision argued that it "casts into darkness the hopes and visions of any woman in this country who has come to believe that the Constitution guaranteed her the right to exercise some control over her unique ability to bear children."

Abortion Battles. The effect of the *Webster* decision was to rekindle contentious debates over abortion in virtually all state capitols. Various legal restrictions on abortions have been passed in the states, including: (1) prohibitions on public financing of abortions; (2) requirements for a test of viability and prohibitions on abortions of viable fetus; (3) laws granting permission to doctors and hospitals to refuse to perform abortions; (4) laws requiring humane and sanitary disposal of fetal remains; (5) laws requiring physicians to inform patients about the development of the fetus and the availability of assistance in pregnancy; (6) laws requiring that parents of minors seeking abortion be informed; (7) laws requiring spouses to be informed; (8) laws requiring that late abortions be performed in hospitals; (9) laws setting standards of cleanliness and care in abortion clinics, (10) laws prohibiting abortion based on the gender of the fetus.

Public Opinion. Public opinion is deeply divided over the issue of abortion. While both "pro–choice" and "pro–life" forces claim to have public opinion on their side, public opinion is in fact almost equally split as to when abortions should be permitted (see Table 3–6). Many of the specific restrictions under consideration in state legislatures have majority support, including the prohibition of public funding for abortions.

SUMMARY

Let us try to set forth some propositions that are consistent with elite theory and assist in describing the development of civil rights policy.

1. Elites and masses in America differ in their attitudes toward blacks. Support for civil rights legislation has come from educated, affluent whites in leadership positions.

2. Mass opinion toward civil rights has generally *followed* public policy, and not led it. Mass opinion did not oppose legally segregated schools until after elites had declared national policy in *Brown* v. *Topeka*.

3. The greatest impetus to the advancement of civil rights policy in this century was the U.S. Supreme Court's decision in *Brown* v. *Topeka*. Thus, it was the Supreme Court, nonelected and enjoying life terms in office, which assumed the initiative in civil rights policy. Congress did not take significant action until ten years later.

4. Resistance to the implementation of *Brown* v. *Topeka* was centered in states and communities. Resistance to national policy was remarkably effective for over a decade; blacks were not admitted to white schools in the South in large numbers until all segments of the national elite—Congress and the executive branch, as well as the judicial branch—acted in support of desegregation.

5. The elimination of legal discrimination and the guarantee of equality of opportunity in the Civil Rights Act of 1964 were achieved largely through the dramatic appeals of middle-class black leaders to the consciences of white elites. Black leaders did not attempt to overthrow the established order, but to increase opportunities for blacks to achieve success within the American system.

6. Elite support for equality of opportunity does not satisfy the demands of black masses for absolute equality. Inequalities between blacks and whites in life chances—income, education, employment, health—persist, although the gap may be narrowing over the long run.

7. Affirmative action programs are pressed upon governments, universities, and private employers by federal agencies seeking to reduce inequalities. But white masses generally reject the notion of compensatory actions which they believe to disadvantage working-class and middle-class white males.

8. From its earliest beginnings, the feminist movement has frequently relied on the tactics of minorities—demonstrations, parades, and occasional civil disobedience—to convince governing elites to recognize women's rights. The Equal Rights Amendment won easy approval in Congress, but failed to win ratification by three-quarters of the states.

9. Abortion was prohibited by most of the states until the Supreme Court decided in *Roe* v. *Wade* in 1973 that women had a constitutional right under the Fifth and Fourteenth Amendments to terminate pregnancies. Thus, the Supreme Court established as a constitutional right what "pro-choice" forces had failed to gain through political processes. Following the Supreme Court's decision in *Webster* v. *Reproductive Health Services* in 1989 permitting some restrictions on abortion, "pro–choice" and "pro–life" forces renewed their political struggle in the states.

BIBLIOGRAPHY

BAXTER, SANDRA, and MARJORIE LANSING. *Women in Politics.* Ann Arbor: University of Michigan Press, 1980.
DECKARD, BARBARA S. *The Women's Movement,* 3rd ed. New York: Harper & Row, 1983.
FRANKLIN, JOHN HOPE. *From Slavery to Freedom.* 5th ed. New York: Knopf, 1978.
GLAZER, NATHAN. *Affirmative Discrimination.* New York: Basic Books, 1975.
KIRKPATRICK, JEANE. *The Politics of the Woman's Movement.* New York: D. McKay, 1975.
SOWELL, THOMAS. *Civil Rights: Rhetoric or Reality.* New York: William Morrow, 1984.
SOWELL, THOMAS. *Preferential Policies: An International Perspective.* New York: William Morrow, 1990.

4

CRIMINAL JUSTICE
rationality and irrationality
in public policy

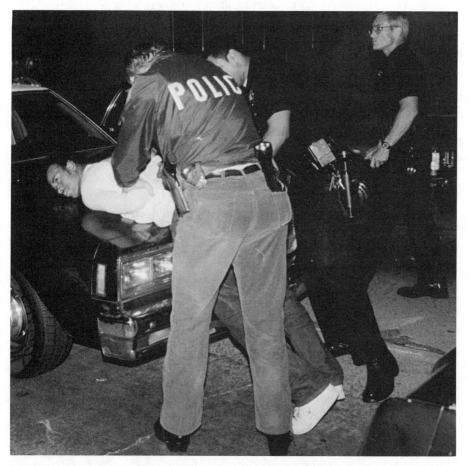

Los Angeles police officers search a person suspected of selling narcotics. (AP/Wide World Photos)

THE PROBLEM OF CRIME

Crime, violence, and social disorder are central problems confronting any society. So also is the problem of government repression. For thousands of years, philosophers and policy makers have wrestled with the question of balancing governmental power against individual freedom. How far can individual freedom be carried without undermining the stability of society and threatening the safety of others?

It is not an easy task to learn exactly how much crime occurs in society. The *official* crime rates are based upon the Federal Bureau of Investigation's *Uniform Crime Reports,* but the FBI reports are based on figures supplied by state and local police agencies (see Table 4–1). The FBI has established a uniform classification of the number of serious crimes per 100,000 people that are reported to the police—murder and nonnegligent manslaughter, forcible rape, robbery, aggravated assault, burglary, larceny, and theft, including auto theft. But one should be cautious in interpreting official crime rates. They are really a function of several factors: (1) the willingness of people to report crime, (2) the adequacy of the reporting system tabulating crime, and (3) the amount of crime itself.

Upward Trends in Crime Rates.   The national crime rate has risen dramatically yet unevenly over the past few decades. From 1960 to 1975 the crime rate more than doubled, and "law and order" became an important political issue. In the early 1980s crime rates leveled off and even declined slightly from their record years. It was widely believed that the early rapid

TABLE 4-1   Crime Rates in the United States: Offenses Known to the Police (Rates per 100,000 Population)

	1960	1965	1970	1972	1975	1978	1980	1983	1988
Murder	5	5	8	9	10	9	10	8	8
Forcible rape	9	12	18	22	26	31	36	34	38
Robbery	52	61	172	180	209	191	244	214	221
Aggravated assault	82	107	162	187	214	256	291	273	370
Burglary	465	605	1068	1126	1429	1424	1668	1334	1309
Larceny and theft	1028	1521	2066	1980	2473	2744	3156	2866	3135
Auto theft	179	251	454	423	461	455	495	429	583
Total crimes against persons	148	185	360	398	459	487	581	529	637
Total crimes against property	1672	2177	3588	3529	4363	4622	5319	4630	5027

Source: Federal Bureau of Investigation, *Uniform Crime Reports,* in *Statistical Abstract of the United States 1990.*

increase and later moderation was a product of age group changes in the population: the early baby boom had expanded the size of the "crime-prone" age group in the population, people fifteen to twenty-four; later, crime rates leveled off when this age group was no longer increasing as a percentage of the population. As late as 1983 many analysts were looking forward to gradual decreases in crime rates based on smaller crime–prone age groups. But in recent years crime rates have unexpectedly soared upward again. The new factor in the crime rate equation appears to be the widespread popularity of "crack" cocaine. Perhaps as many as one-half of all crimes today are drug related.

Victimization.   How much crime is there in America today? We know that the FBI official crime rate understates the real amount of crime. Many crimes are not reported to the police and therefore cannot be counted in the official crime rate. In an effort to learn the real amount of crime in the nation, the U.S. Justice Department regularly surveys a national sample of people asking whether they have been a victim of a crime during the past year.[1] These surveys reveal that the "victimization rate" is many times greater than the official crime rate. The number of forcible rapes is three to five times greater than the number reported to police, burglaries three times greater, and robbery over twice the reported rate. Only auto theft and murder statistics are reasonably accurate, indicating that most people call the police when their car is stolen or someone is murdered.

Why do people fail to report crime to the police? The most common reason given by interviewees is the feeling that police cannot be effective in dealing with the crime. Other reasons included the feeling that the crime was "a private matter" or that the victim did not want to harm the offender. Fear of reprisal was mentioned much less frequently, usually in cases of assaults and family crimes.[2]

Violent Crime.   About 3 percent of Americans are victims of *violent* crime each year. While this percentage might seem small, this represents about six million victims of violent crime. Moreover, this figure applies only to victimizations that take place in a single year. The percentage of persons victimized sometime during their life is much higher. For example, Americans have a 1-in-10,000 chance of being murdered in any one year. But they have a 1-in-133 chance of *ever* becoming a murder victim.[3]

[1]U.S. Department of Justice, *Criminal Victimization in the United States,* published annually. (Washington, D.C.: Bureau of Justice Statistics).

[2]See Wesley G. Skogan, "The Validity of Official Crime Statistics: Empirical Investigation," *Social Science Quarterly,* 55 (June 1974), 25–38.

[3]U.S. Department of Justice, *The Risk of Violent Crime* (Washington, D.C.: Bureau of Justice Statistics, 1985).

Blacks are victimized by crime more often than whites. For example, the lifetime risk of a black male becoming a murder victim is a startling 1-in-21, compared to a 1-in-131 risk for white males (see also Table 4–2). Men are more likely to be murdered, robbed, or assaulted than women, although women are far more likely to be raped than men. The lifetime risk of murder for all males is 1-in-84, compared to 1-in-282 for all females.

"Victimless" Crime.   It is fashionable today to dismiss or ignore crime statistics and to argue that "crime" is merely an activity which some legislative body has chosen to make illegal. But the FBI's Uniform Crime Reports does not count the so-called victimless crimes, including drug abuse, prostitution, and gambling. Murder, rape, robbery, aggravated assault, burglary, and theft are the *only* crimes reported by the FBI, and without question these crimes hurt people. Even if we assume that the "victimless" crimes do not hurt people (a very dubious assumption to anyone familiar with the life of a prostitute, a drug abuser, or a compulsive gambler), we must still be concerned with the rise in violent crime.

TABLE 4–2   Some Facts about Murder: Victims, Motives, Weapons

VICTIMS		MOTIVES		WEAPONS	
	MURDER RATE (1986)		PERCENT (1987)		PERCENT (1987)
Total	9.0	Felony total	19.6	Guns, total	59.2
		Robbery	9.4	Handguns	43.7
White		Narcotics	4.9	Stabbing	20.3
Male	8.6	Sex Abuses	0.3	Blunt Object	5.8
Female	3.0	Other felony	5.0	Strangulation beating	11.1
Black		Suspected felony	1.1	Arson	1.1
Male	55.0	Argument, total	36.7	Other	4.5
Female	12.1	Influence of alcohol, drugs	4.0		
		Property or money	2.6		
		Romantic	2.0		
		Other arguments	32.0		
		Other motives	17.7		
		Unknown, unnoticed	24.9		

Source: U.S. Bureau of the Census, *Crimes in the United States,* in *Statistical Abstract of the United States 1989,* pp. 168–169.

CRIME AND DETERRENCE

A rational strategy for dealing with crime would be to make the costs of committing crimes far greater than any benefits potential criminals might derive from their acts. With advanced knowledge of these costs, rational individuals should be deterred from committing crimes. Deterrence would be enhanced by:

1. The *certainty* that a crime will be followed by costly punishment. Justice must be sure.
2. The *swiftness* of the punishment following the crime. Long delays between crime and punishment break the link in the mind of the criminal between the criminal act and its consequences. And a potential wrongdoer must believe that the costs of a crime will occur within a meaningful time frame, not in a distant, unknowable future. Justice must be swift.
3. The *severity* of the punishment. Punishment which is perceived as no more costly than the ordinary hazards of life on the streets which the potential criminal faces anyhow, will not deter. Punishment must clearly outweigh whatever benefits might be derived from a life of crime in the mind of potential criminals. Punishment must be severe.

These criteria for an effective deterrent policy are ranked in the order of their probable importance. That is, it is most important that punishment for crime be certain. The severity of punishment is probably less important than its swiftness or certainty.

The current system of criminal justice in America is not a serious deterrent to crime. Punishment for crime is neither certain, swift, nor severe. We will argue that the criminal justice system itself, by failing to deter crime, is principally responsible for the fact that *crime in the United States is more common than any other advanced industrial nation of the world.*

Social Heterogeneity.   Of course, there are many other conflicting theories of crime in America. For example, it is sometime argued that this nation's high crime rate is a product of its social heterogeneity—the multiethnic, multiracial character of the American population. Low levels of crime in European countries, Japan, and China are often attributed to their homogeneous populations and shared cultures. Blacks in the United States are both victims and perpetrators of crime far more frequently than whites. While blacks constitute only about 12 percent of the population, they account for 29 percent of all of persons arrested for serious crime (see Table 4–3). A larger segment of the black population is in the young crime-prone age (fifteen to twenty-four years), and these youths are more likely to live outside husband-wife families. It is argued that "the streets" of the nation's black inner cities produces a subculture which encourages crime.

Irrational Crime.   It is also argued that crime is irrational, that is, the criminal does *not* weigh benefits against potential costs before committing the act. Many acts of violence are committed by persons acting in blind rage—murders and aggravated assaults among family members, for example. Many rapes are acts of violence, inspired by hatred of women, rather than efforts to obtain sexual pleasure. More murders occur in the heat of arguments than in the commission of other felonies (see Table 4–2). These are crimes of passion rather than calculated acts. Thus, it is argued, *no* rational policies can be devised to deter these irrational acts.

Age.   Crime is a young man's vocation. The most crime-prone age is eighteen to twenty-four (see Table 4–3), and juveniles under eighteen also account for much of the nation's criminal activity. Much of the increase in crime from 1965 to 1980 may be a product of the fact that the proportion of young people in the population was increasing during those years. And the modest declines in crime rates recently may be a product of the fact that this same crime-prone age group is declining as a percentage of the nation's population.

The youthfulness of most criminal offenders detracts from the effectiveness of deterrent policies. It is sometimes argued that young people do not "think before they act" in crime. Older people are more prone to consider the costs and consequences of their acts than young people. Perhaps all we need to do is wait until the population grows older and crime rates will decline as a result of maturity.

Protecting Individual Liberty.   Finally, we must recognize that the reduction of crime is not the overriding value of American society. Americans

TABLE 4-3   Arrests by Age, Sex, and Race

PERCENT OF TOTAL ARRESTS (1987)	
Male	82.3
Female	17.7
White	68.7
Black	29.5
Other	2.9
Under 18	16.5
18–24	33.6
25–34	33.9
35–44	14.3
45–54	5.2
55 and over	3.1

Source: U.S. Bureau of the Census, *Crime in the United States* in *Statistical Abstract of the United States 1987*, p. 173.

cherish individual liberty. Freedom from repression—from unlawful arrests, forced confessions, restrictions on movement, curfews, arbitrary police actions, unlimited searching of homes or seizures of property, punishment without trial, trials without juries, unfair procedures, brutal punishments, etc.—is more important to Americans than freedom from crime. Many authoritarian governments boast of low crime rates and criminal justice systems which ensure certain, swift, and severe punishment, but these governments fail to protect the personal liberties of their citizens. Indeed, given the choice of punishing all of the guilty, even if some innocents are also punished by mistake, or taking care that innocent persons not be punished, even if some guilty people escape, most Americans would choose the second alternative—protecting innocent persons.

Nonetheless, despite these problems, we shall argue that the frequency of crime in America is largely a product of the failure to adopt rational criminal justice policies.

Certainty.   The best available estimates of the certainty of punishment for serious crime suggests that very few crimes actually result in jail sentences for the perpetrators. Over 13 million serious crimes were reported to police in 1987; but only 2.5 million persons were arrested for these crimes (see Figure 4–1). Some of those arrested were charged with committing more than one crime, but it is estimated that police clear less than 20 percent of reported crimes by arresting the offender. Prosecutors do not charge about half of the persons arrested for serious offenses. Some offenders are handled as juveniles; some are permitted to plead guilty to minor offenses; others are

FIGURE 4-1   Crime and Punishment. (Source: Data from *Statistical Abstract of the United States 1989*, pp. 166, 177, 183).

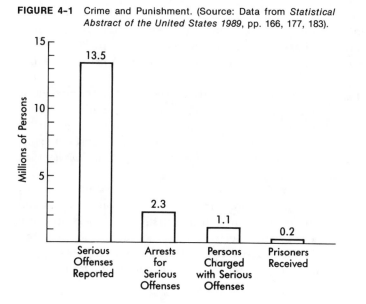

released because witnesses fail to appear or evidence is weak or inadmissible in court. Of the persons charged with serious offenses by prosecutors, fewer than 20 percent receive jail sentences for their crimes. Convicted felons are three times more likely to receive probation instead of a prison sentence. Thus, even if punishment could deter crime, our current criminal justice system does *not* insure punishment for crime.

Swiftness. The deterrent effect of a criminal justice system is lost when punishment is so long delayed that it has little relationship to the crime. The *bail system,* together with *trial delays,* allow criminal defendants to escape the consequences of their acts for long indefinite periods of time. Most criminal defendants are free on bail shortly after their arrest; only persons accused of the most serious crimes and adjudged to be likely to flee before trial are held in jail without bond. In preliminary hearings held shortly after arrest, judges release most defendants pending trial; even after a trial and a guilty verdict, many defendants are free on bail pending the outcome of lengthy appeals. The Constitution guarantees persons accused of crimes freedom from "excessive bail" (Eighth Amendment), and judges may not hold defendants in jail simply because they think the defendants might commit additional crimes while out on bail.

The court system works very slowly and delays favor the criminal defendant. Defendants request delays in court proceedings in order to remain free as long as possible. Moreover, they know that witnesses against them will lose interest, move away, grow tired of the hassle, and even forget key facts, if only the case can be postponed long enough. Some criminal cases are delayed for years.

Justice delayed destroys the deterrent effect, especially in the minds of youthful offenders who are "present oriented" rather than "future oriented." Inner-city youths, with no real prospects for the future anyhow, concentrate their attention on today, tomorrow and perhaps the next day, rather than years into the future. In their limited time frame of reference, they may consider the benefits of their criminal acts to be immediate, while the costs to be so far in the future that they have no real meaning to them. Or the costs may be estimated to be only the arrest itself and a night in jail before release on bail. For deterrence to work, the perceived costs of crime must be greater than the perceived benefits in *the minds of potential wrong-doers.*

Severity. More people are imprisoned today in America than at any previous time. Not only are there more inmates in the nation's prisons, but the *proportion* of the nation's population behind bars is the highest in recent history. (In 1970, 97 of every 100,000 persons was a federal or state prisoner, compared to 228 in 1987). This increase in the prison population suggests that the court system is not really becoming any more lenient over time. On the contrary, in recent years there has been an increase in the likelihood of imprisonment as a punishment following conviction for a serious crime.

Early Releases.   However, prison overcrowding has led to the early release of most prisoners. The deterrent effect of severe sentences is lost, of course, when criminals know that they will not serve their full sentences. Violent criminals on the average serve only half of their sentences, and non-violent offenders less than one-third of their sentences. In some states, due to heavy prison overcrowding, inmates serve only one quarter of their sentences. In many states, early release programs have become institutional-ized. The national average of prison time actually served by convicted murderers is six years.[4]

Thus, the criminal justice system does not succeed in incapacitating criminals for very long. Indeed, it is estimated that about 20 percent of all violent crimes and 30 percent of property crimes are committed by *persons who would still have been in prison on earlier convictions if they had served their full sentences.*[5] These "avertable" crimes are increasing over time as early release is increasingly used to relieve prison overcrowding.

Incapacitation.   Do prison sentences reduce crime? It is clear that re-moving habitual offenders from the streets reduces the crime they commit outside the prison walls for the duration of their sentences. Thus, long sentences can reduce crime rates by "incapacitating" habitual criminals for long periods. (Very few first offenders are sentenced to prison.) But there is no evidence that the prison experience itself deters people from commit-ting more crime after they are released.

Recidivism.   Punishment has no discernible effect on the subsequent criminal behavior of persons who have been convicted and imprisoned. An estimated 61 percent of persons admitted to prison are "recidivists," that is, persons who have previously served a sentence of incarceration as a juvenile, adult, or both. Of those 39 percent entering prisons without a prior record of incarceration, nearly 60 percent have prior convictions that resulted in probation. Thus, a total of 85 percent of all persons admitted to prison have prior convictions.[6] Clearly the criminal justice system did not "rehabili-tate" these persons.

In summary, the severity of punishment does not deter crime, although it may protect the general public by incapacitating criminals.

[4]Richard B. Abell, "Beyond Willie Horton: The Battle of the Prison Bulge," *Policy Review,* 47 (Winter, 1989), 32–35.

[5]John J. DiIulio, Jr., "Punishing Smarter," *Brookings Review* (Summer, 1989), 3–12.

[6]U. S. Department of Justice, Bureau of Justice Statistics, *Examining Readmission.* February, 1985.

POLICE AND LAW ENFORCEMENT

The principal responsibility for law enforcement in America rests with state and local governments. The Federal Bureau of Investigation in the Department of Justice was created in the 1920s and charged with the responsibility of enforcing only federal laws. Today, the role of the federal government in law enforcement is growing, but state and local governments continue to carry the major burdens of police protection, judicial systems, and prison and parole programs. The federal government employs less than 50,000 persons in all law enforcement activities, compared with over one-half million state and local government law enforcement personnel. Federal prisons contain about 40,000 inmates, compared with over 500,000 in state prisons.

Police Functions.   At least three important functions in society are performed by police: law enforcement, keeping the peace, and furnishing services. Actually, law enforcement may take up only a small portion of a police officer's daily activity, perhaps only 10 percent.[7] The service function is far more common—attending accidents, directing traffic, escorting crowds, assisting stranded motorists, and so on. The function of peace keeping is also very common—breaking up fights, quieting noisy parties, handling domestic or neighborhood quarrels, and the like. It is in this function that police exercise the greatest discretion in the application of the law. In most of these incidents, it is difficult to determine blame. Participants are reluctant to file charges and police must use personal discretion in handling each case.

Police are on the front line of society's efforts to resolve conflict. Indeed, instead of a legal or law enforcement role, the police are more likely to adopt a peace-keeping role. Police are generally lenient in their arrest practices; that is, they use their arrest powers less often than the law allows.[8] Rather than arresting people, the police prefer first to reestablish order. Of course, the decision to be more or less lenient in enforcing the law gives the police a great deal of discretion—the police exercise decision-making powers on the streets.

Police Discretion.   What factors influence police decision making? Probably the first factor to influence police behavior is the attitude of the other people involved in police encounters. If a person adopts an acquiescent role, displays deference and respect for the police, and conforms to police ex-

---

[7]James Q. Wilson, *Varieties of Police Behavior* (Cambridge: Harvard University Press, 1968), p. 18; Arthur Niederhoffer, *Behind the Shield* (New York: Doubleday, 1967), p. 71.

[8]Donald J. Black, "Social Organization of Arrest," in *The Criminal Justice Process,* ed. William B. Sanders and Howard C. Davidstel (New York: Holt, Rinehart & Winston, 1976).

pectations, he or she is much less likely to be arrested than a person who shows disrespeci or uses abusive language toward police.[9] This is not just an arbitrary response of police. They learn through training and experience the importance of establishing their authority on the streets.

Police Culture. The tasks assigned to police in an urban society would confound highly trained social scientists. Yet only recently have police officers been recruited from colleges and universities. Formal police training emphasizes self-control and caution in dealing with the public, but on-the-job experiences probably reinforce distrust of others. The element of danger in the police officer's job makes him or her naturally suspicious of others. Police officers see much of the "worst kind" of people, and they see even the "best kind" at their worst.

Police forces are semimilitary organizations engaged in rule enforcement. Police must be concerned with authority themselves, and they expect others to respect authority. One study neatly summarizes "police culture" in terms of the attitudes that police bring to the streets:

> People cannot be trusted; they are dangerous.
> Experience is better than abstract rules.
> You must make people respect you.
> Everyone hates a cop.
> Stronger punishment will deter crime.
> The major job of police is to prevent crime.[10]

Police in the Ghetto. It is often difficult for even the most well-meaning police officer to develop respect or sympathy for inner-city residents. One police officer described this problem as follows:

> The police have to associate with lower-class people, slobs, drunks, criminals, riffraff of the worst sort. Most of these . . . are Negroes. The police officers see these people through middle-class or lower-middle-class eyeballs. But even if he saw them through highly sophisticated eyeballs he can't go in the street and take this night after night. When some Negro criminal says to you a few times, "you white mother-fucker, take that badge off and I'll shove it up your ass," well, it's bound to affect you after a while. Pretty soon you decide they're all just niggers and they'll never be anything but niggers. It would take not just an average man to resist this feeling, it would take an extraordinary man to resist it, and there are very few ways by which the police department can attract extraordinary men to join them.[11]

[9]Stuart A. Sheingold, "Cultural Cleavage and Criminal Justice," *Journal of Politics*, 40, 865–97.

[10]Peter Manning, "The Police" in *Criminal Justice in America* ed. Richard Quinney (Boston: Little, Brown, 1974).

[11]Wilson, *Varieties of Police Behavior*, p. 43.

The police officer's attitude toward ghetto residents is often affected by the high crime rates in ghetto areas. The police officer is suspicious of ghetto residents because crime rates tell him that his suspicions are often justified.

If police are overly suspicious of ghetto blacks, the attitudes of many ghetto blacks toward police are equally hostile. Black novelist James Baldwin writes of police in the ghetto:

> Their very presence is an insult, and it would be, even if they spent their entire day feeding gumdrops to children. They represent the force of the white world, and that world's real intentions are simply to keep the black man corralled up here, in his place. The badge, the gun and the holster and the swinging club make vivid what will happen should his rebellion become overt. . . .
> He has never himself done anything for which to be hated—which of us has? And yet he is facing, daily and nightly, people who would gladly see him dead, and he knows it.[12]

Police and Crime Prevention.   Does increased police protection significantly reduce crime? The common assumption is that increased police presence and increased police expenditures can significantly reduce crime in cities. But, unfortunately, it is very difficult to produce firm evidence to support this assumption. Studies of crime rates in relation to number of police officers and to expenditure have failed to find any strong evidence to support the more-police-activity-equals-less-crime theory.[13] So many other factors may affect crime rates in cities—size, density, youth, unemployment, race, poverty, and so forth—that police activity appears insignificant. Or an increase in police activity may result in increased crime reporting, which tends to obscure any actual reduction in crime in official statistics.

CRIME AND GUNS

Many crimes involve the use of guns. Specifically, the FBI reports that 21 percent of all aggravated assaults, 37 percent of all robberies, and 59 percent of all murders were accomplished with guns.[14] Would registering guns, licensing gun owners, or banning handguns reduce crime?

Gun control legislation is a common policy initiative following murders or assassination attempts on prominent figures. The Federal Gun Control Act of 1968 was a response to the assassinations of Senator Robert F. Kennedy and Martin Luther King, Jr., in that year, and efforts to legislate additional restrictions occurred after attempts to assassinate Presidents Gerald Ford and Ronald Reagan. The rationale for licensing gun owners or ban-

---

[12]James Baldwin, *Nobody Knows My Name* (New York: Dell Pub. Co., Inc., 1962), pp. 61–62.
[13]E. Terrance Jones, "Evaluating Everyday Policies: Police Activity and Crime Incidence," *Urban Affairs Quarterly,* 8 (March 1973), 267–79.
[14]*Statistical Abstract of the United States 1989,* p. 174.

ning guns altogether is that fewer crimes would be committed with guns if guns were less readily available. Murders, especially crimes of passion among family members or neighbors, would be reduced, if for no other reason than that it is physically more difficult to kill someone with only a knife, a club, or bare hands. Proponents of gun control note that the U.S. has less restrictive gun laws than other advanced nations and that it has the highest murder rate.

Federal Law. The Federal Gun Control Act of 1968, as amended, includes the following:

1. A ban on interstate and mail-order sales of handguns.
2. Prohibition of the sale of any firearms to a convicted felon, fugitive, or adjudicated mental defective.
3. A requirement that all firearms dealers must be licensed by the Federal Bureau of Alcohol, Tobacco, and Firearms of the Department of the Treasury.
4. A requirement that manufacturers record by serial number all firearms, and dealers record all sales. Dealers must require proof of identity and residence of buyers, and buyers must sign a statement certifying their eligibility to purchase.
5. Continued restrictions of private ownership of automatic weapons, military weapons, and other heavy ordinance. Prior Treasury Department approval of the purchaser and $200 tax is imposed on each of these weapons.

Federal regulations also bar the importation of "assault weapons," which are generally defined as automatic weapons.

State Laws. State laws, and many local ordinances, also govern gun ownership. Handgun laws are common in the states. Most states require that a record of sale be submitted to state or local government agencies; some states require an application and a waiting period prior to purchase of a handgun; a few states require a license or a permit to purchase one; most states require a license to carry a "concealed" weapon; and four states (Illinois, Massachusetts, New Jersey, and New York) prohibit any handgun ownership except by persons licensed by law enforcement officials.

Gun Ownership. Gun ownership is widespread in the United States. Estimates vary, but there are probably 150 million firearms in the hands of the nation's 236 million people. Half of all American families admit in public opinion surveys to owning guns. A majority of gun owners say their guns are for hunting and sports; about one-third say the purpose of their gun ownership is self-defense. The proportion of gun owners who have ever used their gun in self-defense is infinitesimal. Indeed, the likelihood of being hurt with one's own weapon is far greater than the chance of inflicting harm upon an assailant. Interestingly, *both* those who favor a ban on handguns and those who oppose such a ban cite "crime" as the reason for their position. Those who want to ban guns say they contribute to crime and violence. Those who oppose a ban feel they need guns for protection against crime and violence.

Gun Laws and Crime.   There is no systematic evidence that gun control laws can reduce violent crime. If we compare violent crime rates in jurisdictions with very restrictive gun laws (especially New York, Massachusetts, New Jersey, and Illinois) to violent crime rates in jurisdictions with very loose controls on gun ownership, we find no differences in rates of violent crime that cannot be attributed to social conditions. Gun laws, including purchase permits, waiting periods, carrying permits, and even complete prohibitions, seem to have no effect on violent crime, or even crimes committed with guns.[15] Indeed, gun laws do not even appear to have any effect on gun ownership. Even the Massachusetts ban on handguns, which calls for a mandatory prison sentence for unlicensed citizens found carrying a firearm, did not reduce gun-related crime.[16] The total number of persons imprisoned for gun crimes was essentially unchanged; however, more persons without criminal records were arrested and charged with gun law violations. Of course, it might be argued that state and local laws are inadequate and only a rigorously enforced federal law could effectively ban handguns. But to date we must conclude that "there is little evidence to show that gun ownership among the population as a whole is, per se, an important cause of criminal violence."[17]

Cross-National Comparisons.   Public policies in the United States are seldom argued from a cross-national perspective; but gun control is an exception. A surprising amount of attention is devoted to comparisons between the United States and other nations. Gun control proponents cite the experience of Great Britain and Japan, where ownership of handguns is prohibited and violent crime is very rare (although the situation in Great Britain may be deteriorating). Opponents of gun control can cite the national experience in Israel, where military reservists (eighteen to fifty years of age) keep automatic weapons in their home and violent crime is virtually nonexistent. In short, cultural factors obscure any lessons that cross-national comparisons might teach about the value of gun control.[18]

[15]Douglas R. Murray, "Handguns, Gun Control Laws and Firearm Violence," *Social Problems,* 23 (1975); James D. Wright and Peter H. Rossi, *Weapons, Crime, and Violence in America* (Washington, D.C.: U.S. Department of Justice, National Institute of Justice, 1981).

[16]David Rossman, *The Impact of the Mandatory Gun Law in Massachusetts* (Boston: Boston University School of Law, 1979).

[17]Wright and Rossi, *Weapons, Crime, and Violence in America,* p. 540.

[18]Barry Bruce-Biggs, "The Great American Gun War," *The Public Interest* (Fall 1976), 37–62.

The Right to Bear Arms.   The gun control debate also involves constitutional issues. The Second Amendment to the U.S. Constitution states: "A well regulated militia, being necessary to the security of a free state, the right of the people to keep and bear arms, shall not be infringed." Opponents of gun control view the right "to keep and bear arms" as an *individual* constitutional right, like the First Amendment freedom of speech or press. Proponents of gun control argue that the Second Amendment protects only the *collective* rights of the people to form state militias, that is, the right of the states to maintain National Guard units. Either interpretation can be defended. Opponents of gun control argue that all rights set forth in the Bill of Rights are interpreted as individual rights. The history surrounding the adoption of the Second Amendment reveals the concern of colonists with the attempt by a despotic government to confiscate the arms of citizens and render them helpless to resist tyranny. James Madison writes in *The Federalist No. 46* that "the advantage of being armed which the Americans possess over the people of almost every other nation, . . . forms a barrier against the enterprise of [tyrannical] ambition." Early American political rhetoric is filled with praise for an armed citizenry able to protect its freedoms with force if necessary. And the "militia" was defined as every adult free male able to carry a weapon. Even the early English common law recognized the right of individuals "to have and use arms for self-protection and defense."[19] Proponents of gun control cite the U.S. Supreme Court decision in *United States v. Miller* (1939).[20] In this case, the Court considered the constitutionality of the federal National Firearms Act of 1934, which, among other things, prohibited the transportation of sawed-off shotguns in interstate commerce. The defendant claimed that Congress could not infringe upon his right to keep and bear arms. But the Court responded that a sawed-off shotgun had no "relationship to the preservation or efficiency of a well-regulated militia." The clear implication of this decision is that the right to bear arms refers only to a state's right to maintain a militia.

Ethical Conflict.   Perhaps the argument over gun control really has nothing to do with reducing crime or with constitutional interpretations. Instead, two ethics are in conflict. There is the established upper-class liberal ethic of a civilized, educated, well-ordered society that can resolve conflict through laws, courts, and institutions. There is also the individualist ethic stressing one's own responsibility for the protection of family and property in a tough and sometimes dangerous world. These contrasting ethics in America are clearly in conflict over the gun control issue.

---

[19]William Blackstone, *Commentaries of the Laws of England*, Vol. 1, p. 144.
[20]*United States* v. *Miller*, 307 U.S. 174 (1939).

THE DRUG WAR

Public policy toward drug use in America is ambivalent. Alcohol and cigarettes are legal products, although the Office of the Surgeon General of the United States has undertaken educational campaigns to reduce their use, and Congress has banned the advertising of alcohol and tobacco on radio and television. (See Chapter 6 for a discussion of the effectiveness of these health measures.) Marijuana has been "decriminalized" in several states, making its use or possession a misdemeanor comparable to a traffic offense; a majority of states, however, have retained criminal sanctions against marijuana, and its manufacture and distribution are prohibited everywhere. The potential for drug abuse is found in many prescription medicines—amphetamines, barbiturates, and tranquilizers. The use and possession of cocaine is a criminal offense everywhere in the United States. Heroin is a physically addictive drug, but its use in the United States is declining somewhat.[21]

Drug Use.   It is difficult to estimate the various forms of drug use. According to the U.S. National Institute on Drug Abuse, there are 12 to 14 million "problem drinkers," or about 6 percent of the population. There are an estimated 50 million cigarette smokers, or about 30 percent of the adult population (significantly less than the 45 percent of the population who smoked cigarettes in the 1940s and 1950s). There are an estimated 12 million regular users of marijuana, or about 6 percent of the population, although many more have smoked it at least once.

Recent surveys suggest a modest decline in drug use. The National Institute on Drug Abuse regularly surveys Americans to ask whether they have ever used particular drugs and whether they have used them in the past year or month. These surveys suggest that about 20 million people, or 8 percent of the U.S. population, have used an illicit drug in the previous thirty days (see Figure 4–2). Marijuana is the most commonly used illicit drug, followed by cocaine. According to this survey evidence, the casual use of drugs has declined somewhat in recent years. However, other surveys suggest that hardcore daily use remains high. Thus, while three million Americans may use cocaine at least once a month, two million of these people may be considered "addicted."[22]

Marijuana.   Public policy toward marijuana use illustrates many of the contradictions in drug policy. The medical evidence on the health effects of marijuana is mixed; conflicting reports have been issued about whether

[21]Richard C. Schroeder, *The Politics of Drugs,* 2nd ed. (Washington, D.C.: Congressional Quarterly Inc., 1980), p. 80.

[22]U.S. Senate Judiciary Committee, as reported in the *New York Times,* 10 May 1990.

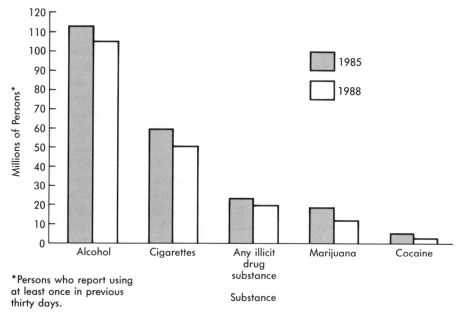

FIGURE 4-2 Drug Use. (Source: National Institute on Drug Abuse.)

or not it is more dangerous than alcohol.[23] The U.S. prohibited the manufacture and use of alcohol for only thirteen years, during Prohibition, 1920 to 1933. Today the manufacture and sale of alcohol is legal in most U.S. jurisdictions, but marijuana is not. Marijuana arrests in the late 1960s and early 1970s approached one-half million per year. The estimates of the number of "problem drinkers" and regular marijuana users are very close. One explanation of the different public policies toward alcohol and marijuana centers on the different generations which use each drug. Marijuana became very popular in the United States in the 1960s, so its users tended to be young. As this generation of Americans grew older, the movement to "decriminalize" marijuana strengthened. "Decriminalizing" marijuana does not make its production or sale legal, but makes its possession (generally of an ounce or less) a civil offense, much like a traffic offense. Oregon was the first state to decriminalize marijuana possession and use in 1973.

Heroin. Public policy toward heroin use has been far more consistent and restrictive over the years. Since the Harrison Narcotic Act of 1916, heroin use has been considered a major law enforcement problem. In contrast, in Great Britain since 1920 heroin use has been considered a medical problem and heroin is dispensed to addicted patients through physicians in the Na-

---

[23]For a summary of this evidence and references to the relevant health literature, see Schroeder, *The Politics of Drugs,* ch. 4.

tional Health Service. Heroin addiction in the United States is estimated to be greater than in Great Britain. Over the years in the United States the extent of heroin addiction has varied with the success or failure of law enforcement. During the 1930s and 1940s with strong federal law enforcement efforts (almost one-third of all federal prisoners in 1928 were violators of the Harrison Act), heroin use declined. It rose again in the 1960s, but in the early 1970s the United States succeeded in pressing the Turkish government to ban opium poppy growing, and law enforcement officials in the United States and France succeeded with their "French Connection" efforts to destroy a major drug smuggling syndicate, and use declined somewhat. In recent years cocaine has replaced heroin as the major drug smuggled into the United States. Most law enforcement officials doubt that heroin or cocaine traffic can ever be eliminated by law enforcement. As Schroeder reports, "It takes only 10 square miles of poppies to feed the entire American heroin market and they grow everywhere."[24]

Cocaine.   The burgeoning market for cocaine currently challenges law enforcement efforts. Cocaine is not regarded as physically addictive, although the psychological urge to continue use of the drug is strong. It is made from coca leaves and imported into the United States. Originally, its high cost, and celebrity use made it favored in upper-class circles. However, cocaine use spread rapidly in the streets with the introduction of "crack" in the 1980s. Crack cocaine can be smoked and a single "hit" purchased for a few dollars. The health problems associated with cocaine use are fairly serious, as reported by the National Institute on Drug Abuse.[25] Death, although rare, can occur from a single ingestion. The power of the coca leaf has been known for hundreds of years; Coca-Cola originally contained cocaine, though the drug was removed from the popular drink in 1903.

Trafficking.   Crime associated with drug trafficking is a serious national problem, whatever the health effects of various drugs. The world of drug trafficking is fraught with violence. Sellers rob and murder buyers and vice versa: neither can seek the protection of police or courts in their dealing with the other. Although some citizens might wish to allow dealers to wipe each other out, the frequency with which innocent bystanders are killed must be considered.

It is very difficult to estimate the total size of the drug market, but 20 to 25 billion dollars per year is a common figure.[26] This would suggest that the drug business is comparable in size to one of the ten largest U.S. industrial corporations. More important, perhaps, drugs produce huge profit margins:

[24]Schroeder, *Politics of Drugs,* p. 148.
[25]Ibid., ch. 9.
[26]*Congressional Quarterly Weekly Report,* 25 June 1988.

a kilo of cocaine purchased in Colombia may cost only $3,600; when sold in the United States, that kilo may retail for $80,000 to $120,000.[27] The price of smuggling a single, easily concealable kilo may run to $15,000. These huge profits allow drug traffickers to corrupt police and government officials as well as private citizens in the United States and other nations.

Drug Policy.   Anti-drug efforts can be divided into three categories: interdiction, enforcement, and education.

Interdiction: Efforts to seal U.S. borders against the importation of drugs have been frustrated by the sheer volume of smuggling. Each year increasingly large drug shipments are intercepted by the U.S. Drug Enforcement Administration, the U.S. Customs Service, the Coast Guard, and state and local agencies. Yet each year the volume of drugs entering the country seems to increase. Drug "busts" are considered just another cost of business to the traffickers. It is not likely that the use of U.S. military forces to augment other federal agencies can succeed in sealing our borders. U.S. pressure against Latin American governments to destroy coca crops and assist in interdiction has already resulted in strained relationships. Our neighboring countries wonder why the U.S. government directs its efforts at the suppliers, when the demand for drugs arises within the United States itself.

Enforcement: The FBI and state local law enforcement agencies already devote great efforts to combating drugs; an estimated 40 percent of all arrests in the United States are drug related. Federal and state prisons now hold a larger percentage of the nation's population than ever before. Sentences have lengthened for drug trafficking and prisons are overcrowded as a direct result of drug-related convictions. Drug testing in government and private employment is increasing, but unless it is random it is not very useful and some courts have prevented random testing of individuals without their consent.

Education: Efforts at educating the public about the dangers of drugs have inspired many public and private campaigns, from former First Lady Nancy Reagan's "Just say no" to Jesse Jackson's "Up with hope, down with dope." But it is difficult to evaluate the effects of these efforts.

Enforcement Responsibilities.   The U.S. Drug Enforcement Administration (DEA) in the Department of Justice was created by Congress in 1973. It has the authority to enforce federal drug laws both in the United States and abroad. (Earlier responsibility had been shared by various agencies, including the Treasury Department's Bureau of Narcotics.) DEA officers may go abroad to collect international intelligence and to cooperate with foreign authorities. The U.S. Customs Service has the responsibility of stopping the entry of narcotics at U.S. borders. The U.S. Coast Guard cooperates in drug

[27]Ethan A. Nadelmann, "U.S. Drug Policy," *Foreign Policy* (Spring, 1988) 83–108.

interception. The FBI monitors drug trafficking that contributes to other federal crimes. Surveillance of low-level buying and selling of drugs is usually left to state and local authorities.

Drug Czar.   Congress created a cabinet-level "drug-czar" position in 1988 to develop and coordinate anti-drug policy in the United States. The first National Drug Control Policy Director, William J. Bennett, submitted his recommendations to President Bush in 1989 and the president's anti-drug program was forwarded to Congress. The program included new funds for federal prison construction and more courts and prosecutors; grants for state and local drug law enforcement; increased money for border control for the Coast Guard, Customs Service, and Immigration and Naturalization Service; authorization for use of the U.S. military in drug enforcement; and additional funds for the Drug Enforcement Administration. Congress added funds for treatment programs in states and cities.

Policy Effectiveness.   It is difficult to assess accurately the effectiveness of anti-drug policies. The National Institute of Drug Abuse has published interview data showing some recent modest declines in self-reported drug use (see Figure 4–2). The DEA reports increasing numbers of cocaine seizures and drug arrests each year, yet there appears to be no significant reduction in the availability of drugs on the street.

Although opinion polls show that Americans consistently rank drugs as one of the most important problems confronting the nation, no effective public policies appear likely to be adopted. As a nation the United States is both wealthy and free, two conditions that make it a perfect market for illicit drugs. The costs of truly effective enforcement, both in terms of dollar expenditures and, more importantly, in terms of lost individual liberty, may be more than our society wishes to pay.

Legalization?   The failure of anti-drug policies to produce any significant reductions in drug supply or demand, coupled with the high costs of enforcement and the loss of civil liberties, have caused some observers to propose the legalization of drugs and government control of their production and sales. Prohibition failed earlier in the century to end alcohol consumption, and crime, official corruption, and the enormous cost of futile efforts to stop individuals from drinking eventually forced the nation to end Prohibition. It is similarly argued that the legalization of drugs would end organized crime's profit monopoly over the drug trade, raise billions of dollars by legally taxing drugs, end the strain on relations with Latin American nations caused by efforts to eradicate drugs, and save additional billions in enforcement costs, which could be used for education and drug treatment.[28] If drugs were legally obtainable under government supervision,

[28]Ethan A. Nadelmann, "The Case for Legalization," *The Public Interest* (Summer, 1988), 3–31.

it is argued that many of society's current problems would be alleviated: the crime and violence associated with the drug trade, the corruption of public officials, the spread of diseases associated with drug use, and the many infringements of personal liberty associated with anti-drug wars.

But even the suggestion of drug legalization offends Americans who believe that legalization would greatly expand drug use in the country. Cheap, available drugs would greatly increase the numbers of addicted persons, creating a "society of zombies" that would destroy the social fabric of the nation. Cocaine and heroin are far more habit forming than alcohol, and legalization would encourage the development of newer and even more potent and addictive synthetic drugs. Whatever the health costs of drug abuse today, it is argued that legalization would produce public health problems of enormous magnitude.[29] Cocaine is very cheap to produce; the current five- to ten-dollar cost of a "hit" is mostly drug dealer profit; legalization, even with taxation, might produce a fifty-cent "hit." Whatever the damages to society from drug-related crime and efforts to prohibit drugs, the damages to society from cheap, available drug usage would be far greater.

CRIME AND THE COURTS

The present system of criminal justice does not deter crime. A major stumbling block to effective law enforcement is the current plight of America's judicial machinery. Former Chief Justice Warren E. Burger listed some of the major problems in America's court system:

> Major congestion on court dockets that delays the hearing of cases months or even years. Moreover, actual trials now average twice as long as ten years ago.
>
> Failure of courts to adopt modern management and administrative practice to speed and improve justice.
>
> Increased litigation in the courts. Not only are more Americans aware of their rights, but more are using every avenue of appeal. Seldom do appeals concern the guilt or innocence of the defendant; they usually focus on procedural matters.
>
> Excessive delays in trials. According to Burger, "Defendants, whether guilty or innocent, are human; they love freedom and hate punishment. With a lawyer provided to secure release without the need for a conventional bail bond, most defendants, except in capital cases, are released pending trial. We should not be surprised that a defendant on bail exerts a heavy pressure on his court-appointed lawyer to postpone the trial as long as possible so as to remain free. These postponements—and sometimes there are a dozen or more—consume the time of judges and court staffs as well as of lawyers. Cases are calendared and reset time after time while witnesses and jurors spend hours just waiting."
>
> Excessive delays in appeals. "We should not be surprised at delay when more and more defendants demand their undoubtedly constitutional right to trial by jury because we have provided them with lawyers and other needs at public

[29] John Kaplan, "Taking Drugs Seriously," *The Public Interest* (Summer, 1988), 32–50.

expense; nor should we be surprised that most convicted persons seek a new trial when the appeal costs them nothing and when failure to take the appeal will cost them freedom. Being human, a defendant plays out the line which society has cast him. Lawyers are competitive creatures and the adversary system encourages contention and often rewards delay; no lawyers want to be called upon to defend the client's charge of incompetence for having failed to exploit all the procedural techniques which we have deliberately made available."

Excessive variation in sentencing. Some judges let defendants off on probation for crimes that would draw five- or ten-year sentences by other judges. Although flexibility in sentencing is essential in dealing justly with individuals, perceived inconsistencies damage the image of the courts in the public mind.

Excessive "plea bargaining" between the prosecution and the defendant's attorney in which the defendant agrees to plead guilty to a lesser offense if the prosecutor will drop more serious charges.[30]

Insufficient Evidence and Dismissal. About half of all felony arrests result in dismissal of the charges against the defendant. This decision is usually made by the prosecutor (the state's attorney, district attorney, or county prosecutor, as the office is variously designated in the states; or a prosecuting attorney in the U.S. Department of Justice in a federal criminal case). The prosecutor may determine that the offense is not serious, or that the offender is not a danger to society, or that the resources of his office would be better spent pursuing other cases. But the most common reason for the dismissal of the charges is insufficient evidence.

The Exclusionary Rule. The exclusionary rule prevents illegally obtained evidence from being used in a criminal case. The rule is unique to the courts in the United States; it was adopted by the U.S. Supreme Court in *Mapp* v. *Ohio* in 1961. Although illegally siezed evidence may prove the guilt of the accused, it cannot be used in court and the accused may go free because the police committed a procedural error. The Fourth Amendment's prohibition against "unreasonable searches and seizures" has been interpreted to mean that police cannot conduct a search on private property without a court warrant. To obtain a warrant from a judge, police must show "probable cause" for their search and describe "the place to be searched and the persons or things to be seized." Errors on warrants are not infrequent; the addresses may be wrong or the names of the persons incorrect, or the articles misspecified. Any error results in exclusion of the evidence. There can be no blanket authorizations in a warrant to find evidence of *any* crime. In a public place, police cannot arrest persons without a warrant unless they have "probable cause" to believe that a crime has been committed. Immediately after making a warrantless arrest, police must take the accused before a magistrate to decide whether a probable cause existed to justify the

[30]Chief Justice Warren Burger, Address on the State of the Federal Judiciary to the American Bar Association, August 10, 1970.

arrest. Police do not have a general right to stop people on the streets or in their automobiles to make random checks or inspections.

Most trial proceedings today are not concerned with the guilt or innocence of the accused, but instead, center on possible procedural errors by police or prosecutors. If the defendant's attorney can show that an error was committed, the defendant goes free, regardless of his or her guilt or innocence. Supreme Court Justice Felix Frankfurter wrote many years ago: "The history of liberty has largely been the history of procedural safeguards." These safeguards protect us all from the abuse of police powers. But Chief Justice Warren Burger attacked the exclusionary rule for "the high price it extracts from society—the release of countless guilty criminals." Why should criminals go free because of police misconduct? Why not punish the police directly, perhaps with disciplinary measures imposed by courts that discover procedural errors, instead of letting guilty persons go free? Releasing criminals because of police misconduct punishes society, not the police.

Right To Counsel.   In a series of cases in the 1960s, the Supreme Court, under the leadership of Chief Justice Earl Warren, greatly strengthened the Sixth Amendment's guarantee of the right to counsel.

> *Gideon* v. *Wainwright* (1963)—Ruling that equal protection under the Fourteenth Amendment requires that free legal counsel be appointed for all indigent defendants in all criminal cases.
>
> *Escobedo* v. *Illinois* (1964)—Ruling that a suspect is entitled to confer with counsel as soon as police investigation focuses on him or her, or once "the process shifts from investigatory to accusatory."
>
> *Miranda* v. *Arizona* (1966)—Requiring that police, before questioning a suspect, must inform the suspect of all his or her constitutional rights, including the right to counsel, appointed free if necessary, and the right to remain silent. Although the suspect may knowingly waive these rights, the police cannot question anyone who at any point asks for a lawyer or indicates "in any manner" that he or she does not wish to be questioned. If the police commit an error in these procedures, the accused goes free, regardless of the evidence of guilt.

It is very difficult to ascertain to what extent these decisions have really hampered efforts to halt the rise in crime in America. Studies of police behavior following the *Mapp* v. *Ohio* decision show that at first police committed many procedural errors and guilty persons were freed; but after a year or so of adjustment to the new rules, successful prosecutions rose to the same level achieved before the decision.[31] The *Miranda* decision appears to have reduced the number of confessions. However, the Supreme Court has not reversed any of these important decisions. So whatever progress is made in law enforcement will have to be made within the current definition of the rights of defendants.

[31]Stephen Wasby, *The Impact of the United States Supreme Court* (Homewood, Ill.: Dorsey Press, 1970).

Plea Bargaining.   Most convictions are obtained by guilty pleas. Indeed, about 90 percent of the criminal cases brought to trial are disposed of by guilty pleas before a judge, not trial by jury. The Constitution guarantees trial by jury (Sixth Amendment) and protects against self-incrimination (Fifth Amendment). All defendants have the right to a trial by jury to determine guilt or innocence. But guilty pleas outnumber trial-by-jury trials by ten to one.[32]

"Plea bargaining," in which the prosecution either reduces the seriousness of the charges, or drops some but not all charges, or agrees to recommend lighter penalties, in exchange for a guilty plea by the defendant, is very common. Some critics of plea bargaining view it as another form of leniency in the criminal justice system which reduces its deterrent effects. Other critics view plea bargaining as a violation of the Constitution's protection against self-incrimination and guarantee of a fair jury trial. Prosecutors, they say, threaten defendants with serious charges and stiff penalties in order to force a guilty plea. Still other critics see plea bargaining as an "under-the-table" process which undermines respect for the criminal justice system.

While the decision to plead guilty or go to jury trial rests with the defendant, the decision is strongly influenced by the policies of the prosecutor's office. A defendant may plead guilty and accept the certainty of conviction with whatever reduced charges the prosecutor offers, and/or accept the prosecutor's pledge to recommend a lighter penalty. Or the defendant may go to trial confronting serious charges with stiffer penalties with the hope of being found innocent. However, the possibility of an innocent verdict in a jury trial is only one in six. This apparently strong record of conviction comes about because prosecutors have already dismissed charges in cases where the evidence is weak or illegally obtained. Thus, most defendants confronting strong cases against them decide to "cop a plea."

It is very fortunate for the nation's court system that most defendants plead guilty. The court system would quickly break down from overload if any substantial proportion of defendants insisted on jury trials.

EVALUATION: DETERRENCE AND CRIMINAL JUSTICE

Does the criminal justice system deter crime? This is a difficult question to answer. First we must distinguish between deterrence and incapacity. *Incapacity* can be imposed by long terms of imprisonment, particularly for habitual offenders; the policy of "keeping criminals off the streets" does indeed protect the public for a period of time, although it is done at a considerable cost ($25,000 per year per prisoner). The object of *deterrence* is to make the

---

[32]U.S. Department of Justice, Bureau of Justice Statistics, *The Prevalence of Guilty Pleas,* December, 1984.

certainty, swiftness, and severity of punishment so great as to inhibit potential criminals from committing crimes.

For many years sociologists scorned the notion of deterrence, arguing that many crimes were committed without any consideration of consequences—particularly "crimes of passion." They argued that urbanization, density, poverty, age, race, and other demographic factors had more effect on crime rates than did the characteristics of the legal system. However, systematic studies have challenged this view. Sociologist Jack P. Gibbs studied criminal homicide rates and related them to the *certainty* and *severity* of imprisonment in the sates.[33] The certainty of imprisonment for criminal homicides (the percentage of persons sent to prison divided by the number of homicides) ranged from 21 percent in South Carolina and South Dakota to 87 percent in Utah. The severity of imprisonment (the average number of months served for a criminal homicide) ranged from a low of 24 in Nevada to a high of 132 in North Dakota. Gibbs was able to analyze statistically these measures of certainty and severity in relation to homicide rates in the states. His conclusions:

1. States above the median-certainty and median-severity rates have lower homicide rates than states below both medians. Indeed, the homicide rate for low-certainty-rate and low-severity-rate states was three times greater than the average rate for high-certainty and high-severity states.

2. Certainty of imprisonment may be more important than severity of punishment in determining homicide rates, but there is conflicting evidence on which of these variables is more influential.

3. Both certainty and severity reduce homicide rates even after controlling for all other demographic variables.

Economists have generally confirmed these findings. Their general premise, of course, is that if you increase the cost of something (crime), less of it will be consumed (there will be fewer crimes). Their own studies confirm the deterrent effect of both the certainty and severity of punishment. Economist Gordon Tullock dismisses the notion that "crimes of passion" cannot be reduced by increasing the certainty and severity of punishment.

The prisoners in Nazi concentration camps must frequently have been in a state of well-justified rage against some of their guards; yet this almost never led to their using violence against the guards, because punishment—which if they were lucky, would mean instant death, but was more likely to be death by torture—was so obvious and certain.[34]

[33]See Maynard L. Erickson and Jack P. Gibbs, "The Deterrence Question," *Social Science Quarterly,* 54 (December 1973), 534–51; and Jack P. Gibbs, "Crime, Punishment, and Deterrence," *Social Science Quarterly,* 48 (March 1968), 515–30.

[34]See Gordon Tullock, "Does Punishment Deter Crime?" *The Public Interest* (Summer 1974), p. 108.

Tullock argues that to increase the deterrent effect of punishment, potential criminals must be given information about it. Indeed, he suggests, governments might even lie—that is, pretend that punishment is more certain and severe than it really is—in order to reduce crime.

PRISONS AND CORRECTIONAL POLICIES

At least four separate theories of crime and punishment compete for preeminence in guiding correctional policies. *Justice:* First, there is the ancient Judeo-Christian idea of holding individuals responsible for their guilty acts and compelling them to pay a debt to society. Retribution is an expression of society's moral outrage and it lessens the impulse of victims and their families to seek revenge. *Deterrence:* Another philosophy argues that punishment should be sure, speedy, commensurate with the crime, and sufficiently conspicuous to deter others from committing crime. *Incapacitation:* Still another philosophy in correctional policy is that of protecting the public from lawbreakers or habitual criminals by segregating these people behind prison walls. *Rehabilitation:* Finally, there is the theory that criminals are partly or entirely victims of social circumstances beyond their control and that society owes them comprehensive treatment in the form of rehabilitation.

Rising Prison Populations.   Over two million Americans each year are prisoners in a jail, police station, juvenile home, or penitentiary. The vast majority are released within one year. There are, however, over 500,000 inmates in state and federal prisons in the United States. These prisoners are serving time for serious offenses: almost all had a record of crime before they committed the act that led to their current imprisonment.

Prison populations have risen dramatically in recent years. As noted earlier, the proportion of the nation's population behind bars has more than doubled in twenty years. Getting "tough on crime"—legislating longer sentences for particular crimes or longer sentences for "career" criminals—is politically very popular. But paying for new prisons is not. And the federal courts have determined that prison overcrowding is a violation of the U.S. Constitution's prohibition on "cruel and unusual punishment." Prison overcrowding has led to a system of early releases, with most inmates serving only one-fourth to one-third of their sentences. So even though more people are put in prison, the deterrent effect is lost because they are released early.

Mandatory Sentencing.   Widespread outrage at these "revolving door" practices have led citizens and their legislators to enact mandatory prison terms for repeat offenders, and determinant sentencing or sentencing guidelines (prescribed specific jail terms for specific criminal offenses). These reforms limit judicial discretion and make punishment policies more explicit. However these policies also increase prison populations. Unless citizens and legislators are also willing to spend tax monies to build more prisons, these policies cannot be implemented.

Failure of Rehabilitation. If correctional systems could be made to work—that is, actually to rehabilitate people as useful, law-abiding citizens—the benefits to the nation would be enormous. Eighty percent of all felonies are committed by repeaters—individuals who have had prior contact with the criminal justice system and were not corrected by it. Penologists generally recommend more education and job training, more and better facilities, smaller prisons, halfway houses where offenders can adjust to civilian life before parole, more parole officers, and greater contact between prisoners and their families and friends. But as Daniel Glaser points out: "Unfortunately there is no convincing evidence that this investment reduces what criminologists call 'recidivism,' the offenders' return to crime.[35] In short, there is no evidence that people *can* be "rehabilitated," no matter what is done. But prison policies now combine conflicting philosophies in a way that accomplishes *none* of society's goals. They do not effectively punish or deter individuals from crime. They do not succeed in rehabilitating the criminal. They do not even protect the public by keeping criminals off the streets. Even the maintenance of order *within* prisons and the protection of the lives of guards and inmates have become serious national problems.

Prison life does little to encourage good behavior, as noted by John DiIulio. "For the most part, the nation's adult and juvenile inmates spend their days in idleness punctuated by meals, violence, and weight lifting. Meaningful educational, vocational, and counseling programs are rare. Strong inmates are permitted to pressure weaker prisoners for sex, drugs, and money. Gangs organized along racial and ethnic lines are often the real 'sovereigns of the cellblock.' "[36]

The Failure of Probation. Whereas the nation's prison population is about one half million persons, over two million people are currently on probation for serious crimes. But probation has been just as ineffective as prison in reducing crime. Even though persons placed on probation are considered less dangerous to society than persons imprisoned, studies indicate that nearly two-thirds of probationers will be arrested and over one-half will be convicted for a serious crime committed *while on probation.*

[35]Daniel Glaser, *Effectiveness of a Prison and Parole System* (New York: Bobbs-Merill, 1969), p. 4.

[36]John J. DiIulio, Jr., "Punishing Smarter," *Brookings Review* (Summer, 1989), 8.

The Failure of Parole.   Over two-thirds of all prisoner releases come about by means of parole. Modern penology, with its concern for reform and rehabilitation, appears to favor parole releases over unconditional releases. The function of parole and post-release supervison is to procure information on the parolees' postprison conduct, and to facilitate and graduate the transition between the prison and complete freedom. These functions are presumaby oriented toward protecting the public and rehabilitating the offender. However, studies of recidivism indicate that up to three-fourths of the persons paroled from prison will be rearrested for serious crimes. There is no difference in this high rate of recidivism between persons released under supervised parole and those released unconditionally. Thus, it does not appear that parole succeeds in its objectives.

Prison Costs Reconsidered.   Taxpayers are understandably upset with the prospect of spending $25,000 per year to keep a prisoner behind bars. But if the costs of incarceration are weighed against its benefits, taxpayers may feel better about prison construction and maintenance. A prisoner's "rap sheet" may list only three or four convictions and a dozen arrests. But interviews with offenders suggest the typical convict has committed hundreds of crimes. Various studies have attempted to estimate the dollars lost to society in the crimes committed by the typical convict in a year.[37] Estimates run from $200,000 to $400,000. This means that a year of crime may be ten to twenty times more costly to society than a year of incarceration.

Efforts are now underway in many states to lower the cost of prison facilities. Not all prisoners need to be housed in maximum security institutions; nonviolent criminals can be safely housed in less costly minimum security facilities. "Privatization" can also dramatically lower the costs of maintaining prisoners. States and counties can contract with private companies both to build and maintain prisons at much lower costs than what the government itself requires to perform these functions. Moreover, initial evaluations suggest that conditions in private prisons are much better than in government prisons. Indeed, even the prisoners prefer privately run prisons.

CAPITAL PUNISHMENT: THE CONSTITUTIONAL ISSUES

Perhaps the most heated debate in criminal justice policy today concerns capital punishment. Opponents of the death penalty argue that it is "cruel and unusual punishment" in violation of the Eighth Amendment of the Constitution. They also argue that the death penalty is applied unequally. A large proportion of those executed have been poor, uneducated, and nonwhite.

[37]See Richard Abell, "Beyond Willie Horton," *Policy Review* (Winter, 1989), 32–35.

In contrast, there is a strong sense of justice among many Americans that demands retribution for heinous crimes—a life for a life. A mere jail sentence for a multiple murderer or rapist-murderer seems unjust compared with the damage inflicted upon society and the victims. In most cases, a life sentence means less than ten years in prison under the current parole and probation policies of many states. Convicted murderers have been set free, and some have killed again. Moreover, prison guards and other inmates are exposed to convicted murderers who have "a license to kill," because they are already serving life sentences and have nothing to lose by killing again.

Prohibition on Unfair Application. Prior to 1971, the death penalty was officially sanctioned by about half of the states. Federal law also retained the death penalty. However, no one had actually suffered the death penalty since 1967 because of numerous legal tangles and direct challenges to the constitutionality of capital punishment.

In *Furman* v. *Georgia* (1971) the Supreme Court ruled that capital punishment as then imposed violated the Eighth and Fourteenth Amendment prohibitions against cruel and unusual punishment and due process of law.[38] The reasoning in the case is very complex. Only two justices, Brennan and Marshall, declared that capital punishment itself is cruel and unusual. The other justices in the majority felt that death sentences had been applied unfairly: a few individuals were receiving the death penalty for crimes for which many others were receiving much lighter sentences. These justices left open the possibility that capital punishment would be constitutional if it was specified for certain kinds of crime and applied uniformly.

After this decision, a majority of states rewrote their death penalty laws to try to ensure fairness and uniformity of application. Generally, these laws mandate the death penalty for murders committed during rape, robbery, hijacking, or kidnapping; murders of prison guards; murder with torture; and multiple murders. Two trials would be held—one to determine guilt or innocence and another to determine the penalty. At the second trial, evidence of "aggravating" and "mitigating" factors would be presented; if there were aggravating factors but no mitigating factors, the death penalty would be mandatory.

Death Penalty Reinstated. In a series of cases in 1976 (*Gregg* v. *Georgia*, *Profitt* v. *Florida*, *Jurek* v. *Texas*)[39] the Supreme Court finally held that "the punishment of death does *not* invariably violate the Constitution." The Court upheld the death penalty, employing the following rationale: the men who drafted the Bill of Rights accepted death as a common sanction for crime. It is true that the Eighth Amendment prohibition against cruel and unusual

---

[38]*Furman* v. *Georgia*, 408 U.S. 238 (1971).
[39]428 U.S. 153 (1976).

punishment must be interpreted in a dynamic fashion, reflecting changing moral values. But the decisions of more than half of the nation's state legislatures to reenact the death penalty since 1972 and the decision of juries to impose the death penalty on hundreds of persons under these new laws are evidence that "a large proportion of American society continues to regard it as an appropriate and necessary criminal sanction." Moreover, said the Court, the social purposes of retribution and deterrence justify the use of the death penalty. This ultimate sanction is "an expression of society's moral outrage at particularly offensive conduct." The Court reaffirmed that *Furman* v. *Georgia* only struck down the death penalty where it was inflicted in "an arbitary and capricious manner." The Court upheld the death penalty in states where the trial was a two-part proceeding, and during the second part the judge or jury was provided with relevant information and standards in deciding whether to impose the death penalty. The Court approved the consideration of "aggravating and mitigating circumstances." The Court also approved of automatic review of all death sentences by state Supreme Courts to ensure that the sentence was not imposed under the influence of passion or prejudice, that aggravating factors were supported by the evidence, and that the sentence was not disproportionate to the crime. However, the court disapproved of state laws making the death penalty mandatory in first degree murder cases, holding that such laws were "unduly harsh and unworkably rigid."

CAPITAL PUNISHMENT: A DETERRENT?

Is the death penalty a deterrent to murder? Does capital punishment save lives because it prevents killings through the threat of execution? This is, indeed, a question of life or death, and it is a question which social science should be able to answer. Unfortunately, however, it is difficult to measure the deterrent effect of the death penalty because we cannot directly observe nonbehavior. We can never know for certain whether the fear of capital punishment was the reason why someone refrained from killing another person. All we can do is compare homicide rates in states which have used the death penalty over time with those states which have not; and in comparing states over time, we must remember than there are many other factors besides capital punishment which can raise or lower the homicide rate: age, race, gun ownership, and so on.

Conflicting Evidence on Deterrent Effects.   Perhaps the most controversial study of the deterrent effect of the death penalty was economist Isaac Ehrlich's analysis of the penalty's use in forty-eight states between 1933 and

1969.[40] He studied execution rates and murder rates, controlling for many other variables, and concluded that the tradeoff between executions of convicted murderers and the reduction of killings was approximately one for eight. In other words, each execution was associated with saving the lives of eight potential victims.

However, other researchers using similar methods have *not* reported the same dramatic findings about the deterrent effects of capital punishment. Indeed, some social scientists specifically deny that the death penalty has any deterrent effect.[41] They attribute increases in the murder rate during the years and in the states which the death penalty was not used to a wide range of factors, including the increased ownership of handguns.[42]

Racial Bias?   The death penalty has also been challenged as a violation of the Equal Protection Clause of the Fourteenth Amendment because of racial bias in the application of the punishment. White murderers are just as likely to receive the death penalty as black murderers. However, some statistics show that if the *victim* is white there is a greater chance that the killer will be sentenced to death than if the victim is black. Nonetheless the U.S. Supreme Court has ruled that statistical disparities in the race of victims by itself does not bar the use of the death penalty in all cases. There must be evidence of racial bias against a particular defendant in order for the Court to reverse a death sentence.

Few Executions.   Today, there are about two thousand prisoners nationwide on "death row," that is, persons convicted and sentenced to death. But only about ten executions are actually carried out each year. The strategy of death row prisoners and their lawyers, of course, is to delay indefinitely the imposition of the death penalty with endless stays and appeals. So far the strategy has been successful for all but a few luckless murderers. As trial judges and juries continue to impose the death penalty, and appellate courts continue to grant stays of execution, the number of prisoners on death row grows. The few who have been executed have averaged ten years of delay between trial and execution.

Symbolic Value.   The death penalty as it is employed today—inflicted on so few after so many years following the crime—has little deterrent ef-

[40]Isaac Ehrlich, "The Deterrent Effect on Capital Punishment: A Question of Life or Death," *American Economic Review*, 65 (June 1975), 397–414.

[41]Hugo Adam Bedau, *The Death Penalty in America* (New York: Doubleday, 1967); Peter Passell, "The Deterrent Effect of the Death Penalty," *Standard Law Review*, 28 (November 1975), 61–80.

[42]Gary Kleck, "Capital Punishment, Gun Ownership, and Homicide," *American Journal of Sociology*, 84 (January 1979), 882–910.

fect. Nonetheless, it serves several purposes. It gives prosecutors some leverage in plea bargaining with murder defendants. The defendants may choose to plead guilty in exchange for a life sentence when confronted with the possibility that the prosecutor may win a conviction and the death penalty in a jury trial. Most importantly, however, the death penalty is symbolic of the value society places on the lives of innocent victims. The death penalty dramatically signifies that society does not excuse or condone the taking of innocent lives. It symbolizes the potential for society's retribution against heinous crime. Public opinion favors the death penalty by three to one. Only for a few years during the mid-1960s did public opinion appear to oppose the death penalty. With increases in the crime rate in the 1970s, heavy majorities swung back in favor of the death penalty. Public support for capital punishment remains high today.

SUMMARY

Crime is a central problem confronting society. We face a conflict between our desire to retain individual freedoms and our desire to ensure the safety of our people.

1. Crime rates have risen unevenly over the past twenty years. After leveling off in the early 1980s as a product of declines in the most crime-prone age groups, crime sored upward again with the spread of "crack" cocaine. The "victimization rate" is several times greater than the reported crime rate. These statistics suggest that the current system of criminal justice is not a serious deterrent to crime.

2. A rational policy toward crime would endeavor to make the costs of crime far outweigh its benefits and in theory defer potential wrongdoers. Effective deterrence requires that punishment be certain, swift, and severe. However certainty and swiftness are probably of more importance to deterrence than severity.

3. But punishment for crime in the United States today is neither certain nor swift. The likelihood of going to jail for any particular crime is probably less than one in a hundred. "Speedy" trial and punishment are rare; criminal defendants usually succeed in obtaining long delays between arrest and trial and most are free on bail while awaiting trial.

4. Police provide many services to society in addition to law enforcement. Indeed, only a small proportion of their time is spent in fighting crime. It is difficult to demonstrate conclusively that increased police protection reduces the actual amount of crime.

5. Guns are used in a large number of violent crimes. Public policy on gun control varies throughout the nation. However, states with strict gun control laws do not have lower rates of violent crime, or even of gun-related crime, than states without such laws.

6. Public policies toward alcohol and drug use are ambivalent. Although the health dangers of cigarettes, alcohol, marijuana, cocaine, and heroin are widely known, the manufacture, sale, and use of each of these substances are treated differently in law enforcement.

7. The judicial system fails to deter criminal conduct. Court congestion, increased litigation, excessive delays, endless appeals, variation in sentencing, and excessive plea bargaining all combine to detract from deterrence.

8. The exclusionary rule, which prohibits the use of illegally obtained evidence in court, has generated controversy since it was first announced by the Supreme Court in *Mapp* v. *Ohio* in 1961. It allows criminals to go free if police make an error.

9. About half of all serious charges are dismissed by prosecutors before trial. But most convictions are obtained by guilty pleas without jury trials. Plea bargaining is the most common means of resolving criminal cases. Without plea bargaining, the court system would break down from overload.

10. Prison and parole policies have failed to rehabilitate prisoners. Prisons can reduce crime only by incapacitating criminals for periods of time. Most prisoners are *recidivists*—persons who previously served a sentence of incarceration before being sentenced again. *Parolees*—persons released by officials for good behavior—are just as likely to commit new crimes as persons released after serving full sentences.

11. Social scientists disagree over whether the severity of the death penalty can be a deterrent to murder. But most agree that capital punishment as currently imposed—on very few persons and after very long delays— is not an effective deterrent.

BIBLIOGRAPHY

HELLMAN, DAVID. *The Economics of Crime.* New York: St. Martin's Press, 1980.

SCHROEDER, RICHARD C. *The Politics of Drugs.* 2nd ed. Washington, D.C.: Congressional Quarterly, 1980.

WILSON, JAMES Q. *Varieties of Police Behavior.* Cambridge, Mass.: Harvard University Press, 1968.

———. *Thinking About Crime.* New York: Basic Books, 1975.

———. *Crime and Public Policy.* New Brunswick, N.J.: Transaction Books, 1983.

5

HEALTH AND WELFARE
the search for a rational strategy

Physicians and hospitals are forced by the threat of malpractice suits to order multiple tests and consultations—many of which may be unnecessary. (Ken Karp)

POVERTY IN AMERICA

A rational approach to policy making requires a clear definition of the problem. But political conflict over the nature and extent of poverty in America is a major obstacle to a rational approach to social welfare policy.

Proponents of programs for the poor frequently make high estimates of the number of poor. They view the problem of poverty as a persistent one, even in an affluent society; they contend that many millions of people suffer from hunger, exposure, and remedial illness, and that some of them even starve to death. Their definition of the problem virtually mandates immediate and massive public welfare programs.

In contrast, others minimize the number of poor in America. They see poverty diminishing over time in a vigorous, expanding, free market economy. They believe the poor in America are considerably better off than the middle class of fifty years ago and even wealthy by the standards of most other societies in the world. They view government welfare programs as causes of poverty, destroying family life and robbing the poor of incentives to work, save, and assume responsibility for their own well-being. They deny that anyone needs to suffer from hunger, exposure, remedial illness, or starvation if they make use of the services and facilities available to them.

How Many Poor?   How much poverty really exists in America? According to the U. S. Social Security Administration there were about 32 million poor people in the United States in 1989. This is approximately 14 percent of the population. This official estimate of poverty includes all those Americans whose annual cash income falls below that which is required to maintain a decent standard of living. The definition of the "poverty line" by the Social Security Administration is derived by calculating "thrifty" food costs for families of various sizes and then multiplying these costs by three, on the assumption that poor families spend one-third of their income on food. The dollar amounts of these lines are flexible to take into account the effect of inflation; the amounts rise each year with the rate of inflation. In 1989 the poverty line for an urban family of four was approximately $12,675 per year (see Table 5–1). The median income for all families for the nation in that year was $28,906.[1]

Liberal Criticism.   This official definition of poverty has many critics. Some *liberal critics* believe poverty is underestimated because: (1) the official definition does not take into account regional differences in the cost of living, climate, or accepted styles of living; (2) the "thrifty" food budget on which the poverty level is based is too low for good nutrition and health; (3) the official definition includes cash income from welfare and social security, and

[1]U.S. Bureau of the Census, *Statistical Abstract of the United States 1990.*

TABLE 5-1   Poverty in America

Poverty definition 1989 for nonfarm family of four	$12,675
Number of poor	31.5 million
Poverty percentage of total population	12.8
Race (% poor)	
White	9.8
Black	31.5
Spanish	26.0
Age (% poor)	
under 18	19.6
over 65	11.4
Family (% poor)	
Married couple	8.2
Female householder, no husband	33.6

Source: *Statistical Abstract of the United States 1990.*

without this government assistance, the number of poor would be much higher, perhaps 25 percent of the total population; (4) the official definition does not count the many "near poor"; there are 40 million Americans or 18.1 percent of the population living below 125 percent of the poverty level; and (5) the official definition does not consider what people think they need to live.

Conservative Criticism.   Some *conservative critics* also challenge the official definition of poverty: (1) it does not consider the value of family assets; people (usually older people) who own their own mortgage-free homes, furniture, and automobiles may have current incomes below the poverty line yet not suffer hardship; (2) there are many families and individuals who are officially counted as poor but who do not think of themselves as "poor people"—students, for example, who deliberately postpone income to secure an education; (3) many persons (poor and nonpoor) underreport their real income and this leads to overestimates of the number of poor; and (4) more importantly, the official definition of poverty excludes "in-kind" (noncash) benefits given to the poor by governments; these benefits include, for example, food stamps, free medical care, public housing, and school lunches. If these benefits were "costed out" (calculated as cash income), there may be only half as many poor people as shown in official statistics. This figure might be thought of as the "net poverty" rate. Net poverty refers to people who remain poor even after counting their in-kind government benefits. The net poverty rate is shown together with the official poverty rate in Figure 5-1.

Latent Poverty.   How many people would be poor if we did *not* have government social security and welfare programs? What percentage of the population can be thought of as "latent poor," that is, persons who would be poor without the assistance they receive from federal programs? Charles

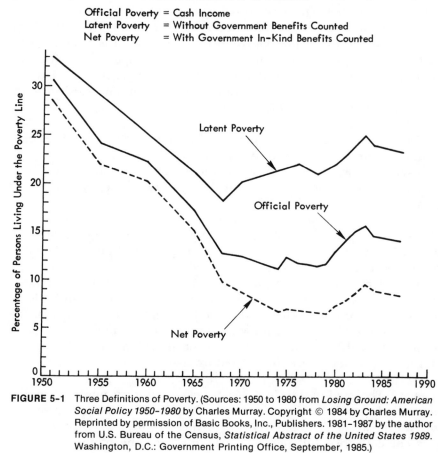

THREE DEFINITIONS OF POVERTY

Official Poverty = Cash Income
Latent Poverty = Without Government Benefits Counted
Net Poverty = With Government In-Kind Benefits Counted

FIGURE 5-1 Three Definitions of Poverty. (Sources: 1950 to 1980 from *Losing Ground: American Social Policy 1950-1980* by Charles Murray. Copyright © 1984 by Charles Murray. Reprinted by permission of Basic Books, Inc., Publishers. 1981-1987 by the author from U.S. Bureau of the Census, *Statistical Abstract of the United States 1989.* Washington, D.C.: Government Printing Office, September, 1985.)

Murray refers to the latent poverty figure as "the most damning statistic," because it counts the number of people in our society who are economically dependent and cannot stand on their own.[2] Latent poverty has been growing rapidly since the late 1960s, when more and more people became dependent on government social security and welfare payment (see Figure 5–1). Latent poverty was estimated to be around 23 percent in 1987, well above the 13.5 percent in official poverty.

Who Are the Poor?

Poverty occurs in many kinds of families and all races and ethnic groups. However, some groups experience poverty in proportions greater than the national average.

---

[2]Charles Murray, *Losing Ground* (New York: Basic Books, 1984).

Family Structure.   Poverty is most common among female-headed families. The incidence of poverty among these families in 1987 was 33.6 percent, compared to only 8.2 percent for married couples (see Table 5–1). These women and their children comprise over two-thirds of all the persons living in poverty in the United States. These figures describe "the feminization of poverty" in America. Clearly, poverty is closely related to family structure. Today the disintegration of the traditional husband-wife family is the single most influential factor contributing to poverty.

Race.   Blacks experience poverty in much greater proportions than whites. Over the years the poverty rate among blacks in the United States has been about three times higher than the poverty rate among whites (see Figure 5–2). Poverty among Hispanics is also significantly greater than among whites.

The relationship between race and family structure is a controversial topic. About 40 percent of all black families in the United States in 1987 were headed by females, compared to about 15 percent of all white families. Over 50 percent of all black female-headed families live in poverty.

These facts are not in dispute, but their implications have generated very controversial debate. U. S. Senator Daniel Patrick Moynihan (D.-N.Y.) ran into a firestorm of criticism when he first suggested in 1965 that the disintegration of black family life was a major cause of poverty. Although Moynihan argued that black families had been victimized by slavery and segregation, his views were interpreted by critics as racist.

Age.   The aged in the United States experience *less* poverty than the non-aged. The aged are not poor, despite the popularity of the phrase "the poor and the aged." The poverty rate for persons over sixty-five years of age is currently two full percentage points *below* the national average. Moreover, the aged are much wealthier than the non-aged. They are more likely than younger people to own homes with paid-up mortgages. A large portion of their medical expenses are paid by Medicare. With fewer expenses, the aged, even with relatively smaller cash incomes, experience poverty in a different fashion than a young mother with children. The lowering of the poverty rate among the aged is a relatively recent occurrence (see Figure 5–2). Continuing increases in social security benefits over the years are largely responsible for this singular "victory" in the war against poverty.

Wealth.   Wealth is the net worth of all one's possessions—home value minus mortgage, auto value minus loan, business value minus debts, money in bank accounts, savings, stocks and bonds, and real estate. All calculations of poverty consider *income* not *wealth*. It is possible for persons to have considerable wealth (for example, to own a mortgage-free home and a loan-free automobile, and have money in savings and investments), yet fall within the

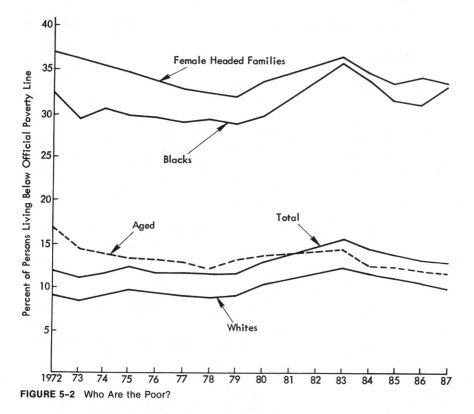

FIGURE 5-2 Who Are the Poor?

official definition of poverty because current cash income is low. Indeed, many of the *aged* who are counted as poor because their incomes are low have substantial accumulations of wealth. The U.S. Census Bureau estimates that in 1984 the net worth of the average householder over age sixty-five was $60,266, compared to a net worth of only $32,667 for all householders (and only $5,784 for householders under age 35). This suggests that the elderly on the average are twice as wealthy as the rest of the population and ten times wealthier than the young!

POVERTY AS INEQUALITY

Poverty can also be defined as "a state of mind"—some people think they have less income or material possessions than most Americans, and they believe they are entitled to more. Their sense of deprivation is not tied to any *absolute* level of income. Instead, their sense of deprivation is *relative* to what most Americans have, and what they, therefore, feel they are entitled to. Even fairly substantial incomes may result in a sense of "relative deprivation" in a very affluent society when commercial advertising and the mass media portray the "average American" as having a high level of consumption and material well-being.

Defining poverty as "relative deprivation" really defines it as *inequality* in society. Thus, eliminating poverty, if it is defined as relative deprivation, would mean achieving absolute equality of incomes and material possessions in the United States.

Measuring Inequality.   Let us try systematically to examine poverty as relative deprivation. Table 5–2 divides all American families into five groups—from the lowest one-fifth, in personal income, to the highest one-fifth—and shows the percentage of total family personal income received by each of these groups over the years. (If perfect income equality existed, each fifth of American families would receive 20 percent of all family personal income, and it would not even be possible to rank fifths from highest to lowest.) The poorest one-fifth received only 3.5 percent of all family personal income in 1929; in 1987 this group was still only receiving 4.6 percent of family personal income. The highest one-fifth of American families in personal income received 54.4 percent of all family personal income in 1929; in 1987, this percentage had declined to 43.7. This was the only income group to lose in relation to other income groups. The middle class improved their relative income position more than the poor. Another measure of income equalization over time is the decline in the percentage of income received by the top 5 percent in America. The top 5 percent received 30 percent of all family income in 1929, but only 16.9 percent in 1987.

Although the income of the lowest fifth of the population appears small (4.8 percent) in comparison to the income of higher fifths, some of the hardships of this lowest fifth are reduced by in-kind government benefits, which are not counted as income.

Recent Increase in Inequality.   While income differences in the United States have declined over the long run, inequality has increased in recent

**TABLE 5-2   The Distribution of Income in the United States
(Percent Distribution of Family Personal Income)**

QUINTILES	1929	1941	1950	1960	1970	1980	1983	1987
Lowest	3.5%	4.1%	4.5%	4.8%	5.4%	5.1%	4.7%	4.6%
Second	9.0	9.5	12.0	12.2	12.2	11.6	11.1	10.7
Third	13.8	15.3	17.4	17.8	17.6	17.5	17.1	16.9
Fourth	19.3	22.3	23.4	24.0	23.9	24.1	24.4	24.1
Highest	54.4	48.8	42.7	41.2	40.9	41.6	42.7	43.7
Total	100.0	100.0	100.0	100.0	100.0	100.0	100.0	100.0
Top 5%	30.0	24.0	17.3	15.9	15.6	15.3	15.8	16.9

Source: *Statistical Abstract of the United States 1990*, p. 451.

years. The income of the poorest quintile declined from 5.4 to 4.6 percent of total income between 1970 and 1987; the income of the highest quintile rose from 40.9 to 43.7 percent of total income.) The increase was slight by historical standards, and the United States remains one of the more equalitarian nations in the world. Nonetheless, this reversal of historical trends has generated both political rhetoric and serious scholarly inquiry about its causes.

Assessing Blame. The political argument that inequality increased because of miserly federal social welfare payments in the 1980s is untrue. Aggregate government social welfare transfer payments did *not* decline, either in real dollars or as a percent of gross national product. (Total social welfare expenditures of the federal government amount to 11.3 percent of the GNP; state and local governments contribute an additional 7.1 percent of the GNP to social welfare spending; total social welfare spending amounts to 18.4 percent of the GNP.[3]) It is true that the *rate of increase* in social welfare spending declined in the 1980s, but total social welfare spending by governments remained at approximately 18.5 percent of the GNP throughout the 1980s.

Recent increases in inequality in the United States are a product of several social and economic trends: (1) the decline of the manufacturing sector of the economy with its relatively high-paying blue collar jobs, and the ascendancy of the communications, information, and service sectors of the economy with a combination of high-paying and low-paying jobs; (2) a rise in the number of two-wage families, making single-wage female-headed household relatively less affluent; and (3) demographic trends, which include larger proportions of aged and larger proportions of female-headed families.

A Solution to Inequality? It is unlikely that income differences will ever disappear completely from a society that rewards skill, talent, risk taking, and ingenuity. If the problem of poverty is defined as relative deprivation—that is, *inequality*—then the problem is not really capable of solution. Regardless of how well-off the poor may be in absolute terms, there will always be a lowest one-fifth of the population receiving something less than 20 percent of all income. Income differences may decline over time, but *some* differences will remain, and even minor differences can be defined as a problem.

WHY ARE THE POOR POOR?

Inasmuch as policy makers cannot even agree on the definition of poverty, it comes as no surprise that they cannot agree on its causes. Yet rationality

[3]U.S. Bureau of the Census, *Statistical Abstract of the United States 1989*, p. 348.

in public policy making requires some agreement on the causes of social problems.

Low Productivity.   Many economists explain poverty in terms of *human capital theory.* The poor are poor because their economic productivity is low. They do not have the human capital—the knowledge, skills, training, work habits, abilities—to sell to employers in a free market. Absence from the labor force is the largest single source of poverty. Over two-thirds of the poor are children, mothers of small children, aged or disabled people, all of whom cannot reasonably be expected to find employment. No improvement in the general economy is likely to affect these people directly. Since the private economy has no role for these people, they are largely the responsibility of government. The poorly educated and unskilled are also at a disadvantage in a free labor market. The demand for their labor is low, employment is often temporary, and wage rates are low.

Economic Stagnation.   Economists also recognize that some poverty results from inadequate aggregate demand. A serious recession and widespread unemployment would raise the proportion of the population living below the poverty line. According to this view, the most effective antipoverty policy is to assure continued economic growth and employment opportunity. Historically, the greatest reductions in poverty have occurred during prosperous times.

Discrimination.   Discrimination plays a role in poverty that is largely unaccounted for by economic theory. We have already observed that blacks are over three times more likely to experience poverty than whites. It is true that *some* of the income differences between blacks and whites are a product of educational differences between the races. However, blacks earn less than whites even at the same educational level. In 1980, black high school graduates earned an average of $12,109 per year, while white high school graduates earned $17,592. Black college graduates earned an average of $21,107, while white college graduates earned $25,071. If the "free" market operated without interference by discrimination, we would expect very little difference in income between blacks and whites with the same education.

The Culture of Poverty.   Yet another explanation of poverty centers on the notion of a "culture of poverty." According to this notion, poverty is a "way of life" which is learned by the poor. The culture of poverty involves not just a low income, but indifference, alienation, apathy, and irresponsibility. The culture of poverty fosters a lack of self-discipline to work hard, to plan and save for the future, and to get ahead. The culture of poverty also encourages family instability, immediate gratification, "present-orientedness," instead of "future-orientedness." All of these attitudes prevent the poor from taking advantage of the opportunities which are available to them. Even cash payments do not change the way of life of these hardcore poor very much. According to this theory, additional money will be spent quickly for nonessential or frivolous items.

Opponents of the culture of poverty idea argue that this notion diverts attention from the conditions of poverty that *foster* family instability, present-orientedness, and other ways of life of the poor. The question is really whether a lack of money creates a culture of poverty or vice versa. Reformers are likely to focus on the condition of poverty as the fundamental cause of the social pathologies that afflict the poor.

Disintegrating Family Structure. Poverty is closely associated with family structure. As we have seen, poverty is greatest among female-headed households and least among husband-wife households. Family structure affects the income of both black and white families:

WHITE	1987 MEDIAN INCOME
Married couple families	$35,355
Female-headed household no husband present	$17,961
BLACK	
Married couple families	$27,238
Female-headed household no husband present	$10,017

It may be fashionable in some circles to view husband-wife families as traditional or even antiquated and to redefine *family* as any household with more than one person. But no worse advice could be given to the poor.

Trends in family composition in the United States are not reassuring. Husband-wife families have declined from 87.5 percent of all families in 1960 to 82.5 percent in 1980, and these families are projected to decline to 75.9 percent of all households by 2000. Female-headed households with no husband present increased from 6.8 percent of all households in 1960 to 14.6 percent in 1980, and they are projected to rise to 20.0 percent of all households in 2000.[4]

Perhaps the most sensitive and controversial topic in social welfare policy is the difference in black and white family structure in America. Racial differences in family composition were observed many years ago; these differences were attributed to the savage effects of slavery and discrimination on black families.[5] Yet as late as 1950 these differences were not very great;

[4]Census Bureau figures cited by U. S. Senator Daniel Patrick Moynihan, "Family and Nation," Godkin Lectures, Harvard University, 1985.

[5]Daniel Patrick Moynihan, *The Negro Family: The Case for National Action* (Washington, D.C.: Government Printing Office, 1965).

census figures for that year show 88 percent of white households headed by a husband and wife, compared to 78 percent of black households. By 1980, husband-wife families among white households had declined only slightly to 85.6 percent. But more significant changes occurred in black households: black husband-wife families declined from 78 percent to 59 percent of all black households. It is significant that almost all of this decline in black husband-wife families occurred in *poor* black households. Husband-wife family structure in black middle- and upper-class households has remained fairly stable at around 80 percent.[6]

Why have husband-wife families declined among poor blacks? Much of this decline has occurred in recent years, following the introduction of many new Great Society programs and huge increases in government welfare spending. Could it be that these government programs discouraged husband-wife family life among the poor, and by doing so actually contributed to an *increase* in poverty? We shall explore this possibility in the next section.

"Capitalist Exploitation."   Finally, we might consider a Marxist explanation of poverty in a capitalist society. Typically Marxists argue that poverty is maintained by the ruling class in order to serve their self-interest. The poor are available to do society's "dirty work," to take jobs which are physically dirty or dangerous, temporary, dead-end, and underpaid. The poor buy old, used, and defective merchandise that others do not want. The poor are often punished and accused of wrong-doing as a means of upholding societal norms. For example, the poor are called lazy because society values hard-working, industrious people. Poverty allows those in the middle and upper classes to maintain their higher status in society. The poor allow others to improve their position in society by providing a market for legal (and illegal) business activities in the slums. The poor help fill the ranks of the "army of unemployed" who function to keep wage rates low by threatening to take the jobs of striking workers. If we accept this Marxist explanation, then the public policy in a capitalist society will be designed to maintain poverty. Welfare programs will not be designed to alleviate poverty or end poverty but rather to "regulate" the poor.[7] In other words, welfare policy will be designed to avoid rioting, violence, or revolution, yet guarantee a continuation of poverty.

PUBLIC POLICY AS A CAUSE OF POVERTY

Does government itself create poverty by fashioning social welfare programs and policies which destroy incentives to work, encourage families to break

[6]U. S. Bureau of the Census, *Characteristics of the Population Below the Poverty Level: 1980* (Washington, D.C.: Government Printing Office, 1982). Cited by Charles Murray, *Losing Ground* (New York: Basic Books, 1985), pp. 129–132 and Appendix Table 25.

[7]Frances Fox Piven and Richard A. Cloward, *Regulating the Poor: The Functions of Public Welfare* (New York: Vintage Books, 1971).

up, and condemn the poor to social dependency? Does the current social welfare system sentence many millions of people to a life of poverty who would otherwise form families, take low-paying jobs, and perhaps with hard work and perseverance, gradually pull themselves and their children into the mainstream of American life?

Losing the War on Poverty.   Poverty in America steadily *declined* from 1950, when about 30 percent of the population was officially poor, to 1970, when about 11 percent of the population was poor. During this period of progress toward the elimination of poverty, government welfare programs were minimal. There were small AFDC programs for women with children who lived alone; eligibility was restricted and welfare authorities checked to see if an employable male lived in the house. There were also federal payments for aged, blind, and disabled poor. Welfare roles were modest; only about 1 to 2 percent of American families received AFDC payments.

With the addition of many new Great Society welfare programs, the downward trend in poverty was ended. Indeed, the numbers and proportion of the population living in poverty began to move upward in the 1970s and early 1980s (see Figure 5–1). This was a period in which AFDC payments were significantly increased and eligibility rules were relaxed. The Food Stamp program was initiated in 1965 and became a major new welfare benefit. Medicaid was initiated in the same year and by the late 1970s became the costliest of all welfare programs. Federal aid to the aged, blind, and disabled were merged into a new SSI program (Supplement Security Income), which quadrupled in numbers of recipients.

Policy-Induced Poverty.   Did poverty increase in spite of, or because of, these new social welfare programs? Poverty increased in the 1970s despite a reasonably healthy economy. Discrimination did not become significantly *worse* during this period; on the contrary, the civil rights laws enacted in the 1960s were opening many new opportunities for blacks. Finally, poverty was reduced among the aged due to generous increases in social security benefits. The greatest increases in poverty occurred in families headed by *working age persons.* In short, it is difficult to find alternative explanations for the rise in poverty. We are obliged to consider the possibility that *policy* changes— new welfare programs, expanded benefits, and relaxed eligibility requirements—contributed to increased poverty.

According to Charles Murray, the persons hurt most by current welfare policies are the poor themselves. In his well-titled yet controversial book *Losing Ground* he argues:

> The most compelling explanation for the marked shift in the fortunes of the poor is that they continued to respond, as they always had, to the world as they found it, but that we—meaning the not-poor and the un-disadvantaged—had changed the rules of their world.... The first effect of the new rules was to make it profitable for the poor to behave in the short term in ways that were

destructive in the long term. Their second effect was to mask these long-term losses—to subsidize irretrievable mistakes.[8]

Welfare Disincentives.   Current social welfare policy provides many disincentives to family life. The break-up of the family, nearly everyone agrees, is closely associated with poverty. The effect of generous welfare benefits and relaxed eligibility requirements on employment has been argued for centuries. Surveys show that the poor prefer work over welfare, but welfare payments may produce subtle effects on the behavior of the poor. Persons unwilling to take minimum-wage jobs may never acquire the work habits required to move into better-paying jobs later in their lives. Welfare may even help to create a dependent and defeatist subculture, lowering personal self-esteem and contributing further to joblessness, illegitimacy, and broken families.

Drastic Solutions?   Murray's policy prescription is a drastic one. He recommends

> . . . scrapping the entire federal welfare and income-support structure for working age persons, including AFDC (Aid to Families with Dependent Children), Medicaid, Food Stamps, Unemployment Insurance; workers compensation, subsidized housing, disability insurance, and the rest. It would leave the working-age person with no recourse whatever except the job market, family members, friends, and public or private locally funded services. . . . cut the knot, for there is no way to untie it.[9]

The result, he argues, would be less poverty, less illegitimacy, more upward mobility, freedom and hope for the poor. "The lives of large numbers of poor people would radically change for the better." The obstacle to this solution, according to Murray, is not only the army of politicians and bureaucrats who want to keep their dependent clients, but more importantly the vast majority of generous and well-meaning middle-class Americans who support welfare programs because they do not understand how badly these programs injure the poor.

WELFARE DYNAMICS: HOW PERSISTENT IS POVERTY?

Is there a large "underclass" of the persistently poor who are dependent upon welfare payments for most of their lives? If welfare payments really *caused* dependency and poverty, then we would expect to see persons who get on

---

[8]Charles Murray, *Losing Ground* (New York: Basic Books, 1983), p. 9.
[9]Ibid., pp. 227–228.

Welfare Recipients Standing In Line for the Federal Cheese Giveaway Program. (UPI/Bettmann Newsphotos.)

welfare rolls to stay there for a long time. But most poverty is *not* long term, and most welfare dependency is relatively brief, lasting less than three years.

Temporary Poverty. Tracing poor families over time presents a different picture of the nature of poverty and welfare from the "snapshot" view taken in any one year. For example, we know that over the last decade 11 to 15 percent of the nation's population has been officially classified as poor in any one year (see Figure 5–1). However, over a decade as many as 25 percent of the nation's population may have fallen under the poverty line at one time or another.[10] Only *some* poverty is persistent: about 6 percent of the population remains in poverty for over five years. This means that *most*

[10]Greg J. Duncan, *Years of Poverty, Years of Plenty* (Ann Arbor: Institute of Social Research, 1984).

of the people who experience poverty in their lives do so for only a short period of time.

Persistent Poverty.   The *persistently poor* are only a minority of the people who ever experience poverty. But the persistently poor place a disproportionate burden on welfare resources. About half of the people on welfare rolls at any one time are persistently poor, that is, likely to remain on welfare for eight or more years. An estimated 73 percent of all black children in the nation will receive welfare benefits sometime during a ten-year period. A smaller but significant 43 percent of all black children will remain on welfare rolls during most of a decade.

Welfare policy must be designed to deal with both persistent and temporary poverty. The Michigan study of 5,000 families showed that of all persons beginning their first spell on the AFDC rolls, 30 percent would go off welfare in two years, 40 percent would remain three to seven years, and 30 percent would remain eight or more years. Thus, for some welfare recipients, welfare payments are a relatively short-term aid that helps people over life's difficult times. For others, welfare is a more permanent part of their lives.

Events Leading to Poverty.   What happens in people's lives that leads to welfare dependency? Divorce or separation is the single most common personal event associated with going onto welfare rolls (see Table 5-3). The second most common event is a child born to an unmarried woman. Getting off of welfare is most often associated with marriage. Finding a job and thereby increasing one's income is less frequent.

How frequent is "intergenerational poverty"? There is a great deal of interest in intergenerational aspects of welfare receipt—especially whether children growing up in households receiving welfare are themselves likely to receive it when they establish their own households. However, the University of Michigan studies report that a parent's reliance on welfare has no significant independent effect on welfare dependency of their children after their children reach adulthood.

Policy Implications.   What implications do these observations about welfare dynamics have for public policy? First of all, for most people who experience poverty, it is only a temporary happening in their lives. It is associated with divorce or separation, job loss, illness or disability, or some other misfortune. Conceivably, in the absence of government welfare programs, some people might remain married who now separate or divorce, knowing that welfare would cushion the financial impact of their decision; and some people may leave an unsatisfactory job knowing that they can rely on welfare. But it is reasonable to assume that most of the *temporary* poverty in America is not a product of any structural characteristic of American society, including government welfare programs. For the temporary poor, welfare

TABLE 5-3 Personal Events Associated with Welfare Reliance (Events Associated with the Beginnings and Endings of AFDC Spells)

BEGINNINGS		ENDINGS	
Divorce/Separation	45%	Marriage	35%
Childless, unmarried woman becomes a female head with children	30	Children leave parental home	11
Earnings of female head fell	12	Earnings of female head increased	21
Earnings of others in family fell	3	Earnings of others in family increased	5
Other income fell	1	Transfer income increased	14
Other (including unidentified)	9	Other (including unidentified)	14
All	100%	All	100%

Source: Greg J. Duncan and Saul D. Hoffman, "Welfare Dynamics and the Nature of Need." Paper presented at Policy Science Program Conference, Florida State University, Tallahassee, Florida March 5–6, 1986; using data from University of Michigan Panel Study of Income Dynamics.

is short term assistance, and welfare programs are more akin to insurance— tiding people over the difficult events of life.

For the persistently poor, who constitute half of the nation's welfare rolls at any one time, welfare is not a temporary expedient but a way of life. Many of the persistently poor are single young women who came onto welfare rolls following the birth of their first child. If the welfare system itself is the cause of poverty, *then* its effects are most likely to be observed among these persistently poor. It is important to remember that most spells of welfare dependency are relatively short. This suggests that a brief experience with the welfare system does *not* necessarily create long-term dependency. However, a significant segment of welfare recipients are persistently poor and dependent. It is by no means certain that the welfare system itself causes this long-term dependence. But a pattern of continuous welfare dependence may indeed be a product of attitudinal and behavioral characteristics toward family, work, and education, which are caused in part by welfare policy itself.

RATIONALITY AND IRRATIONALITY IN THE WELFARE STATE

Nearly one-third of the population of the United States receives some form of government benefit—Social Security, Medicare or Medicaid, disability insurance, veterans' benefits, food stamps, or welfare payments. Since many

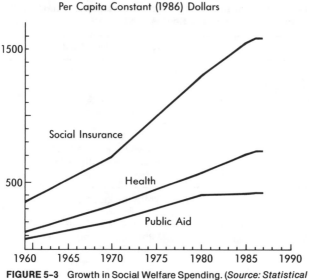

Per Capita Constant (1986) Dollars

FIGURE 5-3   Growth in Social Welfare Spending. (*Source: Statistical Abstract of the United States 1990*, p. 350).

of these programs overlap, it is not really possible to know exactly the total number of people receiving government benefits. We know that in 1986 there were 27 million Social Security retirees, 4 million Social Security disability beneficiaries, 3 million veterans' beneficiaries, 7 million Social Security survivors' beneficiaries, 32 million persons enrolled in Medicare, 23 million persons receiving Medicaid, 20 million persons receiving food stamps, 24 million children receiving free or reduced-price school lunches, and 16 million recipients of cash welfare payments.[11] The "welfare state" now encompasses a very large segment of our society.

Social welfare is now the largest function of the national government. The rise of the social welfare function occurred during both Democratic and Republican administrations and during the nation's longest war (Vietnam). Spending for social welfare and health grew despite rising and falling defense spending; there is *no* relationship between defense and social welfare spending (see Figure 5–3).

It is not really possible in this chapter to describe all the problems of the poor in America or to describe all the difficulties in developing rational social welfare policies. But it is possible to describe the general design of alternative strategies to deal with poverty in America, to observe how these strategies have been implemented in public policy, and to outline some of the obstacles to a rational approach to the problems of the poor.

[11]U. S. Bureau of the Census, *Statistical Abstract of the United States 1989.*

THE PREVENTIVE STRATEGY: SOCIAL SECURITY

The administration of President Franklin D. Roosevelt brought conscious attempts by the federal government to develop rational programs to achieve societal goals. In the most important piece of legislation of the New Deal, the Social Security Act of 1935, the federal government undertook to establish the basic framework for welfare policies at the federal, state, and local levels, and, more importantly, to set forth a strategy for dealing with poverty. The Depression convinced the national leadership and a great many citizens that indigency could result from forces over which the individual had no control—loss of job, old age, death of the family bread-winner, or physical disability. The solution was to require individuals to purchase insurance against their own indigency resulting from any of these misfortunes.

Social Insurance.   The *social insurance* concept devised by the New Deal planners was designed to prevent poverty resulting from uncontrollable forces. Social insurance was based on the same notion as private insurance—the sharing of risks and the setting aside of money for a rainy day. Social insurance was not to be charity or public assistance; it was to be preventive. It relied upon the individual's compulsory contribution to his or her own protection. In contrast, public assistance is only alleviative, and relies upon general tax revenues from all taxpayers. Indeed, when the Roosevelt administration presented the social insurance plan to Congress in the Social Security Act of 1935, it was contended that it would eventually abolish the need for any public assistance program, because individuals would be compelled to protect themselves against poverty!

The distinction between a *social insurance* program and a *public assistance* program is an important one, and has on occasion been a major political issue. If the beneficiaries of a government program are required to make contributions to it before claiming any of its benefits, and if they are entitled to the benefits regardless of their personal wealth, then the program is said to be financed on the *social insurance* principle. On the other hand, if a program is financed out of general tax revenues, and if the recipients are required to show they are poor before claiming its benefits, then the program is said to be financed on the *public assistance* principle.

OASDI.   The key feature of the Social Security Act of 1935 is the Old Age Survivor's Disability and Insurance (OASDI) program, generally known as Social Security. This is a compulsory social insurance program financed by regular deductions from earnings which gives individuals a legal right to benefits in the event of certain occurrences that cause a reduction of their income: old age, death of the head of household, or permanent disability[12]

---

[12]The original Social Security Act of 1935 did not include disability insurance; this was added by amendment in 1950. Health insurance for the aged—Medicare—was added by amendment in 1965; this is discussed later in the chaper.

OASDI is based on the same principle as private insurance—sharing the risk of the loss of income—except that it is a government program and it is compulsory for all workers. OASDI now covers about nine out of every ten workers in the United States, including the self-employed. The only large group outside its coverage are federal employees who have their own retirement system. Both employees and employers must pay equal amounts toward the employees' OASDI insurance. The money is paid into three federal "trust funds"—old age and survivor's disability, and Medicare.

Retirement Benefits.   Upon retirement, an insured worker is entitled to monthly benefit payments based upon age at retirement and the amount earned during working years. The average monthly amount for a retired worker, age sixty-five, with a spouse, was about $950 in 1985. For most recipients this income is tax free. In 1972 Congress ordered automatic cost-of-living adjustments (COLAs) indexed to inflation. The formula for calculating COLAs increases benefits *faster* than actual cost-of-living increases for the elderly.

Survivor and Disability Benefits.   OASDI also provides benefit payments to survivors of an insured worker, including a spouse if there are dependent children. But if there are no dependent children, benefits will not begin until the spouse reaches retirement age. OASDI provides benefit payments to persons who suffer permanent and total disabilities that prevent them from working for more than one year.

Social Security Administration.   OASDI is a completely federal program administered by the Social Security Administration in the Department of Health and Human Services. But it has an important indirect effect on state and local welfare programs: by compelling people to insure themselves against the possibility of their own poverty, Social Security has doubtlessly reduced the welfare problems that state and local governments would otherwise face. The growth of OASDI in numbers of recipients (beneficiaries), average monthly payments, and percentage of the federal government's budget is shown in Table 5–4.

Social Security benefits are specifically exempted from federal income taxes. Persons over sixty-five also receive a double personal exemption on their federal income taxes.

Unemployment Compensation.   A second important feature of the Social Security Act of 1935 was that it induced states to enact unemployment compensation programs through the imposition of the payroll tax on all employers. A federal unemployment tax is levied on the payroll of employers of four or more workers, but employers paying into state insurance programs that meet federal standards may use these state payments to offset most of

TABLE 5-4   Social Security Benefits

	1940	1950	1960	1970	1980	1985	1987
Numbers of Bene- ficiaries (in thousands)	222	3,477	14,845	25,312	35,900	37,058	38,190
Average Monthly Benefit, Single Retired Worker	$18	$36	$63	$101	$305	$420	$515

their federal unemployment tax. In other words, the federal government threatens to undertake an unemployment compensation program and tax if the states do not do so themselves. This federal program succeeded in inducing all fifty states to establish unemployment compensation programs. However, the federal standards are flexible and the states have considerable freedom in shaping their own unemployment programs. In all cases, unemployed workers must report in person and show that they are willing and able to work in order to receive unemployment compensation benefits. In practice, this means that unemployed workers must register with the U. S. Employment Service (usually located in the same building as the state unemployment compensation office) as a condition of receiving their unemployment checks. States cannot deny workers benefits for refusing to work as strike-breakers or refusing to work for rates lower than prevailing rates. But basic decisions concerning the amount of benefits, eligibility, and the length of time that benefits can be drawn are largely left to the states.

EVALUATION: INTENDED AND UNINTENDED CONSEQUENCES OF SOCIAL SECURITY

The framers of the Social Security Act of 1935 created a "trust fund" with the expectation that a reserve would be built up from social insurance premiums from working persons. The reserve would earn interest, and the interest and principal would be used in later years to pay benefits. Benefits for an individual would be in proportion to his or her contributions. General tax revenues would not be used at all. It was intended that the system would resemble the financing of private insurance. But it turned out not to work that way at all.

The "Trust Fund."   The social insurance system is now financed on a pay-as-you-go, rather than a reserve, system. Today, the income from all social insurance premiums (taxes) pays for current Social Security benefits. Today, this generation of workers is paying for the benefits of the last generation, and it is hoped that this generation's benefits will be financed by the next generation of workers. Social Security "trust fund" revenues are now lumped together with general tax revenues in the federal budget.

The "Generational Compact."   Taxing current workers to pay benefits to current retirees may be viewed as a compact between generations. Each generation of workers in effect agrees to pay benefits to an earlier generation of retirees, in the hope that the next generation will pay for their own retirement. But low birth rates (reducing the number of workers), longer life spans (increasing the number of retirees), and very generous benefits, are straining workers' ability to pay. The generational compact is likely to break before younger workers today reach retirement. Many of these workers, for good reason, have lost their confidence and trust in the system to support them in their old age.

The "Dependency Ratio."   Since current workers must pay for the benefits of current retirees and other beneficiaries, the "dependency ratio" becomes an important component of evaluating the future of Social Security. The "dependency ratio" for Social Security is the number of recipients as a percentage of the number of contributing workers. Americans are living longer and increasing the dependency ratio. A child born in 1935, when the Social Security system was created, could expect to live only to age sixty-one, four years *less* than the retirement age of sixty-five. The life expectancy of a child born in 1980 is seventy-four years, nine years *beyond* the retirement age. In the early years of Social Security, there were ten workers supporting each retiree—a dependency ratio of 10 to 1. But today, as the U. S. population grows older—due to lower birth rates and longer life span—there are only three workers for each retiree, and by 2010 the dependency ratio will rise to two workers for each retiree.

Tax Burdens.   Congress has gradually increased the Social Security payroll tax from 3 percent combined employee and employer contributions on the first $3000 of wages, to 15.3 percent combined contribution of the first $51,300 in 1990. The maximum employee contribution has grown from $30 to $3924 since the beginning of the program. The Social Security tax is now *the second largest source of federal revenue*. More important, it is also *the fastest growing source of federal revenue*. Social insurance and welfare payments are now *the largest expenditure of the federal government*, surpassing expenditures for national defense.

Regressive Taxes.   The Social Security tax is regressive. It takes a much larger share of the income of middle- and low-income workers than wealthy investors and others whose income is from sources other than wages. This was not a serious factor when the payments amounted to very little, but to-day the size of Social Security revenues—fully one-quarter of the federal government's income—has an important impact on the total revenue structure. The tax is only on *wages*, not total *income*. And wages above certain levels ($51,300 in 1990) are completely untaxed.

Generous Benefits.   The decline of the insurance concept began in the very first years of the program. The plan to build a large self-financing reserve fund was abandoned in 1939. Benefits are no longer really proportionate to contributions; they are figured more generously for those whose wages are low than for those whose wages are high. The only remaining aspect of an insurance program is that individuals must have paid into the system to receive its benefits, and beneficiaries are not required to prove they are needy. Most Americans view their benefits as a right.

Early Retirement.   Generous benefits also encourage early retirement, thereby reducing the number of tax-paying workers and increasing the number of Social Security beneficiaries. Currently workers may retire at age sixty-two with 80 percent of full benefits or at age sixty-five with full benefits. Fifty years ago, when this retirement age was established, people who reached this age had very few years to look forward to and perhaps had little to contribute to the economy. But today, the average person aged sixty-five has nearly fifteen years of life remaining and can contribute more years of productive work.

COLAs.   Currently social security COLAs are based upon the Consumer Price Index, which estimates the cost of all consumer items each year. These costs include home buying, mortgage interest, child rearing, and other costs which many retirees do not confront. Moreover, most *workers* do not have the same protection against inflation as retirees. Average wage rates do not always match the increases in cost of living. Over the years, the COLAs have improved the economic well-being of Social Security recipients relative to American workers.

Wealthy Retirees.   Social Security benefits are paid to all eligible retirees, regardless of whatever other income they may receive. There is no means test for Social Security benefits. The result is that large numbers of affluent Americans receive government checks each month. Of course, they paid into Social Security during their working years and they can claim these checks as a legal "entitlement" under the insurance principle. But currently their benefits far exceed their previous payments.

Since the aged experience *less* poverty than today's workers (see Figure 5–2) and possess considerably more wealth, social security benefits constitute a "negative" redistribution of income, that is, a transfer of income from poorer to richer people. The elderly are generally better off than the people supporting them.

Social Security in the Federal Budget.   In 1983 a National Commission on Social Security Reform, appointed by President Reagan and made up of equal numbers of Democrats and Republicans, recommended increases in Social Security taxes to build a "reserve" for large numbers of "baby-boom" generation retirees expected after the year 2000. Congress raised the social security tax, and the trust fund began to build a "surplus". That is to say, income from the social security tax currently exceeds payments to beneficiaries. The surplus is officially used to purchase U.S. government bonds.

However, Social Security taxes are shown in the federal budget as current revenues (see Chapter 10), and current revenues offset all current expenditures of the federal government. The federal government runs high deficits each year: current federal spending regularly exceeds current federal revenues by $100 to $200 *billion* per year. The social security "surplus" hides some of this deficit in overall federal spending, and the use of the "trust fund" to purchase debt aids the federal government in its deficit financing. In short, the "trust fund surplus" is merely an accounting gimmick; current social security taxes are being used to finance current spending, and future retirement benefits will have to be paid from future revenues.

How could we insure that the social security surplus be saved? Unfortunately there is no way to prevent Congress from spending the money, except perhaps to remove the temptation altogether by cutting the payroll tax and returning to pay-as-you-go financing. Senator Daniel Patrick Moynihan (D.—NY) proposed such a cut in 1990, much to the embarrassment of the Bush Administration. Eliminating the Social Security "surplus" by cutting the tax would expose the full amount of annual federal deficit spending.

THE ALLEVIATIVE STRATEGY: PUBLIC ASSISTANCE

The Social Security and Unemployment Compensation programs were based upon the insurance strategy for preventing indigence, but the federal government also undertook in the Social Security Act of 1935 to help the states in providing public assistance payments to certain needy persons. This strategy was designed to alleviate the conditions of poverty; there was no effort to attack the causes of poverty. The notion was to provide a minimum level of subsistence to certain categories of needy adults—the aged, blind, and disabled—and to provide for the care of dependent children. This was to be done by providing small amounts of cash in monthly payments through state-administered welfare programs. The federal grant-in-aid device was employed because welfare functions traditionally had been the responsibility of state and local governments. The entire federal effort in public assistance was supposed to be temporary in duration, declining in importance as social insurance took over the burden of assuring security.

Cash Programs: SSI and AFDC.   Today the federal government directly aids three categories of welfare recipients—the aged, the blind, and the disabled—under the Supplemental Security Income program (SSI). The federal government also provides grants to the states to assist the fourth and largest category—families with dependent children. Within broad outlines of the federal policy, states retain considerable discretion in the Aid to Families with Dependent Children (AFDC) program in terms of the amounts of money appropriated, benefits to be paid to recipients, rules of eligibility, and rules of the programs. Each state may choose to grant assistance beyond the amounts supported by the national government. Each state establishes its own standards to determine need. As a result, there is a great deal of variation among the states in ease of access to welfare rolls and in the size of welfare benefits.

Federal standards for state AFDC programs, established as a prerequisite to receiving federal aid, allow considerable flexibility in state programs. Federal law requires the states to make financial contributions to their public assistance programs and to supervise these programs either directly or through local agencies. Whatever standards a state adopts must be applicable throughout the state, and there must be no discrimination in these welfare programs. The federal government demands periodic reporting from the states, insists that states administer federally supported programs under a merit personnel system, and prevents the states from imposing unreasonable residence requirements on recipients. But in important questions of administration, standards of eligibility, residence, types of assistance, and amounts of payments, the states are free to determine their own welfare programs. Beginning in 1972, the federal government required "employable" welfare recipients to register for the Work Incentive (WIN) program; individuals prepared for work are referred to jobs while others are enrolled in training or job experience programs. But the definition of "employable" generally excludes the aged, the ill, and mothers of preschool children; indeed, only a tiny fraction of all welfare recipients have participated in the WIN program.

General Assistance.   It is important to note that the federal government helps provide cash assistance to only four categories of needy persons— aged, blind, disabled (through SSI), and families with dependent children (through AFDC). Aid to persons who do *not* fall into any of these categories but who, for one reason or another, are "needy," is referred to as "general assistance." General assistance programs are entirely state-financed and state-administered. Without federal participation, these programs differ radically from state to state in terms of the persons aided, the criteria for eligibility, the amount and nature of benefits, and administration of financing. The average general assistance payment is lower than comparable payments in federally supported programs.

States also continue to maintain institutions to care for those individuals who are so destitute, alone, or ill that money payments cannot meet their needs. These institutions include state orphanages, homes for the aged, and homes for the mentally ill. They are, for the most part, state-financed as well as state-administered. However, persons living in these tax-supported institutions may be eligible for federal assistance—Social Security, SSI, and Medicare and Medicaid, for example.

In-Kind Programs.   Public assistance in the form of in-kind (noncash) benefits expanded very rapidly between 1965 and 1980. *Medicaid* is the costliest of these in-kind programs, providing federally assisted medical care for the poor. Over 23 million people or 10 percent of the population of the United States receive Medicaid benefits. The Food Stamp program, administered by the Department of Agriculture, now costs more than either SSI or AFDC. Eligible persons may obtain free food stamps, generally from the county welfare department. The stamps may then be used to purchase food at supermarkets. This program enrolls about 20 million people or 8 to 9 percent of the population. Eligibility for both food stamps and Medicaid now extends to many low-income persons who are not poor enough to qualify for cash payments under SSI or AFDC.

Housing Assistance.   Housing assistance is also a major in-kind benefit program for the poor. An estimated six million people live in two million low-income public housing units in the nation and many more benefit from various federal housing subsidies.

Other Assistance.   Public assistance recipients are generally eligible for participation in a variety of other social programs. These include school lunches and milk; job training; various educational and childcare programs and services; special food programs for women, infants, and children (WIC); home heating and weatherization assistance; free legal services; and more.

EVALUATION: THE WELFARE MESS

While the social insurance programs (OASDI, Medicare, and Unemployment Compensation) are politically popular and enjoy the support of large numbers of active beneficiaries, the public assistance programs are far less popular. They are disliked by many national, state, and local legislators who must vote the appropriations for them; they are resented by many taxpayers who must bear ever-increasing burdens; they are denounced by the officials and caseworkers who must administer them; and they are accepted with bitterness by those who are intended to benefit from them.

Social Dependency. Certainly our public assistance programs have not succeeded in reducing dependency. Between 1965 and 1978 the number of welfare recipients more than tripled. It was the Aid to Families with Dependent Children (AFDC) and the Medicaid and Food Stamp programs, that became the largest and most expensive of all welfare programs, and the most controversial. In the 1980s enrollments leveled off in most major programs.

The Working Poor. Despite these levels of dependency upon welfare and the growing burden of welfare costs, many of the nation's poor do not receive public assistance. There were over 33 million poor people in the United States in 1987, perhaps 10 million of whom receive no federal welfare benefits. Many of these poor are working poor, who are ineligible for welfare assistance because they hold jobs, even though these jobs pay very little.

Disparities Among States. State administration of welfare has resulted in wide disparities among the states in eligibility requirements and benefits levels. For example, in 1986 average AFDC monthly payments ranged from a high of $535 per family in California to a low of $114 per family in Alabama.[13] In terms of welfare payments, it is far better to be poor in a wealthy high-tax state than in a poor low-tax one.

Cash Versus In-Kind Assistance. The merits of cash versus goods and services as a form of public assistance have long been debated. It is frequently argued that cash payments are ineffective in alleviating poverty because recipients are often unable to manage household money. They fall prey to advertising which encourages them to spend money for nonessential items and to overlook the food and clothing needs of themselves and their children. Assistance in the form of goods (for example, food stamps which can only be used to purchase basic food items) and services (for example, health care, daycare for children, home management counseling) might represent a more effective approach. However, recipients themselves resent the goods and services approach, charging that it is paternalistic, that it curtails flexibility in family spending, and that it implies irresponsibility on the part of the recipient. Today most caseworkers argue for joint provision of cash and goods and services; they contend that cash is more effective when accompanied by services, and services are more effective when accompanied by cash.

Casework. Welfare administration is made difficult by the heavy load assigned to caseworkers, many of whom are recent college graduates. They

[13]*Statistical Abstract of the United States 1989, p. 367.*

spend much of their time determining eligibility, computing payments, and filling out an avalanche of forms. With caseloads averaging up to 100 or 200 families, their contacts with recipients must be hurried, infrequent, and impersonal. Caseworkers are unable to develop any close bonds of friendship or rapport with persons in need of help. Recipients often come to view caseworkers with distrust or worse. The strain on caseworkers is very great; bigcity welfare departments report high turnover among caseworkers.

Work Disincentives.   In most states, if a recipient of assistance takes a full-time job, assistance checks are reduced or stopped. If the recipient is then laid off, it may take some time to get back on the welfare roll. In other words, employment is uncertain, while assistance is not. More importantly, the jobs available to most recipients are very low-paying jobs which do not produce much more income than does assistance, particularly when transportation, childcare, and other costs of working are considered. All these facts discourage people from looking for work.

Social dependency and disincentives to work are magnified by the "pyramiding effect" of separate public assistance and social service programs. A family on the welfare rolls is generally entitled to participate in the Food Stamp program, to receive health care through Medicaid, to gain access to free or low-rent public housing, to receive free lunches in public schools, and to receive a variety of other social and educational benefits at little or no cost to themselves. These benefits and services available to the poor are not counted as income, yet the nonpoor must pay for similar services out of their own earnings. If a family head on welfare takes a job, he or she not only loses welfare assistance, but, more importantly perhaps, becomes ineligible for food stamps, Medicaid, public housing, and many other social services. Thus, only a fairly well-paying job would justify going off the welfare rolls.

Slowing the Growth of Welfare.   The Reagan administration attempted *to slow the rate of growth* in social insurance and public assistance programs. Despite widespread publicity given to welfare "cuts" during the Reagan years, more dollars were spent for the major programs than during previous administrations. Expenditures for Social Security, unemployment compensation, Medicare, Medicaid, SSI, AFDC, and food stamps continued to rise each year. However, their *rate of increase* was less than in previous years (see Table 5–5). Thus, the nation's social welfare system remained intact even during a conservative presidential administration. It is easy for liberal commentators to overlook this most important observation about social welfare policy in America: *major social welfare programs were virtually unchanged during the Reagan administration and spending for social welfare continued to rise.*

Workfare.   In recent years liberals and conservatives in the states have begun to come together in a consensus in support of changing welfare rules.

TABLE 5-5   Social Welfare Program Expenditures

	BILLIONS $	
	1980	1987
Social Insurance		
Social Security OASDI	152.1	288.5
Medicare	35.0	82.0
Federal Employee Retirement	27.0	44.1
Railroad Retirement	4.8	6.5
Unemployment Compensation	18.3	18.0
Workmans Compensation	13.3	27.0
Public Assistance		
SSI	6.4	13.7
AFDC	15.0	18.4
General Assistance	2.0	3.8
Food Stamps	9.1	12.5
School lunch	2.0	3.3
Women, Infants, Children	1.4	1.7
Emergency food	1.1	0.9
Elderly nutrition	0.7	0.6
Medicaid	23.5	50.0
Housing assistance	14.1	13.1
Energy Assistance	2.1	2.1
Other		
Head Start	1.3	1.4
Jobs and training	3.9	3.8
Social services	4.2	4.2

Source: *Statistical Abstract of the United States 1990,* pp. 351–353.

Both have come to agree that a large "underclass" of single mothers and their children have become dependent on welfare and that breaking this "cycle of poverty" requires getting these mothers into the work force. The fact that most nonpoor mothers now work has convinced many liberals that welfare mothers have no special claim to stay at home. And conservatives have come to understand that some transitional aid—education, job training, continued health care, and daycare for children—may be necessary to move welfare mothers into the work force.

In 1981 President Ronald Reagan convinced Congress to *allow* the states to require welfare recipients to work in exchange for their AFDC checks. The states began experimenting with "workfare" programs in the 1980s. Most of the new state workfare programs offered welfare recipients options of job training with child care and transportation, going back to school, or work with transitional medical care, child care, and other benefits for extended time periods. However, none of the new state programs required all recipients to work. Most programs allowed mothers with preschool children to opt out altogether. Moreover, state and local welfare bureaucracies generally resisted reform. Some opposition was philosophical, calling it "slavefare"; other barriers arose in providing the necessary funds for casework supervision, realistic job training, and effective job placement. By 1988 fewer than 5 percent of welfare recipients were participating in workfare programs. Congress has required the states gradually to increase the percentage of workfare participants.

Welfare for the Middle Class.   Why does poverty persist in a nation where total social welfare spending is more than three times the amount needed to eliminate poverty? If the approximately $500 billion spent per year for social welfare were directly distributed to the nation's 33 million poor people, each poor person—man, woman, and child—would receive over $15,000 per year! The answer, of course, is that most social welfare spending, including the largest programs—Social Security and Medicare—goes to the nonpoor. Even the means-tested aid, amounting to over $100 billion per year combined federal and state spending for SSI, AFDC, Food Stamps, Medicaid and public housing, often finds its way to the nonpoor. The middle classes are the major beneficiaries of the nation's social welfare system.

THE CURATIVE STRATEGY: THE WAR ON POVERTY

"This Administration today, here and now, declares unconditional war on poverty in America." President Lyndon B. Johnson made this declaration in his 1964 State of the Union message and followed with a wide range of Great Society programs.[14] The "War on Poverty" promised a new *curative* strategy in dealing with the problems of the poor. In contrast to the alleviative strategy of public assistance, or the preventive strategy of social insurance, the curative strategy was supposed to break the cycle of poverty and provide escape routes by which the poor could become self-supporting and capable of earning adequate incomes. The emphasis was on "Rehabilitation, not Relief." Programs were aimed, whether accurately or inaccurately, at curing the cause of poverty rather than alleviating its symptoms.

Job Training.   Federal job training programs were a very important part of the curative strategy. These programs were designed to increase the skills and employment opportunities of the poor through both classroom and on-

---

[14]Major social legislation of the Great Society included the Elementary and Secondary Education Act (1965), Medicare (1965), Medicaid (1965), and the Food Stamp Act (1964), all of which are discussed elsewhere in this book. The Great Society also included the Economic Opportunity Act (1964) and the many programs and services that evolved from it.

the-job training. A variety of programs begun in the Kennedy and Johnson administrations were brought together in 1973 under the Comprehensive Employment and Training Act (CETA). Originally CETA provided federal funds to both private and governmental employers who agreed to recruit and train low-skilled persons to fill regular job vacancies. The employers were reimbursed for the costs of training, remedial education, counseling, and supporting services. In addition, federal funds provided allowances for trainees to support themselves during the training period.

CETA was never a very popular program in Washington. Public service jobs were viewed as dead-end, make-work, temporary jobs, which really did not assist the poor in becoming permanent productive members of the labor force. The public service jobs component of CETA was ended altogether in 1982. Federal allowances for trainees in job training programs were viewed as handouts which "enticed people to enter training programs for short-term income rather than long-term employability gains."[15]

The Reagan Administration believed that general employment-training block grants to the states would be more effective than CETA-administered grants for individual training programs throughout the country. The Job Partnership Training Act (JPTA) in 1982 authorized block grants for employment training in the states. Each state receives JPTA funds based on its number of poor and unemployed. Governors are required to establish private industry councils composed of business, labor, and community representatives in local areas. These councils are supposed to guide job training efforts and distribute federal funds.

Measuring Unemployment.   One major problem in dealing with unemployment is accurately assessing the meaning of the U. S. Labor Department's official "unemployment rate." The official unemployment rate is determined by a national survey conducted by the Bureau of Labor Statistics. The BLS asks a national sample of persons sixteen years of age and over, "Are you employed?" If the answer is no, BLS asks, "Are you looking for work?" If the answer is yes, then this person is counted as unemployed. Today's officially unemployed include teenagers, second and third wage earners in the same household, and individuals who sign up for jobs at the U. S. Employment Service because doing so is a requirement to receive certain welfare benefits. Years ago, the officially unemployed were almost exclusively heads of households with no other source of income. Hence, unemployment today is not the equivalent of unemployment a few decades ago. However, it should also be noted that the official rate does not include "discouraged workers"—those who say they are not currently looking for work because they have no hope of finding a job.

---

[15]U.S. Office of Management and Budget. *Budget of the United States Government 1983.* Washington: U.S. Government Printing Office, 1982, p. 5–120.

Legal Services.   The Legal Services Corporation also grew out of the War on Poverty. It is a nonprofit corporation financed by Congress from tax revenues to provide free legal services to the poor—to assist them in rent disputes, contracts, welfare rules, minor police action, housing regulations, and so on. More than 5000 attorneys throughout the nation are supported by the corporation. But over the years many of these attorneys have undertaken to launch "class action" suits—civil suits on behalf of broad classes of people rather than individual clients—in support of various liberal causes. Many of these suits have been brought against federal, state, and local government agencies. Efforts by conservatives and the Reagan Administration to end Legal Services were unsuccessful.

Head Start.   The most popular program to emerge from President Johnson's War on Poverty was Head Start. This is a program for disadvantaged preschool children to provide them special preparation before they enter kindergarten or first grade. It is very popular among parents and in the Congress. President Bush budgeted large increases in federal funding to Head Start following his well-publicized "educational summit" with the nation's governors early in his term. Yet the value to children of Head Start preparation largely disappears after the first two to three year of schooling. Studies comparing poor children who attended Head Start with poor children who had not, show that differences in achievement levels disappear after several years. Nevertheless, Head Start remains politically very popular.

Failed Experiment in Community Action.   President Lyndon B. Johnson's Great Society also included the Economic Opportunity Act of 1964. Communities were urged to form "community action agencies," composed of representatives of government, private organizations, and, most importantly, the poor themselves. A federal Office of Economic Opportunity (OEO) gave financial support to anti-poverty programs devised by the local community action agency. Projects might include (but were not limited to) literacy training, health services, homemaker services, neighborhood service centers, vocational training, and childhood development activities. The act also envisioned that a community action agency would help organize the poor so that they could become participating members of the community and avail themselves of the many public programs designed to serve them.

Even before President Johnson left office in 1969, the War on Poverty had become another unpopular war. The Nixon Administration "reorganized" OEO in 1973, turning over some programs like Head Start to other agencies. In 1975, the Ford Administration and Congress abolished OEO altogether. The reasons for the failure of the War on Poverty are complex.

The Office of Economic Opportunity was always the scene of great confusion. New and untried programs were organized at breakneck speed. There was a high turnover in personnel. There was scandal and corruption, particularly at the local level. Community action agencies with young and inexperienced personnel frequently offended experienced governmental administrators as well as local political figures. Congressional action was uncertain, the project's life was extended for a year at a time, and appropriations were often delayed. But most damaging of all, even though programs were put in operation, there was little concrete evidence that these programs were successful in their objectives, that is, in eliminating the causes of poverty.[16]

HOMELESSNESS AND PUBLIC POLICY

For a pitiful few in America, sickness, hardship, and abandonment have risen dramatically in recent years. These few are the nation's homeless "street people," suffering exposure, alcoholism, drug abuse, and chronic mental illness while wandering the streets of the nation's larger cities. No one knows the total number of homeless; but the best systematic estimate is 250,000 to 350,000.[17] In most large cities, street people are the most visible social welfare problem.

The issue of homelessness has become so politicized that an accurate assessment of the problem and a rational strategy for dealing with it have become virtually impossible.[18] The term "homeless" is used to describe many different situations. There are the street people who sleep in subways, bus stations, parks, or the streets. Some of them are temporarily traveling in search of work; some have left home for a few days or are youthful runaways; others have roamed the streets for months or years. There are the sheltered homeless who obtain housing in shelters operated by local governments or private charities. As the number of shelters has grown in recent years, the number of sheltered homeless has also grown. But most of the sheltered homeless come from other housing, not the streets. These are people who have been recently evicted from rental units or have previously lived with family or friends. These sheltered homeless often include families with children; the street homeless are virtually all single persons.

The ranks of the street homeless expand and contract with the seasons. The homeless are difficult subjects for systematic interviewing; many do not wish to admit to alcoholism, drug dependence, or mental illness. The television networks sensationalize the topic, exaggerate the number of homeless, and incorrectly portray the homeless as middle class, white, families victimized by economic misfortune and the high cost of housing.

---

[16]Daniel P. Moynihan, *Maximum Feasible Misunderstanding: Community Action in the War on Poverty* (New York: The Free Press, 1969), pp. 1324–1325.

[17]Peter H. Rossi, *Down and Out in America* (Chicago: University of Chicago Press, 1989).

[18]Robert C. Ellickson, "The Homelessness Muddle," *The Public Interest* (Spring, 1990) 45–60.

Who Are the Homeless?   Serious studies indicate that close to half of the street homeless are chronic alcoholic and drug abusers and an additional one-fourth to one-third are mentally ill.[19] The alcohol and drug abusers, especially "crack" cocaine users, are the fastest growing groups among the homeless. Moreover, the alcohol and drug abusers and mentally ill among the homeless are likely to remain on the streets for long periods of time. Among the 15 to 25 percent of the homeless who are neither mentally ill nor dependent on alcohol or drugs, homelessness is more likely to be temporary.

Public Policy as a Cause of Homelessness.   The current plight of the homeless is primarily a result of various "reforms" in public policy, notably the "deinstitutionalization" of care for the mentally ill, the "decriminalization" of vagrancy and public intoxication, newly recognized rights to refuse treatment, and the renewal of central cities and the elimination of low-rent apartments and cheap hotels.

Deinstitutionalization.   Deinstitutionalization was a reform advanced by mental health care professionals and social welfare activists in the 1960s and 1970s to release chronic mental patients from state-run mental hospitals. It was widely recognized that aside from drugs, no psychiatric therapies have much success among the long-term mentally ill. Drug therapies can be administered on an outpatient basis; they usually do not require hospitalization. So it was argued that no one could be rightfully kept in a mental institution against his or her will; people who had committed no crimes and who posed no danger to others should be released. Federal and state monies for mental health were to be directed toward community mental health facilities which would treat the mentally ill on a voluntary outpatient basis. The nation's mental hospitals were emptied of all but the most dangerous mental patients. The population of mental hospitals declined from over 500,000 in 1960 to about 100,000 in 1984.[20]

Decriminalization.   Vagrancy (homelessness) and public intoxication are no longer crimes. Involuntary confinement has been abolished for the mentally ill and for substance abusers, unless a person is adjudged in court to be "a danger to himself or others," which means a person must commit a serious act of violence before the courts will intervene. For many homeless this means the freedom to "die with their rights on." The homeless are victimized by cold, exposure, hunger, the availability of alcohol and illegal drugs, and violent street crimes perpetrated against them, in addition to the ravages of their illness itself.

---

[19]As reported in a twenty-seven-city survey by the U.S. Conference of Mayors. See *U.S. News and World Report,* 15 January 1990, pp. 27–29.

[20]*Newsweek,* 6 January 1985, p. 16.

The Failure of Community Care.   Community-based care is largely irrelevant to the plight of the chronic mentally ill persons and alcohol and drug abusers in the streets. Most are "uncooperative"; they are isolated from society; they have no family members or doctors or counselors to turn to for help. For them, community "care" is a Salvation Army meal and cot, or a night in a city-run refuge for the homeless, or a ride to the city hospital psychiatric ward for a brief period of "observation" after which they must be released again to the streets. The nation's vast social welfare system provides them little help. They lose their social security, welfare, and disability checks because they have no permanent address. They cannot handle forms, appointments, or interviews; the welfare bureaucracy is intimidating. Welfare workers seldom provide the "aggressive care management" and mental health care that these people need.

Housing Policy.   Thus, for most of the homeless, their problems are far more intractable than the availability of low-cost housing. Nonetheless, government policies in many cities create shortages of low-cost housing. Rent controls assist a few older middle-class families who occupied apartments when controls were imposed, but controls discourage new housing construction and thus guarantee housing shortages and inflated rents within a few years of their imposition. Urban renewal destroys low-rent apartments as well as single-room-occupancy (SRO) hotels and "flophouses." Building and housing codes make its economically more advantageous for owners to abandon buildings than to rent them at low rates. Contrary to common political rhetoric, homelessness is *not* a result of cuts in public housing payments. Public housing units expanded from 1.2 to 1.4 million from 1980 to 1987 and the number of households receiving housing assistance doubled.[21]

HEALTH CARE OR MEDICAL CARE?

There is no better illustration of the dilemmas of rational policy making in America than in the field of health. Again, the first obstacle to rationalism is in defining the problem. Is our goal to have *good health*—that is, whether we live at all (infant mortality), how well we live (days lost to sickness), and how long we live (life spans and adult mortality)? Or is our goal to have *good medical care*—frequent visits to the doctor, well-equipped and accessible hospitals, and equal access to medical care by rich and poor alike?

Perhaps the first lesson in health policy is understanding that good medical care does *not* necessarily mean good health. Good health correlates best with factors over which doctors and hospitals have no control: heredity, lifestyle (smoking, eating, drinking, exercise, worry), and the physical en-

---

[21]*Statistical Abstract of the United States 1989,* p. 713.

vironment (sewage disposal, water quality, conditions of work, and so forth). Most of the bad things that happen to people's health are beyond the reach of doctors and hospitals.

Of course, doctors can set broken bones, stop infections with drugs, and remove swollen appendixes. And if you happen to be suffering from these or similar problems you want the careful attention of a skilled physician. But in the long run, infant mortality, sickness and disease, and life span are affected very little by the quality of medical care.[22] If you want a long healthy life, choose parents who have lived a long healthy life, and then do all the things your mother always told you to do: don't smoke, don't drink, get lots of exercise and rest, don't overeat, relax, and don't worry. You can spend millions on medical care, and you will not enjoy the same good health as you will by following these traditional guidelines.

Leading Causes of Death.   Historically, most of the reductions in infant and adult death rates have resulted from public health and sanitation including immunization against smallpox, clean public water supply, sanitary sewage disposal, improved diets, and increased standards of living. Many of the leading causes of death today (see Table 5–6) including heart disease, stroke, cirrhosis of the liver, accidents, and suicides are closely linked to personal habits and lifestyles and are beyond the reach of medicine. Thus, the greatest contribution to better health is likely to be found in altered personal habits and lifestyles, rather than in more medical care. Nonetheless, health policy in America is largely centered around the questionable notion that better medical care means better health.

The overall death rate in the United States (the number of deaths per 100,000 people) continues to decline. Considerable progress is being made by the nation in reducing death rates for many of the major killers—heart disease, stroke, pneumonia, diabetes, and emphysema. However, the cancer death rate continues to rise despite increased medical spending.

Health Care for the Poor.   Society feels a special responsibility for providing health care to the poor. No one should be denied medical care for lack of money; no one should suffer or die for lack of financial resources to obtain adequate food; nor should anyone suffer desperation or pain for the lack of medical care that money can buy. We can find general agreement on these broad ethical principles. The tough questions arise when we try to find a way of implementing these principles.

It is not difficult to demonstrate that the poor and the black in America

---

[22]The literature on this point is extensive. See, for example, Victor R. Fuchs, *Who Shall Live? Health, Economics, and Social Choice* (New York: Basic Books, 1974); Nathan Glazer, "Paradoxes of Health Care," *The Public Interest* (Winter 1971), 62–77; Leon R. Kass, "Regarding the End of Medicine and the Pursuit of Health," *The Public Interest* (Summer 1975), 11–42.

TABLE 5-6   Leading Causes of Death[a]

	1960	1970	1980	1988
All Causes	954.7	945.3	883.4	883.0
Heart disease	369.0	362.0	334.3	312.2
Stroke (cerebrovascular)	108.0	101.9	80.5	61.1
Cancer	149.2	162.8	181.9	198.6
Accidents	52.3	56.4	48.4	39.7
Pneumonia	37.3	30.9	26.7	31.5
Diabetes	16.7	18.9	15.5	16.1
Cirrhosis	11.3	15.5	13.8	10.6
Emphysema, asthma	[b]	15.2	10.0	8.3
Suicide	10.6	11.6	12.5	12.3
Homicide	4.7	8.3	9.4	9.0

[a]Deaths per 100,000 population per year.
[b]Not separately recorded.
Source: *Statistical Abstract of the United States 1990,* p. 79.

have higher mortality rates than the affluent and the white. For example, the infant mortality rate is used frequently as a general indicator of the adequacy of health care. Infant mortality rates have been consistently higher for blacks than for whites (see Table 5–7). Infant mortality rates have declined for both races since 1950, but black infant deaths have continued to be significantly higher than white infant deaths. These and other figures clearly suggest that the poor do not enjoy the same good health as the affluent. But is this a product of inadequate medical care, or is it a product of nutrition, lifestyle, environment, and other nonmedical factors?

Contrary to popular stereotypes, the poor in America see doctors *more often* than the nonpoor. This situation has come about since 1965 with the beginning of the Medicaid program for the poor and Medicare for the aged. Yet despite the increase in medical care for the poor, the health of the poor remains below the health of the nonpoor. Thus, *access to medical care* for the poor has indeed been improved by government policies and programs, but this is largely irrelevant to health.

TABLE 5-7   Death Rates by Race

	WHITE	BLACK
Total	518.0	781.0
Male	679.0	1026.9
Female	387.7	588.2
Infant	8.9	18.0

Source: *Statistical Abstract of the United States 1990,* pp. 75, 78.

Medicaid: Health Care As Welfare.　　Medicaid is the federal government's largest single welfare program for the poor. The costs of Medicaid now exceed the costs of all other public assistance programs—including AFDC, SSI, and the Food Stamp program. Medicaid was begun in 1965 and grew quickly into the nation's largest welfare program.

Medicaid is a combined federal and state program. The states exercise fairly broad administrative powers and carry almost half of the financial burden. Medicaid is a welfare program designed for needy persons: no prior contributions are required, monies come from general tax revenues, and most recipients are already on welfare roles. Although states differ in their eligibility requirements for Medicaid, states must cover all AFDC families and most states also cover SSI recipients. In addition, a majority of states extend coverage to other "medically needy"—individuals who do not qualify for public assistance but whose incomes are low enough to qualify as needy. About half of the states extend Medicaid to families whose head is receiving unemployment compensation.

States also help set benefits under Medicaid. All states are required by the federal government to provide inpatient and outpatient hospital care, physicians' services, family planning, laboratory services and X-rays, and nursing and home health care. States must also develop an early and periodic screening, diagnosis, and treatment program for all children under Medicaid. However, states themselves generally decide upon the rate of reimbursement to hospitals and physicians. Low rates can discourage hospitals and physicians from providing good care under Medicaid. To make up for low payments, hospitals and doctors may schedule too many patients in too short a span of time or prescribe unnecessary tests and procedures designed to make treatment more expensive.

Medicare: Health Care As Insurance.　　Medicare, like Medicaid, was enacted in 1965 as an amendment to the nation's basic Social Security Act. Medicare provides prepaid hospital insurance for the aged and low-cost voluntary medical insurance for the aged, directly under federal administration. Medicare includes HI—a compulsory basic health insurance plan covering hospital costs for the aged, which is financed out of payroll taxes collected under the Social Security system; and SMI—a voluntary, supplemental medical insurance program that will pay 80 percent of "allowable" charges for physicians' services and other medical expenses, financed in part by contributions from the aged and in part by general tax revenues.

Only *aged* persons are covered by Medicare provisions. Eligibility is *not* dependent on income; *all* aged persons eligible for Social Security are also eligible for Medicare. No physical examination is required and preexisting conditions are covered. The costs of SMI are so low to the beneficiaries that participation by the elderly is almost universal.

Both the HI and SMI provisions of Medicare require patients to pay small *initial* charges or "deductibles." The purpose is to discourage unnecessary hospital or physician care. HI generally pays the full charges for the first sixty days of hospitalization each year after a deductible charge equivalent to one day's stay; but many doctors charge higher rates than allowable under SMI. Indeed, it is estimated that only about half of the doctors in the nation accept SMI allowable payments as payment in full. Many doctors bill Medicare patients for charges *above* the allowable SMI payments. Medicare does *not* pay for prescription drugs, eyeglasses, hearing aids, or routine physical examinations.

Catastrophic Coverage.   For a few victims of long-term "catastrophic" illness, Medicare is inadequate. Medicare covers only the first sixty days of hospitalization; it covers nursing home for one hundred days only if the patient is released there from a hospital; it covers only 80 percent of allowable physician charges; and it does not cover drugs. Congress attempted to remedy these problems in 1988 with catastrophic health care coverage under Medicare. Coverage would have included *all* hospital charges after one day's deductible, *all* physician allowable charges after a deductible amount, 150 days of skilled nursing-home care, and 80 percent of the costs of drugs, plus other associated benefits. Congress proposed to pay for these added benefits with a 15 percent income tax surcharge on Medicare enrollees, the elderly. But a year after the program was initiated, opposition to the tax surcharge among the elderly was so strong that Congress was forced to jettison the program. The politically powerful senior voters deluged Congress with their objections to the surtax. They wanted their added benefits paid for by working people; if they were forced to pay for them themselves, they would rather not have them.

Long-Term Care.   As the number and proportion of the elderly population grows in the United States (eighty years and over is the fastest growing age group in the nation), the need for long-term nursing-home care grows. Current Medicare insurance coverage is limited to acute rather than chronic illness and thus provides little support for nursing homes or care in the home. Medicaid assistance to the needy is paid to nursing-home patients. But middle-class people cannot qualify for Medicaid without first "spending down" their savings. Long-term nursing-home care threatens their assets and their children's inheritance. Private insurance policies covering long-term care are said to be too expensive. So senior citizen groups have lobbied heavily for long-term nursing-home care to be paid for by taxpayers under Medicare. The U.S. Commission on Comprehensive Health Care, labeled the "Pepper Commission" for the late U.S. Representative Claude Pepper, a Florida Democrat who represented the affluent aged in Congress for many years, called for a new comprehensive program for nursing-home care for everyone under Medicare at an additional cost of $42 *billion* per year.[22]

EVALUATION: HEALTH-CARE COSTS AND BENEFITS

There is no doubt that Medicaid and Medicare have *improved access* to medicine for the poor and the aged. The nation's health, as measured by infant mortality rates, death rates due to specific causes, and average life spans, is improving over time. *But there is no indication that Medicaid or Medicare has been mainly or even partly responsible for these improvements.* Indeed, declines in the leading causes of death (shown in Table 5–6) were just as great *prior* to the enactment of Medicaid and Medicare as they have been after the enactment of these programs. As Aaron Wildavsky observes:

> If the question is, "Does health increase with government expenditure on medicine?" the answer is likely to be "No." Just alter the question: "Has access to medicine been improved by government programs?" and the answer is most certainly with a little qualification, "Yes."[23]

No Constraints on Costs.   No system of health care can provide as much as people will use. Each individual, believing his or her health and life are at stake, will want the most thorough diagnostic testing, the most constant care, the most advanced treatment. And doctors have no strong incentive to try to save on costs; they want the most advanced diagnostic and treatment facilities available for their patients. Under conditions of uncertainty in a medical situation—and there is always some uncertainty—physicians can always think of one more thing which might be done—one more consultation, one more test, one more therapeutic approach. The patient wants the best, and the doctor wants it too. Any tendency for doctors to limit testing and treatment is countered by the threat of malpractice suits; it is always easier to order one more test or procedure than to risk even the chance that the failure to do so will some day be cause for a court suit. So both patients and doctors push up the costs of health care, particularly when the public or private insurance pays.

"Third-Party Payers."   There is little cost constraint on patients and physicians when they know "third-party payers" will foot the bill. About 85 percent of the U.S. population is covered by health insurance—either private insurance, generally provided through group employment plans, or government insurance under Medicare or Medicaid. Both private insurers and the

[22]*New York Times,* March 29, 1990.

[23]Aaron Wildavsky, *Speaking Truth to Power* (Boston: Little, Brown, 1979), p. 286.

government have undertaken various efforts to control costs. Their cost-control regulations and restrictions have created a mountain of paperwork for physicians and hospitals and created frustrations and anger among both care givers and patients. And these efforts have not had much success in limiting overall medical costs.

Health Care Inflation.   The costs of health care in the United States have risen much faster than prices in general. Medical costs have tripled over the last ten years. The nation's total medical bill is over 10 percent of the Gross National Product (see Figure 5–4).

Certainly third-party payment by government and private insurance has contributed to this inflation. But there are other causes of inefficiency and inflation in America's health-care system. Advances in medical technology have produced elaborate and expensive equipment. Hospitals that have made heavy financial investment in this equipment must use it as often as possible. Physicians trained in highly specialized techniques and procedures wish to use them. Physicians and hospitals are forced by the threat of malpractice litigation to use the most advanced tests and treatments. Malpractice suits force doctors to practice "defensive medicine"—to order multiple tests and consultations to guard against even the most remote medical possibilities. The system encourages the provision of unnecessary tests and services. An unnecessary expansion of hospital facilities in the nation also contributes to inefficiency. About 40 percent of hospital beds are empty, yet overhead costs of maintaining these facilities must be paid.

FIGURE 5–4 Total National Health Expenditures, Selected Years 1965 to 1990, in Billions of Dollars and Percentage of Gross National Product. (Source: *Statistical Abstract of the United States 1989*, p. 90.)

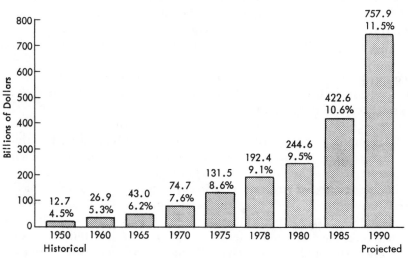

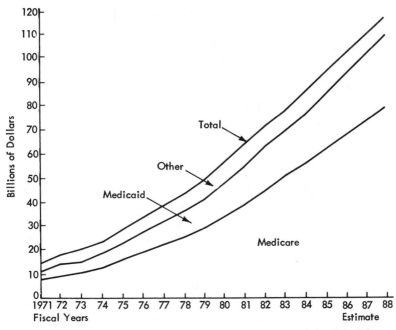

FIGURE 5-5   Federal Outlays for Health. (Source: *The Budget of the United States Government FY 1986*. Washington, D.C.: Government Printing Office, 1985.)

Coping with Medical Costs.   Medical care is a "scarce resource." There will never be enough of it available to satisfy the unlimited demands of every individual in society. If unlimited health care is right and all costs are eliminated, then each patient and doctor can order the most elaborate diagnostic procedures (extensive lab work, CAT scanning, consultations with specialists), extraordinary treatments (renal dialysis, organ transplants), long hospital stays, extensive nursing care, frequent office visits, and so on. With potentially unlimited demand, medical care must be rationed in *some* fashion.

Payments for Diagnosis-Related Groups.   Controlling Medicare costs is a direct responsibility of the federal government. In 1983, the Reagan administration won congressional approval for a system of Medicare payment by "diagnosis-related groups" (DRGs). Prior to this reform, Medicare generally reimbursed hospitals for the total amount billed for each patient. This was a retrospective (after the fact) method of paying for hospital care. Now a prospective method of payment is being utilized in which the federal government specifies in advance what it will pay for the treatment of five hundred different illnesses or diagnosis-related groups. Hospitals that spend more to treat Medicare patients must absorb excess costs, but if the hospital spends less than the amount allotted to treat a patient, it is allowed to keep the difference. Hospitals may not charge Medicare patients more than DRG allotment. Obviously, the idea behind DRGs is to encourage hospitals to be more efficient in their treatment of Medicare patients.

Prospective Payment Systems. Both government and private insurers are moving rapidly to prospective payment system (PPS) as a means of cost control. These plans establish computerized guidelines for "appropriate" care for various injuries and illnesses. Physicians who go beyond these guidelines in tests or treatments must specify unusual circumstances or risk being denied payment by the insurers. But many physicians complain that PPS is a cumbersome and restrictive "cookbook" approach to medicine that often leads to undertreatment.

HMOs. Health maintenance organizations (HMOs) are membership organizations that hire doctors and other health professionals at fixed salaries to serve dues-paying members. HMOs typically provide comprehensive health care for enrolled members. The members pay a regular fee and are entitled to hospital care and physicians' services at no extra cost. Advocates of HMOs says that this is less costly than fee-for-service medical care because doctors have no incentive to overtreat patients. Moreover, HMOs emphasize preventive medicine and therefore minimize serious illnesses. Many of the complaints about HMOs correspond to complaints about service in other bureaucratic settings: patients see different doctors on different days; doctors in HMOs do not work as hard as private physicians; care is "depersonalized"; and so forth.

NEW STRATEGIES: MANDATED HEALTH INSURANCE

When the original Social Security Act of 1935 was passed, efforts were made in Congress to include "a comprehensive national health insurance system with universal and mandatory coverage." But President Franklin D. Roosevelt backed off when he was convinced by representatives of the American Medical Association that the plan would not work without the support of the nation's physicians. President Harry Truman pushed hard for a national health insurance program tied to Social Security, but again opponents led by the American Medical Association were successful in defeating the proposal. In 1965 President Lyndon Johnson opted for a somewhat narrower goal—government health insurance for the poor and the aged (Medicaid and Medicare). But the decades-old debate over national health care continues.

Health Insurance Coverage. Today about 85 percent of the nation's population is covered by either government or private health insurance. Governments pay about 41 percent of all health care costs—17 percent through Medicare, 10 percent through Medicaid, and 14 percent through

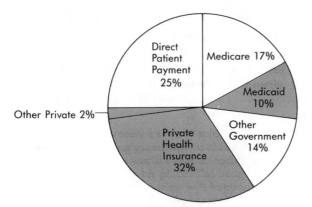

FIGURE 5-6 Who Pays the Medical Bills.

other government programs including military and veteran care. Private insurance pays for 32 percent of the nation's health costs; direct patient payments account for only 25 percent. (See Figure 5–6.)

There are an estimated 37 million Americans, or 15 percent of the population, who have no medical insurance. These people may postpone or go without needed medical care, or be denied medical care by hospitals and physicians in all but emergency situations. Confronted with serious illness, they may be obliged to impoverish themselves in order to become eligible for Medicaid. Their unpaid medical bills must be absorbed by hospitals or shifted to paying patients and their insurance companies. Many of the uninsured work for small businesses or are self-employed or unemployed. Private insurance is very expensive when purchased individually, that is, outside of an employer or group plan.

Mandated Health Insurance. In recent years, proponents of national health insurance have altered their tactics, shifting from support of government insurance programs to mandating that all employers provide health insurance. At the state level, Massachusetts requires that employers provide medical insurance and that an additional tax on employers be used to finance a state-administered insurance fund for the unemployed. Of course, the burden of mandated insurance falls on small businesses, which may close as a result, and on minimum-wage workers, who may lose their jobs because of the added costs of employment.

PREVENTIVE STRATEGIES: SUCCESSES AND FAILURES

Governments have long concerned themselves with the general health and safety of their citizens. Nonetheless, government efforts to reduce deaths due to accident or preventable illness have not always been successful.

Speed Limits.   Occasionally government actions improve health or safety without setting out specifically to do so. When the United States adopted a national 55 MPH speed limit to save gasoline, the initial result was a reduction in annual highway accident deaths from over 56,000 per year to 46,000 per year—a saving of 10,000 lives each year. Rarely is any public health program so successful. Yet this program was adopted in 1973 to save gas, rather than to save lives. No giant Washington bureaucracy was established to implement this particular law and relatively little federal money was spent to enforce it. Yet no other single action of the federal government has ever been so successful in saving so many lives. Over time average highway speeds increased (even before the 55 MPH speed limit was raised) and highway deaths began to creep up toward the levels of earlier years.

OSHA.   Just the opposite experience occurred with the creation of the Occupational Safety and Health Administration (OSHA) in 1970. OSHA was established as a large Washington bureaucracy with a substantial budget, amid a great deal of fanfare. Its responsibilities included the tasks of drawing up safety regulations for virtually every type of private employment and then enforcing these regulations with 2,500 inspectors issuing citations against businesses, large or small, found to be in violation of the regulations.

Approximately 11,000 persons die in work-related accidents each year. But there is no indication that OSHA ever affected this statistic. The number of work-related deaths declines slightly each year, but the declines were the same both before and after the creation of OSHA. Moreover, OSHA imposes requirements on businesses without weighing the benefits against the costs of these regulations. In recent years, OSHA has been instructed to concentrate its attentions on a few of the more dangerous industries (construction, heavy manufacturing, transportation, and petrochemicals) and to drop its more trivial safety rules. But it appears as if the bureaucratic command-control approach to safety and health is ineffective.

Smoking.   In contrast to the government's failure with the bureaucratic approach in occupational health and safety, it is interesting to observe the government's success with the public education approach to smoking and health. The decrease in the percentage of adult smokers in recent years has been substantial. And yet, the federal government has not banned smoking or the manufacturing of cigarettes; no federal bureaucracy has been created specifically to implement anti-smoking laws; and relatively few tax dollars have been spent to curtail smoking. (On the contrary, the federal government spends millions each year to support the price of tobacco in its agricultural commodity credit program.)

According to the U.S. Public Health Service, the proportion of

American adults who smoke decreased from 42.5 percent in 1965 to 32.5 percent in 1985.[24]

	1965	1980	1985
Men	52.8%	36.8	32.5
Women	31.5	29.6	27.8
Total	42.5	33.5	30.1

What could account for this significant change in a health-related habit?

The American Cancer Society persuaded President John F. Kennedy to establish a special advisory commission to the surgeon general of the United States to undertake a comprehensive review of all the data relating to smoking and health. The famous "Surgeon General's Report" was published in 1964.[25] It concluded that cigarette smoking was a serious health hazard and that cigarette smoking was causally related to lung cancer. It also reported that cigarette smoking was associated with coronary disease, chronic bronchitis, and emphysema. The tobacco industry vainly tried to discredit the report, but cigarette sales dropped sharply. Although sales recovered after several years, increasing percentages of adults gave up smoking, or never started the habit.

The Federal Cigarette Labeling and Advertising Act of 1966 required all cigarette packages (and later all cigarette advertising) to be marked with the statement: "Caution: Cigarette Smoking May Be Dangerous to Your Health." In 1970, Congress approved legislation banning all cigarette commercials on radio and television. In 1971, the Interstate Commerce Commission restricted smoking to certain sections of buses and trains, and the Civil Aeronautics Board did the same on airlines in 1973.

Note that the federal government's actions in smoking have been largely *educational*. In this case, these efforts have met with significant success.

SUMMARY

A "rational" approach to social welfare policy requires a clear definition of objectives, the development of alternative strategies for achieving these objectives, and a careful comparison and weighing of the costs and benefits of each alternative. But there are seemingly insurmountable problems in developing a completely "rational policy":

---

[24]*Statistical Abstract of the United States 1989*, p. 118.

[25]Report of the Advisory Committee to the Surgeon General of the Public Health Service, *Smoking and Health* (Washington, D.C.: Government Printing Office, 1964).

1. Contrasting definitions of the problem of poverty constitute one obstacle to rational policy making. Official government sources define poverty in terms of minimum dollar amounts required for subsistence. Poverty, by this definition, declined steadily in America prior to 1965, but rose with the introduction of many new social welfare programs. In recent years 12 to 14 percent of the population has remained below the official poverty line.

2. Latent poverty refers to people who would fall below the poverty line in the absence of government assistance. Latent poverty has also risen over the last twenty-five years, as more people have become dependent on government.

3. Contrasting explanations of poverty also make it difficult to formulate a rational policy. Is poverty a product of a lack of knowledge, skills, and training? Or recession and unemployment? Or a "culture of poverty"? Certainly the disintegration of the traditional husband-wife family is closely associated with poverty. How can government devise a rational policy to keep families together, or at least not encourage them to dissolve?

4. Government welfare policies themselves may be a significant cause of poverty. Poverty in America had steadily declined prior to the development of new Great Society programs, the relaxation of eligibility requirements for welfare assistance, and the rapid increase of welfare expenditures of the 1970s. To what extent do government programs themselves encourage social dependency and harm the long-term prospects of the poor?

5. The social insurance concept was designed as a preventive strategy to insure persons against indigence arising from old age, death of a family breadwinner, or physical disability. But the Social Security "trust fund" idea remains in name only. Today each generation of workers is expected to pay the benefits for each generation of retirees. Yet after the year 2000 the "dependency ratio" will rise to a point where it will be very difficult for workers then to support the large number of Social Security recipients.

6. The federal government also pursues an alleviative strategy in assisting the poor with a variety of direct cash and in-kind benefit programs. The Supplemental Security Income program (SSI) provides direct federal cash payments to the aged, the blind, and disabled. As a welfare program, SSI is paid from general tax revenues, and recipients must prove their need. The federal government also provides assistance to the states for the Aid to Families with Dependent Children (AFDC) welfare program. The largest in-kind welfare programs are the federal Food Stamp and Medicaid programs.

7. The paramount objective in national health policy has never been clearly defined. Is it *good health,* as defined by lower death rates, less illness, and longer life? Or is it *better medical care,* as defined by easy access to inexpensive hospital and physician care? If good health is the objective, then preventive efforts to change people's personal habits and lifestyles are more likely to improve health than anything else.

8. Medical care does not contribute directly to good health. However, our ethical commitments require that we ensure adequate medical care for all, particularly the poor and the aged. Medicaid is now the nation's costliest welfare program. The poor visit doctors more often and stay in hospitals longer than the nonpoor. But the health of the poor is still not as good as the health of the nonpoor. This suggests the public policy has succeeded in improving access to medical care but not necessarily in improving the nation's health.

9. Medicare offers prepaid medical insurance for the aged under Social Security. Prior to the adoption of Medicare in 1965, the aged found it difficult to obtain medical insurance from private firms. Medicare removes the fear of impoverishment through hospital bills, even if it does not increase life span.

10. Both Medicaid for the poor and Medicare for the aged, together with private medical insurance, have contributed to inflation in medical care costs. The *success* of these programs (in terms of numbers of beneficiaries) has led to a new policy problem—medical care cost containment. In other words, solving one policy problem created another.

BIBLIOGRAPHY

DUNCAN, GREG, J. *Years of Poverty, Years of Plenty.* Ann Arbor: Institute for Social Research, University of Michigan, 1984.

HARRINGTON, MICHAEL. *The Other America.* New York: Macmillan, 1962.

MOYNIHAN, DANIEL PATRICK. *Maximum Feasible Misunderstanding: Community Action and the War on Poverty.* New York: Free Press, 1969.

MURRAY, CHARLES. *Losing Ground.* New York: Basic Books, 1984.

PIVEN, FRANCES FOX, and RICHARD A. CLOWARD. *Regulating the Poor: The Functions of Public Welfare.* New York: Random House, 1971.

WILSON, WILLIAM J. *The Truly Disadvantaged.* Chicago: University of Chicago Press, 1987.

6

EDUCATION
the group struggle

There is strong public support for national standardized testing of students in the United States. (Laima Druskis)

MULTIPLE GOALS IN EDUCATIONAL POLICY

Perhaps the most widely recommended "solution" to the problems that confront American society is more and better schooling. If there ever was a time
when schools were only expected to combat ignorance and illiteracy, that
time is far behind us. Today schools are expected to do many things: resolve
racial conflict and build an integrated society; inspire patriotism and good
citizenship; provide values, aspirations, and a sense of identity to disadvantaged children; offer various forms of recreation and mass entertainment
(football games, bands, choruses, cheerleading, and the like); reduce conflict in society by teaching children to get along well with others and to adjust to group living; reduce the highway accident toll by teaching students
to be good drivers; fight disease and poor health through physical education, health training, and even medical treatment; eliminate unemployment
and poverty by teaching job skills; end malnutrition and hunger through
school lunch and milk programs; fight drug abuse and educate children about
sex; and act as custodians for teenagers who have no interest in education
but whom we do not permit either to work or to roam the streets unsuper-
vised. In other words, nearly all the nation's problems are reflected in
demands placed on the nation's schools. And, of course, these demands are
frequently conflicting.

It is important to note at the outset, however, that some of the pressures
which have confronted American education are changing as total enrollments
decline. Elementary and secondary school enrollments peaked around 1970;
since then, declines in the birth rate (beginning in the 1960s) have gradually reduced the total number of children in school. Of course, enrollments
are uneven across the nation: some school districts still face burgeoning
enrollments, while others must close down classrooms and stop hiring new
teachers. But overall, the problems confronting the nation's schools do not
now include increasing enrollments. Even colleges and universities, which
still managed small enrollment gains in the 1970s, have leveled off in enrollment in the 1980s (see Figure 6–1).

Educational policy affects a wide variety of interests, and stimulates
a great deal of interest group activity. We will describe the major interests
involved in federal educational policy. We will examine the constitutional
provisions and court policies dealing with religion in the public schools. We
will observe how both racial and religious group interests are mobilized in
educational policy making, and we will see the importance of resolving group
conflict in the development of educational policy. We shall also describe the
structure of educational decision making and the resulting multiple points
of group access in a fragmented federal-state-local educational system. We
shall attempt to describe the broad categories of group interests—teachers,
taxpayers, school board members, school administrators, and finally,
parents—involved in educational policy at the local level. Finally, we will

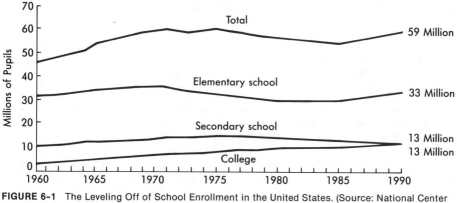

FIGURE 6-1   The Leveling Off of School Enrollment in the United States. (Source: National Center for Education Statistics, *American Education at a Glance,* 1989).

examine the governing and financing of public higher education—the nation's investment in state colleges and universities.

BATTLING OVER THE BASICS

Citizens groups with an interest in education—parents, taxpayers, and employers—have confronted professional educators—school administrators, state education officials, and teachers' unions—over the vital question of what should be taught in public schools. Public sentiment is strongly in favor of teaching the "three Rs" ("reading, 'riting, and 'rithmetic"), enforcing minimum standards with tests, and even testing teachers themselves for their mastery of the basics. Indeed, there is strong public support for standardized *national* testing of all U.S. students, as in Japan (see Table 6–1). Parents are less enthusiastic than professional educators about emotional growth, "getting along with others," self-expression and self-image, cultural enrichment, good citizenship, and various "innovative" programs of education.

The SAT Score Controversy.   For many years critics of modern public education cited declining scores on standardized tests, particularly the Scholastic Aptitude Test (SAT), required by many colleges and universities, as evidence of the failure of the schools to teach basic reading and mathematics skills. The end of the decline in 1982 (see Table 6–2) was attributed to increasing emphasis on basic skills and standardized testing. But in all likelihood, changes in these test scores were really a function of how many students took the test. During the years of declining test scores, increasing numbers and proportions of students were taking the test—students who never aspired to college in the past and whose test scores did not match those of the earlier smaller group of college-bound test takers. Scores have crept

TABLE 6-1   Public Opinion on School Standards

	FAVOR	OPPOSE
Would you favor or oppose much more stress on teaching basic skills to children?	98%	2%

	AGREE	DISAGREE
All students should be required to pass a standardized basic skill test before they can graduate.	79%	21%

	AGREE	DISAGREE
Teachers should be required to pass a standardized test in the subject they will teach before they can teach in the public school.	90%	10%
Public schools in this community should use standardized national testing programs to measure the academic achievement of students.	77%	14%
All high school students should be required to pass a standard nationwide examination to get a high school degree.	72%	21%

Source: *The New York Times,* 26 December 1989.

upward since 1982, with black and Hispanic students narrowing the gap with white students.

A Nation At Risk.   The "back to basics" citizens' reform movement in education was given impetus by an influential report by the National Commission on Excellence in Education entitled "A Nation At Risk."[1]

> Our nation is at risk. Our once unchallenged prominence in commerce, industry, science, and technological innovation is being overtaken by competitors throughout the world. . . .
> If an unfriendly foreign power had attempted to impose on America the mediocre educational performance that exists today, we might well have viewed it as an act of war.

The commission cited as evidence of the nation's decline in educational achievement:

> international comparisons of student achievement among industrialized nations which often rank American students last and never first

[1]National Commission on Excellence in Education, *A Nation At Risk* (Washington, D.C.: Government Printing Office, 1983).

TABLE 6-2   The SAT Score Controversy

ALL STUDENTS AVERAGE			AVERAGES BY GROUP		
YEAR	VERBAL	MATHEMATICAL	COMBINED SCORE		
1963	478	502		1978	1988
1965	473	498	Black	686	737
1970	460	488	Mexican-American	772	810
1975	437	473	White	931	935
1980	424	466			
1981	424	466			
1982	426	467			
1985	431	475			
1989	427	476			

Source: College Entrance Examination Board, New York.

marked declines in student achievement over the preceding twenty years

declining high school enrollments in courses in science, mathematics and foreign language, and increasing enrollments in cooking, marriage, driving, health, and recreational courses

declining amounts of school homework

rising school grades despite declining achievement scores

the recruitment of new teachers from the bottom quarter of college graduates

the concentration of college credits of future teachers in educational courses, reducing the time spent in subject matter courses

shortages of teachers in mathematics and science

The commission's recommendations set the agenda for educational policy debate in the states. Among the many recommendations were these:

a minimum high school curriculum of four years of English, three years of mathematics, three years of social science, and one-half year of computer science

four to six years of foreign language study beginning in the elementary grades

standardized tests for achievement for all of these subjects

more homework, a seven-hour school day, and a 200- to 220-day school year

reliable grades and standardized tests for promotion and graduation

"performance-based" salaries for teachers and rewards for "superior" teaching

Testing.   Many state legislatures responded to the commission's report and the demand for greater achievement in basic skills by requiring minimum competence testing (MCT examinations) in the schools. These tests may be used as diagnostic tools to determine the need for remedial education, or minimum scores may be required for promotion or graduation. Currently, about half of the states require students to pass a minimum competency test in order to receive a high school diploma. These tests usually require performance at an eighth or ninth grade level.

Minimum competence tests force schools and teachers to place greater emphasis on the "basics." Professional educators have been less enthusiastic about testing than citizen groups and state legislators. Educators contend that MCT leads to narrow "test-taking" education rather than broad preparation for life. MCT requires teachers to devote more time to coaching students on how to pass an exam rather than preparing them for productive lives after graduation.

But the most serious opposition to MCT has come from minority group leaders who charge that the tests are racially biased. Average black student scores are frequently lower than average white students scores, and larger percentages of black students are held back from promotion and graduation by testing than white students. Some black leaders charge that racial bias in the examination itself, as well as racial isolation in the school, contribute to black-white differences in exam scores. Denying a disproportionate number of black students a diploma because of the schools' failure to teach basics may be viewed as a form of discrimination. However, to date federal courts have declined to rule that MCT itself is discriminatory, as long as sufficient time and opportunity have been provided all students to prepare for the examination.

Testing Teachers.   Professional education groups have opposed teacher competency tests on the grounds that standardized tests cannot really measure competency in the classroom. The National Education Association has opposed all testing of teachers; the American Federation of Teachers is willing to accept competency testing only for new teachers. The Educational Testing Service (which prepares the SAT, GRE, LSAT, and other standardized national examinations) offers a National Teacher Examination (NTE), which measures general knowledge and basic comprehension and mathematical skills. Today, only a few states have adopted teacher competency tests, but the results have been disquieting. Large numbers of experienced teachers have failed the tests; black teachers have failed more often than white teachers.

Pay and Recruitment.   Another concern of the National Commission on Excellence in Education is the inability of the teaching profession to attract quality students. The commission noted that the average SAT scores of education majors were lower than the average scores of other students. Average starting salaries for teachers nationwide is less than 75 percent of the average starting salaries for other graduates. Years ago, when women were excluded from many other professions, teaching attracted many people of high ability even though salaries were low. But today, with expanded opportunities for women, the teaching profession cannot expect to attract quality graduates without offering competitive salary levels.

Merit Pay.   Few state legislators are willing or able to raise all teachers' salaries to the level of other professionals. The commission's recommendation for the adoption of "merit pay" provides a less costly option, yet one that promises to reward good teaching. Ideally, merit pay would help retain exceptional teachers and encourage quality teaching, without rewarding mediocrity through general (across-the-board) salary increases to all teachers. But the professional education groups fear that merit pay will become a substitute for adequate teachers' salaries. They also argue that there are no objective criteria for measuring "merit" in classroom teaching. Using student test scores would unfairly penalize teachers who taught disadvantaged students. And teacher scores on "pencil-and-paper" tests do not really measure classroom performance. And of course, the allocation of merit pay by principals and superintendents is attacked as potentially arbitrary. In short, merit pay plans often founder on an age-old question: What is good teaching?

THE EDUCATIONAL GROUPS

Interest group activity in education includes many racial, religious, labor, and civil rights organizations, as well as educational groups.

Professional Education Lobby.   The professional educational groups are at the heart of most educational issues. The largest educational organization is the National Education Association (NEA), which claims a membership of two million teachers and school administrators. The NEA maintains a large Washington office for lobbying Congress and the executive branch and makes substantial campaign contributions to political candidates. The American Federation of Teachers has a smaller membership, concentrated in big-city school districts, but as an affiliate of the AFL-CIO it can call upon assistance from organized labor. Because of the frequent involvement of racial and religious issues in education, such groups as the National Association for the Advancement of Colored People (NAACP), National Catholic Education Conference, the American Jewish Congress, Americans United for the Separation of Church and State, and the American Civil Liberties Union all become involved in educational policy. Support for federal aid to education is generally forthcoming from the NEA and AFT, organized labor (AFL-CIO), school-related organizations such as the National Congress of Parents and Teachers and the American Library Association, and liberal groups such as Americans for Democratic Action. The educational groups not only lobby Congress but also the executive branch, particularly the Department of Education. Indeed, the Department of Education was created in 1979 largely because of President Carter's campaign pledge to the educational groups to create a separate education department.

Voters and Taxpayers.   School politics at the community level differ from one community to another, but it is possible to identify a number of political groups that appear on the scene in school politics almost everywhere. There is, first of all, that small band of voters who turn out for school elections. It is estimated that, on the average, only about one-third of the eligible voters bother to cast ballots in school elections. Voter turnout at school bond and tax elections also demonstrates no groundswell of public interest in school affairs. Perhaps even more interesting is the finding that the larger the voter turnout in a school referendum, the more likely the *defeat* of education proposals. In general, the best way to defeat a school bond referendum is to have a large turnout. Proponents of educational expenditures are better advised not to work for a large turnout, but for a better-informed and more educationally oriented electorate.

School Boards.   School board members constitute another important group of actors in local school politics. School board members are generally better educated than their constituents. They are selected largely from among business owners, proprietors, and managers. There is some evidence that people who are interested in education and have some knowledge of what the schools are doing tend to support education more than do the less informed citizens. However, the occupational background of school board members suggests that they are sensitive to tax burdens placed upon business people and property owners.[2]

Educators.   The professional educators can be divided into at least three distinct groups. Numerically, the largest group (2.5 million) is the schoolteachers. But perhaps the most powerful group is the professional school administrators, particularly the superintendents of schools. A third group consists of the faculties of teachers colleges and departments of education at universities. This latter group often has contacts with state departments of education, diffuses educational innovations and ideologies to each generation of teachers, and influences requirements for teacher certification within the states.

Citizens Versus Professionals.   Democratic theory assumes that schools are public institutions that should be governed by the local citizenry through their elected representatives. This was the original concept in American public education developed in the nineteenth century. But as school issues became more complex, the knowledge of citizen school boards seemed insufficient to cope with the many problems confronting the schools—teaching innovations, curricular changes, multimillion-dollar building programs, special educational programs, and so forth. In the twentieth century, the

[2]See Harmon Ziegler and M. Kent Jennings, *Governing American Schools* (Boston: Duxbury Press, 1974).

school superintendent and his or her administrative assistants came to exercise more and more control over day-to-day operations of the schools. Theoretically, the superintendent only implements the policies of the board, but in practice he or she has assumed much of the policy making in education. The superintendent is a full-time administrator, receiving direct advice from attorneys, architects, accountants, and educational consultants, and generally sets the agenda for school board meetings.

The resulting "professionalism" in education tangles directly with the "democratic" notion of control of school. There are few meetings of local school boards which do not involve at least some tug-of-war between board members and the superintendent. Professional educators often support the idea that "politics" should be kept out of education; this means that elected school board members should not interfere in educational decisions. But school board members and interested citizens generally believe that popular control of education is a vital component of democracy. Schools should be "responsive" to community needs and desires. Frequently, citizen criticism has focused on the schools' failure to teach basic skills—reading, writing, and arithmetic. These issues have in turn raised the underlying question— who should govern our schools, professional educators or interested citizens?

Teachers' Unions.   The struggle for power over the schools between interested citizens, school board members, and professional educators has now been joined by still another powerful force—the nation's growing teachers' unions. Most of the nation's two million teachers are organized into either the older, larger National Education Association (NEA), or the smaller but more militant American Federation of Teachers (AFT), an affiliate of the AFL-CIO. State and district chapters of both the NEA and AFT have achieved collective bargaining status in most states and large urban school districts. Both AFT and NEA chapters have shut down schools to force concessions by superintendents, board members, and taxpayers—not only in salaries and benefits, but also in pupil-teacher relations, classroom conditions, school discipline, and other educational matters.

THE FEDERAL GOVERNMENT'S ROLE IN EDUCATION

Traditionally, education in the United States was a community responsibility. But over the years state governments have assumed major responsibility for public education. The federal government remains largely an interested spectator in the area of educational policy. While it has taken the lead in guaranteeing racial equality in education and separating religion from public schools, it has never assumed any significant share of the costs of education. State and local taxpayers have always borne over 90 percent of the costs of public elementary and secondary education; the federal share has never ex-

TABLE 6-3   Sources of Funds for Education in the United States

	PERCENTAGE OF SCHOOL EXPENDITURES BY SOURCE			
	1960	1970	1980	1986
Elementary and Secondary				
Federal	3.9	7.4	9.1	6.1
State	31.1	34.6	43.3	45.2
Local	53.3	47.7	40.3	40.2
Private	11.7	10.3	7.3	8.4
Higher Education				
Federal	7.5	9.7	8.6	6.9
State	23.9	25.5	30.7	29.2
Local	3.0	3.2	2.4	2.3
Other (inc. tuition)	22.4	25.5	24.5	26.6
Private	43.3	36.0	33.6	34.9

Source: *Statistical Abstract of the United States 1990*, p. 129.

ceeded 10 percent (see Table 6–3). Similarly, federal expenditures for higher education have never exceeded 10 percent of the total costs.

Nonetheless the federal government's interest in education is a long-standing one. In the famous Northwest Ordinance of 1787, Congress offered land grants for public schools in the new territories and gave succeeding generations words to be forever etched on grammar school cornerstones: "Religion, morality, and knowledge, being necessary to good government and the happiness of mankind, schools and the means for education should ever be encouraged." The earliest democrats believed that the safest repository of the ultimate powers of society was the people themselves. If the people made mistakes, the remedy was not to remove power from their hands but to help them in forming their judgment through education. If the common people were to be granted the right to vote, they must be educated for the task. This meant that public education had to be universal, free, and compulsory. Compulsory education began in Massachusetts in 1852 and was eventually adopted by Mississippi in 1918.

Early Federal Aid.   In 1862 the Morrill Land Grant Act provided grants of federal land to each state for the establishment of colleges specializing in agricultural and mechanical arts. These became known as "land-grant colleges." In 1867 Congress established a U.S. Office of Education; in 1979, a separate, cabinet-level Department of Education was created. The Smith-Hughes Act of 1917 set up the first program of federal grants-in-aid to promote vocational education, enabling schools to provide training in agriculture, home economics, trades, and industries. In the National School Lunch and Milk programs, begun in 1946, federal grants and commodity donations were made for nonprofit lunches and milk served in public and private schools. In the Federal Impacted Areas Aid program, begun in 1950, federal aid was authorized for "federally impacted" areas of the nation. These are areas in which federal activities create a substantial increase in school enrollments or a reduction in taxable resources because of a federally owned property. In response to the Soviet Union's success in launching the first satellite into space in 1957, Congress became concerned that the American educational system might not be keeping abreast of advances being made in other nations, particularly in science and technology. In the National Defense Education Act of 1958, Congress provided financial aid to states and public school districts to improve instruction in science, mathematics, and foreign languages. Congress also established a system of loans to undergraduates, fellowships to graduate students, and funds to colleges— all in an effort to improve the training of teachers in America.

ESEA. The Elementary and Secondary Education Act of 1965 established the single largest federal aid to education program. "Poverty-impacted" schools were the beneficiaries of ESEA, receiving instructional materials and educational research and training. ESEA provided for federal financial assistance to "local educational agencies serving areas with concentrations of children from low-income families" for programs "which contribute particularly to meeting the special needs of educationally deprived children." Grants were made on application to the Office of Education and were awarded on the basis of the number of children enrolled from poverty-stricken families.

Educational Block Grants. Early in the Reagan Administration, the Education Consolidation and Improvement Act of 1981 consolidated ESEA and other federal educational grant programs into single "block" grants for states and communities. The purpose was to give states and local school districts greater discretion over the use of federal educational aid.

President Reagan tried throughout his administration to limit the federal government's role in education. At one point he even proposed abolishing the U.S. Department of Education (DOE) in order to emphasize that education should be the responsibility of state and local governments and not the federal government. But educational interests were too well organized in Congress to permit DOE to dissolve. Reagan's active Secretary of Education, William Bennett (later President Bush's chief coordinator in the war on drugs), believed that the federal government's role should be one of advising the states and stimulating and encouraging educational reform.

Most of the cuts in federal school aid recommended by President Reagan were restored by Congress, but the president succeeded in *limiting the growth* of federal educational spending. The result was a gradual decline in the 1980s of the federal percentage of total educational funding in the nation (see Table 6–3).

Federal Aid and Educational Quality.   It is difficult to demonstrate that federal aid programs improved the quality of education in America. Indeed, during the years in which federal aid was increasing, student achievement scores were *declining* (see Table 6–2). In its report "A Nation At Risk," the National Commission on Excellence in Education reaffirmed that "state and local government officials, including school board members and governors, and legislators, have *the primary responsibility* for funding and governing the schools." Raising the educational achievement levels of America's youth depends less on how much is spent than on how it is spent.

Bush and Educational Summitry.   George Bush pledged in his campaign to be the "education president." But this pledge does not appear to include significant increases in federal spending for education. President Bush has suggested that the problem of education has little to do with spending and more to do with educational reform in the nation's schools. He has used his office to marshal public support for reform, to set national goals for education, and to encourage state and local officials to "restructure" public schools. Well-publicized "education summit" meetings with the nation's governors appear to be the focus of Bush's efforts.

Educational Goals for America.   President Bush and the nation's governors have generally agreed on a set of goals of education in the United States:

> Every child must start school ready to learn.
> The high school graduation rate will be increased to at least 90 percent.
> U.S. students will become first in the world in mathematics and science achievement.
> Every adult American will become literate.
> Every school in the United States will be free of drugs and violence and will offer a disciplined environment conducive to learning.

It is not altogether clear how these goals are to be achieved. President Bush has suggested that the federal government is prepared to spend additional money on the first preschool goal through Head Start, but that the remaining goals are the principal responsibilities of states, communities, schools, teachers, and citizens.

THE STRUGGLE OVER EDUCATIONAL FINANCE

Spending for education varies enormously across the United States. As a state and local responsibility, educational spending varies from state to state and from one school district to another even in the same state. For example, in 1988 public spending per pupil for elementary and secondary schools varied from $7,038 in Alaska and $6,910 in New Jersey, to $2,410 in Arkansas (see Table 12–1 in Chapter 12). Regional wealth is the principal determinant of the amount of money being spent on the education of each child.

Variations in spending for education are even greater at the local level. Most local school revenues are derived from *local* property taxes. In every state except Hawaii, local school boards must raise money from property taxes to finance their schools. This means that communities that do *not* have much taxable property cannot finance their schools as well as communities that are blessed with great wealth. Frequently, wealthy communities can provide better education for their children at *lower* tax rates than poor communities can provide at *higher* tax rates, simply because of disparities in the value of taxable property from one community to the next.

Representatives of poor, black, and Spanish-speaking groups have charged that reliance on local property taxation for school finance discriminates against poor communities. The California Supreme Court held that the California system of public school finance, "with its substantial dependence on local property taxes and resultant wide disparities in school revenue, violates the equal protection clause of the Fourteenth Amendment (of the U.S. Constitution)."[3] However, the United States Supreme Court declined to intervene in this struggle over educational finance. In 1973 the Court ruled that disparities in property values between jurisdictions relying on property taxes to finance education did *not* violate the equal protection clause of the Fourteenth Amendment.[4] The Supreme Court declined to substitute its own judgement about how schools should be financed for the judgment of forty-nine states.

In recent years state courts have become increasingly active in mandating greater equality in educational spending among school districts within their states. At least a dozen *state* Supreme Courts have challenged the earlier reasoning of the U.S. Supreme Court that inequality in educational finance does not violate the constitutional guarantee of "equal protection of the law." These state courts have held that inequalities in school spending between wealthy and poor districts within a state violate equal protection guarantees in their *state constitutions*. (Although state Supreme Courts can interpret the meaning of their own state constitutions, these decisions do not directly overturn the U.S. Supreme Court's decision that equal spending is not mandated

[3]*Serrano* v. *Priest*, 5 Cal. 3rd 584 (1971).
[4]*Rodriquez* v. *San Antonio Independent School District*, 411 U.S. 1 (1973).

by the U.S. Constitution.) Increasingly state governments have been obliged to undertake equalization programs among schools in their states.

EDUCATIONAL REFORM AND PARENTAL CHOICE

Social science research suggests that educational performance is enhanced when the schools are perceived by children to be extensions or substitutes for their family (see Chapter 1 "Policy Analysis in Action"). Academic achievement and graduation rates improve for all students, but especially for students from disadvantaged backgrounds, in schools where there is a high expectation for achievement, an orderly and disciplined environment for learning, an emphasis on basic skills, frequent monitoring of student progress, and teacher-parent interaction and agreement on values and norms. When parents choose schools for their children, as in the case of private and Catholic schools, these values are strengthened.[5]

Parental Choice.   Parental choice among schools and the resulting competition among schools for enrollment not only improves academic achievement and graduation rates but also increases parental satisfaction and teacher morale. Principals and teachers are encouraged to work directly with parents to set clear goals, develop specialized curricula, impose discipline, and demand more from the students. Choice plans do more than just benefit the parents who have the knowledge to choose schools wisely for their children. They also send a message to educators to structure their schools to give parents what they want for their children or risk losing enrollment and funding.

Opposition.   Yet there is strong opposition to the choice idea. The most vocal opposition comes from professional school administrators and state educational agencies. They argue that giving parents the right to move their children from school to school disrupts educational planning and threatens the viability of schools that are perceived as inferior. It may lead to a stratification of schools into popular, magnet schools that would attract the best students, and the less popular schools that would be left with the task of educating students whose parents were unaware or uninterested in their children's education. Other opponents of choice plans fear that public education might be undermined if the choice available to parents includes the option of sending their children to private, church-related schools.

Educational Vouchers.   The most controversial choice plans involve educational vouchers that would be given to parents to spend at any school

[5]James S. Coleman and Thomas Hoffer, *Public and Private High Schools* (New York: Basic Books, 1987).

they choose, public or private. State governments would redeem the vouchers submitted by schools by paying specified amounts. All public and private schools would compete equally for students and state education funds would flow to those schools that enrolled more students. Competition would encourage all schools to satisfy parental demands for excellence. But allowing private schools to compete equally with public schools for students may undermine the nation's long tradition of public education. Even if racial or religious or ethnic discrimination was strictly prohibited in a voucher system, there would still be a tendency for students to become isolated from those different from themselves.

Choice within Public Schools. Choice plans can also be implemented *within* public school systems. States or school districts may provide open enrollment among public schools, with educational funds flowing to those schools on the basis of the enrollment they attract. Competition involves magnet school programs with freedom for principals and teachers to determine goals, curriculum, discipline, and structure in their schools.[6] No school would be guaranteed students or funds; enrollments and financing would come only when students and parents chose to go to particular schools. Parents could choose any school in a district, or perhaps even schools in other districts; pupils would not be assigned on the basis of attendance boundaries. The "best" schools would have excess demand and might have to turn pupils away; parents would have second and third choices. Some schools might end up with very few students; they would be forced either to improve themselves or close. Over time, high schools would tend to specialize, some emphasizing math and science, others the fine arts, others business, and still others vocational training. Some schools might be "adopted" by business, professional organizations, or universities. Including private schools in a system of choice and competition would improve the likelihood of success, but such a system could be operated wholly within the public school system.

Experiments with Choice. Several states and school districts have experimented with choice plans. Minnesota is the first state to allow parents to decide which school district their children will attend. Funding follows the student and transportation is provided for low-income students. Parents can opt for any public school in the state. Earlier parental choice plans were carried out within school districts. An especially noteworthy plan was devised for East Harlem in New York City, where the school superintendent, Sy Fliegel, argued that low-income parents should have a choice of schools just as high income parents have that choice through private schools:

> Parental choice can provide the catalyst for educational reform by introducing a market mechanism to the public educational system—a market place for

[6]See John E. Chubb and Terry M. Moe, "Politics Markets and the Organization of Schools," *American Political Science Review* 82 (December, 1988), 1065–1087.

ideas innovations and investments. It also increases a sense of ownership for parents, teachers and administrators, providing a framework for improvement efforts. . . .

Inner-city minority parents are no less concerned than their middle-class counterparts to see their children educated in stimulating, orderly, vigorous schools and no less capable of choosing those schools when information is made available to them.[7]

PUBLIC POLICY AND HIGHER EDUCATION

State governments have been involved in public higher education since the colonial era. State governments in the Northeast frequently made contributions to support private colleges in their states, a practice that continues today. The first state university to be chartered by a state legislature was the University of Georgia in 1794. Before the Civil War, Northeastern states relied exclusively on private colleges, and the Southern states assumed the leadership in public higher education. The antebellum curricula at Southern state universities, however, resembled the rigid classical studies of the early private colleges—Greek and Latin, history, philosophy, and literature.

Growth of Public Universities. It was not until the Morrill Land Grant Act of 1862 that public higher education began to make major strides in the American states. Interestingly, the Eastern states were slow to respond to the opportunity afforded by the Morrill Act to develop public universities; Eastern states continued to rely primarily on their private colleges and universities. The Southern states were economically depressed in the post–Civil War period, and leadership in public higher education passed to the Midwestern states. The philosophy of the Morrill Act emphasized agricultural and mechanical studies rather than the classical curricula of Eastern colleges, and the movement for "A and M" education spread rapidly in the agricultural states. The early groups of Midwestern state universities were closely tied to agricultural education, including agricultural extension services. State universities also took the responsibility for the training of public school teachers in colleges of education. The state universities introduced a broad range of modern subjects in the university curricula—business administration, agriculture, home economics, education, engineering. It was not until the 1960s that the Eastern states began to emphasize public higher education, as evidenced by the development of the huge, multicampus State University of New York.

Today public higher education enrolls three-fourths of the nation's college and university students (see Table 6–4). Perhaps more importantly, the nation's leading state universities can challenge the best private institutions

[7]Sy Fliegel, "Parental Choice in East Harlem," *Florida Policy Review* 5 (Summer, 1989), pp. 27–28.

TABLE 6-4 Higher Education in America

	1970	1980	1987
Institutions			
Four-year colleges and universities	1,665	1,957	2,135
Two-year colleges	891	1,274	1,452
Faculty (thousands)	573	846	736
Enrollment (thousands)			
Total	8,581	12,097	12,768
Four-year colleges and universities	6,290	7,571	7,992
Two-year colleges	1,630	4,526	4,776
Public	5,800	9,457	9,975
Private	2,120	2,640	2,793
Graduate	1,031	1,343	1,452
Undergraduate	7,376	10,475	11,048

Source: *Statistical Abstract of the United States 1990*, p. 153.

in academic excellence. The University of California at Berkeley and the University of Michigan are deservedly ranked with Harvard, Yale, Princeton, Stanford, and Chicago.

Federal Aid. Federal aid to colleges and universities has come in a variety of forms. Yet, overall, the federal share of higher education finance remains under 10 percent. State governments carry the major burden of higher education in America through their support of state colleges and universities.

Historically, the Morrill Act of 1862 provided the groundwork for federal assistance to higher education. In 1890 Congress activated several federal grants to support the operations of the land-grant colleges, and this aid, although very modest, continues to the present. The GI bills following World War II and the Korean War (enacted in 1944 and 1952 respectively) were not, strictly speaking, aid-to-education bills, but rather a form of assistance to veterans to help them adjust to civilian life. Nevertheless, these bills had a great impact on higher education in terms of the millions of veterans who were able to enroll in college. Congress continues to provide educational benefits to veterans but at reduced levels from the wartime GI bills. The National Defense Education Act of 1958 also affected higher education by assisting students, particularly in science, mathematics, and modern foreign languages.

Federal Research Support. Federal support for scientific research has also had an important impact on higher education. In 1950 Congress established the National Science Foundation to promote scientific research and education. NSF has provided fellowships for graduate education in the sciences, supported the development of science teachers at all levels, supported many specific scientific research projects, and supported miscellaneous scientific enterprises. In 1965 Congress established a National Endowment for the Arts and Humanities, but funded these fields at only a tiny fraction of the amount given to NSF. In addition to NSF, many other federal agencies have granted research contracts to universities for specific projects. Thus, with federal support, research has become a very big item in university life.

Student Assistance.   The federal government directly assists institutions of higher education through federal grants and loans for construction and improvement of both public and private higher educational facilities. It directly assists students through Basic Educational Opportunity Grants, commonly called "Pell Grants" for its sponsor Senator Claiborne Pell (D.-R.I.). The program, which offers college students in good standing a money grant each year, is calculated minus the amount their families could reasonably be expected to contribute to their educational expenses. A Guaranteed Student Loan program seeks to encourage private banks to make low-interest loans to students. The federal government pays the interest charges while the student is in school and guarantees repayment in the event the student defaults on the payment after graduation. A National Direct Student Loan Program allows students to borrow from the financial aid offices of their own universities. Again, no interest is charged while the student is in school; repayment is delayed until after the student leaves school. Finally, a national work-study program uses federal funds to allow colleges and universities to employ students part-time while they continue to go to school.

GROUPS IN HIGHER EDUCATION

There are many influential groups in public higher education—aside from the governors and legislators who must vote the funds each year.

Trustees.   First of all, there are the boards of trustees (often called regents) that govern public colleges and universities. Their authority varies from state to state. But in nearly every state they are expected not only to set broad policy directions in higher education but also to insulate higher education from direct political involvement of governors and legislators. Prominent citizens who are appointed to these boards are expected to champion higher education with the public and the legislature.

The Presidents.   Another key group in higher education is composed of university and college presidents and their top administrative assistants. Generally, university presidents are the chief spokespersons for higher education, and they must convince the public, the regents, the governor, and the legislature of the value of state colleges and universities. The president's crucial role is one of maintaining support for higher education in the state; he or she frequently delegates administrative responsibilities for the internal operation of the university to the vice-presidents and deans. Support for higher education among the public and its representatives can be affected by a broad spectrum of university activities, some of which are not directly related to the pursuit of knowledge. A winning football team can stimulate legislative enthusiasm and win appropriations for a new classroom building. University service-oriented research—developing new crops or feeds, assessing the state's mineral resources, advising state and local government agencies on administrative problems, analyzing the state economy, advising local school authorities, and so forth—may help to convince the public of the practical benefits of knowledge. University faculty may be interested in advanced research and the education of future Ph.D.s, but legislators and their constituents are more interested in the quality and effectiveness of undergraduate teaching.

The Faculty.   The faculty of the nation's 3400 colleges and universities traditionally identified themselves as professionals with strong attachments to their institutions. The historic pattern of college and university governance included faculty participation in policy making—not only academic requirements but also budgeting, personnel, building programs, and so forth. But governance by faculty committee has proven cumbersome, unwieldy, and time-consuming in an era of large-scale enrollments, multimillion-dollar budgets, and increases in the size and complexity of academic administration. Increasingly, concepts of public "accountability," academic "management," cost control, and centralized budgeting and purchasing have transferred power in colleges and universities from faculty to professional academic administrators.

The Unions.   The traditional organization of faculty has been the American Association of University Professors (AAUP); historically this group confined itself to publishing data on faculty salaries and officially "censuring" colleges or universities that violate longstanding notions of academic freedom or tenure. (Tenure is the tradition that a faculty member who has demonstrated his or her competence by service in a college or university position for three to seven years cannot thereafter be dismissed except for "cause"—serious infraction of established rules or dereliction of duty, to be proved in an open hearing.) In recent years, the American Federation of Teachers (AFT) succeeded in convincing some faculty that traditional patterns of individual bargaining over salaries, teaching load, and working conditions in colleges and universities should be replaced by collective bargaining in the manner of unionized labor. The growth of the AFT has spurred the AAUP on many campuses to assume a more militant attitude on behalf of faculty interests. The AAUP remains the largest faculty organization in the nation, but most of the nation's faculty are not affiliated with either the AAUP or the AFT. Faculty collective bargaining is complicated by the fact that faculty continue to play some managerial role in academic governance—for example, in choosing deans and department heads and sitting on salary committees.

The Students.   The nation's 12 million students are the most numerous yet least influential of the groups directly involved in higher education. Students can be compared to other "consumer" groups in society which are generally less well organized than the groups that provide goods and services. American student political activism has been sporadic and generally directed toward broad symbolic issues—the Vietnam War, the nuclear freeze movement, environmental issues. Most students view their condition in life as a short-term one; organizing for effective group action requires a commitment of time and energy which most students are unwilling to subtract from their studies and social life. Nonetheless, student complaints are often filtered through parents to state legislators or university officials.

READING, WRITING, AND RELIGION

The First Amendment of the Constitution of the United States contains two important guarantees of religious freedom: (1) "Congress shall make no law respecting an establishment of religion. . ." and (2) "or prohibiting the free exercise thereof." The due process clause of the Fourteenth Amendment made these guarantees of religious liberty applicable to the states and their subdivisions as well as to Congress. Most of the debate over religion in the public schools centers around the "no establishment" clause of the First Amendment rather than the "free exercise" clause. However, it was respect for the "free exercise" clause that caused the Supreme Court in 1925 to declare unconstitutional an attempt on the part of a state to prohibit private and parochial schools and to force all children to attend public schools. In the words of the Supreme Court: "The fundamental theory of liberty upon which all governments in this Union repose excludes any general power of the state to standardize its children by forcing them to accept instruction from public teachers only. The child is not the mere creature of the state."[8] It is this decision that protects the entire structure of private religious schools in this nation.

A great deal of religious conflict in America has centered around the meaning of the "no establishment" clause, and the public schools have been the principal scene of this conflict. One interpretation of the clause holds

[8]*Pierce* v. *The Society of Sisters,* 268 U.S. 510 (1925).

that it does not prevent government from aiding religious schools or encouraging religious beliefs in the public schools, as long as it does not discriminate against any particular religion. Another interpretation of the "no establishment" clause is that it creates a "wall of separation" between church and state in America to prevent government from directly aiding religious schools or encouraging religious beliefs in any way.

Government Aid to Church-Related Schools

Those favoring government aid to church-related schools frequently refer to the language found in several cases decided by the Supreme Court, which appears to support the idea that government can *in a limited fashion* support the activities of church-related schools. In an early case the Court upheld a state law providing free textbooks for children attending both public and parochial schools on the grounds that this aid benefited the *children* rather than the Catholic Church and hence did not constitute an "establishment" of religion with the meaning of the First Amendment.[9]

In *Everson v. Board of Education* (1974), the Supreme Court upheld bus transportation for parochial school children at public expense on the grounds that the "wall of separation between church and state does not prohibit the state from adopting a general program which helps *all* children." Interestingly in this case, even though the Supreme Court permitted the expenditure of public funds to assist children going to and from parochial schools, the Supreme Court voiced the opinion that the "no establishment" clause of the First Amendment should constitute a wall of separation between church and state. In the words of the Court:

> Neither a state nor the federal government can set up a church. Neither can pass laws which aid one religion, aid all religions, or prefer one religion over another. Neither can force nor influence a person to go to or to remain away from church against his will, or force him to profess a belief or disbelief in any religion. No person can be punished for entertaining or professing religious beliefs or disbeliefs, for church attendance or nonattendance. No tax in any amount, large or small, can be levied to support any religious activities or institutions, whatever they may be called, or whatever form they may adopt to teach or practice religion. Neither a state nor the federal government can, openly or secretly, participate in the affairs of any religious organizations or groups, and vice versa.[10]

So the *Everson* case can be cited by those interests which support the allocation of public funds for assistance to children in parochial schools, as well as those interests which oppose any public support, direct or indirect, of religion.

[9]*Cochran* v. *Board of Education*, 281 U.S. 370 (1930).
[10]*Everson* v. *Board of Education*, 330 U.S. 1 (1947).

The question of how much government aid can go to church schools and for what purposes is still unresolved. Some states have passed bills giving financial support to nonpublic schools for such purposes as textbooks, bus transportation, and remedial courses. Proponents of public aid for church schools argue that these schools render a valuable public service by instructing millions of children who would have to be instructed by the state, at great expense, if the church schools were to close. There seem to be many precedents for public support of religious institutions: Church property has always been exempt from taxation; church contributions are deductible from federal income taxes; federal funds have been appropriated for the construction of religiously operated hospitals; chaplains are provided in the armed forces as well as in the Congress of the United States; veterans' programs permit veterans to use their educational subsidies to finance college educations in Catholic universities; federal grants and loans for college construction are available to Catholic as well as to public colleges, and so on.

Opponents of aid to church schools argue that free public schools are available to the parents of all children regardless of religious denomination. If religious parents are not content with the type of school that the state provides, they should expect to pay for the establishment and operation of special schools. The state is under no obligation to finance the religious preferences in education of religious groups. In fact, they contend that it is unfair to compel taxpayers to support religion directly or indirectly; furthermore, the diversion of any substantial amount of public education funds to church schools would weaken the public school system. The public schools bring together children of different religious backgrounds and by so doing supposedly encourage tolerance and understanding. In contrast, church-related schools segregate children of different backgrounds, and it is not in the public interest to encourage such segregation. And so the dispute continues.

One of the most important Supreme Court decisions in the history of church-state relations in America came in 1971 in the case of *Lemon v. Kurtzman*.[11] The Supreme Court held that it was unconstitutional for a state (Pennsylvania) to pay the costs of teachers' salaries or instructional materials in parochial schools. The Court acknowledged that it had previously approved the provision of state textbooks and bus transportation directly to parochial school children. But the Court held that state payments to parochial schools involved "excessive entanglement between government and religion" and violated both the "no establishment" and "free exercise" clauses of the First Amendment. State payments to religious schools, the Court said, would require excessive government controls and surveillance to ensure that funds were used only for secular instruction. Moreover, the Court expressed the fear that state aid to parochial schools would create "political divisions along religious lines . . . one of the principal evils against which the First Amend-

---

[11]*Lemon* v. *Kurtzman*, 403 U.S. 602 (1971).

ment was intended to protect." However, in *Roemer* v. *Maryland* (1976) the Supreme Court upheld general public grants of money to church-related *colleges:* "Religious institutions need not be quarantined from public benefits which are neutrally available to all."[12]

Prayer in Public Schools

Religious conflict in public schools also centers around the question of prayer and Bible-reading ceremonies conducted in public schools. A few years ago the practice of opening the school day with prayer and Bible reading ceremonies was widespread in American public schools. Usually the prayer was a Protestant rendition of the Lord's Prayer and Bible reading was from the King James version. In order to avoid the denominational aspects of the ceremonies, the New York State Board of Regents substituted a nondenominational prayer, which it required to be said aloud in each class in the presence of a teacher at the beginning of each school day.

> Almighty God, we acknowledge our dependence upon Thee, and we beg Thy blessings upon us, our parents, our teachers, and our country.

New York argued that this prayer ceremony did not violate the "no establishment" clause, because the prayer was denominationally neutral and because student participation in the prayer was voluntary. However, in *Engle* v. *Vitale* (1962), the Supreme Court stated that "the constitutional prohibition against laws respecting an establishment of a religion must at least mean in this country it is no part of the business of government to compose official prayers for any group of the American people to recite as part of a religious program carried on by government." The Court pointed out that making prayer voluntary did not free it from the prohibitions of the "no establishment" clause; that clause prevented the establishment of a religious ceremony by a government agency, regardless of whether the ceremony was voluntary or not:

> Neither the fact that the prayer may be denominationally neutral, nor the fact that its observance on the part of the students is voluntary can serve to free it from the limitations of the establishment clause, as it might from the free exercise clause, of the First Amendment, both of which are operative against the states by virtue of the Fourteenth Amendment. . . . The establishment clause, unlike the free exercise clause, does not depend on any showing of direct governmental compulsion and is violated by the enactment of laws which establish an official religion whether those laws operate directly to coerce nonobserving individuals or not.[13]

[12]*Roemer* v. *Maryland,* 415 U.S. 382 (1976).
[13]*Engle* v. *Vitale,* 370 U.S. 421 (1962).

One year later in the case of *Abbington Township* v. *Schempp,* the Court considered the constitutionality of Bible-reading ceremonies in the public schools.[14] Here again, even though the children were not required to participate, the Court found that Bible reading as an opening exercise in the schools was a religious ceremony. The Court went to some trouble in its opinion to point out that it was not "throwing the Bible out of the schools," for it specifically stated that the study of the Bible or of religion, when presented as part of a secular program of education, did not violate the First Amendment, but religious *ceremonies* involving Bible reading or prayer, established by a state or school district, did so.

State efforts to encourage "voluntary prayer" in public schools have also been struck down by the Supreme Court as unconstitutional. When the state of Alabama authorized a period of silence for "meditation or voluntary prayer" in public schools, the Court ruled that this was an "establishment of religion." The Court said the law had no secular purpose, that it conveyed "a message of state endorsement and promotion of prayer," and that its real intent was to encourage prayer in public schools.[15] In a stinging dissenting opinion, Chief Justice Warren Burger noted that the Supreme Court itself opened its session with a prayer, that both houses of Congress opened every session with prayers led by official chaplains paid by the government. "To suggest that a moment of silence statute that includes the word *prayer* unconstitutionally endorses religion, manifests not neutrality but hostility toward religion."

The Supreme Court's interpretation of the "no establishment" clause ruling out prayer in the public schools is politically unpopular. Large majorities of Americans would prefer to see prayers in public schools and would support a constitutional amendment to reverse the Supreme Court's decision (see Table 6–5).

SUMMARY

Let us summarize educational policy issues with particular reference to the group conflicts involved:

1. American education reflects all of the conflicting demands of society. Schools are expected to address themselves to virtually all of the nation's problems, from racial conflict to drug abuse, to highway accidents. They are also supposed to raise the verbal and mathematical performance levels of students better to equip the nation's workforce in a competitive global economy. Various interests give greater priority to these diverse and sometimes conflicting goals.

[14]*Abbington Township* v. *Schempp,* 374 U.S. 203 (1963).
[15]*Wallace* v. *Jaffree,* June 4, 1985.

TABLE 6-5   Public Opinion on School Prayer

	AGREE	DISAGREE
Do you mostly agree or disagree with this. . .The Supreme Court and Congress have gone too far in keeping religious and moral values like prayer out of our laws, our schools, and our lives.	73%	27%

	APPROVE	DISAPPROVE
Generally speaking, do you approve or or disapprove of allowing prayer in public schools?	80%	20%

	FAVOR	OPPOSE
Do you favor or oppose a constitutional amendment to allow daily prayers to be recited in school classrooms?	71%	29%

Source: *Public Opinion* (June/July 1982), p. 40.

2. In recent years, citizen groups, parents, taxpayers, and employers, have inspired a back to basics movement in the schools, emphasizing reading, writing, and mathematical performance, calling for frequent testing of student skills, and the improvement of teacher competency. Professional educators—school administrators, state education officials, and teachers' unions—have tended to resist test-oriented reforms, emphasizing instead the education of the whole child.

3. Conflict between citizens and professional educators is reflected in arguments over "professionalism" versus "responsiveness" in public schools. Parents, taxpayers, and locally elected school board members tend to emphasize responsiveness to citizen demands; school superintendents and state education agencies tend to emphasize professional administration of the schools. Teachers unions, notably state and local chapters of the National Education Association (NEA) and American Federation of Teachers (AFT) represent still another group interest in education—organized teachers.

4. Federal aid to education grew with the Elementary and Secondary Education Act of 1965, but the federal share of the nation's educational spending never exceeded 10 percent. State and local governments continue to bear the major burden of educational finance.

5. Professional education groups and teachers' unions have long lobbied in Washington for increased federal financing of education. Federal aid to education grew with the Elementary and Secondary Education Act of 1965, but the federal share of educational spending never exceeded 10 percent. The creation of a cabinet-level Department of Education in 1977 also reflected the influence of professional educators.

6. Increased federal involvement in education has coincided with declines in educational achievement levels. Citizen groups and independent study commissions recommended major reforms in education. The Reagan and Bush administrations emphasized reforms in education rather than increased federal spending.

7. Current reforms in education center on choice plans. Choice would empower parents and end the monopoly power of public school administrators. But choice plans that allow parents to choose private over public schools threaten American traditional reliance on public education. Choice *within* public school systems is somewhat less controversial, and various states have undertaken to experiment with limited open enrollment and magnet school plans.

8. Public higher education in the states involves many diverse groups— governors, legislators, regents, college and university presidents, and faculty. State governments, through their support of state colleges and universities, bear the major burden of higher education in the United States. Federal support for research, plus various student loan programs, are an important contribution to higher education. Yet federal support amounts to less than 10 percent of total higher education spending.

9. Religious groups, private school interests, and public school defenders frequently battle over the place of religion in education. The U.S. Supreme Court has become the referee in the group struggle over religion and education. The Court must interpret the meaning of the "no establishment" clause of the First Amendment of the U.S. Constitution as it affects government aid to church-related schools and prayer in the public schools.

BIBLIOGRAPHY

CHUBB, JOHN E. and TERRY M. MOE. *Politics, Markets, and America's Schools.* Washington: Brookings Institution, 1990.

COLEMAN, JAMES S. *Equality of Education Opportunity.* Washington, D.C.: Government Printing Office, 1966.

COLEMAN, JAMES S., THOMAS HOFFER, and SALLY KILGORE. *High School Achievement.* New York: Basic Books, 1982.

COLEMAN, JAMES S. and THOMAS HOFFER. *Public and Private High Schools.* New York: Basic Books, 1987.

NATIONAL COMMISSION ON EXCELLENCE IN EDUCATION. *A Nation at Risk.* Washington, D.C.: Government Printing Office, 1983.

7

ENVIRONMENTAL POLICY
externalities and interests

An officer in the Coast Guard Reserve cleans oil from the beach after a barge ran aground off the mouth of the Cuyahoga River. (Official U.S. Coast Guard Photograph)

PUBLIC CHOICE AND THE ENVIRONMENT

All human activity produces waste. Environmentalists, the mass media, politicians, and bureaucrats may portray pollution as a "moral evil," but in fact it is a cost of production. We can no more "stop polluting" than we can halt our natural bodily functions. As soon as we come to understand that we cannot outlaw pollution and come to see pollution as a cost of human activity, we can begin to devise creative environmental policies.

Environmental "Externalities."   Typically pollution becomes a "problem" when it is *not* a cost to its producer—that is, when producers can ignore the cost of their pollution and shift these costs onto others or society in general. An "externality" occurs when one individual, firm, or government undertakes an activity that imposes unwanted costs on others. A manufacturing firm or local government that discharges waste into a river shifts its own costs to individuals, firms, or local governments downstream, who must forego using the river for recreation and water supply or else undertake the costs of cleaning it up themselves. A coal-burning electricity-generating plant that discharges waste into the air shifts its costs to others, who must endure irritating smog. By shifting these costs to others, polluting firms lower the costs of production to themselves, which allows them to lower their prices to customers and/or increase their own profits. Polluting governments have lower costs of disposing their community's waste, which allows them to lower taxes for their own citizens. As long as these costs of production can be shifted to others, polluting individuals, firms, and governments have no incentive to minimize waste or develop alternative techniques of production. And because the prices charged by polluting firms and governments are lower than they would otherwise be, people are encouraged to buy more of their goods and services, thus adding even more to pollution.

Costs of Regulation.   Environmental policies are costly. These costs are often ignored when environmental regulations are considered. Direct spending by business and government for pollution abatement and control has grown rapidly over recent years (see Table 7–1), and today exceeds $100 billion per year. Yet governments themselves—federal, state, and local governments combined—pay only about one-fifth of the environmental bill.

TABLE 7-1   Spending for Pollution Abatement and Control

	1975	1980	1987
Total ($ billions)	$30.2	$53.5	$81.1
Percent government	28.9%	25.3%	20.5%

Source: *Statistical Abstract of the United States 1989.*

Businesses and consumers pay four-fifths of the environmental bill. Governments can shift the costs of its policies onto private individuals and firms by enacting regulations requiring pollution control. A government's own budget is unaffected by these regulations, but the costs are paid by society. Indeed, as environmental costs multiply for American businesses, the costs of their products rise in world markets. Unless other nations impose similar costs on their businesses, U.S. firms face a competitive disadvantage. In other words, pollution is a global issue, not only because air and water pollution does not stop at national boundaries, but also because polluting nations can "free ride" on the environmental safeguards of other nations.

Benefits in Relation to Costs.   Environmental policies should be evaluated in terms of their net benefits to society—that is, the costs of environmental policies should not exceed their benefits to society. It is much less costly to reduce the first 50 to 75 percent of any environmental pollutant or risk than it is to reduce it to zero. As any pollutant or risk is reduced, the cost of further reductions rise and the net benefits to society of additional reductions decline. Indeed, removing the last traces of any environmental pollution or risk is extremely costly. It is impossible to remove all environmental risks, just as it is impossible to remove all risk of accident or illness. As the limit of zero pollution or zero environmental risk is approached, additional benefits are minuscule but additional costs are astronomical. Ignoring these economic realities simply wastes the resources of society, lowers our standards of living, and in the long run impairs our ability to deal effectively with any societal problem, including environmental protection.

"Command and Control."   Traditionally, environmental regulations rely on centralized and uniform controls—administrative or legislative rules and regulations that require the use of pollution control devices or that apply rigid emission standards to specified pollution sites and sources. But this "command and control" approach has failed to create the necessary incentives for individuals, private firms, and local governments to clean up the environment. First of all, the bureaucrats or legislators who impose specific regulations lack detailed knowledge of production processes and alternative methods of pollution abatement. Moreover, individuals, firms, or local governments that do succeed in reducing pollution increase their risk of being targeted by the regulators for even tougher (and much more costly) emission standards. This creates a disincentive to innovate in pollution control—a disincentive that magnifies inefficiencies over time. Finally, specific controls give polluters an incentive to meet the requirements of the law or regulation, but not actually to reduce pollution.

Market Incentives.   Where government action is necessary to curb environmental externalities, it is better to establish private economic incentives to reduce pollution than to rely on centralized, uniform, and specific regulations. Market-based approaches that provide flexibility, encourage innovation, and support economic growth are more cost effective in achieving environmental goals than regulations devised in Washington. These approaches may involve setting overall pollution limits, while permitting industries, utilities, and state and local governments to determine how to meet these limits. They may also involve permitting specific pollution sources— factories, refineries, utilities, governments—to trade allowable emissions among themselves to achieve the most efficient use of the emissions. Yet to date environmental policy in the United States relies principally on centralized command and control, with the U.S. Environmental Protection Agency accumulating vast power over virtually every segment of economic activity in the nation.

ENVIRONMENTAL EXTERNALITIES

The air and water in the United States are far cleaner today than in previous decades. This is true despite growth in population and even greater growth in waste products. Nonetheless, genuine concern for environmental externalities centers on the disposal of solid wastes (especially hazardous wastes), water pollution, and air pollution.

Solid Waste Disposal

Every American produces about 3.5 pounds of solid waste per day (see Table 7–2). The annual load of waste dumped on the environment includes 48 billion cans, 26 billion bottles and jars, 2 billion disposable razors, 16 billion disposable diapers, and 4 million automobiles and trucks. The nation spends billions of dollars annually on hauling all this away from homes and businesses. Over time, the types of solid wastes disposed of as municipal garbage have changed, with plastic and paper replacing metal in the municipal garbage pail.

There are essentially three methods of disposing of solid wastes—landfills, incineration, and recycling. Modern landfills have nearly everywhere replaced town dumps. Landfills are usually lined with clay so that potential-

TABLE 7–2   Growth in Solid Wastes

	1960	1970	1980	1986
Gross waste (millions of tons)	87.5	120.5	142.6	157.7
Waste per person per day (lbs)	2.65	3.22	3.43	3.58

Source: *Statistical Abstract of the United States 1990.*

ly toxic wastes do not seep into the water system. Even so, hazardous wastes are separated from those that are not hazardous and handled separately. Given a reasonable site, there is nothing especially wrong with a landfill that contains no hazardous wastes. However, people do not want landfills near their residence. Landfill sites need to meet strict environmental standards (for example, they cannot be located where there is a noticeable slope to the site). These conditions combine to make it difficult to develop new landfills. And new landfills—or some other solution—are always required, for the old ones invariably become full. Some communities today resort to paying to use another community's landfill—often hundreds of miles from where the garbage originated—but no one thinks of this as a long-term solution.

Another alternative is to burn the garbage. Modern incinerators are special plants, usually equipped with machinery to separate the garbage into different types, with scrubbers to reduce air pollution from the burning, and often with electrical generators powered by heat from the garbage fire. Garbage is put through a shredder to promote even burning; metal is separated out by magnets; and the garbage is passed over screens that separate it further. At this point about half the garbage has been removed and hauled to a landfill. The remaining garbage is shredded still further into what is called fluff, or perhaps is compressed into pellets or briquets. This material is then burned, usually at another site and perhaps together with coal, to produce electricity. The ash is handled by the public utility as it would handle any other ash, which often means selling it to towns to use on roads.

The problem with this method is the substances emitted from the chimney of the incinerator or the utility that is burning the garbage. A massburn incinerator may emit the following wastes: soot or smoke, sulfur dioxide, nitrogen oxides, hydrogen chloride, hydrogen fluoride, carbon monoxide, arsenic, cadmium, chromium, lead, mercury, dioxin, and furnace. Finally, because the garbage separated during the screening phase still has to be disposed of, the problem of diminishing landfill sites is only reduced, not eliminated.

A third method of reducing the amount of solid waste is recycling. Recycling is the conversion of wastes into useful products. Most of the time, waste cannot be recycled into the same product it was originally, but rather, into some other form. Most newspapers are recycled into cardboard, insulation, animal bedding, and cat litter, but, in an exception to the general rule, some is recycled into newsprint.

Americans buy 13 million tons of newspapers and set out 5 million tons, or about 35 percent, for recycling. Roughly 3 million tons are actually recycled, the remainder is either piled up as excess inventory in paper mills or dumped or burned. There is at present more paper available for recycling than existing plants have capacity to use. Despite problems of supply and demand, newspaper recycling is more successful than many other types of recycling. Although newspapers account for only 10 percent of non-commercial solid waste, they make up 25 percent of recycled waste. This eases pressure on landfills, reduces gases produced by incineration, eases water pollution caused by paper mills, and saves trees.

Contrary to popular rhetoric, there is no "landfill crisis"; the nation is not "running out of land." However, both government agencies and private waste disposal firms are being stymied by the powerful NIMBYs—"not in my back yard" organized interests. Landfill sites are plentiful but local opposition is always strong. Timid politicians cannot confront the NIMBYs, so they end up overusing old landfills or trying to ship their garbage elsewhere.

Hazardous Waste

Hazardous wastes are those which pose a significant threat to public health or the environment due to their "quantity, concentration, or physical, chemical, or infectious characteristics."[1] The Resource Conservation and Recovery Act of 1976 gave the U.S. Environmental Protection Agency the authority to determine which substances are hazardous, and the EPA has classified several hundred substances as hazardous. Releases of more than a specified amount must be reported to the National Response Center. Substances are considered hazardous if they easily catch fire, are corrosive, react easily with other chemicals, or are poisonous (toxic). Some substances, such as asbestos, are hazardous because they cause cancer. Toxic chemicals must also be reported annually, and extremely hazardous substances require emergency planning. Thus far the U.S. has avoided any toxic releases comparable to the accident in Bhopal, India, which killed almost 3,000 people. However, smaller toxic releases have caused death and injury.

Nuclear wastes create special problems. These are the wastes from nuclear fission reactors and nuclear weapons plants. They have been in existence for over forty years. Because the waste is radioactive and some of it stays radioactive for thousands of years, it has proven very difficult to dispose of. Current plans to store some wastes in deep, stable, underground sites have run into local opposition. Most nuclear waste in the United States is stored at the site where it was generated, pending some long-term plan for handling it.

Hazardous wastes from old sites also constitute an environmental problem. These wastes need to be incinerated or moved to more secure landfills. Otherwise, they can affect the health of people living near the waste site, often by seeping into the water supply. The U.S. Environmental Protection Agency is committed to cleaning up such sites under the Superfund laws of 1980 and 1986. As a first step, they have developed a National Priorities List of sites that need attention, ranking them on a hazard ranking system.

---

[1] Resource Conservative and Recovery Act, PL 94–580 Section 4001 (1976).

Water Pollution

Debris and sludge, organic wastes, and chemical effluents are the three major types of water pollutants. These pollutants come from (1) domestic sewage, (2) industrial waste, (3) agricultural runoff of fertilizers and pesticides, and (4) "natural" processes including silt deposits and sedimentation, which may be increased by nearby construction. A common standard for measuring water pollution is "biochemical oxygen demand" (BOD), which identifies the amount of oxygen consumed by wastes. This measure, however, does not consider chemical substances that may be toxic to humans or fish. It is estimated that domestic sewage accounts for 30 percent of BOD, and industrial and agricultural wastes for 70 percent.

Primary sewage treatment—which uses screens and settling chambers where filth falls out of the water as sludge—is fairly common. Secondary sewage treatment is designed to remove organic wastes, usually by trickling water through a bed of rocks three to ten feet deep, where bacteria consume the organic matter. Remaining germs are killed by chlorination. Tertiary sewage treatment uses mechanical and chemical filtration processes to remove almost all contaminants from water. Many Northeastern cities, including New York City, dump sewage sludge into the ocean after only primary treatment or no treatment at all. While federal law prohibits dumping raw sewage into the ocean, it has proven difficult to secure compliance from coastal cities. Federal water pollution abatement goals call for the establishment of secondary treatment in American communities. In most industrial plants, tertiary treatment ultimately will be required to deal with the flow of chemical pollutants. But tertiary treatment is expensive; it costs two or three times as much to build and operate a tertiary sewage treatment plant as it does a secondary plant. Even today, however, one-third of all Americans live in communities where their sewage gets nothing but primary treatment.

Phosphates are major water pollutants that overstimulate plant life in water, which in turn kills fish. Phosphates run off from fertilized farm lands. Farming is the major source of water pollution in the United States. Paper manufacturing is another major industrial polluter.

Waterfronts and seashores are natural resources. The growing numbers of waterfront homes, amusement centers, marinas, and pleasure boats are altering the environment of the nation's coastal areas. Marshes and estuaries at the water's edge are essential to the production of seafood and shellfish, yet they are steadily shrinking with the growth of residential-commercial-industrial development. Oil spills are unsightly. Although pollution is much greater in Europe than in America, America's coastal areas still require protection. Federal law makes petroleum companies liable for the cleanup costs of oil spills, and outlaws flushing of raw sewage from boat toilets. The *EXXON Valdez* oil spill in Alaska in 1989 focused attention on the environmental risks of transporting billions of barrels of foreign and domestic oil each year in the United States.

The federal government has provided financial assistance to states and cities to build sewage treatment plants ever since the 1930s. Efforts to establish national standards for water quality began in the 1960s and culminated in the Water Pollution Control Act of 1972. This act reinforced earlier laws against oil spills and thermal (heat) pollution. More importantly, it set "national goals" of elimination of the discharge of *all* pollutants into navigable waters; it required industries and municipalities to install "the best available technology"; it gave the EPA authority to initiate legal actions against polluting caused by firms and governments; and increased federal funds available to municipalities for the construction of sewage treatment plants. The EPA was authorized by the Safe Drinking Water Act of 1974 to set minimum standards for drinking water throughout the nations.

Water quality in the United States has improved significantly over the last two decades (see Table 7–3). The problem, of course, is that removing *all* pollutants may not be cost effective. There is a law of diminishing returns at work in environmental efforts which tells us that removing the last 1 percent of pollution is more costly than removing the first 99 percent. Setting unrealistic standards for clean air and clean water is self-defeating.

Air Pollution

The air we breathe is about one-fifth oxygen and a little less than four-fifths nitrogen, with traces of other gases, water vapor, and the waste products we put into it. Most air pollution is caused by the gasoline-powered internal combustion engines of cars, trucks, and buses. Motor vehicles account for over 51 percent of the total polluting material sent into the atmosphere every year. Industries and government contribute another 20 percent: the largest industrial polluters are petroleum refineries, smelters (aluminum, copper, lead, and zinc), and iron foundries. Electrical power plants also contribute about 20 percent of total air pollutants by burning coal or oil for electrical power. Heating is also a major source of pollution; homes, apartments, and offices use coal, gas, and oil for heat. Another source of pollution is the incineration of garbage, trash, metal, glass, and other refuse by both governments and industries.

TABLE 7-3   Improvements in Water Quality

	1975	1980	1985	1988
Fecal coliform bacteria	36	31	28	22
Dissolved oxygen	5	5	3	2
Phosphorous	5	4	3	4
Lead	NA	5	0	0

Figures are violations rates—the proportion of measures which violate EPA standards.
Source: *Statistical Abstract of the United States 1990.*

TABLE 7-4   Decline in Air Pollution Emissions

	1970	1980	1987
SO Sulfur Dioxide	28.4	23.9	20.4
NO Nitrogen Oxide	18.1	20.3	19.5
CO Carbon Monoxide	98.7	76.1	61.4
Particular matter	18.5	8.5	7.0
Lead	0.20	0.07	0.01

Figures are millions of metric tons.
Source: *Statistical Abstract of the United States 1990.*

Air pollutants fall into two major types: particles and gases. The particles include ashes, soot, and lead, the unburnable additive in gasoline. Often the brilliant red sunsets we admire are caused by large particles in the air. Less obvious but more damaging are the gases: (1) sulfur dioxide, which in combination with moisture can form sulfuric acid; (2) hydrocarbons—any combination of hydrogen and carbon; (3) nitrogen oxide, which can combine with hydrocarbons and the sun's ultraviolet rays to form smog; and (4) carbon monoxide, which is produced when gasoline is burned.

It is difficult at the present time to assess the full impact of air pollution on health. We know that when the smog or pollution count rises in a particular city there are more deaths due to emphysema than would normally have been expected. In the streets of certain cities at certain hours of heavy traffic, carbon monoxide can deprive the body of oxygen; persons exposed to it may exhibit drowsiness, headache, poor vision, impaired coordination, and reduced capacity to reason. Nitrogen oxide irritates the eyes, nose, throat, and respiratory system; it damages plants, buildings, and statues. Finally, urban residents have been found to be twice as likely to contract lung cancer as rural residents.

On the other hand, it is known that smoking is much more hazardous than the worst pollution. As one expert testified: "If you want to pass all of these regulations because smog stinks, or because it burns your eyes, or because it blocks your view of the mountains, OK—fine. But if you are trying to pass all of these regulations because smog is a health hazard—forget it—because it is not."[2] Early reports published by the government that pollution is a health hazard were later discredited.[3]

The air we breathe is significantly cleaner today than twenty years ago. All major air pollution emissions are declining (see Table 7–4). Federal clean air legislation (described later in this chapter) is generally credited with causing these improvements.

[2]Quote from Richard J. Lescoe, M.D., former director of the California Lung Association, in *World Research Ink* (November/December 1979), 10.
[3]Richard J. Tobin, *The Social Gamble* (Boston: Lexington, 1979).

INTEREST GROUP EFFECTS

Americans live longer and healthier lives today than at any time in their country's history. Life expectancy at birth is now seventy-five years, up four full years since 1970. Concentrations of pesticides in human tissue have fallen 75 percent in those same years, and lead concentrations in the blood have fallen 40 percent. Cancer deaths are up slightly but not due to environmental hazards: the National Cancer Institute estimates that only 2 percent of all cancer deaths can be attributed to environmental sources. The primary cases of premature death are what they have always been: smoking, diets rich in fat and lean in fiber, lack of exercise, and alcohol abuse. Yet public opinion generally perceives the environment as increasingly contaminated and dangerous and this perception drives public policy.

Interest Group Economics. Organized environmental interests must recruit memberships and contributions (see Table 7–5). They must justify their activities by publicizing and dramatizing environmental threats. When Greenpeace boats disrupt a U.S. Navy exercise, they are attracting the publicity required for a successful direct mail fund-raising drive. The mass media, especially the television networks, welcome stories that capture and hold audience attention. Stories are chosen for their emotional impact; and threats to personal life and safety satisfy the need for drama in the news. Statistics that indicate negligible risks, or scientific testimony that minimizes threats or presents ambiguous findings, do *not* make good news stories. Politicians wish to be perceived as acting aggressively to protect citizens from any risk, however minor. Politicians want to be seen as "clean" defenders of the pristine wilderness. And government bureaucrats understand that the greater

TABLE 7-5   The "Environmentalists" Ranked by Estimated Annual Budget

National Wildlife Education
  Budget: $85 million
  Membership: 5.6 million
  Staff: 700
	Wilderness Society
	  Budget: $20 million
	  Membership: 0.3 million
	  Staff: 130

Greenpeace
  Budget: $34 million
  Membership: 1.4 million
  Staff: 1200
	National Resources Defense Council
	  Budget: $13 million
	  Membership: 0.1 million
	  Staff: 125

National Audobon Society
  Budget: $33 million
  Membership: 0.5 million
  Staff: 337
	Environmental Defense Fund
	  Budget: $13 million
	  Membership: 0.1 million
	  Staff: 100

Sierra Club
  Budget: $28 million
  Membership: 0.5 million
  Staff: 185	

the public fear of environmental threat, the easier it is to justify expanded powers and budgets.

Shaping Public Opinion.   Interest group activity and media coverage of environmental threats have succeeded in convincing most Americans that environment pollution is getting "worse." Evidence that the nation's air and water are measurably cleaner in 1990 than in 1970 is ignored. Catastrophic predictions of impending environmental doom create a climate of opinion that precludes rational discussion of the benefits and costs of environmental policies. Opinion polls now report that 74 percent of Americans agree with the statement: "Protecting the environment is so important that requirements and standards cannot be too high and continued environmental improvements must be made *regardless of cost.*"[4] If taken seriously, such attitudes would prevent economic, scientific, or technological considerations from guiding policy. "Environmentalism" threatens to become a moral crusade that dismisses science and economics as irrelevant or even wicked. In such a climate of opinion, moral absolutism replaces rational public policy.

Serious and reliable scientific information on environmental questions is difficult to find on television. Scientists give poor interviews; they use technical language, cite statistics, speak of complexities and uncertainties, and seldom see issues as one-sided. In contrast, environmental activists, from Robert Redford to Barry Comminer, simplify and dramatize issues and exaggerate environmental threats. The public itself appears to tolerate familiar and common risks to health and safety more easily than the unknown and unfamiliar risks of environmental contaminates. For example, individuals easily tolerate very great risks when they can choose to avoid them, such as skiing and mountain climbing, and risks that are familiar to them, such as smoking. But people appear unwilling to tolerate even minor risks when they are involuntarily exposed to them, for example, nuclear radioactivity and when the risks have long delayed or unknown effects, for example, chemicals, insecticides.

Interest Group Politics.   Everyone is opposed to pollution. It is difficult publicly to oppose clean air or clean water laws—who wants to stand up for dirt? Thus, the environmentalists begin with a psychological and political advantage: they are "clean" and their opponents are "dirty." The news media, Congress, and executive agencies can be moved to support environmental-protection measures with little consideration of their costs—in terms of job loss, price increases, unmet consumer demands, increased dependence on foreign sources of energy. Industry—notably the electric power companies, oil and gas companies, chemical companies, automakers, and coal companies—must fight a rearguard action, continually seeking delays,

[4]*The New York Times*, 27 April 1990.

amendments, and adjustments in federal standards. They must endeavor to point out the increased costs to society of unreasonably high standards in environmental protection legislation. But industry is suspect; the environmentalists can charge that industry opposition to environmental protection is motivated by greed for higher profits. And the charge is partially true, although most of the cost of antipollution effort is passed on to the consumer in the form of higher prices.

The environmentalists are generally upper-middle-class or upper-class individuals whose income and wealth are secure. Their aesthetic preferences for a no-growth, clean, unpolluted environment takes precedence over jobs and income, which new industries can produce. Workers and small businesspeople whose jobs or income depend upon energy production, oil refining, forestry, mining, smelting, or manufacturing are unlikely to be ardent environmentalists. But there is a psychological impulse in all of us to preserve scenic beauty, protect wildlife, and conserve natural resources. It is easy to perceive industry and technology as the villain, and "man against technology" has a humanistic appeal.

NIMBY Power.   Environmental groups have powerful allies in the nation's NIMBYs—local residents who feel inconvenienced or threatened by specific projects. Even people who otherwise recognize the general need for new commercial or industrial developments, highways, airports, power plants, pipelines, or waste disposal sites, nonetheless voice the protest "not in my back yard," earning them the NIMBY label. While they may constitute only a small group within a community, they become very active participants in policy-making—meeting, organizing, petitioning, parading, and demonstrating. NIMBYs are frequently the most powerful interests opposing specific developmental projects and are found nearly everywhere. They frequently take up environmental interests, using environmental arguments to protect their own property investments.

The "Greenhouse Effect"

Gloomy predictions about catastrophic warming of the Earth's surface have been issued by the media and environmental interest groups in support of massive new regulatory efforts. This global warming is theorized to be a result of emissions of carbon dioxide and other gases that trap the sun's heat in the atmosphere. As carbon dioxide increases in the atmosphere as a result of increased human activity, more heat is trapped in the atmosphere. Deforestation contributes to increased carbon dioxide by removing trees, which absorb carbon dioxide and produce oxygen. *Time* magazine featured as its "Man of the Year" for 1988 a doomed Planet Earth perishing from human waste and greenhouse heating. The dire consequences of the greenhouse effect include droughts and crop destruction, the melting of the polar ice caps, and ocean flooding. These predictions have become widely believed; people now blame any heat wave on the "greenhouse effect." New environmental regulations and increased powers for the EPA are justified by reference to halting "the greenhouse effect."

Yet despite the widespread popularity of the "greenhouse" theory, there is no evidence that the earth is warming. It is true, of course, that the earth's atmosphere creates a greenhouse effect: if not, temperatures on the Earth's surface would be like those on the moon—unbearably cold ($-270\,°F$) at night and unbearably hot ($+212\,°F$) during the day. The greenhouse gases, including carbon dioxide, moderate the Earth's surface temperature. And it is true that carbon dioxide is increasing in the atmosphere, an increase of about 25 percent since the beginning of the Industrial Revolution in 1850. And it is true that various computer simulations of the effect of increased dioxides in the atmosphere have predicted increases in the average $57\,°F$ temperature on the Earth. But average temperatures on the Earth's surface have not increased over the last hundred years. Ocean temperatures have remained constant since the first reasonably accurate measurement at the beginning of the twentieth century; and sophisticated satellite measurement of global temperatures over the past ten years fails to show any warming whatsoever. The last ice age, when average temperatures were nine degrees cooler, ended 15,000 years ago; the Earth's temperature changes very, very slowly. Warming estimates by computer simulations are very unreliable; they range from one degree (not significant) to eight degrees (significant only if it occurs rapidly). Few scientists believe that greenhouse warming can now be detected in normal climatic variations from year to year.

Carbon dioxide is produced from the respiration of all living things, as well as from decaying vegetation and the burning of fossil fuels. Human activity accounts for about half of the production of carbon dioxide. Hydrocarbons also contribute to the greenhouse effect; these are produced by growing plants, especially evergreens (causing the blue haze of the Great Smoky Mountains), and are found in industrial and automobile emissions. Methane, another greenhouse gas, is produced by the rotting of vegetation and the flatulence of cows.

Whatever the merits of reducing fossil fuel emissions—such as auto exhaust, coal burning, electric energy plants—predictions of catastrophic warming of the earth are based more on speculation than reality. Nonetheless, popular belief in the "greenhouse effect" strengthens the influence of environmental interests and bureaucrats calling for drastic restrictions on emissions.

"Acid Rain"

All water has some acid content. Rainwater is normally slightly acid, as is the water in lakes and streams. Acidity is higher in some regions and bodies of water than in others. An increase in acidity can change the vegetation and wildlife of lakes and streams. Indeed, if acidity increased to the levels of residential swimming pools, most forms of animal life would be lost. The effect of nitric acid, which is found in most crop fertilizers, is to promote plant growth in water. Excessive growth of algae in water fed from fertilized land can choke out fish.

The term "acid rain" refers to increases over the normal acidity of rainwater attributable to emissions from motor vehicles, electrical power plants, and other industries. Rainwater in certain parts of Northeastern United States and Canada is slightly more acidic than rainwater elsewhere. (Acidity and alkalinity are measured on a pH scale from 0 to 14 with 7.0 being neutral. Average rainwater pH is 5.0; rainwater in affected areas has been measured at 4.2.) It is widely speculated that this increase in acidity is a product of sulfur and nitrogen emissions from coal-burning power plants. But lakes and streams are *not* "dying from acid rain." Indeed, it is difficult to demonstrate that any adverse effects occur to streams or lakes or forests or human health, from acidity in rainwater.

Environmental groups and the mass media have largely ignored serious studies of the effects of rainwater acidity. A massive ten-year, $500 million study, the National Acid Precipitation Assessment Project (NAPAP), reported that: (1) there is no evidence that acid rain has affected American forests except for damage to red spruce at high elevations in the Eastern mountains; (2) there is no evidence of acid rain damage to crops; (3) there is no evidence of human health risks from acid rain to healthy individuals, but it could pose a risk to asthmatics, people with heart and lung disease, and the elderly; and (4) overall, less than 5 percent of the nation's lakes and 10 percent of its streams have elevated acid levels.[5] In general, the NAPAP report indicates that "acid rain" is not a serious environmental issue.

Nonetheless, public concern about acid rain drives environmental policy in Washington and inspires multibillion dollar regulatory programs.

The "Ozone Hole"

Ozone is a gas similar to oxygen. Some chemicals in automobile exhaust can catalyze oxygen in the air to break down into ozone. Ozone is a principle ingredient in smog. It makes the air hazy or even brown. In heavy concentrations in some cities and under certain weather conditions, it can cause eye and lung irritation. Some cities declare a "smog alert" when ozone levels become too high. Persons with respiratory diseases, the elderly, and children are advised to stay indoors to avoid inflammation of the lungs. There is no question that ozone production is an "externality."

A more recent, widely publicized story is that ozone levels in the upper atmosphere are declining. Ozone in the upper atmosphere is believed to reflect some of the sun's ultraviolet light and prevent it from reaching

---

[5]National Acid Precipitation Assessment Project, "Draft for External Review," (Washington, D.C.: NAPAC), September 5, 1990.

the earth. Ultraviolet light can contribute to skin cancer. Fluorocarbons (including freon in air conditioners) breaks down ozone into ordinary oxygen. So the theory has been advanced that the release of fluorocarbons is creating an "ozone hole" in the atmosphere, allowing more ultraviolet light to reach earth and cause more skin cancer.

While it is true that fluorocarbons break down ozone, it is not clear whether they contribute to a decline in ozone levels in the upper atmosphere or not, or indeed whether ozone in the upper atmosphere is in fact declining. An "ozone hole" is reported to exist during the Antarctic summer. A modest reduction in sunbathing would be many thousand times more effective in reducing skin cancer than eliminating fluorocarbons. Yet belief in the catastrophic effects of an "ozone hole" drives environmental policy.

THE NUCLEAR INDUSTRY MELTDOWN

Nuclear power is the cleanest and safest form of energy available. But the political struggle over nuclear power has all but destroyed early hopes that nuclear power could reduce the United States' dependence on fossil fuels. Nuclear power now provides about 18 percent of the nation's total electricity. Many early studies recommended that the United States strive for 50 percent nuclear electric generation by 1990. But under current policies it is unlikely that nuclear power will ever be able to supply any more energy than it does today. The nuclear industry itself is in a state of "meltdown" and the cause of the meltdown is political, not technological.

In its developmental stages, nuclear power was a government monopoly. The Atomic Energy Act of 1946 created the Atomic Energy Commission (AEC), which established civilian rather than military control over nuclear energy. The AEC was responsible for research, development, and production of nuclear weapons, as well as the development of the peaceful uses of nuclear energy. The AEC contracted with the Westinghouse Corporation to build a reactor and with the Duquesne Light Company to operate the world's first nuclear power plant at Shippingport, Pennsylvania, in 1957. Under the Atomic Energy Act of 1954 the AEC granted permits to build, and licenses to operate, nuclear plants; the AEC also retained control over nuclear fuel.

The AEC promoted the growth of the nuclear industry for over twenty years. By the late 1970s there were seventy nuclear power plants licensed to operate and eighty-five construction permits issued. But opponents of nuclear power succeeded in the Energy Reorganization Act of 1974 in separating the nuclear regulatory function from the research and development function. Today a separate agency, the Nuclear Regulatory Commission (NRC), regulates all aspects of nuclear power. Only 104 nuclear power plants are operating in the United States today. Many planned plants were cancelled and no new plants have been started in over a decade.

Nuclear power has long been under attack by a wide assortment of "no-nuke" groups. The core opposition to nuclear power is found among environmental activist groups. But fear plays the most important role in nuclear politics. The mushroom cloud image of the devastation of Japanese cities at the end of World War II is still with us. The mass media cannot resist dramatic accounts of nuclear accidents. The public is captivated by the "China Syndrome" story—an overheated nuclear core melts down the containing vessels and the plant itself and releases radioactivity that kills millions.

Nuclear power offers a means of generating electricity without discharging any pollutants into the air or water. It is the cleanest form of energy production. It does not diminish the world's supply of oil, gas, or coal. However, used reactor fuel remains radioactive for hundreds of years and there are potential problems in burying this radioactive waste. Spent fuel is now piling up in storage areas in specially designed pools of water at nuclear power sites. When these existing storage places are filled to capacity, spent fuel will have to be transported somewhere else, adding to new complaints about the dangers of radioactive waste. There are many technical alternatives in dealing with waste, but there is no political consensus about which of these alternatives to choose.

The nuclear power industry in the United States has a forty year record of safety. No one has ever died or been seriously harmed by radioactivity from a nuclear power plant in the United States.[6] Despite sensational media coverage, the failure of the nuclear reactor at Three Mile Island, Pennsylvania, in 1979 did not result in injury to anyone or cause damage beyond the plant. There are over 300 nuclear power plants in operation outside of the United States. France, Japan, Taiwan, and the Soviet Union are gradually switching from fossil fuels to nuclear generation of electricity. The worst nuclear accident in history occurred at Chernobyl in the Soviet Union in 1986; it resulted in thirty-one deaths from radiation.

Zero risk is an impossible standard, and the costs of efforts to approach zero risk are astronomical. Under popular pressure to achieve near-zero risk, the Nuclear Regulatory Commission has imposed licensing requirements that now make nuclear plants the most expensive means of generating electricity. No new nuclear plants have been proposed in over a decade, and private utilities have cancelled dozens of planned nuclear plants. The nation's largest nuclear plant complex, the Washington Public Power Service, was forced into bankruptcy. Indeed, the existing nuclear power industry in the United States may be driven to extinction by ever-increasing costs of near-zero risk regulatory policy. The *stated policy* of the national government may be to keep open the nuclear power option, but the *actual effect* of nuclear regulatory policy is to foreclose that option.

---

[6]This record includes the 107 nuclear power plants operated in the United States, and hundreds of nuclear-powered surface and submarine ships operated by the U.S. Navy. For an excellent, unbiased discussion of nuclear safety, see Harold W. Lewis, "The Safety of Fission Reactors," *Scientific American*, 242 (March, 1980), 53–65.

POLITICIANS AND BUREAUCRATS:
REGULATING THE ENVIRONMENT

Federal environmental policy making began in earnest in the 1970s with the creation of the Environmental Protection Agency, now the U.S. Department of Environmental Protection, and the passage of clean air and water quality acts. Potentially, the Department of Environmental Protection is the most powerful and far-reaching bureaucracy in Washington today, with legal authority over any activity in the nation that affects the air, water, or ground. The Department's power has gradually increased over two decades.

The Environmental Protection Agency.   The EPA was created in an executive order by President Richard Nixon in 1970 to reorganize the federal bureaucracy to consolidate responsibility for (1) water pollution, (2) air pollution, (3) solid waste management, (4) radiation control, and (5) hazardous and toxic substance control. The EPA is a regulatory agency with power to establish and enforce policy.

The National Environmental Protection Act.   The NEPA in 1970 created the Council on Environmental Quality to advise the President and Congress on environmental matters. The CEQ is an advisory agency. However, the act requires all federal agencies as well as state, local, and private organizations receiving federal monies to file lengthy "environmental impact statements." If the CEQ wants to delay or obstruct a project, it can ask for endless revisions, changes, or additions in the environmental impact statement. The CEQ cannot by itself halt a project, but it can conduct public hearings for the press, pressure other governmental agencies, and make recommendations to the president. The courts have ruled that the requirement for an environmental impact statement is judicially enforceable.

The Clean Air Act of 1970.   This act authorized the EPA to identify air pollutants that cause a health threat and to establish and enforce standards of emission. The EPA began by focusing on automobile emissions and requiring the installation of pollution equipment on all new cars. These requirements were delayed several years, owing to oil shortages in the early 1970s. In addition, lead was removed from auto fuel and engines were redesigned for lead-free gasoline. More radical solutions advanced by the EPA (for example, to halt driving in certain cities) were blocked by courts and Congress. The EPA was even more aggressive in pursuing stationary sources of air pollution with requirements for "smoke-stack scrubbers," low-sulfur coal, and other very costly devices. Industry opposition led to some relaxation of these requirements in the Clean Air Act Amendments of 1977.

The Water Pollution Control Act of 1972.   This early antipollution law set an unrealistic goal: "that the discharge of pollutants into the navigable

---

1990   The creation of the U.S. Department of Environmental Protection by President George Bush gave greater symbolic importance to the federal government's environmental efforts.

---

waters be eliminated by 1985." After a flood of lawsuits the EPA was forced to abandon the "zero discharge" standard. Forcing municipal governments to clean up their discharges proved more difficult than forcing industry to do so. Many municipalities remain in violation of federal water quality standards.

Toxic Substances Control Act of 1976.   This Act authorized the EPA to designate hazardous and toxic substances and to establish standards for their release into the environment.

The Comprehensive Environmental Response Act of 1980.   This Act established a "superfund" for cleaning up old toxic and hazardous waste sites. Over 20,000 sites have been identified; full cleanup of all of the sites could cost many billions of dollars, far more than the President or Congress is willing to appropriate to the superfund.

MORE REGULATION FROM WASHINGTON

Although the air and water in the nation are much cleaner today than in previous decades (see Tables 7–3 and 7–4), Americans believe just the opposite—that overall environmental quality is declining. In response to the question, "In the past twenty years has the environment gotten better, gotten worse, or stayed about the same?," 73 percent of the American public said "worse," 18 percent said "the same," and only 9 percent said "better."[7] These poll results have not gone unnoticed by politicians, from George Bush to Mikhail Gorbachev. The new "greening" of the political landscape in the United States was watered by George Bush's self-description as an "environmentalist" and his reopening of the debate on clean air.

Clean Air Act 1990.   The Clean Air Act Amendments of 1990 reflect the political popularity of "green" initiatives and the influence of environmental interests and the mass media in shaping public policy. New regulations are aimed at a variety of perceived threats to the environment:

> *Acid rain.* Sulfur dioxide emissions must be cut from 20 to 10 million tons annually, and nitrogen oxide emissions must be cut by 2 million tons. Midwestern

[7]*The Washington Post*, 20 April 1990.

coal burning utilities must burn low sulphur coal and install added smoke-scrubbing equipment at increased costs to their consumers.

Ozone hole. Production of chlorofluorocarbons and hydrochlorofluorocarbons (aerosol sprays, insulating materials, etc.) is outlawed, and new regulations are placed on chemicals used in air conditioners and refrigerators.

Urban smog. Additional mandated pollution control equipment is required on new automobiles. Oil companies must produce cleaner burning fuel. There is also a special requirement that automobile companies produce an experimental fleet of cars to be sold in Southern California.

Toxic air pollutants. New definitions and regulations govern over 200 substances as "toxic air pollutants" released into the air from a wide variety of sources from gas stations to dry cleaners. The EPA is given authority to require all of these sources to install "the best available control technology" and to provide "an ample margin of safety" for nearby residents.

Costs.   It is difficult to estimate the overall costs to society of these tighter standards. The Bush administration has claimed they would cost only $16 billion a year, but the Business Roundtable, composed of chief executives of the nation's largest industries, has estimated the costs to exceed $100 billion. High sulfur-content coal from West Virginia would be virtually banned and many mining jobs in that state lost. It is even more difficult to estimate the benefits to society of additional reductions in air pollutants. We can reasonably expect that cleaner air would improve health and reduce medical costs, but no reliable estimate can be made as to the amount of these benefits, if any.

ALTERNATIVE SOLUTIONS

Pollution is a cost of production, a cost that producers externalize to others. Once we view pollution in this fashion, it becomes possible to envision a variety of market-based environmental policies that hold much more promise of success than centralized governmental commands and regulations. If more attention is given to the generation of pollution rather than its control, if pollution becomes a cost to its producers, then it will be reduced through the ordinary operations of a free-market economy.

Regulatory Problems.   The current "command and control" approach to environmental policy is inefficient. Pollution abatement practices are many and varied; the best practice depends on circumstances that can vary from one plant to another. The cost of reducing pollution varies enormously; some sources can reduce pollution cheaply while some can do so only at great cost. A centralized government bureaucracy in Washington cannot efficiently supervise practices in every location in the nation. And uniform nationwide regulations discourage innovation. New pollution abatement methods are discouraged by government rules requiring older methods.

Moreover, government regulation encourages interest groups to pursue special advantages in influencing government action. Lobbyists for different industries or companies, unions, and regions of the country, will all seek to gain advantage over their competitors by imposing regulatory costs on them and escaping such costs themselves. Frequently Congress imposes regulations on *new* plants or products, giving advantage to existing firms. Plants that exist have more political clout than plants that do not yet exist. The effect is to discourage growth.

Pollution Taxes.   A more effective alternative is pollution taxation. Taxes on pollutants, imposed on those who generate them, would provide economic incentives for individuals, firms, and local governments to find the cheapest and most effective method to limit pollution. A tax on each firm that generates pollution, based on amount and type of pollution generated, would substitute economic incentives for pollution abatement for central directories of politicized bureaucracies. By imposing a per unit tax on the emission of pollutants, such as sulfur dioxide, any feasible amount of abatement can be achieved depending on the level of the tax. Each polluter would be given the information and motivation to reduce pollution as cheaply and efficiently as possible in order to reduce the tax. Those who do so would be rewarded with lower taxes and higher profits. Those who do not would be obliged to pass the tax on to customers in the form of higher prices. Customers would be given an incentive to reduce their use of high-pollution products and search for alternatives.

Pollution taxes offer a far less expensive approach to environmental policy than centralized rules and regulations. Governmental bureaucracies and enforcement costs would be reduced. Taxes could be levied not only on air and water pollutants but also on consumer products that create disposal problems. When consumers are forced to pay the full environmental costs of the products they buy, their market choices will incorporate the full cost of production. By shifting environmental policy away from centralized bureaucratic control and toward decentralized market economic incentives, it is possible to increase environmental quality while at the same time promoting economic growth.

Tradable Emission Allowances.   A positive development in recent environmental policy proposals has been the greater attention given to tradable emission allowances. The total emission allowances reflect the overall goal of environmental policy, for example, a cap of 10 million tons of SO_2 emissions. Emission allowances would be distributed to existing utilities, refineries, and other sources of pollution. Plant owners would be free to buy or sell these allowances among themselves. Thus emission rates among individual plants would vary, while overall emissions would be held at the target level. Tradable allowances reduce the overall costs of compliance by allowing flexibility. They encourage innovation in technology; innovative plants can sell their excess allowances at a profit. Plants that could only reduce emissions at a very high cost to their customers could purchase emission allowances and continue operations. Bureaucratic enforcement would be kept to a minimum, simply measuring emissions rather than dictating plant operations.

Waste Charges.   Another effective alternative is charging businesses and households by the amount of garbage collected. Governments rarely reflect the true costs of garbage collection and landfill operations in their pricing of services. Direct charges based on the volume of garbage collected would inspire businesses and households to buy less unnecessary packaging and to undertake recycling efforts voluntarily.

Economic Growth.   Policies that retard economic growth are usually counterproductive to environmental protection. The world's worst polluters are underdeveloped nations. As income increases, people make greater efforts to improve environmental quality. Market economies are more successful at environmental protection than socialist economies. The socialist economies of Eastern Europe produced severe environmental degradation because there were no market incentives guiding production.

SUMMARY

Public choice theory views environmental pollution as an "externality" of human activity. Individuals, firms, and governments frequently impose unwanted costs on others. The environment, especially air and water, is a common pool resource: access is unrestricted; there are no cleary defined property rights to it; no one has the individual responsibility of caring for it; individuals, firms, and governments tend to use it to carry off waste materials, thus generating unwanted costs or externalities on everyone else. Government has a legitimate interest in managing environmental externalities. Public choice theory offers valuable guidelines in dealing with them.

1. Economic growth is not incompatible with environmental protection. On the contrary, increases in wealth and advances in technology provide the best hope for a cleaner environment.

2. Effective pollution control and risk reduction must be balanced against its costs. Environmental policies whose costs exceed benefits will impair society's ability to deal effectively with environmental problems.

3. The costs of removing additional environmental pollutants and risks rise as we approach zero tolerance. Total elimination of pollutants from air, water, or ground involves astronomical costs and wastes the resources of society.

4. Traditionally "command and control" approaches to environmental protection are less effective than market incentives. Legislatures and bureaucrats that endeavor to devise laws and regulations to reduce pollution, are less effective than individuals, firms, and local governments with strong market incentives to reduce pollution in a cost-effective manner.

5. The air and water in the United States is measurably cleaner today than in 1970, when the first major environmental policies were enacted. Improvements in air and water quality have occurred despite growth in the population and growth in waste products.

6. Nonetheless, most Americans believe that pollution is growing "worse." Interest group activity and media coverage of environmental "crises," together with economic prosperity and the end of the Cold War, have pushed environmental issues to the forefront of American politics. Predictions of global doom create a climate of opinion that precludes rational analyses of the benefits and costs of environmental policies.

7. Current policy initiatives center on emissions of sulfur dioxide and nitrogen oxide from coal-burning and utilities, emissions of ozone and carbon monoxide from automobiles and stationary sources, and "toxic air pollutants" released from a wide variety of sources.

8. If firms were taxed on the basis of the pollutants they emit, a strong market incentive would be created for a reduction in pollution. A pollution tax would capture the "externalities" and force producers and consumers to incorporate the full environmental costs of products in the price. It would encourage polluters to find ways themselves to reduce pollution rather than simply comply with government regulations. Waste charges would encourage consumers to reduce their use of waste-producing goods.

BIBLIOGRAPHY

HAHN, ROBERT W. *A Primer on Environmental Policy Design.* London: Harwood Academic Publishers, 1989.

SINGER, S. FRED, ed. *Global Climate Change: Human and National Influences.* New York: Paragon House, 1989.

WILDAVSKY, AARON. *Searching for Safety.* New Brunswick, N.J.: Transaction Publishers, 1988.

8

DEFENSE POLICY
strategies for serious games

After the Vietnam war, the United States ended the draft. It now relies on an all-volunteer force. (Marc Anderson)

DETERRENCE STRATEGY AND NUCLEAR WAR

Game theory provides an interesting way of thinking about defense policy. Defense policies of major world powers are interdependent. Each major power must adjust its own defense policies to reflect not only its own national objectives but also its expectations of what other major powers may do. Outcomes depend on the combination of choices made in world capitals. Moreover, it is not unreasonable to assume that major powers strive for rationality in defense policy making. Nations choose defense strategies (policies) that are designed to achieve an optimum payoff even after considering all their opponents' possible strategies. Thus, national defense policy making conforms to basic game-theoretic notions. Our use of game-theoretic ideas is limited, however, to suggesting interesting questions, posing dilemmas, and providing a vocabulary for dealing with policy making in a competitive, interdependent world.

In order to maintain peace and protect the national interest of the United States, primary reliance is placed upon the strategy of *deterrence*. In a general sense, deterrence means that war and aggression are prevented by making the consequences of such acts clearly unacceptable to rational leaders of other nations. This is the irony of deterrence: massive destruction of civilization is prevented by maintaining weapons capable of inflicting the massive destruction they seek to prevent. The United States does not wish to use its nuclear deterrent *physically*, but rather *psychologically*, to inhibit potential enemies from engaging in war or aggression.

For over forty years, following the nuclear destruction of Hiroshima and Nagasaki in 1945, nations have added nuclear weapons to their arsenals. Yet they have not been used in war. Why? Because nations are peace-loving, God-fearing, humane, trusting, caring, compassionate? Or because fear of retaliation has prevented nuclear war?

The strategy of deterrence assures that peace is maintained through mutual fear of retaliation. It is based on the rational self-interest of national leaders. It does not depend on their love of peace, or fear of God, or sense of humanity. We are not willing to risk the lives of hundreds of millions of people on anything other than rational self-interest. If America loses its deterrent—its ability to threaten retaliation—then peace would rest on the fragile hope that our potential enemies would be merciful, kind, and compassionate. No national leader can afford to take such a risk.

Assured Destruction Deterrence

Assured destruction deterrence is the notion that a nation can dissuade a potential enemy from aggression or war by maintaining the capability to destroy the enemy's society *even after absorbing a well-executed surprise attack*. Assured destruction deterrence considers the enemy's most menacing attack—a surprise, full-salvo, first-strike against our own offensive forces.

It emphasizes our "second-strike capability"—the ability of our forces to survive such an attack by the enemy and then to inflict an unacceptable level of destruction on the aggressor's homeland in retaliation.

Note that the "second-strike capability" required for assured destruction deterrence is far more than the mere possession of nuclear weapons. It is not sufficient to merely count missiles or megatonnage or "overkill" capacity. The key question is the *survivability* of an effective retaliatory strike force. Assured destruction deterrence considers what can be done *after* a successful surprise attack by the enemy. The surviving forces will be damaged and not fully coordinated because of the enemy's attacks on communications and command installations. These forces must operate in the confusion of a post-attack environment. The enemy's defenses will be alerted. Yet the surviving forces must still retain a credible capability of penetrating the best-alerted defenses and inflicting unacceptably high casualties.

It is extremely important to realize that second-strike capability must be *communicated* to the enemy if it is to serve as a deterrent. It would be irrational to keep your second-strike capacity a secret. (Even if you did not have such a capability, you might bluff that you did.) Hence, U.S. policy makers regularly publicize the strength and size of U.S. strategic offensive forces. Deterrence is achieved only if the enemy knows that you have the capacity to deliver unacceptable damage even after absorbing a first strike.

Moreover, a second-strike deterrent must be *credible*. A potential enemy must never begin to suspect that in the event of attack you would lack the will to use your weapons. Even if you doubt the morality of a retaliatory strike which would kill millions of people, you must hide this doubt in order to preserve deterrence.

Finally, deterrence strategy assumes that potential enemies are *rational*. In this context, rationality means that an enemy would not deliberately choose a course of action that would produce mass death and destruction in his own country. Needless to say, an irrational leader (or a terrorist group) with nuclear weapons is an immense danger to the world.

Mutual Assured Destruction—MAD

If *both* sides possess second-strike capability, each side can deter the other from launching a first strike. The mutual development of second-strike capability by both the United States and the USSR provides *stability* in strategic nuclear relations between the superpowers. *If* (1) both the United States and the USSR possess sufficient, protected retaliatory forces, so that either side could absorb any conceivable first strike by the other and still retain sufficient power to strike back and destroy the other; and *if* (2) each side communicates this retaliatory power to the other side; and *if* (3) both sides believe that the other side can survive a first strike; *then* the situation is one of mutual assured destruction or "MAD." MAD's balance of terror— each side restrained by knowledge of the second-strike capability of the other side—has maintained stability and protected the world from nuclear war for the past several decades. MAD produces stability because each side knows that any nuclear attack it might launch could lead to *its own destruction* and thus be suicidal. MAD removes the need for trust and replaces it with the calculated self-interest in not being devastated. World peace under MAD does not rest on trust or love or brotherhood, but on rational calculation of what is in each side's self-interest.

In summary, assured destruction deterrence is a psychological concept. It requires (1) second-strike capability, (2) communication, (3) credibility, and (4) a rational opponent. The capability of this nation's forces to survive a surprise, full-salvo, nuclear attack must not be allowed to erode; potential aggressors must be informed of these capabilities; and the threat to use these capabilities in case of attack must be credible. If these requirements are met, then there should never be any need to use our nuclear weapons physically. Peace should be the outcome.

MAD has the effect of holding the populations of each nation hostage against the possibility of a first-strike attack. The population of the USSR can be destroyed by a retaliatory strike by the United States, and the population of the United States can be destroyed by a retaliatory strike by the USSR. Hence, both nations are threatened with the annihilation of their own populations if they launch a first-strike attack.

Flexible Strategic Response

Assured destruction deterrence strategy threatens a potential attacker with a massive retaliatory strike—a strike which would be targeted on population and industrial centers. But is such a threat really creditable, particularly in response to an attack on only our offensive missile and bomber bases? If deterrence fails, and the Soviets launch an attack at military targets in the United States that causes relatively few civilian casualties, would it be rational to retaliate with a full-salvo city-busting attack? Such a retaliatory strike would certainly cause the Soviets to reply in a similar fashion, using whatever missiles they have left to kill millions of Americans. The Soviet threat of a second attack on our cities might "deter our deterrent." Knowing that we cannot really use our nuclear forces against Soviet cities without incurring great loss of life ourselves, the Soviet leadership might be tempted to launch a limited-salvo attack against our offensive missile and bomber bases.

In the 1970s, U.S. defense policy makers became increasingly concerned about the threat of a *limited* Soviet attack against our offensive nuclear forces. Some officials believed that a massive U.S. response to such a limited attack would be irrational, and, more importantly, that the Soviet Union would not consider the threat of a massive U.S. retaliatory strike to be creditable. It was argued that to deter the Soviets from a limited attack on U.S. offensive nuclear forces, the United States must develop a more *flexible strategic response*, including "limited nuclear options."

A limited nuclear options strategy allows the United States to respond to a limited Soviet attack with a limited attack of our own. A limited U.S. attack would be directed at "counterforce targets"—Soviet missile and bomber bases. Civilian casualties and damage to industry would be avoided. An effort would be made *not* to kill Soviet leaders, so that some resolution to conflict could be achieved before it escalates into an even more damaging nuclear war against cities. "What we need is a series of measured responses to aggression which bears some relation to the provocation, prospects of terminating hostilities before general nuclear war breaks out, and some possibility of restoring deterrence. . . . To be creditable, and hence effective over the range of possible contingencies, deterrence must rest on many options and on a spectrum of capabilities to support these options. . . . Flexibility of response is essential."[1]

Of course, there are many dangerous elements in a policy of limited nuclear options. First of all, by suggesting that the destruction caused by nuclear war might be controlled and limited primarily to military targets, the likelihood of nuclear war may be increased. As nuclear war becomes "thinkable," it becomes more acceptable; and the psychological barriers inhibiting political leaders from engaging in nuclear war would be weakened. Second, there is the fear that nuclear war can never be controlled. Once the nuclear threshold is crossed, there is no way to limit or manage the resulting destruction. Even limited nuclear attacks on military targets would kill millions of people in the United States and the Soviet Union. Escalation would be inevitable. Third, counterforce targeting threatens the second-strike capability of the enemy. It is the equivalent of the United States pursuing a disarming first-strike capability. If we achieve significant counterforce capability against the Soviets they will be encouraged to launch on warning to preserve *their* deterrent. This would create an even more delicate and dangerous world nuclear balance. Fourth, the pursuit of counterforce capability will lead to a very expensive and uncontrollable arms race between the superpowers. Counterforce weapons must have "hard target-kill capability," and this means great accuracy, higher yields, and larger numbers of warheads.

STRATEGIC WEAPONS: THE EMBATTLED TRIAD

In striving to maintain assured destruction deterrence, the United States, over the past thirty years, has relied on a "TRIAD" of weapons systems: land-based missiles (ICBMs), submarine-launched missles (SLBMs), and manned bombers. The strategic concept of the TRIAD includes the notion that any

---

[1]Former Secretary of Defense James R. Schlesinger, "Flexible Strategic Options," in *American Defense Policy,* ed. John E. Endicott and Roy W. Stafford, 4th ed. (Baltimore: Johns Hopkins University Press, 1977), p. 82.

one of three sets of forces would give the United States assured destruction deterrence: if the ICBMs were destroyed in their silos by an enemy first strike, and all of the manned bomber force were destroyed, the United States could still retaliate with an SLBM attack, which would itself inflict unacceptable damages on the enemy. Each "leg" of the TRIAD is supposed to be an independent, survivable, second-strike force. Each "leg" of the TRIAD poses separate and unique problems for an enemy in devising a way to destroy the U.S. second-strike deterrent.

ICBMs

Both the United States and the Soviet Union have developed long-range intercontinental ballistic missiles (ICBMs) that can travel between the United States and USSR in less than forty minutes. To improve their survivability, both sides have placed their ICBMs in "hardened" (concrete and steel) underground silos—designed and constructed so that they can be destroyed only by a direct hit. The United States built 1,000 Minuteman ICBMs in the early 1960s. These aging missiles continue to be this nation's primary ICBM force. The Minuteman is a solid-fuel missile that can be launched on short notice and can strike within one-quarter mile of any target in the Soviet Union. About half of the Minuteman force carries multiple independently targeted reentry vehicles (MIRVs), which are smaller nuclear warheads that separate from the missle itself and can be accurately directed to separate targets.

Soviet Superiority.   Beyond replacing earlier Minuteman missiles with the MIRV-carrying Minuteman III, and improving the accuracy of the Minuteman guidance system, the United States did not deploy any new ICBMs for twenty-five years. In contrast, the Soviet Union continued the development of newer, larger, and more accurate MIRVed missiles. The result is a diversified Soviet Strategic Rocket Force, which includes about 1400 ICBMs of various types, as shown in Table 8–1. The SS-18 is currently the Soviets' major land-based ICBM. It dwarfs the Minuteman III in that it carries *ten* MIRV warheads, each with a *one-megaton* weapon, and there is no reason to doubt its accuracy. The Soviets have 308 of these large ICBMs, which means that their SS-18 force can deliver over 3,000 one-megaton weapons. The SS-18 gives the Soviets "hard target-kill capability"—the ability to destroy U.S. missile silos and thus threaten to eliminate our retaliatory capability in a well-planned first strike. With their improved accuracy, the Soviets can now destroy the entire U.S. land-based missile force using only a small portion of their own ICBM force. This danger to the survivability of our ICBM force compelled President Carter and later President Reagan to announce plans for the development of a new ICBM system called the MX. Modernization of our land-based ICBMs, and the search for a *survivable* basing mode for them, continues to occupy defense policy planners, the president, and the Congress.

TABLE 8-1 U.S. and Soviet Strategic Nuclear Forces

UNITED STATES			SOVIET UNION		
LAND-BASED ICBM'S					
	MISSILES	WARHEADS		MISSILES	WARHEADS
Minuteman II (1)	450	450	SS-11 (1)	400	400
Minuteman III (3)	500	1,500	SS-13 (1)	60	60
MX (10)	50	500	SS-17 (4)	138	552
			SS-18 (10)	308	3080
			SS-19 (6)	350	2100
			SS-24 rail mobile (1)	30	300
			SS-25 land mobile (1)	165	165
Totals	1000	2450		1451	6657
SLBM'S					
	MISSILES	WARHEADS		MISSILES	WARHEADS
Poseidan C-3	224	3,136	SS-N-6	240	240
Trident C-4	384	3,072	SS-N-8	286	286
			SS-N-17	12	12
			SS-N-18	224	1568
			SS-N-20	100	900
			SS-N-23	80	800
Totals	608	6208		942	3806
STRATEGIC BOMBERS					
	AIRCRAFT	WARHEADS		AIRCRAFT	WARHEADS
B-1 B	97	1,164	Bear	75	1500
B-52	69	828	Bear with ALCM	100	200
B-52 with ALCM	194	3,880	Blackjack	20	240
Totals	360	5,875		195	1940

Source: International Institute for Strategic Studies, *The Military Balance 1989–1990* (London: International Institute for Strategic Studies, 1990).

MX. The MX missile is a land-based, intercontinental, solid-fueled missile that can carry ten MIRVed warheads. The MX gives the U.S. hard target-kill capability and partially restores the strategic imbalance created by the SS-18. However, the central problem remains that of finding a *survivable* basing mode for land-based missiles. Congress refused to buy more than fifty MXs because they are vulnerable to attack. For over a decade various plans were discussed to make the MX survivable, but each plan was rejected. President Bush has proposed placing MXs on railroad cars that would be moved about in the event of a crisis and thus made difficult for an enemy missile to target and destroy.

Midgetman.   To help resolve the basing problem, President Reagan established an independent and bipartisan Commission on Strategic Alternatives in 1983, headed by former national security advisor General Brent Scowcroft. The Commission recommended deployment of 100 MXs, arguing that the MX was required in order to threaten at least a portion of Soviet offensive missile forces. The Commission also recommended the development of small, single-warhead, mobile missiles (quickly dubbed the "Midgetman" by the press); these smaller missiles could be easily and quickly moved about the countryside, making them difficult targets for an attacker. Originally 500 to 600 were planned, but Congress has not yet approved the purchase of any Midgetman missiles. It is not certain that Congress will approve both a rail-based MX and a land-mobile Midgetman in an era of reduced military spending. However, the Soviets under President Gorbachev have deployed both a new rail-mobile SS-24 and land-mobile SS-25 (see Table 8-1).

Manned Bombers

The second "leg" of the TRIAD is the intercontinental bomber. Manned bombers can survive a first strike if they are in the air. A certain portion of a manned bomber force can be kept in the air during crisis periods. Given adequate warning (knowledge that the enemy has fired its ICBMs or SLBMs), a significant percentage of bombers can get off the ground before incoming missiles arrive. Unlike missiles, manned bombers can be called back if the alert is an error; they can be redirected to other targets in flight; and they can be used in conventional nonnuclear war if needed.

B-52.   The U.S. intercontinental manned bomber force is composed mainly of aged, slow, and large B-52s. This bomber was developed in 1952 as a high-penetration aircraft (a plane that would fly high over enemy air defenses), with a 6000-mile range and a capability of carrying large numbers of nuclear weapons as bombs and short-range air-to-surface missiles. But the B-52 is subsonic, that is, it flies at a maximum speed of 550 miles per hour. It is large and it presents a large target on radar for enemy air defense missiles and interceptor aircraft. It was produced between 1952 and 1962, and was predicted to "wear out" in the 1980s. Indeed, many of the original force of 600 B-52s have been cannibalized to keep 250 aircraft "operational." The B-52 has undergone eight major improvements (through the B-52G and B-52H models) to try to offset Soviet air defenses. Soviet surface-to-air missiles (SAMs) now make high-altitude penetration very risky. Low-altitude penetration (as low as 100 to 200 feet) is preferred in order to make radar detection difficult and radar-guided SAMs less effective.

The Cruise Missile.   Cruise missiles are small, air-breathing, subsonic, low-flying guided missiles that can be fired from the ground (Ground-Launched Cruise Missiles, GLCMs), or from the air (Air-Launched Cruise Missiles, ALCMs), or from surface ships or submerged submarines (Sea-Launched Cruise Missiles, SLCMs). Cruise missiles are very inexpensive to build compared to other weapons; tens of thousands could be built to over-whelm any possible air defense system. Cruise missiles are very small (under thirty feet long); their size makes them mobile and difficult to locate; a single B-52 can carry twenty of them; and attack submarines can fire them under water from torpedo tubes. Although cruise missiles are very slow-flying, their radar guidance system allows them to fly close to the ground; very few could be intercepted in a large-scale attack; and they are very accurate. Currently the United States is extending the life of the B-52 by arming many of these with ALCMs. These ALCMs will allow the old slow-flying and vulnerable B-52s to avoid flying over the heaviest enemy air defenses.

B-1 Bomber.   A more advanced manned bomber, the B-1 was developed and tested in the mid-1970s as a replacement for the aging B-52s. The B-1 is a small, intercontinental, supersonic (over 2000 miles per hour) bomber, designed for low-altitude penetration of modern air defenses. After successful test flying of this aircraft, President Jimmy Carter cancelled production in 1977 arguing that the program was too costly and that Cruise missiles could extend the useful life of the B-52s. Criticism of this decision was widespread in Congress and the military. President Ronald Reagan restored funding for the B-1, but only 100 of the aircraft were built. The B-1 currently maintains U.S. capability to penetrate modern air defenses and overfly target areas.

B-2 Bomber.   Successful penetration of enemy air defenses after the year 2000 will require highly sophisticated aircraft employing the most advanced "stealth" (radar evading) technology. As Soviet SAMs become increasingly deadly at all altitudes and speeds, avoiding radar detection becomes the key to target penetration. Stealth technology refers to airframe design and con-struction materials that minimize the aircraft's reflection on enemy radar screen. While no aircraft can be invisible, a very small radar "signature" or "blip" may go undetected in background clutter, or make accurate tracking and targeting by SAMs very difficult. Beginning in the late 1970s, the U.S. made rapid strides in secret stealth research. A stealthy fighter, the F117A was built and deployed with little public attention. In 1989 the Air Force rolled out its first stealth bomber, the B-2, with its revolutionary flying wing design. But the Air Force also revealed the high cost of the new bomber and its sophisticated technology. The B-2's future is very much in doubt in an era of reduced defense spending.

SLBMs

The third "leg" of the TRIAD is the submarine-launched ballistic missile (SLBM) force. At present, this is the most "survivable" force and therefore the best second-strike component of the TRIAD. Most defense analysts believe that Soviet antisubmarine warfare (ASW) capability is not now, nor will it be in the foreseeable future, capable of destroying a significant portion of our SLBM force on a surprise first strike.

Poseidon C-3.   The first SLBM carrying submarines (SSBNs) went to sea in 1960. SSBNs are nuclear powered; they can remain undersea for long periods; and they can launch missiles from underwater. During the 1960s the U.S. deployed a force of forty-one SSBNs each carrying sixteen Polaris missiles, or a total force of 656 SLBMs. These early SLBMs had a relatively short range and therefore the submarines had to "patrol" near Soviet shores. In the 1970s the U.S. developed a longer-range (4000 miles) Poseidon C-3 missile in advanced *Lafayette, Madison* and *Franklin* SSBNs. The longer range gave the SSBNs more ocean in which to hide and lengthened the time each boat could be on patrol. Currently the U.S. deploys fourteen SSBNs carrying 224 Poseidon C-3 missiles. Each of these missiles carrys ten to fourteen MIRVed warheads.

Trident I C-4.   The Trident submarine program is designed to eventually replace earlier SSBNs, each with their sixteen SLBM launch tubes, with the newer, quieter, *Ohio* class SSBNs, each with twenty-four launch tubes. At the same time a longer-range (5000 miles) missile, the Trident I C-4, is replacing the Poseidon C-3. Currently the Navy has twelve older SSBNs retrofitted to carry 192 Trident C-4 missiles. More importantly, the Navy now has nine *Ohio*-class "Trident" submarines in the water, eight of which are each carrying twenty-four missiles, a total of 192 Trident C-4s each with MIRVed warheads.

Trident II D-5.   Generally SLBMs are not as accurate as land-based missiles and the warheads they carry are much smaller. (An SLBM warhead may have a yield of 40 to 50 Kilotons compared to a yield of 335 Kilotons for the Minuteman III warhead and 1000 Kilotons for the MX warhead.) This means that SLBMs generally lack "hard target-kill capability"—the ability to put at risk enemy missile silos. However, technological advances on the Trident II D-5 missile are designed to give that missile sufficient accuracy and yield to destroy hardened targets. Thus the Trident II D-5, like the MX, will give the U.S. some limited hard target-kill capability.

STAR WARS—THE STRATEGIC DEFENSE INITIATIVE

For over forty years, since the terrible nuclear blast of Hiroshima and Nagasaki, in 1945, the world has avoided nuclear war. Peace has been maintained by deterrence—by the threat of devastating nuclear attacks which would be launched in retaliation to an enemy first strike. While this balance of terror has kept the peace, many scholars, soldiers, and citizens have tried to think of a better way of avoiding nuclear war. Instead of deterring war through fear of retaliation, perhaps we should seek a technological defense against nuclear missiles, one that will eventually render them "impotent and obsolete."

According to President Reagan,

> Our nuclear retaliating forces have deterred war for forty years. The fact is, however, that we have no defense against nuclear ballistic missile attack . . . In the event that deterrence failed, a president's only recourse would be to surrender or to retaliate. Nuclear retaliation whether massive or limited, would result in the loss of millions of lives. . . .
>
> If we apply our great scientific and engineering talent to the problem of defending against ballistic missiles, there is a very real possibility that future presidents will be able to deter war by means other than threatening devastation to any aggressor—and by a means which threatens no one. . . .
>
> Emerging technologies offer the possibilities of non-nuclear options for destroying missiles and the nuclear warheads they carry in all phases of their flight. New technologies may be able to permit a layered defense by providing: sensors for identifying and tracking missiles and nuclear warheads; advanced ground and spaceborne intercepters and direct energy weapons to destroy both missiles and nuclear warheads; advanced ground and spaceborne intercepters and directed energy weapons to destroy missiles and nuclear warheads; and the technology to permit the command control and communication necessary to operate a layered defense. . . .[2]

"Star Wars."   The Strategic Defense Initiative (SDI) is a research program designed to explore means of destroying enemy nuclear missiles in space before they can reach their targets. Following the President's initial announcement of SDI in March 1983, the press quickly labeled the effort "Star Wars." At present, SDI is only a research program. The Soviets have two small ABM (antiballistic missile) systems permitted by SALT I. But at present neither side can stop any significant portion of the other side's missiles once they have been fired. For many years to come, deterrence will continue to rest upon fear of retaliation.

Ballistic Missile Defenses.   As a broad research program, the SDI is not yet based on any single type of ballistic missile defense. A *boost phase defense*

---

[2]President Ronald Reagan, *The President's Strategic Defense Initiative*, The White House, January 3, 1985.

might attempt to destroy enemy missiles shortly after they are launched. Sophisticated battle management satellites might keep watch over known Soviet missile fields. Antimissiles might be placed in orbit over Soviet missiles, ready to destroy these missiles during their initial boost phase. Or lasers or particle beams might be directed to mirrors orbiting over Soviet missile fields and bounced toward Soviet missiles in flight. If Soviet missiles escape these early boost phase defenses, perhaps *a layered defense* in space might be constructed in an effort to destroy missiles and warheads while they are traveling toward the United States. Defensive missiles or beams would have to locate, identify, track, and destroy perhaps thousands of separate missiles and warheads. Finally, those enemy warheads which survive a layer defense in space might be attacked in the *terminal phase* of their flight. Antiballistic missile defense might be set up specifically to defend expected targets, for example, the Capitol and command centers, or our own offensive missile sites. (Currently the Soviet Union has one ABM system defending Moscow and one defending their offensive ICBM fields; the U.S. has no operating ABM systems.)

Technologies. Several different technologies are currently being explored for ballistic missile defenses. (1) *Conventional ABM* technologies featuring rocketpowered missile intercepters have been available for years; conceivably this "off-the-shelf" technology could be placed in space orbit over Soviet ICBM fields, as well as based on the ground to protect ICBM sites and command centers. (2) In the past, ABMs have contained conventional explosives and were guided by radar and heat sensors. Today research is proceeding on *electromagnetic rail guns,* which would fling nonexplosive projectives ("smart rocks")—later advanced versions have been named "brilliant pebbles" along a magnetic beam in space. (3) *Chemical lasers* get their energy from combustion of fuels; this energy can be concentrated in beams which may destroy enemy missiles. Since chemical lasers can be distorted by the atmosphere, these weapons would also have to be placed in space. Perhaps "fighting mirrors" could be located in space over the Soviet Union, prepared to reflect laser beams generated by a chemical laser elsewhere in space. (4) However, more powerful *X-ray lasers* might be generated from the ground, somewhere in the United States, and projected by space-based mirrors toward Soviet missile sites. X-ray lasers are untroubled by atmospheric conditions. But X-ray lasers require an intense power source—perhaps an underground nuclear device.

Battle Management. SDI requires the development of the most sophisticated and reliable computers ever developed. "Star Wars" weapons must be preprogrammed to fire at Soviet offensive missiles within seconds of their launch. Sophisticated battle management computations must be made—detecting, tracking, aiming, firing, assessing damage, coordinating firings, distinguishing decoys, and so on—for a giant space battle that would last less than thirty minutes. Reliable computer programs must be written for large and complex tasks.

Soviet Reaction.   In addition to proving its feasibility, any ballistic missile defense technology must meet two important strategic tests in order to be effective. First, it must be cost-effective at the margin: it must be cheaper for the United States to add additional defenses than for the Soviet Union to add additional offensive missiles to overcome these defenses. A ballistic missile defense which is not cost-effective will simply encourage the Soviet Union to add additional offensive weapons. Secondly, it must be survivable itself and able to overcome Soviet countermeasures. This concern may give rise to a preference for ground-based lasers located in the United States over space-based lasers vulnerable to Soviet attack. Soviet ASAT (antisatellite) technology has already progressed for many years. Only recently has the United States begun ASAT research. Soviet ASAT capability is virtually indistinguishable from a capability to attack our proposed orbiting ballistic missile defenses.

Confusion Over Goals.   Currently there is some confusion about the goals of SDI. Is the goal to create an impenetrable shield that will protect not only the population of the United States but the population of our European allies as well? Will this shield allow us to dismantle our retaliatory nuclear forces because deterrence will no longer be necessary? Or is the goal of SDI simply to enhance deterrence by protecting our second-strike forces against a surprise disarming strike by the Soviets? If a completely impenetrable shield is not possible, will we not be required to keep some retaliatory forces as a deterrent? Will SDI reduce reliance on retaliation and allow some reduction in offensive weapons? If we eventually developed an effective defense against ballistic missiles, would we share this technology with the Soviets in order to calm their fears about a nuclear attack from a defended United States? It is important to remember that SDI is now only a research program; these questions will confront policy makers in the twenty-first century.

Opposition.   Opponents of President Reagan's Strategic Defense Initiative have made several important arguments:

1. U.S. efforts to defend itself against ICBMs may prompt the Soviets to build more and better ICBMs. SDI may simply stimulate an arms race. Even supporters of SDI acknowledge that missile defenses must be survivable, or else the Soviets

will simply attack the defense before launching their ICBMs. Supporters of SDI also acknowledge that defenses must be cheaper to build than ICBMs, or else the Soviets will simply build more ICBMs than we can build defenses.

2. The SDI might be interpreted by the Soviets as an effort by the U.S. to gain a "first-strike" capability—the ability to launch a nuclear attack against the USSR and then defend ourselves against their weakened retaliatory response. This is the official line taken by the Soviets in objecting to "Star Wars." They claim we are seeking to "militarize space" in an effort to gain an advantage over them.

3. SDI might destabilize the balance of terror currently existing between the U.S. and the USSR. If the U.S. could defend itself against ICBMs and the Soviet Union could not, the U.S. could launch an attack without fear of retaliation. This is the major argument advanced against SDI by the Soviets.

4. SDI is technologically infeasible; efforts to build missile defenses will waste tens of billions of dollars. A complete protective "superdome" over the United States and its allies is impossible. Even a few nuclear weapons can cause millions of deaths.

5. SDI threatens to violate the SALT I Treaty prohibiting anti-ballistic missiles. Moreover, the SDI program may stand in the way of future agreements with the Soviet Union for promoting or reducing nuclear weapons. The Soviets have stated repeatedly that the U.S. must give up its SDI before any agreement on nuclear arms can be reached.

Support.   In contrast, supporters of the strategic defensive initiative argue that:

1. Technological advances offer the promise of maintaining peace by means of space defense, rather than by the threat of nuclear retaliation. SDI is only a research program. Decisions about actually deploying a ballistic missile defense are many years in the future.

2. A ballistic missile defense is preferable to threats of retaliation for maintaining peace. What if deterrence fails someday? What if an irrational leader ignores our threat of retaliation and proceeds to attack the United States regardless of the consequences? A ballistic missile defense would provide the president and the nation with a means of defending ourselves in an actual attack.

3. A ballistic missile defense does not threaten millions of lives in the fashion of our current deterrent strategy. Defensive weapons would be nonnuclear; they would be targeted on missiles and warheads, not cities. A defensive strategy is morally preferable to threatening millions of lives.

4. A ballistic missile defense can offset the Soviet superiority in numbers and size of missiles. An effective missile defense may someday convince them that continuing increases in numbers of ICBMs are pointless. Indeed, the Soviets may be pressured to make reductions in their ICBMs in exchange for limiting the U.S. "Star Wars" program.

5. A ballistic missile defense, when employed in conjunction with our retaliatory forces, would improve deterrence. Any Soviet plans for a first strike against our retaliatory forces would be frustrated by the uncertainties created by our new defenses. Soviet generals could not guarantee that all of our retaliatory forces would be destroyed in a surprise attack.

ARMS LIMITATION GAMES

Overview. The United States and the Soviet Union have engaged in negotiations over strategic arms for many years. These negotiations began in 1970 under President Richard Nixon and his national security advisor Henry Kissinger and were originally labeled the Strategic Arms Limitation Talks (SALT). These talks produced the SALT I agreement in 1972, which was ratified by the U.S. Senate. Later, under President Jimmy Carter, they produced the SALT II agreement of 1979, which was *not* ratified by the U.S. Senate. President Reagan described SALT II as a "flawed" agreement, but he pledged that the U.S. would continue to honor its terms as long as the Soviets did so. Reagan called for talks aimed at arms "reduction" rather than "limitation," and renamed the talks Strategic Arms Reduction Talks or START. In 1983 the Soviets walked out of these talks, protesting NATO's decision to deploy U.S. medium-range missiles in Europe to counter an earlier Soviet deployment of European missiles. However, the Soviet walkout failed to intimidate the Western European nations; a heavy-handed Soviet "nuclear freeze" offensive failed; Reagan was reelected; and the "Star Wars" ballistic missile defense program was announced. In early 1985 the Soviets agreed to return to the bargaining table for new talks on nuclear and space arms at Geneva, Switzerland. These negotiations led to the Intermediate-range Nuclear Force (INF) Treaty in 1987 that eliminated an entire class of intermediate-range nuclear missiles threatening Europe. General agreement on a START Treaty, reducing the strategic nuclear weapons of both sides, was announced in 1990 by President George Bush and President Mikhail Gorbachev at a Washington summit meeting.

SALT I. SALT I in 1972 was a milestone in that it marked the first effort by the superpowers to limit strategic weapons. SALT I consisted of a formal treaty halting further development of anti-ballistic missile systems (ABMs), and an executive agreement placing numerical limits on offensive missiles. The ABM treaty limited each side to one ABM site for defense of its national capital and one ABM site for defense of an offensive ICBM field. The total number of ABMs permitted was 200 for each side, 100 at each location. (The USSR maintains both of its ABM sites; the United States had one site at the Grand Forks, North Dakota, Minuteman Field, which was deactivated in 1975.) Under the offensive arms agreement, each side was frozen at the total number of offensive missiles completed or under construction. The Soviet Union was permitted 1618 land-based missiles. The United States was permitted to maintain 1054 land-based missiles. Both sides were limited to the missile-carrying submarines operational or under construction at the time of the agreement; this also allowed the Soviets to gain an edge on the total number of SLBMs. Each nation agreed not to interfere in the electronic and satellite intelligence-gathering activities of the other nation.

Experience with SALT I.   Soviet weapons development after SALT I continued at a rapid pace and soon began to threaten U.S. second-strike capability. SALT I did *not* limit MIRVs, nor the size or accuracy of missiles, nor the number of manned bombers. In all these areas, the Soviets made impressive gains. The Soviets deployed the world's largest missile, the SS-18, which carries *ten* one-megaton weapons. The Soviets built over 300 of these giant missiles—enough to carry over 3000 one-megaton warheads. The Soviets acquired the capability of destroying our ICBM forces using only their new SS-18s, while keeping the bulk of their ICBM and SLBM forces in reserve for threatened use against American cities if the United States attempted to retaliate. Finally, the Soviets deployed new supersonic manned bombers, the Backfire and Blackjack, which are capable of penetrating weak U.S. air defenses and hitting any remaining targets.

SALT II.   The SALT II agreement in 1979 was a complex one. Its major provisions included:

1. An overall limit on the number of strategic nuclear delivery vehicles (ICBMs, SLBMs, manned bombers) at 2250.
2. An overall limit on the total number of MIRVed ballistic missiles, ICBMs, and SLBMs and strategic bombers with long-range Cruise missiles.
3. A ban on the construction of *heavy* ICBMs. (This was a controversial item because the USSR already had 314 heavy ICBMs (the SS-18) while the United States had none. The treaty prevents the United States from building a heavy missile and recognizes the USSR monopoly in this weapon.)
4. A ban on the testing or deployment of new types of ICBMs, with the exception of one new type of ICBM for each side.
5. A limit of ten MIRVed warheads on a single ICBM; a limit of fourteen MIRVed warheads on a single SLBM; and a limit of twenty Cruise missiles on a single bomber. (These limits represented current technology; they did not require changes in programs of either side.)
6. A ban on the rapid reload of ICBM launchers. (This affected the USSR program because only Soviet ICBMs can refire. Soviet reload missiles must be kept away from launch sites.)
7. An agreement by both sides not to interfere with national technical means (NTM) of verification of the provisions of the treaty. Neither side will interfere with photo-reconnaissance satellites or use deliberate concealment measures which impede verification. Electronic signals from test missiles, known as telemetry, cannot be encoded.

The Failure of SALT II.   Initially American leaders hoped that SALT would modify Soviet behavior and improve the political relationship between the United States and the USSR, a relationship commonly called *détente.* But Soviet expansionism was unchecked by the SALT agreements and SALT II was officially withdrawn from the U.S. Senate by President Carter in response to the Soviet invasion of Afghanistan. But objections were also raised to various strategic arrangements in SALT II. The treaty recognized the Soviet monopoly in "heavy" missiles (SS-18s). The treaty did not require the dismantling of this destabilizing Soviet ICBM force. With its SS-18s, the Soviets continue to have a first-strike capability against our aging Minuteman ICBM force. SALT II did not deal directly with warheads; both sides continued to maintain over 12,000 strategic warheads each. SALT II did not bring about any reductions in nuclear forces nor slow the building of new strategic weapons on either side.

A New START.   Early in his administration President Reagan called for "a substantial reduction in nuclear arms that would result in levels that are equal and verifiable."[3] The Reagan administration rejected the approach represented in earlier SALT negotiations that only future growth in nuclear arms be "limited." Instead, the goal in U.S. policy became "reductions" in nuclear arms. To symbolize this change, arms negotiations were relabeled START (Strategic Arms Reduction Talks). Moreover, President Reagan insisted that any new agreement must result in equal levels of nuclear arms, even if this meant the Soviets would have to destroy more of their larger arsenal to reach equality. Finally, Reagan insisted on stringent verification measures, including onsite inspections.

The U.S. Position.   The U.S. position in the START negotiations was based on the premise that the Soviet Union had acquired "a definite margin of superiority—enough so that there is risk."[4] If the U.S. and Soviet arsenals were frozen at current levels, not only would the United States be endangered, but also the prospects for negotiated reductions would disappear. With the United States frozen in a position of inferiority, there would be no incentive for the Soviets to negotiate reductions. Indeed, the Soviets would have no incentive to reduce their current arsenal unless convinced that the United States would rebuild its defenses to match the Soviet level. This meant that the success of the START negotiations depended on convincing the Soviets that the United States was really prepared to modernize its own forces if no agreement was reached. Thus under President Reagan, U.S. strategic force modernization efforts—the MX, Trident, B-1, and cruise weapons—were defended as a means of forcing the Soviets to agree to arms reductions.

The Soviet Position.   In the arms talks the Soviets sought to count British and French nuclear missiles and aircraft against any limits placed on the U.S. side. They also sought to count all U.S. nuclear forces located in Europe,

---

[3]Text of the address of President Ronald Reagan on U.S. foreign policy, 18 November 1981.

[4]President Ronald Reagan, March 31, 1982, reported in *Congressional Quarterly Weekly Report,* April 3, 1982, p. 725.

including short- and medium-range battlefield nuclear weapons and all European-based U.S. aircraft, against any limits on U.S. "strategic" weapons. In short, the Soviets wanted to be equal or superior to any *combination* of forces that could be arrayed against them anywhere in the world. According to the Soviets, their 1983 walkout of the START talks was a protest against NATO's decision to carry out the deployment of U.S. medium-range missiles in Europe. The original NATO decision regarding U.S. ground-launched Cruise and Pershing II missiles in Europe had been made in 1979 in response to the earlier deployment of Soviet mobile, multiwarhead, medium-range, SS-20 missiles targeted on the Western European nations. NATO had postponed the actual deployment of U.S. missiles in the hope that the Soviets would agree instead to withdraw their SS-20s.

Changes in the Soviet Position.   What brought the Soviets back to the negotiating table in 1985? The walkout failed to intimidate Western European governments; despite Soviet threats these governments went forward with the deployment of U.S. medium-range missiles. A Soviet "peace" offensive resulted in noisy demonstrations in European capitals, but failed to break up the NATO alliance. The reelection of Ronald Reagan promised a continuation of the U.S. defense modernization program. Finally, the president's announcement that the U.S. intended to begin a program of research on advanced ballistic missile defenses—the program labeled "Star Wars" by the press and the Soviets—seemed to motivate the Kremlin leaders to reopen talks. Although the Soviets publicly ridiculed the prospect of an effective ballistic missile defense and claimed to be able to defeat it with more and better ICBMs, the prospect of a race against the United States in advanced technology weapons appeared to worry them.

The Geneva Talks.   The United States and the Soviet Union agreed in the Geneva Talks to discuss three broad topics:

1. Strategic nuclear arms, including ICBMs, SLBMs, and long-range aircraft.
2. Intermediate nuclear forces in Europe, including U.S. ground-launched Cruise and Pershing II missiles and Soviet SS-20s.
3. Space arms, including ground-based and space-based ballistic missile defenses.

Initially the Soviets insisted that all three of these topics had to be considered "in their interrelatedness," implying that they would not agree to any reductions in nuclear weapons unless the U.S. gave up its "Star Wars" research on ballistic missile defense. A meeting at Reykjavik, Iceland, between President Reagan and President Gorbachev broke up over the Soviet leader's insistence that no agreement could be reached until the U.S. ended its SDI program. But in 1987 the Soviet position softened and a separate agreement was reached on intermediate nuclear forces in Europe.

INF Treaty. The Intermediate-range Nuclear Force (INF) Treaty marked a major breakthrough in relations between the superpowers. It was the first agreement that actually resulted in a reduction of existing nuclear weapons. It eliminated an entire class of nuclear missiles—those with intermediated range, between 300 and 3,800 miles. It was also the first treaty that resulted in equal levels (zero) of arms for the United States and the USSR. To reach equality, the Soviets were required to destroy more missiles and warheads than the United States. Finally the INF Treaty was the first treaty to provide for verification by onsite inspection. The INF Treaty represented a personal triumph for President Reagan and a vindication of his approach to arms control. The proportion of each side's nuclear weapons covered by the INF was small, but the treaty established the principals for future arms control agreements—reductions, equality, verification.

Agreement on START. The long-awaited agreement on long-range strategic nuclear weapons was formally announced at a Washington summit meeting in 1990 of presidents George Bush and Mikhail Gorbachev. While details of the Treaty remained to be finalized, the "agreed major provisions" included the following:

> The total number of deployed strategic nuclear delivery systems (ICBMs, SLBMs and manned bombers) will be reduced to no more than 1600, a 30 percent reduction from the SALT II level.
>
> The Soviet Union will reduce by one half its force of heavy SS-18 ICBMs (leaving 154), and carry no more than ten warheads on each of them.
>
> The total number of strategic nuclear warheads will be reduced to no more than 6,000, a nearly 50 percent reduction.
>
> No more than 1100 warheads will be carried on manned bombers and no more than 1100 will be carried by mobile ICBMs.
>
> The U.S. will be permitted 150 long-range bombers, each with no more than twenty ALCMs; the Soviet Union may have 210 long-range bombers each with no more than twelve ALCMs.
>
> Verification will include onsite and short-notice inspections, as well as "national technical means" (satellite surveillance).

The START agreement not only reduces the total numbers of nuclear warheads and launch vehicles, but more importantly reduces the plausibility of a surprise nuclear first strike. Its most crucial provision is the reduction of half of the Soviet's SS-18 hard target-kill weapons. Of course, the complete elimination of all first-strike missiles (including the fifty U.S. MXs) would provide even greater stability. But the USSR was unwilling to agree to a total elimination of their SS-18 force. Nonetheless, the Soviet dismantlement of half of this force is a significant achievement in arms control. Both sides can continue "modernization" of their missile forces, except that no new types of "heavy" ICBMs can be developed, nor can any ICBMs that carry more than ten warheads. It is expected that the Soviet Union will continue to place ICBMs on mobile launchers, as the U.S. may do if Congress approves either the rail-based MX or the ground-mobile Midgetman. While air-launched cruise missiles (ALCMs) are covered by the treaty, sea-launched cruise missiles (SLCMs) remain outside of the treaty's limits, except that each side agrees to "declare" its planned deployments. SLCMs aboard ships and submarines are very difficult to verify, and there is no easy way to determine if an SLCM has a nuclear or a conventional warhead. Finally, it is important to note that the Soviets gave up on their insistence that the U.S. halt its "Star Wars" research as a condition for signing the START treaty.

DEFENDING WESTERN EUROPE

The preservation of democracy in Western Europe has been the centerpiece of U.S. foreign and military policy for most of the twentieth century. The United States fought in two world wars and suffered one-quarter million battle deaths to preserve democracy in Europe. Today the combined economic output of the Western European nations exceeds the economic output of the Soviet Union. Nowhere in the world does the United States have a greater stake in the preservation of national independence and democratic government than in Western Europe.

Origins of NATO. In response to aggressive Soviet moves in Europe after World War II, the United States, Canada, Belgium, Britain, Denmark, France, Iceland, Italy, Luxembourg, the Netherlands, Norway, and Portugal joined in the North Atlantic Treaty Organization (NATO). Each nation pledged that "an armed attack against one . . . shall be considered an attack against them all." Greece and Turkey joined in 1952 and West Germany in 1955. More importantly, to give this pledge credibility, a joint NATO military command was established with a U.S. commanding officer (the first was General of the Army Dwight D. Eisenhower) to command the defenses of Western Europe. After the formation of NATO, the Soviets made no further advances in Western Europe. The Soviets themselves, in response to NATO, drew up a comparable treaty among their own Eastern European satellite nations—the "Warsaw Pact."

Developing NATO Strategies. NATO is an international organization whose members are democracies. The fundamental difficulty in such an organization is finding agreement among the fifteen member nations on a common strategy. U.S. presidents continually assured Western Europeans that a Soviet attack on them would be regarded as an attack on the United States itself. But when the Soviet Union acquired the ability to strike the U.S. homeland with nuclear weapons, skepticism in Western Europe about the U.S. commitment grew. In 1966, France withdrew from the NATO military command (although not the NATO treaty) in order to develop its own independent nuclear war capability. The overwhelming Soviet advantage in conventional armies had forced NATO to introduce tactical nuclear weapons in 1957. These nuclear weapons were designed for battlefield use; their purpose was to offset huge Soviet imbalances in tanks, artillery, and infantry. It was hoped that the threat of tactical nuclear weapons would help dissuade the Soviets from an attack on Western Europe. Tactical nuclear weapons are used *primarily* as psychological deterrents. However, tactical nuclear warfare is not unthinkable. It is a more likely possibility than strategic nuclear warfare.

European Concerns.   The potential destructiveness of a war in Western Europe, particularly a war involving tactical nuclear weapons, created serious political and strategic problems in Western European capitals. Resisting Soviet aggression with nuclear weapons would cause great destruction and loss of life in Europe. A limited war on European territory would not be "limited" for most Europeans; it would probably result in massive numbers of civilian casualties. Neutralist and leftist parties argued that it would be better to submit to Soviet demands, to avoid provoking the Soviets in any way, and to disarm and disband NATO, than to risk the damages of war. But, the elected leadership of the Western European democracies stood firm in their commitment to resist Soviet intimidation.

Flexible Response and First Use.   Confronted with overwhelming Soviet and Warsaw Pact superiority in conventional forces—troops, tanks, armored personnel carriers, artillery, and combat aircraft (see Table 8–2)—NATO was forced to rely on the threat of nuclear weapons to deter Soviet aggression. A "flexible response" strategy envisioned that NATO's conventional forces would try to halt an initial Soviet thrust until reserves from the United States and other European nations could be brought into the battle. But if Soviet forces overran NATO defenses, the NATO command would be authorized to use battlefield nuclear weapons against Soviet armored columns and troop concentrations. Note that this strategy implies NATO's "first use" of *nuclear* weapons against Soviet *conventional* weapons.

Intermediate-Range Nuclear Forces.   The Soviets deployed over 300 intermediate-range nuclear missiles in the late 1970s (notably their mobile multi-warhead SS-20s) aimed at the cities of Western Europe. The implied threat was that any attempt to resist Soviet aggression militarily would result in the massive destruction of European cities. But the NATO nations responded by deploying new U.S. Pershing II and ground-launched cruise missiles in Europe to neutralize the Soviet threat. At the same time NATO offered the Soviets the "zero option"—NATO would cancel deployment of

TABLE 8-2   The United States and the Soviet Union Balance of Conventional Forces

	U.S.	USSR
Armed Forces Personnel	2.1 million	4.3 million
Army		
Divisions	16 full	216[a]
	2 light	
Tanks	15,992	53,300
Artillery and Missiles	5,397	31,500
Helicopters	8,376	4,500
Marines		
Divisions	3	[b]
Aircraft	174	
Tanks	716	
Air Force		
Aircraft	3,577	4,595
Air Defense		
Aircraft	[c]	2,225
SAM	[c]	8,500
Navy		
Major Combat Surface Ships	229	264
Attack Submarines	96	280
Aircraft Carriers	14	4
Aircraft	1,579	739

[a]At full strength, Soviet combat divisions include about 8,000 men, compared to 14,000-16,000 men in U.S. combat divisions.

[b]U.S.S.R. has only small "Naval Infantry" units assigned to fleets.

[c]U.S. has no separate Air Defense Force. U.S. SAM included in Army Artillery.

Source: International Institute for Strategic Studies, *The Military Balance 1989–1990* (London: Institute for Strategic Studies, 1990).

these missiles if the Soviets would withdraw their SS-20s. Initially the Soviets doubted NATO's resolve and launched their "nuclear freeze" movements in Europe to prevent the deployment of new American missiles. They walked out of arms negotiations in 1983 protesting the missile deployment, but came back to the bargaining table when confronted with NATO's firm stance. In 1987 the INF Treaty incorporated the zero option—the elimination of all intermediate nuclear weapons on both sides. Thus, NATO's resolve succeeded in bringing about the world's first arms reduction treaty.

THE FUTURE OF NATO

The Soviet Union and its Warsaw Pact armies vastly outnumbered the U.S. and NATO forces in Europe in conventional troops, tanks, artillery, and aircraft. Warsaw Pact forces outnumbered NATO 3 to 1 in tanks, 4 to 1 in artillery, 2 to 1 in combat aircraft, and 3 to 2 in total troop strength. The Soviet

Union itself maintains a total armed force of 4.3 million persons, with a large arsenal of tanks, artillery, and surface-to-air missiles. The U.S. maintains a total armed force of 2.1 million, with less than one-third the arsenal of tanks, artillery, and other ground combat weapons (see Table 8–2). Achieving reductions and equality in *conventional* forces is an even more complex and difficult task than doing so in *nuclear* force.

The Collapse of Communism in Eastern Europe.   The dramatic collapse of the communist governments of Eastern Europe in 1989—Poland, Hungary, Romania, Bulgaria, and East Germany—vastly reduces the threat of a Soviet military attack in Western Europe. While large Soviet troop concentrations remain in Europe, particularly in East Germany, their ability to launch an attack against the West is undermined by the new independence of their Warsaw Pact allies.

The dismantling of communist governments in Eastern Europe came about as a direct result of President Michail Gorbachev's decision to renounce the use of Soviet military force to keep these communist governments in power. For over forty years, the communist governments of Eastern Europe were kept in power by Soviet tanks; bloody Soviet military operations put down civilian uprisings in Hungary in 1956 and Czechoslovakia in 1968. The threat of Soviet military intervention crushed the Solidarity movement in Poland in 1981, yet that same movement became the government of Poland in 1989. Any effort today by a Soviet leader to reimpose communist governments on Eastern European nations by military force would probably result in widespread bloodshed.

Conventional Force Reductions.   In an important speech at the United Nations in December 1988, President Gorbachev announced that the Soviet Union would reduce its total troop strength by 500,000 and remove 50,000 troops and 5,000 tanks stationed in Eastern Europe. These are significant reductions that reduce the plausibility of a "short-warning" Soviet attack on Western Europe. These pledges were made without any demand for matching cuts by the U.S. or NATO, suggesting that Gorbachev recognized the existing heavy military imbalance on the Soviet side. At the same time Gorbachev put forward broad proposals for further *mutual* reductions in conventional forces in Europe. President George Bush later responded with a plan to reduce U.S. and Soviet troops stationed in central Europe to 195,000 on each side. Such a reduction would mean the withdrawal of nearly half of the Soviet troops stationed in Germany. Soviet troops in Poland, Czechoslovakia, and Hungary may also be withdrawn at the request of those governments.

Germany United.   The collapse of the Berlin Wall in 1989 and the formal unification of Germany in 1990 rearranged the balance of military power in central Europe. West Germany, with 61 million people, is economically strong. Uniting with 17 million less prosperous people in East Germany is causing temporary economic dislocations; but over the long run a united Germany is likely to become the strongest power in Europe. Germany remains a member of NATO, although by agreement with the Soviet Union NATO troops will not enter Eastern Germany. Soviet troops, numbering about 350,000 remain in East Germany; their future is to be decided in conventional force reduction talks and direct negotiations between Germany and the USSR. The once powerful Warsaw Pact forces of East Germany are being absorbed into the army of united Germany. But Germany has reached agreement with the Soviet Union on overall limits on German military forces.

Diminishing Soviet Threat.   Thus, the Soviet military threat to Western Europe has been diminished through:

1.   significant reductions in Soviet troops and tanks available for a short-warning attack.
2.   political realignments of the Warsaw Pact nations that undermine Soviet reliance on their former allies.
3.   Soviet agreement to withdraw troops from Poland, Hungary and Czechoslovakia, and pledge to negotiate the fate of 350,000 Soviet troops remaining in East Germany.

Sound defense policy must also consider the possible "reversibility" of these changes. President Gorbachev could be replaced and traditional Soviet military doctrines reimposed. If the United States and its NATO allies reduce their own military forces at a disproportionate rate, the resulting imbalance might tempt a hardline Soviet regime to reassert its military power in Europe again by simply moving its forces westward from the Russian border.

RESTRUCTURING THE U.S. MILITARY

The collapse of communist governments in Eastern Europe and the new willingness of the Soviet Union to consider conventional force reductions in Europe require a restructuring of U.S. defense policy. The Soviet Union continues to maintain the world's most powerful military forces, but political liberalization in that nation appears to reduce the threat of a direct military confrontation with the West. It is prudent to remind ourselves that changes in the Soviet Union are not "irreversible"; ten years of political and economic liberalization in China were reversed in a single night in Tiananmen Square. Yet as the Soviet threat to Western Europe diminishes, the U.S. must revise its own strategies and force levels.

European Forces.   For over four decades U.S. military forces and strategies were designed primarily to confront the large heavy armor and artillery forces of the Soviet Union on the European battleground. This mission required the development of heavy and technologically sophisticated armored weapons, such as the 60-ton M-1 Abrams tanks and the armored AH-64 Apache helicopters. The U.S. Army committed ten of its sixteen heavy divisions to NATO, with four of these divisions stationed in Europe and six in the United States with pre-positioned weapons and supplies in Europe. The Air Force also dedicated over half of its conventional forces to the defense of Western Europe. But a reduced U.S. military role in Europe suggests that these heavy forces can be reduced over time. U.S. military forces are far more likely to be called upon to fight in smaller conflicts in distant parts of the world.

Regional Forces.   The United States has found it necessary to employ military force in many regional conflicts over the years. The largest of these conflicts, of course, were the Korean War (1950–53) with 38,000 U.S. battle deaths and the Vietnam war (1965–73) with 48,000 battle deaths. But U.S. forces have also been used in the Dominican Republic (1965), the Mayaquez incident in Cambodia (1975), Lebanon (1982), Grenada (1982), Libya (1984), the Persian Gulf (1987), and Panama (1989). As frequent and as bloody as these regional conflicts have been, U.S. defense policy has always placed primary emphasis on deterring a Soviet nuclear strike and countering a massive Soviet conventional invasion of Europe. But now planning for regional conflicts may become the primary task of the U.S. military. Regional conflicts generally require highly mobile, light forces capable of being transported rapidly to any part of the world. While these forces may not directly confront Soviet armies, the military forces of various less-developed nations are increasingly deploying very sophisticated weapons.

U.S. Navy.   Traditionally the principal responsibility for extending U.S. military power throughout the world rested with the U.S. Navy. The Navy's principal weapon is the carrier battle group—one or more large aircraft carriers, each deploying seventy-five to ninety-five combat aircraft, with cruisers, destroyers, and attack submarines providing defense. The U.S. Marine Corps specializes in amphibious operations—moving conventional troops, tanks, and artillery from ships to shore to capture and secure territory. U.S. Navy and Marine forces now include fourteen aircraft carriers, over 1700 combat aircraft, and three marine divisions with 195,000 troops. These forces were designed more for regional conflict than for the defense of Western Europe; the reduced Soviet threat in Europe does not significantly affect the continuing need for these forces.

234 *Defense Policy*

U.S. Army and Air Force. It is likely that U.S. Army and Air Force planning will increasingly emphasize quick reaction to regional conflict around the world. For the Army this would mean increased emphasis on airborne and air-mobile forces and light divisions; for the Air Force it would mean transporting Army troops quickly anywhere in the world and providing close ground support and air superiority over distant battlefields.

Lessons from Desert Storm The spectacular success of U.S. military operations in the Persian Gulf war reaffirmed the value of high quality air, land, and sea forces capable of fighting anywhere in the world and armed with the most modern weaponry. Decisive military victory in the Gulf buried the "Vietnam syndrome"—national self-doubt about the role and effectiveness of our military forces. Advanced high-tech weapons proved their worth on the battlefield, spared American lives, and silenced many critics of expensive weapons programs. The Patriot anti-ballistic-missile demonstrated that incoming missiles could be intercepted and destroyed, thus inspiring the national effort to develop and deploy ABM's. Stealth technology also proved its worth early in the air war, destroying SAM-defended Iraqi nuclear and chemical facilities. Superiority in the air and smart bombs and missiles destroyed enemy units on the ground at low casualty rates. The Army's AirLand Battle doctrine, emphasizing highly mobile, heavy firepower, coordinated air and ground operations and multiple points of attack demonstrated its effectiveness. Superiority in intelligence, training, and morale proved their value against a very large enemy army. But the Gulf war also exposed weaknesses in rapid airlift and sealift capabilities; the U.S. may not always have a prolonged period to build up its forces before a conflict breaks out. Above all, the nation's political leadership demonstrated that it had learned its lesson: once the fateful decision to use force is made, military actions should be overwhelming, swift, and decisive.

Special Operations Forces. Guerilla wars will continue. Indeed, as direct U.S.-Soviet military confrontation diminishes, the number of indirect clashes through Third-World "proxies" may increase. The Soviets have continued to provide advanced military equipment training, "advisors," and logistics to Vietnam, Cambodia, Cuba, Nicaragua, Angola, Ethiopia, Somalia, Mozambique, Syria, Libya, Iraq, and South Yemen.[5] Traditionally the U.S. military overlooked guerilla warfare, or "low-intensity conflict," in favor of conventional warfare. Special operations forces (SOF) today number less than 2 percent of U.S. military forces. Yet it is likely that in the future SOF will be required to protect U.S. interests in a wide variety of situations, from guerilla wars to terrorist activity.

[5]See International Institute for Strategic Studies, *The Military Balance 1989–1990* (London: Brassy's 1989), p. 42.

EVALUATION: THE PRICE OF PEACE

The United States' investment in national defense over the past half-century succeeded in its most vital objective—deterring nuclear war. It also maintained the peace and security of Western Europe, which had experienced two world wars in the first half of the Twentieth Century. The decline in American military strength following the Vietnam War in the 1970s led directly to the expansion of Marxist military regimes throughout the world—not only in Vietnam, Laos, and Cambodia, but also in Angola, Ethiopia, Mozambique, Somalia, and South Yemen, and in Cuba, Nicaragua, Grenada. In contrast, the restoration of U.S. military strength in the 1980s encouraged the Soviet Union to seek more constructive relations with the West, provided the necessary conditions for genuine arms reduction negotiations, and gave encouragement to democratic forces throughout the world. U.S. military intervention in Grenada in 1984 and Panama in 1990 not only restored democratic governments in those nations but also strengthened democratic resolve throughout Latin America.

Lessening Threats to National Security.   Today democratic forces in the world are in the ascendancy. The Berlin Wall has collapsed and the nations of Eastern Europe have thrown out their communist rulers. Soviet President Gorbachev's renunciation of the use of military force to maintain communist governments led directly and speedily to the collapse of communist governments in Poland, Hungary, Czechoslovakia, Bulgaria, Romania, and East Germany. These Warsaw Pact nations can no longer be considered assets to Soviet military strength in Europe. The Soviets themselves withdrew their troops from Afghanistan and announced unilateral reductions in military strength in Europe. The Marxist military rulers of Nicaragua, "the Sandinistas," have been forced to share power with a democratically elected government, after years of pressure from U.S.-backed "contra" guerillas. Aging communist rulers of China must rely on military force to contain the popular democracy movement in that nation. Marxist dictatorships in Cuba and North Korea remain the most heavily militarized societies in the world, increasingly isolated from world developments.

The achievement of many of the objectives of U.S. national defense policy leads to a welcome yet paradoxical result—a lessening of the threat to our national security and a reduction in national defense needs. U.S. defense spending has declined in real dollars steadily since 1986, and current projections indicated that U.S. military strength may be cut in half before 2000.

Trends in Defense Spending.   U.S. defense spending has always been well below that of the Soviet Union. (For many years the C.I.A. estimated Soviet defense spending at 14 to 15 percent of its Gross National Product; but recent, more informed estimates of a smaller Soviet GNP suggest that defense spending in that nation may be consuming up to 25 percent of its GNP.) In 1955 defense spending in the United States claimed 58 percent of all federal expenditures and equaled 10.5 percent of the Gross National Product. Ten years later, in 1965, defense spending had shrunk to 40.1 percent of federal spending and to 7.2 percent of the GNP. By 1978 defense spending had declined to only 23 percent of federal spending and 4.5 percent of the GNP. This was the lowest defense "effort" the United States had made since before World War II.

The United States' political leadership acknowledged the strategic and conventional military imbalances by the end of the Carter administration. Figure 8–1 shows that defense spending as a percent of the GNP began to creep upward in 1980. Reagan's defense "buildup" occurred during his first years in office. Defense spending rose to 6.5 percent of the GNP and 29 percent of the total federal budget in 1986. But President Reagan was unable to maintain the momentum of the U.S. defense buildup in his second term in office. Secretary of Defense Caspar Weinberger fought a losing battle against a Congress determined to limit military spending. President Bush and Defense Secretary Richard Cheney have attempted to preempt congressional cuts in defense by paring down the defense budget themselves. But Congress inevitably cuts the President's lowered requests even more. In 1990 Secretary Cheney announced plans for a 25 percent reduction in U.S. military forces over a five-year period.

FIGURE 8-1 National Defense Outlays as a Percent of GNP. (*Source: The Budget of the United States Government FY 1991.* Washington, D.C.: Government Printing Office, 1990).

Defense and Social Welfare.   Defense outlays have no effect on either social welfare spending or inflation. Total spending for welfare, social security, and health is more than double the defense budget. There is no evidence that increases in the defense budget come at the expense of social spending. "Great Society" social welfare spending increased dramatically during the same years (1965-70) that military spending for the Vietnam War increased. Nor is defense spending inflationary: from 1955 to 1965, when defense spending was heavy, there was very little inflation in the country; likewise inflation declined dramatically during the Reagan military buildup.

Personnel and Weapons Costs.   The United States relies on an All Volunteer Force. The draft was ended following the Vietnam War. The All Volunteer Force is expensive, because pay and benefits must be made attractive. Personnel costs account for over one-half of the defense budget. An additional one-quarter of the budget is spent on operations. This leaves only one-quarter of the defense budget (only about 5 percent of the total federal budget) for the purchase of *all* new weapons—missiles, warheads, tanks, planes, ships, submarines, rifles.

Future Directions.   U.S. strategic forces must continue to deter nuclear attack. The United States cannot rely on internal political developments in the Soviet Union to insure against nuclear war. As long as the Soviets maintain nuclear forces capable of destroying American society in a single attack, the U.S. must maintain survivable, second-strike, retaliating forces as a deterrent to war. And these forces must be modernized over time. Thus, debates over the land-based missiles and their survivability—specifically, debate over a rail-mobile MX and a land-missile Midgetman—will continue. Consensus over the Trident submarine program may continue, but the B-2 "stealth" bomber program may fall victim to defense budget cuts.

Conventional military forces in the future will be smaller yet hopefully more mobile and ready to respond to regional conflicts around the world. Cuts in U.S. Army forces in Europe, and greater reliance on reserve rather than active duty units, will reduce expenditures. But modern, well-equipped, and well-trained air and naval forces are still required to confront global threats. The real question is whether the euphoria brought on by the collapse of communism in Eastern Europe will cause Congress to cut U.S. military strength so severely that the nation is unable to respond to future threats.

SUMMARY

Decisions about defense policy in Washington, Moscow, Peking, and other world capitals are interdependent—the future of humankind depends on what is done at each of these major power centers and how each responds to the decisions of others. Game theory provides a vocabulary and a way of thinking rationally about decision making in competitive interdependent situations. Let us set forth several summary ideas about defense policy.

1. Assured destruction deterrence strategy seeks to prevent nuclear war by making the consequences of a nuclear attack unacceptable to a rational enemy. The key to assured destruction deterrence is the *survivability* of one's forces—what can be done on a second strike after absorbing a successful surprise first strike by the enemy.

2. To maintain peace through assured destruction deterrence requires (1) second-strike capability, (2) communication of that capability to the enemy, (3) the enemy's belief in the credibility of the threat, and (4) a rational enemy.

3. If both sides maintain second-strike capability—that is, *mutual* assured destruction, or MAD—then a stable "balance of terror" is said to exist. Each side is restrained from launching an attack because it knows the second-strike capability of the other side. World peace does not rest on trust or love or brotherhood, but on a rational calculation of what is in each side's self-interest.

4. To implement its assured destruction deterrence, the United States has attempted to maintain a "TRIAD" of strategic forces—land-based missiles, submarine-launched missiles, and manned bombers. However, Soviet technological developments in the 1970s threatened the survivability of land-based missiles and manned bombers. The U.S. strategic weapons modernization program included "hard target-kill" capability weapons—the MX and Trident II D-5 missiles—and bombers capable of penetrating modern SAM defenses—the B-1 and B-2. Submarine-based missiles remain the most survivable of nuclear deterrent forces.

5. President Reagan began a large-scale research program into ballistic missile defense. The Strategic Defense Initiative, or "Star Wars," is designed to reduce reliance on deterrence through retaliation and instead defend the U.S. by destroying enemy missiles in space. SDI will require the development of very sophisticated weapons and computer technologies. Opponents of SDI argue that it will encourage the Soviet to build more offense missiles, that the Soviets will interpret SDI as an attempt by the U.S. to gain a first-strike capability against them, and that it will destabilize the balance of terror. Supporters of SDI argue that it promises to maintain peace through defense against missiles rather than the threat of nuclear retaliation against people.

6. In SALT I (1972) both sides renounced ABM programs and placed overall numerical limits on strategic weapons. But the arms race continued, and so did Soviet momentum in new heavy missiles, especially SS-18s, which threaten to destroy the entire U.S. ICBM force on a first strike. The SALT II (1979) agreement placed a series of limits on strategic nuclear-launch vehicles, and guaranteed noninterference in "national technical means"

(satellite intelligence) of verification. However, it has also recognized Soviet monopoly in heavy ICBMs. SALT II failed to win Senate ratification, but both sides pledged to honor its provisions.

7. President Reagan revised the U.S. arms negotiations strategy by calling for reductions, equality, and verification. Initially the Soviets rejected the new American position and walked out of arms control negotiations in 1983, only to return in 1985 when missile threats and "peace movements" failed to intimidate the U.S. or its NATO allies. New talks began in Geneva on strategic arms reductions, intermediate nuclear forces in Europe, and missile defenses.

8. The INF Treaty in 1987 reflected the U.S. principles of reductions, equality, and verification. For the first time in history an entire class of nuclear weapons—missiles with a range of 300 to 3000 miles—were completely eliminated. To reach this equal-zero level, the Soviets were obliged to destroy more missiles and warheads than the U.S. And for the first time, onsite verification was provided for.

9. The START agreement promises to significantly reduce not only missiles and warheads, but more importantly the likelihood of a first-strike nuclear attack. The Soviets agreed to reduce by one-half their SS–18 hard target-kill capabilities weapons. Both sides agreed to reduce missiles by 30 percent and warheads by almost 50 percent, and both sides agreed to onsite short-notice inspections.

10. Rational thinking in conventional war requires that the political purposes of the war should guide military operations. Unlimited, uncontrolled violence is not a rational strategy. For conventional war to be a rational policy, the benefits must outweigh the costs. Conventional forces also have a deterrent value, when potential aggressors know they must attack U.S. military forces to capture territory, the potential risks may dissuade them. U.S. forces in Europe and South Korea have both a deterrent value and the physical capability of resisting aggression.

11. Soviet conventional forces far outnumber U.S. conventional forces. This poses a conventional military threat to Western Europe and allows the Soviets to supply arms to satellite nations in the Middle East, Asia, Africa, and Latin America.

12. The preservation of democracy in Western Europe has been a central goal of U.S. policy for most of the twentieth century. In the NATO alliance the United States and Western European nations pledge that an armed attack against one will be considered an armed attack against all. A joint NATO military command is designated to implement this pledge.

13. The collapse of communist governments in Eastern Europe, combined with unilateral Soviet troop reductions, have lessened the threat to European security. These developments, together with German unification, require reconsideration of the security role of the NATO alliance and the purpose and number of U.S. troops stationed in Western Europe.

14. U.S. military strategies and forces must be restructured to confront changing threats. The U.S. may not need to maintain the same heavy armored forces in Europe. It may need to restructure its forces to confront regional conflicts, guerilla wars, and terrorist activity. U.S. Navy and Marine forces, and conventional U.S. Air Force tactical fighters and bombers, together with lighter U.S. Army divisions capable of rapid air deployment around the world, appear better to match future military requirements.

15. Defense spending has declined steadily in recent years and additional deep cuts are envisioned. Yet U.S. forces must continue to deter nuclear attack rather than rely on internal politics in the Soviet Union. And U.S. forces must be able to deal effectively with a variety of other types of conflicts. Future U.S. military forces will be smaller and more global in their reach. Weapons modernization will continue as will the requirement to maintain high quality and morale among military personnel. Military forces are a hedge against an uncertain future.

BIBLIOGRAPHY

HARTMAN, FREDERICK H. and ROBERT L. WENDZEL, *Defending America's Security.* New York: Pergamon, 1988.
INTERNATIONAL INSTITUTE FOR STRATEGIC STUDIES, *The Military Balance.* London: Brassey's. (Annual.)
KEGLEY, CHARLES W., and EUGENE R. WITTKOPF (eds.), *The Nuclear Reader,* 2nd ed. New York: St. Martin's, 1989.
KRUZEL, JOSEPH (ed.), *American Defense Annual 1989–1990.* Lexington MA: Lexington Books, 1989.
SNOW, DONALD M., *National Security.* New York: St. Martin's, 1987.

9

PRIORITIES
AND PRICE TAGS
incrementalism at work

The Budget and Accounting Act of 1921 gave the president responsibility for budget formulation; prior to that the president had not had formal powers over taxing and spending. (David Valdez/The White House)

DIMENSIONS OF GOVERNMENT SPENDING

Too often we think of budgeting as the dull province of accountants and statisticians. Nothing could be more mistaken. The budget is the single most important policy statement of any government. The expenditure side of the budget tells us "who gets what" in public funds, and the revenue side of the budget tells us "who pays the cost." There are few government activities or programs that do not require an expenditure of funds, and no public funds may be spent without budgetary authorization. Deciding what goes into a budget (the budgetary process) provides a mechanism for reviewing government programs, assessing their cost, relating them to financial resources, making choices among alternative expenditures, and determining the financial effort that a government will expend on these programs. Budgets determine what programs and policies are to be increased, decreased, lapsed, initiated, or renewed. The budget lies at the heart of public policy.

Governments do many things that cannot be measured in dollars. Nevertheless, government expenditures are the best available measure of the overall dimensions of government activity. Budgets represent government policies with price tags attached.

The expenditures of *all* governments in the United States—the federal government, together with fifty state governments and eighty thousand local governments—grew from $1.7 billion in 1902 to over $1.8 *trillion* in 1990 (see Table 9–1). Some of the increase in government activity can be attributed to growth in the nation's population. And a great deal of the increase in

TABLE 9–1   Growth in Population, GNP, and Government Activities Over Nine Decades

	POPULATION MILLIONS	GNP BILLIONS	ALL GOVERNMENT SPENDING BILLIONS	PERCENT OF GNP
1902	79.2	21.6	1.7	7.7
1922	110.1	74.0	9.3	12.5
1932	124.9	58.5	12.4	21.3
1940	132.6	100.6	20.4	20.3
1944	138.9	211.4	109.9	52.0
1950	152.3	284.6	70.3	24.7
1960	180.7	502.6	151.3	30.1
1970	203.2	959.6	312.1	32.5
1980	226.0	2626.1	959.0	36.5
1985	238.0	3869.4	1348.5	34.8
1990	248.8	5337.0	1815.6	34.0

Source: U.S. Bureau of the Census, *Historical Statistics on Governmental Finances and Employment* (Washington, D.C.: Government Printing Office, 1967); updated from *Economic Report of the President 1990.*

dollar amounts spent by government is exaggerated by the diminishing value of the dollar—that is, by inflation. However, government activity has grown much faster than both the population and inflation.

A better yardstick of the growth of government activity is found in the relationship of government expenditures to the Gross National Product (GNP). The GNP is the dollar sum of all goods and services produced in the nation's economy. The growth of the GNP in the twentieth century reflects the expansion of the nation's economy: the GNP in dollar amounts grew from $21.6 billion in 1902 to over $5 *trillion* today.

Government expenditures in relation to the Gross National Product had risen, somewhat bumpily, from 7.7 percent in 1902 to 35 percent in the late 1970s. If public programs financed by the government had grown at the same rate as private economic activities, this percentage figure would have remained at the same level over the years. But government activity over the long run has grown even *faster* than private enterprise. By any yardstick, then, we find the growth of government activity in America has been substantial. Government activity now accounts for one-third of all economic activity in the nation.

WHY GOVERNMENTS GROW

What accounts for the growth of government activity? There are many theories which offer explanations of government growth. We shall examine "incrementalism" in some detail, but first we should take note of some of the other leading theories of government growth. These theories are *not* mutually exclusive; indeed, probably all of the forces identified by these theories contribute to government growth.[1]

Wagner's Law.   Years ago, a European economist, Adolph Wagner, set forth a "law of increasing state activity" roughly to the effect that government activity increased faster than economic output in all developing societies.[2] He attributed his law to a variety of factors: increasing regulatory services required to control a more specialized, complex economy; increasing involvement of government in economic enterprise; and increasing demands in a developed society for social services such as education, welfare, and public health. Thus the "law of increasing state activity" portrayed growth in government activity as an inevitable accompaniment of a developing society.

[1]For a thorough survey of the literature on government growth, see P.D. Larkey, C. Stolp, and M. Winer, "Theorizing About the Growth of Government," *Journal of Public Policy* 1 (February 1981), 157–220. See also D. Lowrey and W. Berry, "The Growth of Government in the United States," *American Journal of Political Science*, 27 (April 1980), 189–201.

[2]Adolph Wagner's major work is *Grundelgung der Politischen Oekonomie* (Leipzig, 1883). This work is discussed at length in Alan T. Peacock and Jack Wiseman, *The Growth of Public Expenditures in the United Kingdom* (Princeton, N.J.: Princeton University Press, 1961).

FIGURE 9-1   All Government Expenditures as a Percentage of the Gross National Product in the U.S.

The Displacement Effect Hypothesis.   This theory assumes that government is responsive to public opinion and that public opinion usually limits government growth. However, during periods of social upheaval, especially war or economic dislocation, the public will accept higher than normal levels of taxation.[3] During these periods, then, government grows. After the stressful period is over, government size does not decline to its previous levels. Instead, new expenditures are substituted for those accepted during the crisis. There is some support for this theory in examining U.S. government expenditures in Figure 9-1: expenditures increase during crisis periods but never return to precrisis levels after the crises are over.

Fiscal Illusion Explanation.   This explanation assumes that government officials can increase revenues, and then expenditures, by altering the revenue structure and tax-collecting devices so that voters do not realize how much money government is actually taking from them.[4] The federal income tax grew very rapidly *after* the introduction of "withholding" in 1943; wage earners never receive the money they earned and come to perceive it as "belonging" to the federal government. This illusion may also be accomplished through complex or indirect tax systems, for example social security payroll taxes, sales taxes, and value added taxes. These taxes make

[3]Peacock and Wiseman, *The Growth of Public Expenditures in the United Kingdom.*

[4]R.E. Wagner, "Revenue Structure, Fiscal Illusion and Budgetary Choice," *Public Choice,* 25 (Spring 1976), 45–61.

it difficult for taxpayers directly to associate the amount they pay in taxes to the cost of the services they receive.

Bureaucratic Decision Making.   Both bureaucrats and the legislators who decide upon their budgets are personally interested in expanding government budgets.[5] Bureaucrats are interested in increasing the amount of money they can spend and the number of employees under their supervision. Legislators want to increase the resources over which they have jurisdiction and enhance the government's capacity to deal with their own constituents.

Interest Group Interaction.   This explanation assumes that interest groups will want to increase the size of government programs that benefit their own members. Benefits are visible and concentrated. Costs, even though they may exceed the benefits, are diffused. All interests might prefer that no one gets these benefits at government expense, but each interest group is motivated to act on behalf of its own members.

The Median Voter.   The median voter explanation of public sector growth assumes that the level of government chosen by voters will be the level preferred by the median voter. However, it is highly unlikely that this level will be the most efficient level of government expenditures. The *median* voter will have less income than the *mean* income of all people, because income is unevenly distributed. Thus, the median voter would choose a level of government high enough to redistribute income from the richer to the poorer. The position of the median voter is also influenced by the fact that government employees, who in their own self-interest would support expanded government, are also voters.

Electoral Competition.   This explanation assumes that politicians in competitive elections will be motivated to expand the size of government by offering specific groups of voters visible and exaggerated benefits while hiding or minimizing the costs to other voters.[6] Moreover, competitive elections maximize incentives to pursue policies that will win the votes of the "have nots"—in particular, to increase social welfare services.

Leftist Party Control of Government.   Another explanation of government growth centers on the control of government by liberal or left parties. Party activists in liberal and conservative parties hold strong and divergent views about the role of government in combating unemployment and controlling inflation. In most Western European democracies control of government

[5] W.A. Niskanen, *Bureaucracy and Representative Government* (Chicago: Aldine and Atherton, 1971).

[6] E.R. Tufte, *Political Control of the Economy* (Princeton, N.J.: Princeton University Press, 1978).

by the liberal party is associated with significant increases in the public budget.[7]

Cumulative Unintended Consequences.   This explanation suggests that the size of the public sector is the result of previous efforts to solve other, often unrelated, problems. Since our comprehension capabilities are limited, we are unable to view the size of government in a holistic manner, taking all revenues and expenditures and their future consequences into account. Thus, manageable decisions are limited to relatively simple problems. However, even seemingly simple decisions have consequences for present and future expenditures. Over the years, the effects of all these decisions accumulate until the previously made commitments push the size of government beyond what anyone originally intended. Future generations are thus forced to live with the unintended consequences of previous decisions.

INCREMENTALISM IN BUDGET MAKING

The incremental model of public policy making is particularly well suited to assist in understanding the budgeting process. Budgeting is *incremental* because decision makers generally consider last year's expenditures as a base. Active consideration of budget proposals is generally narrowed to new items or requested increases over last year's base. The attention of presidents, members of Congress, governors, legislators, mayors, and councils is focused on a narrow range of increases or decreases in a budget. A budget is almost never reviewed as a whole every year, in the sense of reconsidering the value of all existing programs. Departments are seldom required to defend or explain budget requests which do *not* exceed current appropriations; but requested increases in appropriations require extensive explanation.

Budget decisions are made incrementally because policy makers do not have the time, energy, or information to review every dollar of every budget request every year. Nor do policy makers wish to refight every political battle over the establishment of existing programs every year. So they generally accept last year's *base* spending level as legitimate and focus attention on proposed increases for each program.

Reformers have proposed the "zero-base" budget to force agencies to justify every penny requested—not just requested increases. In theory, zero-base budgeting would eliminate unnecessary spending protected by incrementalism. But in practice, zero-base budgeting requires so much wasted effort in justifying already accepted programs each year that executive agencies and legislative committees will grow tired of the effort and return to incrementalism.

[7]Ibid.; and D. Hibbs, "Political Parties and Macroeconomic Policy," *American Political Science Review*, 72 (December 1977), 467–87.

Budgeting Is Political.   Political scientist Aaron Wildavsky was told by a federal executive, "It's not what's in your estimates, but how good a politician you are that matters."[8] Being a good politician involves (1) the cultivation of a good base of support for requests among the public at large and among people served by the agency, (2) the development of interest, enthusiasm, and support for a program among top political figures and legislative leaders, and (3) skill in following strategies that exploit opportunities to the maximum. Informing the public and the clientele of the full benefit of the services they receive from the agency may increase the intensity with which they will support the agency's request. If possible, the agency should inspire its clientele to contact members of Congress, governors, mayors, legislators, and council members, and to help work for the agency's request. This is much more effective than the agency trying to promote its own requests.

Budgeting Is Fragmented.   In theory, the Office of Management and Budget (OMB) in the executive branch, and the Congressional Budget Office (CBO) in the legislative branch, are supposed to bring together budget requests and fit them into a coherent whole, while at the same time relating them to revenue estimates. But it is very difficult for the president, and almost impossible for Congress, to view the total policy impact of a budget. Wildavsky explains that the fragmented character of the budgetary process helps to secure agreement on the budget as well as reduce the burden of calculation. If each congressional subcommittee challenged the result of the others, conflict might be so great that no budget would ever be passed. It is much easier to agree on a small increase or decrease to a single program than it is to compare the worth of one program to that of all others. However, to counter the fragmentation in the federal budget, Congress not only established the Congressional Budget Office, but also House and Senate budget committees to examine the budget as a whole. We will describe their operation in the next section. But it is interesting to note that their purpose is to try to overcome the fragmentation in federal budget making.

Budgeting Is Nonprogrammatic.   Agency budgets typically list expenditures under the ambiguous phrases "personnel services," "contractual services," "travel," "supplies," "equipment." It is impossible to tell from such a listing exactly what programs the agency is spending its money on. Such a budget obscures policy decisions by hiding programs behind meaningless phrases. Reform-oriented administrators have called for budgeting by programs for many years; this would present budgetary requests in terms of end products or program packages, like aid to dependent children, vocational rehabilitation, administration of fair employment practices laws, and highway

[8]Aaron Wildavsky, *The Politics of the Budgetary Process*, 4th ed. (Boston: Little, Brown, 1984), p. 19.

patrolling. Chief executives generally favor *program budgeting* because it will give them greater control over policy. But Wildavsky points out that there are some political functions served by *non*program budgeting. He notes that

> Agreement comes much more readily when the items can be treated in dollars instead of basic differences in policy. Calculating budgets in monetary increments facilitates bargaining and logrolling. It becomes possible to swap an increase here for a decrease there or for an increase elsewhere without always having to consider the ultimate desirability of the programs blatantly in competition.[9]

"UNCONTROLLABLE" GOVERNMENT SPENDING

Government budgeting is incremental in part because of "uncontrollables" in the federal budget. "Uncontrollables" are items that are determined by past policies of Congress and represent commitments in future federal budgets. Most federal spending is "uncontrollable," that is, based on previous decisions of Congress and not easily changed in annual budget making. Sources of uncontrollable spending include:

"Entitlement" Programs. Federal programs that provide classes of people with a legally enforceable right to benefits are called "entitlement" programs. Entitlement programs account for over half of all federal spending, including social security, welfare, Medicare and Medicaid, food stamps, federal employees' retirement, and veterans' benefits. These entitlements are benefits that past Congresses have pledged the federal government to pay. Entitlements are not *really* uncontrollable: Congress can always amend the basic laws that established them; but this is politically difficult and might be regarded as a failure of trust.

Indexing of Benefits. One reason that spending increases each year is that Congress has authorized automatic increases in benefits tied to increases in prices. Benefits are "indexed" to the Consumer Price Index under social security, SSI, food stamps, and veterans' pensions. This indexing pushes up the cost of entitlement programs each year, even when the number of recipients stays the same. Indexing, of course, runs counter to federal efforts to restrain inflation. Moreover the Consumer Price Index (which includes interest payments for new housing, the cost of new cars and appliances) generally overestimates the needs of recipients for cost-of-living increases.

Increasing Costs of In-Kind Benefits. Rises in the cost of major in-kind (noncash) benefits, particularly medical costs of Medicaid and Medicare, also

[9]Ibid., p. 136.

guarantee growth in federal spending. These in-kind benefit programs have risen faster in cost than cash benefit programs.

Interest on the National Debt. Interest payments have grown rapidly as a percentage of all federal spending. The federal government has a long history of deficits. Only one year in the past thirty has the government balanced the budget. The result is a national debt approaching $4 *trillion*. Each year the deficit increases, interest payments go up. Interest payments also rise with increases in interest rates. Interest payments are now over 15 percent of total federal spending.

Backdoor Spending. Some federal spending does not appear on the budget. For example, spending by the Postal Service is not included in the federal budget. No clear rule explains why some agencies are in the budget and others are not. But "off-budget" agencies have the same economic effects as other government agencies. Another form of backdoor spending is found in government-guaranteed loans. Initially government guarantees for loans—FHA housing, Guaranteed Student Loans, veterans' loans, and so forth—do not require federal money. The government merely promises to repay the loan if the borrower fails to do so. Yet these loans create an obligation against the government.

Savings and Loan Bailout. Government guarantees of loans are not cost free, as the financial disaster in the savings and loan industry demonstrates. As a result of federal guarantees of deposits through the Federal Savings and Loan Insurance Corporation (FSLIC), the U.S. government is now saddled with perhaps as much as $500 billion in loan defaults. The federal Regulation Trust Corporation has assumed the heavy liabilities and meager assets of bankrupt savings and loan companies throughout the nation. The cost of this enormous bailout is kept "off budget" to spare both Congress and the president the embarrassment of even higher annual deficits.

CHANGING BUDGET PRIORITIES

Incrementalism may help to explain the process of budgetary decision making. But incrementalism appears unable to explain major changes in budgetary priorities over time. Incrementalism views public policy as a continuation of past government activities, with only incremental modifications from year to year. Yet increments add up over time: some programs, like Social Security and Medicare, expand over the years, taking even larger shares of federal spending; other programs, like national defense, gradually contract as a share of federal spending.

"Revolutions" in spending patterns are not anticipated by incremental theory. Nonetheless, the United States experienced a "revolution" in spending priorities during the 1970s. In a single decade America's "national priorities" in defense and social welfare were reversed. In 1965 national defense expenditures accounted for 40.9 percent of the federal budget, while social security and welfare expenditures accounted for only 8.7 percent of the budget (see Table 9-2). While the mass media focused attention on the war in Vietnam and on Watergate, these national priorities were reversed. By 1975, only a decade later, defense accounted for only 26.0 percent of the federal budget, while social security and welfare expenditures had grown to 38.4 percent of the budget. This reversal of national priorities occurred

TABLE 9-2   Federal Budget Priorities over the Years

FUNCTION	(BILLIONS OF DOLLARS)								
	1960	1965	1970	1975	1980	1985	1989	1990*	1991*
National Defense	45.9	49.6	81.7	86.5	134.0	252.7	303.6	296.3	303.3
Income Security†	3.7	9.1	15.6	50.2	86.5	128.2	136.0	146.6	153.7
Social Security	4.3	16.4	30.3	64.7	118.5	188.6	232.5	248.5	264.8
Medicare	—	—	6.2	12.7	32.1	65.8	85.0	96.6	98.6
Agriculture	3.3	4.8	5.2	3.0	8.8	25.6	16.9	14.6	14.9
Natural Resources	1.0	2.1	3.1	7.3	13.9	13.4	16.2	17.5	18.2
Energy	0.5	0.7	1.0	2.9	10.2	5.7	3.7	3.2	3.0
Veterans Benefits	5.4	5.1	8.7	16.6	21.2	26.3	30.1	28.9	30.3
Interest on Debt	8.3	10.4	14.4	23.2	52.5	129.4	169.1	175.6	173.0
All Other ††	9.8	17.1	29.4	65.2	113.2	110.6	148.5	169.4	173.5
Total	92.2	118.3	195.6	332.3	590.9	946.3	1141.6	1197.2	1233.3

FUNCTION	PERCENTAGE DISTRIBUTION								
	1960	1965	1970	1975	1980	1985	1989	1990	1991
National Defense	55.8	43.0	41.8	26.0	22.7	26.7	26.6	24.7	24.6
Income Security †	4.5	7.9	8.0	15.1	14.6	13.5	11.9	12.2	12.5
Social Security	5.2	14.2	15.5	19.5	20.1	19.9	20.4	20.8	21.5
Medicare	0.0	0.0	3.2	3.8	5.4	7.0	7.4	8.1	8.0
Agriculture	4.0	4.2	2.7	0.9	1.5	2.7	1.5	1.2	1.2
Natural Resources	1.2	1.8	1.6	2.2	2.4	1.4	1.4	1.5	1.5
Energy	0.6	0.6	0.5	0.9	1.7	0.6	0.3	0.3	0.2
Veterans Benefits	6.6	4.4	4.4	5.0	3.6	2.8	2.6	2.4	2.5
Interest on Debt	10.1	9.0	7.4	7.0	8.9	13.7	14.8	14.7	14.0
All Other ††	11.9	14.8	15.0	19.6	19.2	11.7	13.0	14.1	14.1
Total	100.0	100.0	100.0	100.0	100.0	100.0	100.0	100.0	100.0

*Estimates

†This includes public assistance, food stamps, railroad and governmental employee retirement benefits, and unemployment compensation.

††This includes international affairs, science, space, transportation, education, commerce, community development, justice, and general government.

Sources: *Statistical Abstract of the United States 1990;* and *The Budget of the United States Government—Fiscal Year 1991.*

during both Democratic (Johnson) and Republican (Nixon and Ford) administrations in Washington, *and* during the nation's longest war. In short, what we thought we "knew" about the effects of politics and war on social welfare spending turned out to be wrong.

Interestingly, not many people really noticed this reversal of national priorities. Many people still believe the federal government spends more on defense than anything else. Old beliefs die hard.

Federal budget outlays over two decades for major programs are shown in Table 9–2, in both dollar and percentages of the total federal budget. Note how spending for *national defense* has grown very slowly in dollars and declined very rapidly as a percentage of total federal spending. In contrast, spending for social security, welfare, and Medicare has grown very rapidly, both in dollars and in percentages of the federal budget.

The Reagan defense "buildup" reached its peak in 1985. But this effort only expanded defense spending from a low of 23 percent to 27 percent of total federal spending. Defense spending has declined as a share of total federal spending ever since 1985, and steeper declines are expected in the next few years with the waning of the Cold War.

Today social security, Medicare, and welfare payments account for 42 percent of all federal spending. It is likely that these expenditures will continue to grow, not only in dollars but also in shares of the federal budget. Medical costs are the most rapidly growing sector of the federal budget. And during the past decade, when the total federal debt grew from $1 to $3 trillion, interest costs were growing rapidly. Interest costs will continue to grow unless the president and Congress succeed in eliminating annual federal deficits.

FIGURE 9-2   The Federal Government Dollar. (*Source: The Budget of the United States Government Fiscal Year 1991.*)

Where It Goes . . .

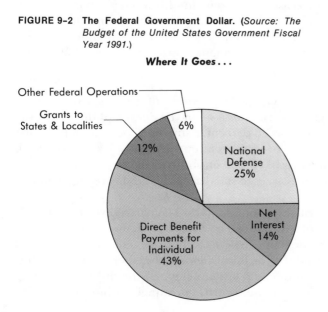

GOVERNMENT SPENDING AND ECONOMIC THEORY

Various economic theories compete for preeminence as guides to government fiscal and monetary policy. "Macroeconomic" theory, when applied to the government's influence on the economy, focuses on aggregate amounts of spending, taxes, borrowing, and money. Macroeconomic theory tries both to explain economic cycles and to prescribe government policies to counter inflation and recession.

Classical Theory.   Classical economists generally view a market economy as a self-adjusting mechanism that will achieve an equilibrium of full employment, maximum productivity, and stable prices if left alone by the government. The price mechanism will adjust the decisions of millions of Americans to bring into balance the supply and demand of goods and labor. Regarding recessions, if workers are temporarily unemployed because the supply for workers exceeds the demand, wages (the price of labor) will fall; eventually it will again become profitable for business to have more workers at lower wages and thus end unemployment. Similarly, if the demand for goods (automobiles, houses, clothing, kitchenware, and so on) falls, business inventories will rise and businesspeople will reduce prices (often through rebates, sales, and so forth) until demand picks up again. Regarding inflation, general increases in prices will reduce demand and automatically bring it back into line with supply unless government interferes. Inflation is caused by government expansion of the money supply; if too much money is available in bank loans and currency, both prices and wages will rise. But if the money supply is stable, increases in the demand for money will push up interest rates thus raising the "price" of money. An increase in interest rates will reduce the demand for money and cool inflation. In short, classical economic theory relies on the free movement of prices to counter both recession and inflation.

Keynesian Theory.   The Great Depression of the 1930s shattered popular confidence in classical economics. For the decade of the 1930s, the average unemployment rate was 18 percent, rising to 25 percent in the worst year, 1933. But even in 1936, seven years after the great stock market crash in 1929, unemployment was still 18 percent of the workforce, raising questions about the ability of the market to stabilize itself and insure high employment and productivity.

According to the British economist John Maynard Keynes, economic instability was a product of fluctuations in *demand.* Both unemployment and lower wages reduced the demand for goods; business cut production and laid off more workers to adjust for lower demand for their goods; but cuts and layoffs further reduced demand and accelerated the downward spiral. Reducing interest rates would not necessarily encourage businessmen to borrow money to build new plants and create new jobs if there was no demand for their products. Increasing the supply of money was like trying to push with a string; the economy would not expand unless demand were increased. Keynesian theory suggested that the economy could fall into a recession and stay there. Only government could take the necessary "counter cyclical" steps to expand demand by spending more money itself and lowering taxes. Of course, government cannot add to aggregate demand if it balances the budget. Rather, during a recession government must incur deficits to add to total demand, spending more than it receives in revenue. To counter inflationary trends, government should take just the opposite steps. During inflations when strong consumer demand is pushing up prices, government should cut its own spending, raise taxes, and run a surplus in the budget, thus reducing aggregate demand.

"We Are All Keynesians." Keynesian ideas dominated policy making for nearly a half century. Keynesian counter cyclical policies were written into the Employment Act of 1946, specifically pledging the federal government "to promote maximum employment production and purchasing power" through its aggregate taxing and spending. The Act created the Council of Economic Advisors to "develop and recommend to the president national economic policies" and required the president to submit to Congress an annual economic report assessing the state of the economy. While arguments continued over whether policy should tilt toward fighting recession or fighting inflation, by 1970 President Richard Nixon announced that "we are all Keynesians."

Yet while most economists endorsed government deficits to counter recessions, it became increasingly clear that politicians were unable to end deficit spending after the recession was over. Politicians were more fearful of unemployment than inflation, and since Keynesian theory portrayed these events as opposite ends of a seesaw, politicians were given a rationale for continued deficit spending. Even during inflation, politicians cannot bring themselves to enact the spending cuts and tax increases recommended by Keynes.

There were other problems with Keynesian economic analysis. Throughout the 1970s unemployment and inflation occurred simultaneously in defiance of Keynesian theory. In the 1976 presidential campaign, Jimmy Carter attacked the performance of the nation's economy under President Gerald Ford by inventing a new phrase, "misery index"—a combination of the unemployment rate and inflation rate, which then stood at 13.5 percent. Later, candidate Ronald Reagan used Carter's phrase to embarrass the embattled incumbent: in 1980 the misery index stood at 20 percent.

Forty years of Keynesian efforts to manipulate aggregate demand had produced "stagflation" in the 1970s: inflation and high interest rates, unemployment, and stagnant economic growth rates. While politicians had no difficulty *increasing* spending during recessions, it turned out to be impossible for them to reduce spending during inflation periods. The result was continuing government deficit spending during both recession and inflation, runaway, "double-digit" (over 10 percent) annual inflation rates, and declining rates of economic growth. Keynesian economics was labeled by President Reagan as "the failed policies of the past."

Supply-Side Economics.   Supply-side economists argue that attention to long-term economic growth is more important than short-term manipulation of demand. Economic growth requires an expansion in the productive capacity of society. All economists agree that this requires an increase in one or more of the following: (1) natural resources, (2) labor, (3) capital, or (4) technology. Economic growth requires that we find and develop our natural resources, improve the productivity of our labor force, provide incentives for savings and capital investment, and improve our technology through continuing research and development.

Economic growth increases the overall supply of goods and services, and thereby holds down prices. Inflation is reduced or ended altogether. More importantly, everyone's standard of living is improved with the availability of more goods and services at stable prices. Economic growth even increases government revenues over the long run.

Most supply-side economists believe that the free market is better equipped than government to bring about lower prices and more supplies of what people need and want. Government, they argue, is the problem, not the solution. Government taxing, spending, and monetary policies have promoted immediate consumption, instead of investment in the future. High taxes penalize hard work, creativity, investment, and savings. Government should provide tax incentives to encourage investment and savings; tax rates should be lowered to encourage work and enterprise. Overall government spending should be held in check; if possible, the governmental proportion of the GNP should be reduced over time. Government regulations should be minimized in order to increase productivity and growth. Overall, government should act to stimulate production and supply rather than demand and consumption.

"Reaganomics."   Economic policy in the 1980s under President Reagan reflected these supply-side views. According to Reagan, the most important cause of the nation's economic problems—inflation, unemployment, low productivity, low investment—was the government itself. "The federal government, through taxes, spending, regulating, and monetary policies, has sacrificed long-term growth and price stability for ephemeral, short-term goals."[10] Government efforts to reduce unemployment simply added to inflation.

[10]Office of the President, *A Program for Economic Recovery*, 18 February 1981 (Washington, D.C.: Government Printing Office).

Upon taking office the Reagan Administration set forth a package of four sweeping directions:

Budget reform to cut the rate of growth in federal spending.

Tax reductions, lowering of the top marginal tax rates, as well as additional tax reductions to encourage business investment.

Relief from government regulations that cost industry large amounts of money for small increases in safety or environmental protection.

Slower growth of the money supply, to be achieved with the cooperation of the Federal Reserve Board.

It is very difficult to assess accurately the effects of Reagan's economic policies, or any government economic policies for that matter. The problem is that the economy is constantly changing, independently of government policies. For example, as more women enter the labor force, the economy must create many new jobs just to absorb the larger percentage of the population who are seeking work. The unemployment rate may increase even though many more people are working, simply because jobs cannot be created as fast as new workers enter the job market.

Another problem is that the economy often requires one or two years to respond to government policies. The first two years of the Reagan administration, 1981-1983, saw the deepest recession in the United States since the 1930s. Did this recession occur because of Reagan policies, or did it occur as a product of high inflation and high interest rates in the preceding Carter administration? Finally, government policies can have different effects, some good and some bad. Political opponents of the administration in power will emphasize the bad effects, while the administration itself emphasizes the good.

On the positive side, the Reagan administration ushered in *the longest continuous period of growth in the GNP in modern history.* The annual *inflation rate* declined from 14.5 percent to 4.5 percent, a truly impressive performance. Unemployment declined from 10 percent to 6 percent of the workforce, even while the economy absorbed about 10 million new workers. The *participation rate* in the labor force (the percentage of the population who are working) also increased. Real growth in the GNP (growth measured in constant dollars) rebounded from the sluggishness of the late 1970s to about 3 percent per year, a very healthy growth rate if it can be sustained.

The Reagan administration failed to cut government spending; on the contrary, government spending continued to increase during the Reagan years, although the rate of growth was slowed. Tax cuts did *not* result in greatly increased revenues as predicted by some supply-side economists. Instead, the tax cuts slowed the rate of growth of government revenue. Government spending was not slowed sufficiently to offset these lost revenues, and defense spending was increased. Reagan had promised a balanced budget, but it was impossible to cut taxes, increase defense spending, and maintain social security and other popular domestic spending programs without increasing the federal deficit. Indeed, in recent years the federal government has run *the largest peacetime deficits in history.*

These deficits threaten the future of the economy. As the federal government borrows high amounts of capital to fund its debts, less capital is available to the private market for economic growth. Interest rates are kept high by the government's own demand for loans.

Monetarist Economics. Keynesian theory not only recommended increased government spending, reduced taxes, and larger deficits during recessions, but also an expansion of the money supply. Expanding the supply of money, by easing bank reserve requirements and lowering bank interest rates, was expected to add to demand. Similarly, during inflationary periods, government was supposed to tighten the supply of money by increasing bank reserve requirements and increasing interest rates. Thus, by increasing or decreasing the overall supply of money, government could "fine tune" the economy.

The independent Federal Reserve Board, commonly called "the Fed," can expand or contract the money supply through its oversight of the operation of banks participating in the Federal Reserve System. The Fed is headed by a seven-person board of governors, appointed by the president for overlapping terms of fourteen years. By controlling the amount of money banks can lend, the Fed can regulate the money supply and influence interest rates. Many economists credit the defeat of runaway inflation of the 1970s to the stern policies of Fed Chairman Paul Volker. Despite heavy political pressure from Congress and occasionally from the Reagan administration, Volker pursued extremely tight money policies in the early 1980s, allowing interest rates to rise above the previously unimaginable rate of 20 percent. This bitter medicine probably deepened the 1981-83 recession but it brought inflation under control.

However, monetarist economic theory contends that economic stability can only be achieved by holding the rate of monetary growth to the same rate as the economy itself. Led by the Nobel-prize winning economist Milton Friedman, monetarists challenge the view that manipulating the money supply can effectively influence economic activity. They argue that over the long run real income is a function of actual economic output. Increasing the supply of money faster than output only creates inflation. The value of each dollar declines because there is more money to buy the same amount of goods. Government manipulation of the money supply can only produce short-term economic effects. Monetarists believe that the extraordinarily high interest rates of the early 1980s were not a result of the Fed's operations but rather a product of investor fears of continued inflation. As soon as investors came to believe that the Fed would stick to noninflationary policies, interest rates came down. In short, monetarists believe that government tinkering with money supply is the problem not the solution.

THE BURDEN OF GOVERNMENT DEBT

Traditional Keynesian economics encouraged government deficit spending during recessions. In theory, Keynesian economics called for surpluses during expansionary periods, but in practice Congresses hardly ever wished to tax more than they spent. The U.S. government has incurred a deficit in every one of the past thirty years. The total federal debt approaches 4 *trillion* dollars, or $16,000 for every man, woman and child in the nation (see Figure 9–3).

Debt and the GNP.   Liberal economists traditionally minimized the burdens of government debt. The U.S. government debt is owed mostly to banks and financial institutions and private citizens who buy U.S. Treasury bonds. As old debt comes due, the U.S. Treasury Department sells new bonds to pay off the old, that is, it continues to "roll over" or "float" the debt. The debt today is smaller as a percentage of the gross national product than at some periods in U.S. history (see Figure 9–3). Indeed, in order to pay the costs of fighting World War II, the U.S. government ran up a debt of 110 percent of GNP; the current debt is the highest in history in dollar terms but only about 50 percent of the GNP. This suggest that the debt is still manageable, because of the size and strength of the U.S. economy.

The ability to float such a huge debt depends on public confidence in the United States government—confidence that it will continue to pay interest on its debt, that it will pay off the principal of bond issues when they come due, and that the value of the bonds will not decline over time because of inflation.

Interest Burden.   Interest payments on the national debt are now 14 percent of total federal expenditures and the third largest expenditure of the federal government, after social security and national defense. These payments come from current taxes and they divert money away from all other government programs. Even if the federal government manages to balance its current budgets, these payments will remain obligations of the children and grandchildren of the current generation of policy makers and taxpayers. In short, today's high spending and low taxing is shifting the burden of debt from the current generation to future generations.

Default, Hyperinflation.   No one expects the United States ever to default on its debt—that is, to refuse to pay interest or principal when it comes due, although other debt-ridden nations have done so in the past and many threaten to do so today. But there is always the possibility that a future administration in Washington might "monetarize" the debt, that is, simply print currency and use it to pay off bondholders. Of course, this currency would flood the nation and soon become worthless. Hyperinflation would leave U.S. bondholders with worthless money. These financial disasters—default

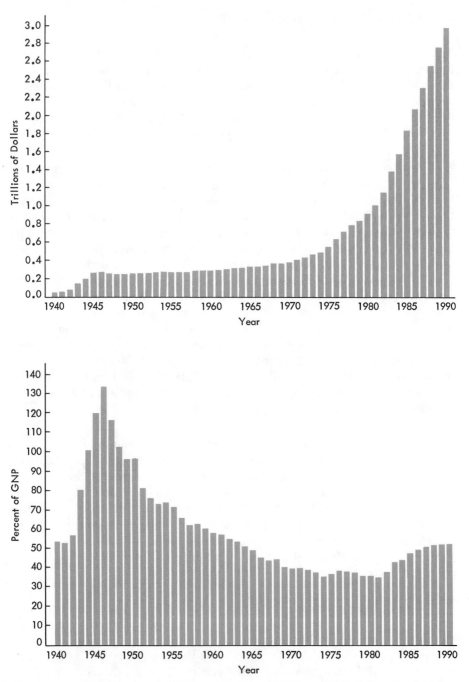

FIGURE 9-3 Top Graph Shows the Federal Debt Between 1940 and 1990; Bottom Graph Shows Federal Debt As Percentage of GNP During the Same Period.

or hyperinflation—are unlikely, but the existence of a high federal deficit means that such disasters are not unthinkable.

Dealing with Deficits. The simple and responsible solution to the federal deficit is to have the president and Congress prepare and pass only balanced budgets. But that solution has eluded policy makers for over thirty years. Neither presidents nor Congresses, Democrats nor Republicans, have been willing to reduce expenditures or raise taxes to balance budgets. American politics has reached a level of irresponsibility at which calls for a balanced budget are considered "naive" and "unrealistic." So Washington searches for politically "painless" remedies.

The Balanced Budget Constitutional Amendment. Constitutions govern government. Presumably, if "the people" wish to discipline their government they can do so by amending the Constitution to restrict the actions of officials. Indeed, according to the National Taxpayers Union, some thirty-one states have petitioned Congress to call a constitutional convention to balance the budget. Under Article V of the Constitution, a convention must be called if two-thirds of the states (thirty-four) request one. However, no procedure exists to force Congress to do so, or to determine when or how such a convention would be held, how delegates would be elected, or what the authority of the convention would be. Realistically, the call for a constitutional convention to balance the budget is only a means of pressuring Congress to pass a constitutional amendment itself to require balanced budgets.

President Ronald Reagan led an unsuccessful effort to get Congress to pass a balanced budget amendment and send it to the states for ratification. Yet, even during the years that the Republican president proposed this amendment, he also submitted budgets with the largest peacetime deficits in history! Congressional Democrats viewed the amendment as a partisan attempt by Reagan to shift attention away from his own red ink.

Gramm-Rudman-Hollings. Congress devised its own deficit reduction plan in 1985 calling for "mandatory" reductions in annual federal deficits each year until a balanced budget is reached. The plan was originally proposed by Senators Phil Gramm (R.–Tex.), Warren B. Rudman (R.–N.H.), and Ernest F. Hollings (D.–N.C.). Of course, no Congress can really "mandate" that future Congresses do anything they do not wish to do. But "Gramm-Rudman" established automatic budget cuts that would take effect if Congress and the president could not agree on deficit reductions.

The Gramm-Rudman-Hollings deficit reduction plan was supposed to work as follows:

> Gradually lowered ceilings were to be placed in the annual federal deficit from 1986 to 1991, when a balanced budget would be required.

The president's OMB and Congress's CBO would jointly predict the size of the projected deficit each year. (The independent General Accounting Office was to resolve any differences in estimates.)

If Congress and the president failed through the ordinary budget process to achieve these targeted deficit amounts, the president would be required to order spending cuts in all nonexempt programs.

However, Congress exempted about half of all federal spending programs from the mandatory provisions of the plan. The privileged programs included:
—Social Security, including generous cost of living allowances
—Welfare: SSI and AFDC
—Food Stamps
—Medicaid
—Veterans benefits
—Interest on the national debt.
Half of the automatic cuts were to come from military spending and the other half from domestic programs that were not exempted.

Why was Congress willing to give up part of its constitutional powers over spending in favor of "automatic" cuts by budgetary bureaucracies? Obviously Congress did not have the political courage to make the decisions that it was elected to make—that is, to decide to raise taxes or cut spending or both. They wanted an "invisible hand" to make the tough taxing and spending decisions. Perhaps the threat of "meat-ax" automatic cuts in defense and domestic spending would be enough to force Congress itself to confront the hard budget choices. Gramm-Rudman did not rule out tax increases as a means of reaching the targeted deficit ceilings. In short, it was hoped that Gramm-Rudman would force responsible budget policies on both the president and Congress.

Gramm-Rudman in Action.   The Gramm-Rudman plan failed to bring about a balanced budget, although it might be argued that recent annual deficits would have been larger without the plan. Both the president and Congress frequently resorted to "smoke and mirrors" to obscure the real size of the deficit and to claim that Gramm-Rudman ceilings were being met. Some deficit spending, including the massive bail-out of the savings and loan industry, was placed "off budget"; revenue estimates were inflated, thus obscuring deficits until after the fiscal year was over and the ceilings bypassed; and Congress itself set back the deficit reduction schedule year after year.

Budget Summits.   While the reluctance of politicians to raise taxes or cut spending to balance budgets is the principal cause of the nation's continuing deficit woes, partisan conflict between Republican presidents and Democratic-controlled Congresses prevents the adoption of meaningful remedies. Even when political and economic pressures build to reduce the size of these deficits, Republican presidents and Democratic Congresses offer opposing budget solutions. Republican presidents Ronald Reagan and

George Bush generally sought to reduce deficits through cuts in domestic spending, not tax increases. Democratic Congresses generally sought to reduce deficits through reductions in defense spending as well as tax increases. Inasmuch as the American constitutional system gives both the president and Congress a check on the actions of the other, some agreement is necessary to achieve deficit reductions. Hence the frequent call for a "budget summit" between leaders of Congress, president, and his budget director and key advisors.

Yet budget summits have failed to achieve significant reductions in annual federal deficits. In 1990, President George Bush was forced to retract his campaign pledge, "Read my lips, no new taxes!" and agree to an increase in the top marginal income tax rate from 28 to 31 percent (see Chapter 10). Military spending was cut dramatically, and there were token reductions in Medicare spending. But these modest efforts were washed away in a sea of red ink; slowing economic growth, with lower projected government revenues and higher interest rates promised the nation continuing deficits in excess of $200 billion per year.

THE POWER OF THE PURSE

The Constitution of the United States places all *taxing, borrowing,* and *spending* powers in the hands of Congress in Article I:

> Section 8, Paragraph 1 grants Congress the power "to lay and collect taxes, duties, imposts and excises, to pay the debts and provide for the common defense and general welfare of the United States. . . ."
>
> Section 8, Paragraph 2 grants Congress the power "to borrow money on the credit of the United States."
>
> Section 9, Paragraph 7 declares that "no money shall be drawn from the Treasury, but in consequence of appropriations made by law. . . ."

The power to tax was greatly enlarged by the Sixteenth Amendment in 1913 authorizing the federal government to tax income. For nearly 150 years the power to spend was interpreted in a limited fashion: Congress could only spend money to perform its *delegated* powers. But the Constitution also contained the more expensive phrase "to pay the debts and provide for the common defense and general welfare of the United States". This phrase was interpreted by Alexander Hamilton to mean that Congress could spend money broadly for the "general welfare." This broad interpretation was ultimately adopted by the U.S. Supreme Court (*U.S.* v. *Butler*, 297 U.S. 1, 1936), and today there are no constitutional limits on Congress' spending power. Congress' borrowing power is also constitutionally unlimited. There is no constitutional requirement for a balanced budget.

The Constitution gives the president no formal powers over taxing and spending. Constitutionally all the president can do is "make recommendations" to the Congress. It is difficult to imagine that prior to 1921 the president played no direct role in the budget process. The Secretary of the Treasury compiled the estimates of the individual agencies, and these were sent, without revision, to Congress for its consideration. It was not until the Budget and Accounting Act of 1921 that the president acquired responsibility for budget formulation, and thus developed a means of directly influencing spending policy.

THE FORMAL BUDGETARY PROCESS

The president, through the Office of Management and Budget (OMB), located in the Executive Office, has the key responsibility for budget preparation. In addition to this major task, the OMB has related responsibilities for improving the organization and management of the executive agencies, for coordinating the extensive statistical services of the federal government, and for analyzing and reviewing proposed legislation to determine its effect on administration and finance.

OMB—Preparing the Presidential Budget.   Preparation of the fiscal budget starts more than a year before the beginning of the fiscal year for which it is intended. OMB, after preliminary consultation with the executive agencies and in accord with presidential policy, develops targets or ceilings within which the agencies are encouraged to build their requests. This work begins a full sixteen to eighteen months before the beginning of the fiscal year for which the budget is being prepared. In other words, work would begin in January 1991 on the budget for the fiscal year beginning October 1, 1992 and ending September 30, 1993. Budgets are named for the fiscal year in which they *end*, so this example describes the work on *The Budget of the United States Government Fiscal Year 1993* or more simply "FY93."

Budget materials and instructions go to the agencies with the request that the forms be completed and returned to OMB. This request is followed by about three months' arduous work by agency-employed budget officers, department heads, and the "grass roots" bureaucracy in Washington and out in the field. Budget officials at the bureau level check requests from the smaller units, compare them with previous years' estimates, hold conferences, and make adjustments. The process of checking, reviewing, modifying, and discussing is repeated on a larger scale at the department level.

The heads of agencies are expected to submit their completed requests to OMB by mid-September or early October. Occasionally a schedule of "over ceiling" items (requests above the suggested ceilings) will be included.

With the requests of the spending agencies at hand, OMB begins its own budget review. Hearings are given each agency. Top agency officials support their requests as convincingly as possible. On rare occasions dissatisfied agencies may ask the budget director to take their cases to the president.

In December, the president and the OMB director will devote time to the document, which by now is approaching its final stages of assembly. They and their staffs will "blue-pencil," revise, and make last-minute changes, as well as prepare the president's message, which accompanies the budget to Congress. After the budget is in legislative hands, the president may recommend further alterations as needs dictate.

Although the completed document includes a revenue plan with general estimates for taxes and other income, it is primarily an expenditure budget. Revenue and tax-policy staff work centers in the Treasury Department and not in the Office of Management and Budget. On January 15th the president presents *The Budget of the United States Government* for the fiscal year beginning October 1st to Congress (see Figure 9–4).

House and Senate Budget Committees.   In an effort to consider the budget as a whole, Congress has established House and Senate budget committees and a Congressional Budget Office (CBO) to review the president's budget after its submission to Congress. These committees draft a first budget resolution (due May 15th) setting forth target goals to guide committee actions on specific appropriation and revenue measures. If appropriations measures exceed the targets in the budget resolution, it comes back to the floor in a reconciliation measure. A second budget resolution (due September 15th) sets binding budget figures for committees and subcommittees considering appropriations. In practice, however, these two budget resolutions have been folded into a single measure, because Congress does not want to reargue the same issues twice.

Gramm-Rudman Deficit Reduction.   Proposed spending and revenue laws, together with economic forecasts for the coming budget year, are then reviewed by the president's Office of Management and Budget (OMB) and the Congressional Budget Office (CBO). This review is to determine how large the projected *deficit* may be. (This process was introduced in 1985 by the Gramm-Rudman-Hollings Act discussed earlier.) Their estimates of the deficit are sent to the independent General Accounting Office to resolve any differences and to declare whether or not the deficit exceeds limits set in the Gramm-Rudman-Hollings Act. If the deficit limits are exceeded, Congress and the president have thirty days to reduce spending or increase taxes in order to reduce the deficit. Otherwise, automatic cuts will be made in defense and domestic spending levels, although social security and most welfare programs are exempted from these automatic cuts.

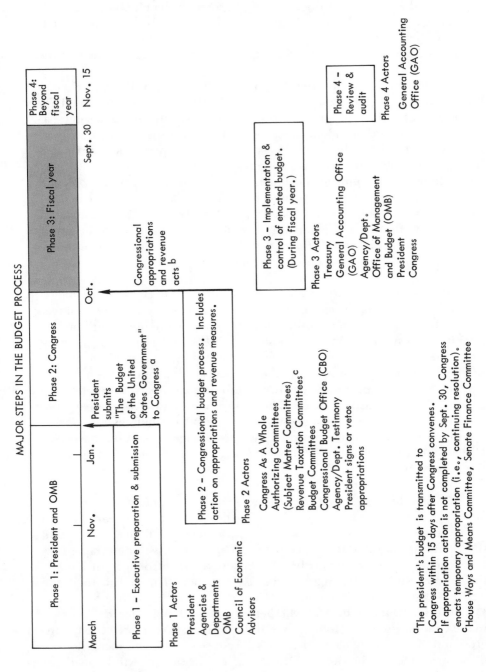

MAJOR STEPS IN THE BUDGET PROCESS

| Phase 1: President and OMB | Phase 2: Congress | Phase 3: Fiscal year | Phase 4: Beyond fiscal year |

March   Nov.   Jan.   Oct.   Sept. 30   Nov. 15

President submits "The Budget of the United States Government" to Congress [a]

Congressional appropriations and revenue acts [b]

Phase 1 – Executive preparation & submission

Phase 1 Actors

President
Agencies & Departments
OMB
Council of Economic Advisors

Phase 2 – Congressional budget process. Includes action on appropriations and revenue measures.

Phase 2 Actors

Congress As A Whole
Authorizing Committees
(Subject Matter Committees)
Revenue Taxation Committees [c]
Budget Committees
Congressional Budget Office (CBO)
Agency/Dept. Testimony
President signs or vetos appropriations

Phase 3 – Implementation & control of enacted budget. (During fiscal year.)

Phase 3 Actors

Treasury
General Accounting Office (GAO)
Agency/Dept.
Office of Management and Budget (OMB)
President
Congress

Phase 4 – Review & audit

Phase 4 Actors

General Accounting Office (GAO)

[a] The president's budget is transmitted to Congress within 15 days after Congress convenes.
[b] If appropriation action is not completed by Sept. 30, Congress enacts temporary appropriation (i.e., continuing resolution).
[c] House Ways and Means Committee, Senate Finance Committee

FIGURE 9–4

264

Appropriations Acts.   Congressional approval of each year's spending is usually divided into thirteen separate appropriations bills, each covering separate broad categories of spending. These appropriations bills are drawn up by the House and Senate appropriations committees and their specialized subcommittees. Indeed, House appropriations subcommittees function as overseers of the agencies included in their appropriations bill. The appropriations committees must stay within overall totals set forth in the budget resolutions adopted by Congress. All appropriations bills *should* be passed by both houses and signed by the president into law before October 1st, the date set for the start of the fiscal year. However, it is rare that Congress meets its own deadlines. The government usually finds itself beginning a new fiscal year without a budget. Legally the U.S. government is obliged to shut down if Congress does not pass an appropriations measure. However, Congress gets around this problem by adopting a "continuing resolution" authorizing government agencies to keep spending money for a specified period at the same level as the previous fiscal year.

An *appropriations* act provides money for spending and no funds can be spent without an appropriations act. An *authorization* is an act of Congress establishing a government program and defining the amount of money which it may spend. Authorizations may be for several years. However, the authorization does not actually provide the money which has been authorized; only an appropriations act can do that. Appropriations acts are almost always for a single fiscal year. Congress has its own rule that does not allow appropriations for programs which have not been authorized. However, appropriations frequently provide less money for programs than earlier authorizations.

Appropriations acts include both obligational *authority* and *outlays*. An obligation of authority permits a government agency to enter into contracts calling for payments into future years (new obligated authority). Outlays are to be spent in the fiscal year for which they are appropriated.

Appropriations Committees.   Considerations of specific appropriations measures are functions of the appropriations committees in both houses. Committee work in the House of Representatives is usually more thorough than it is in the Senate; the committee in the Senate tends to be a "court of appeal" for agencies opposed to House action. Each committee, moreover, has about ten largely independent subcommittees to review the requests of a particular agency or a group of related functions. Specific appropriations bills are taken up by the subcommittees in hearings. Departmental officers answer questions on the conduct of their programs and defend their requests for the next fiscal year; lobbyists and other witnesses testify.

Revenue Acts.   The House Committee on Ways and Means and the Senate Finance Committee are the major instruments of Congress for consideration of *taxing* measures. Through long history and jealous pride they have maintained formal independence of the appropriations committees, further fragmenting legislative consideration of the budget.

Presidential Veto.   In terms of aggregates, Congress does not regularly make great changes in the executive budget, rarely changing it more than 5 percent. The budget is approved by Congress in the form of appropriations bills, usually thirteen of them, each ordinarily providing for several departments and agencies. The number of revenue measures is smaller. As with other bills that pass Congress, the president has ten days to approve or veto appropriations legislation. He lacks the power to veto items in bills, and only rarely exercises his right to veto appropriations bills in their entirety.

SUMMARY

Government budgeting lies at the heart of public policy making. Budgets tell us "who gets what" from government, and "who pays the cost." The theory of incrementalism helps us to understand the budget process and budget outcomes.

1. Government activity has grown in relation both to the size of the population and the economy. Government activity now accounts for over one-third of all economic activity in the United States.

2. Government expenditures as a proportion of all economic activity in the nation spurt upward in response to wars and depressions. When these crises subside, government expenditures associated with them decline somewhat, but stabilize at levels higher than before the crises. War forces citizens to tolerate major increases in government activity. During war, government domestic spending declines; but after a war, domestic spending displaces defense spending and achieves a higher plateau than before the war.

3. The budgetary *process* itself is incremental, political, fragmented, and nonprogrammatic. Policy makers generally consider last year's expenditure as a base and focus their attention on a narrow range of increases and decreases in expenditures. Evaluating the desirability of *every* public program *every* year might create politically insoluble conflict as well as exhaust the energies of budget makers.

4. The range of decisions available to policy makers in the development of an annual budget is really quite small. "Uncontrollable" items account for over two-thirds of the federal budget.

5. Among public expenditures, income security (social security, welfare, and social services) now takes highest priority. Defense spending, which was once the largest share of all federal spending, is now much less than spending for social programs. This shift in national priorities occurred between 1965 and 1975, during both a Democratic and a Republican administration

and during the nation's longest war. This reversal of federal budget priorities raises questions about whether budgeting is truly "incremental."

6. Various macroeconomic theories compete as guides to government fiscal and monetary policy. Keynesian economic theory urged government manipulation of aggregate demand by raising spending, lowering taxes, and incurring debt during recessions, and pursuing the opposite policies during inflations. But "supply-side" economists in the Reagan administration viewed these traditional countercyclical taxing and spending policies as "the failed policies of the past," which produced inflation, high interest rates, and a stagnant economy. Higher government taxing and spending levels promoted immediate consumption instead of investment in the future, and penalized hard work, creativity, and savings. President Reagan's Program for Economic Recovery included cutting the rate of growth of government spending, reducing personal income tax rates, reducing government regulations, and slowing the growth of the money supply.

7. The economic record of the Reagan years was very impressive: continuous growth in the GNP, lower inflation, lower taxes, and a slower rate of growth of government spending. The economy absorbed many millions of new workers, but the federal government incurred the highest annual deficits in history.

8. Huge federal deficits direct federal tax dollars away from defense and domestic needs and into interest payments. These deficits and interest payments burden future generations. Americans today are spending at the expense of their children.

9. In over thirty-five years neither presidents nor Congresses, Republicans or Democrats, have acted responsibly regarding deficits. Washington has been politically unable and unwilling to reduce spending (or to raise taxes) in order to balance the federal budget.

10. A constitutional amendment requiring a balanced budget is lost in political controversy and might not succeed in its objective even if it were to pass. An effort by Congress to discipline itself—the Gramm-Rudman-Hollings Act—promises gradually reduced deficits through automatic cuts in defense and nonprivileged domestic programs until a balanced budget is reached. But Congress can ignore, repeal, or amend its own law.

BIBLIOGRAPHY

CONGRESSIONAL QUARTERLY. *Budgeting for America.* Washington, D.C.: Congressional Quarterly, Inc., 1982.
FENNO, RICHARD. *The Power of the Purse.* Boston: Little, Brown, 1966.
WILDAVSKY, AARON. *The Politics of the Budgetary Process.* 4th ed. Boston: Little, Brown, 1984.

10

TAX POLICY
battling the special interests

For the most part, Americans who itemize their deductions fall into the middle- and upper-income tax brackets. (Van Bucher/Photo Researchers)

INTEREST GROUPS AND TAX POLICY

The interplay of interest groups in policy making is praised as "pluralism" by many political scientists. Robert A. Dahl, for example, proclaimed the "central guiding thread of American constitutional development" to be "the evolution of a political system in which all the active and legitimate groups in the population can make themselves heard at some critical stage in the process of decision."[1] Public policy is portrayed by interest group theory as the equilibrium in the struggle between interest groups (see Chapter 2). While this equilibrium is not the same as majority preference, it is considered by pluralists to be the best possible approximation of the public interest in a highly organized society.

But what if only a small proportion of the American people are organized into politically effective interest groups? What if the interest group system represents well-organized, economically-powerful, producer groups, who actively seek immediate tangible benefits from the government? What if the interest group system leaves out a majority of Americans, particularly the less-organized, economically dispersed consumers and taxpayers, who wish for broad policy goals such as fairness, simplicity, and general economic well-being? Most serious social scientists acknowledge that the interest group system in Washington fails to represent the mass public in policy making. Political scientist E.E. Schattschneider writes: "The business or upper-class bias of the pressure system shows up everywhere."[2] Even the so-called "public interest" groups are really "models of elitism" representing a tiny group of administrators, lobbyists, and lawyers, who make their living claiming to represent the public in Washington.

There is no better illustration of the influence of organized interest groups in policy making than national tax policy. Every economics textbook tells us that the public interest is best served by a tax system which is universal, simple, and fair, and which promotes economic growth and well-being. But until recently the federal tax system was very nearly the opposite: it was complex, unfair, and nonuniversal. About *one-half* of all personal income in the United States escaped taxation through various exemptions, deductions, and special treatments in tax laws. Most of these tax breaks benefited businesses and upper-income individuals. Tax laws treated different types of income differently. They penalized work, savings, and investment, and diverted capital investment into nonproductive tax shelters and an illegal "underground economy."

The unfairness, complexity, and inefficiency of the tax laws were directly attributable to organized interest groups. The nation's elected policy

[1]Robert A. Dahl, *A Preface to Democratic Theory* (Chicago: University of Chicago Press, 1956), p. 124.

[2]E.E. Schattschneider, *The Semi-Sovereign People* (New York: Holt, Rinehart & Winston, 1960), p. 31.

makers were fully aware of this. Representative Dan Rostenkowski of Chicago, chairman of the House Ways and Means Committee, which writes the nation's tax laws, admitted:

> We gave oil companies breaks to fuel our oil industry. We gave real estate incentives to build more housing. We sharpened our technology with research and development credits. We gave tax breaks to encourage people to save. We pile one tax benefit on top of another—each one backed with good intention.
>
> Unfortunately it didn't take too long before those with the best accountants and lawyers figured out how to beat the system . . . and the cost of government was shifted to families like those in my neighborhood who don't have the guile to play the game of hide-and-seek with the IRS. . . .
>
> In the end tax reform comes down to a struggle between the narrow interests of the few—and the broad interests of working American families.[3]

Indeed, the influence of the special interests in federal tax policy was so great that few observers expected that tax reform efforts would ever succeed. For years congressional advocates of tax reform—Representatives Jack Kemp (R.–N.Y.) and Richard Gephardt (D.–IN) and Senator Bill Bradley (D.–N.J.)— were ignored. And President Reagan's tax reform proposals were said to be doomed. But in a dramatic turnabout in the Tax Reform Act of 1986, the special interests suffered a rare but major defeat on tax policy. The president and Congress, Republicans and Democrats, joined together in a sweeping reform of the nation's tax laws.

In this chapter, we will examine the nation's tax laws and the influence of the special interest on these laws. We will describe how reform was accomplished over the opposition of the special interests and how the special interests continue to influence tax policy today.

TAX BURDENS: DECIDING WHAT'S FAIR

The politics of taxation centers around the question of who actually bears the burden or incidence of a tax—that is, which income groups must devote the largest proportion of their income to taxes. Taxes that require high-income groups to pay a larger percentage of their incomes in taxes than low-income groups are said to be *progressive*, while taxes that take a larger share of the income of low-income groups are called *regressive*. Taxes that require all income groups to pay the same percentage of their income in taxes due are said to be *proportional*. Note that the *percentage of income* paid in taxes is the determining factor. Most taxes take more money from the rich than the poor, but a progressive or regressive tax is distinguished by the *percentages*

---

[3]Text of address by U.S. Representative Dan Rostenkowski, 28 May 1985. *Congressional Quarterly Weekly Report*, 1 June 1985, p. 1077.

of income taken from various income groups. The percentage of income paid in taxes is called the *effective tax rate.*

Various exemptions and deductions in tax laws can also be considered progressive or regressive, depending on whether they benefit the rich or the poor. For example, a personal exemption of $2,000 is considered progressive. Even though both rich and poor can claim their personal exemptions, four $2,000 exemptions for a poor family whose income is under $10,000 exempts 80 percent of their income from taxation; whereas the same four $2,000 exemptions for a family whose income is $100,000 exempts only 8 percent of their income from taxation. In contrast, the deduction for state and local taxes is considered regressive, because wealthy taxpayers who pay heavy state and local income and property taxes are more likely to claim large deductions for these items than poorer taxpayers.

The Argument for Progressivity.   Progressive taxation is generally defended on the principle of ability to pay; the assumption is that high-income groups can afford to pay a large percentage of their incomes into taxes at no more of a sacrifice than that required of lower-income groups to devote a smaller proportion of their income to taxation. This assumption is based on what economists call *marginal utility theory* as it applies to money: each additional dollar of income is slightly less valuable to an individual than preceding dollars. For example, a $5,000 increase in the income of an individual already earning $100,000 is much less valuable than a $5,000 increase to an individual earning only $3,000 or to an individual with no income. Hence, added dollars of income can be taxed at higher *rates* without violating equitable principles.

The Argument for Proportionality.   Opponents of progressive taxation generally assert that equity can only be achieved by taxing everyone at the *same* percentage of their income, regardless of the size of their income. A tax which requires all income groups to pay the same percentage of their income is called a *proportional* or *flat tax.* Progressivity penalizes initiative, enterprise, and risk, and reduces incentives to expand and develop the nation's economy. Moreover, by taking incomes of high-income groups, governments take money that would otherwise go into business investments and stimulate economic growth. Highly progressive taxes curtail growth and make everyone poorer.

Reducing the Progressivity of the Federal Income Tax.   Certainly the most dramatic change in federal tax laws during the Reagan years was the reduction in the progressivity of tax rates. The top marginal tax rate was reduced from 70 percent when President Reagan took office to 28 percent following enactment of tax reform in 1986. (*Marginal* is a term used by economists to mean additional; a progressive tax taxes additional increments of income at higher rates; these increments are often referred to as "brackets"; the top marginal rate refers to the rate applied to the highest tax bracket.) This reduction in progressivity in the rate structure occurred in two major tax enactments: the Economic Recovery Tax Cut Act of 1981 reduced the rate structure from 14–70 percent to 11–50 percent; the Tax Reform Act of 1986 reduced the fourteen rate brackets varying from 11–50 percent to only two rate brackets, 15 and 28 percent.

"Soak the Rich."   In 1990 Congressional Democrats returned to the politically popular theme of "soak the rich," insisting on an increase in the top rate as part of a "deficit reduction" summit compromise with President George Bush. The president abandoned his firm campaign pledge "Read my lips, no new taxes!" Reversing the trend of the previous decade, the top marginal income tax rate was raised from 28 to 31 percent.

Universality.   Americans have also come to associate *universality* with fairness. Universality means that all types of income should be subject to the same tax rates: income earned from stocks, bonds, and real estate, and the buying and selling of these investments, should be taxed at the same rate as income earned from wages. Moreover, Americans have become somewhat more skeptical of exemptions, deductions, and special treatment in the tax laws. It is true that most people wish to retain the widely used tax breaks— the personal exemption, charitable deductions, and home mortgage deductions. But there is a growing sentiment that tax laws should not be used to promote social policy objectives by granting a wide array of tax preferences.

Economic Growth.   Americans also appear to have a new appreciation of the effect of high tax rates on *economic growth*. Excessively high rates cause investors to seek "tax shelters"—to use their money not to produce more business and employment but rather to produce tax breaks for themselves. High tax rates discourage work, savings, and productive investment; they also encourage costly "tax avoidance" (legal methods of reducing or eliminating taxes) as well as "tax evasion" (illegal means of reducing or eliminating taxes.).

Simplicity.   Finally, *simplicity* in taxation is also recognized both as a means of reducing the costs of paying taxes and a way of reassuring taxpayers that the tax structure is fair, reasonable, and understandable.

WHO REALLY BEARS THE TAX BURDEN?

The federal tax burden is about 20 percent of the nation's GNP. (State and local taxes add an additional 12 percent of GNP to create a total tax burden—federal state and local taxes combined—of over 32 percent of GNP.) But this tax burden is *not* distributed evenly among all income classes, that is to say it is not proportional. The federal individual income tax is progressive; the federal corporate income tax is also progressive, if we assume it is paid mainly from shareholders' dividend payments; but the social security tax (F.I.C.A.) is regressive. The overall distribution of the federal tax burden is mildly progressive.

Total v. Taxable Income. About half of all personal income escapes federal taxation through exemptions, deductions, and special treatments. Total *adjusted gross income* reported on federal income tax returns in 1988 was $3 trillion, while total personal income was estimated at $4 trillion. Legal deductions from Adjusted Gross Income in 1988 resulted in *taxable income* of $2 trillion.

Tax Burdens. The progressivity of the federal individual income tax is shown in Table 10–1. Taxpayers with less than $25,000 adjusted gross income paid an average effective tax rate of 7.8 percent, while the 65,303 taxpayers with over $1 million of income in 1988 paid 25.4 percent. Thus, wealthy taxpayers bear a burden over three times heavier than lower income taxpayers. And persons with incomes below $12,000 pay no federal income taxes at all.

Tax Payments. Wealthy taxpayers pay a very large share of total federal income taxes collected. The nation's $1 million income earners constitute only 0.06 percent of total taxpayers, but they contribute 10.5 percent of total income tax collections—almost as much as the 62 percent of taxpayers earning less than $25,000. These tax payments by the wealthy increased markedly after the Tax Reform Act of 1986.

TAXATION AND ECONOMIC GROWTH

The goal of any tax system is not only to raise sufficient revenue for the government to perform its assigned tasks, but also to do so simply, efficiently, and fairly, and in a way that does not impair economic growth. The argument on behalf of tax reform in the 1980s was that the federal tax system failed to meet *any* of these criteria:

> It was so complex that a majority of taxpayers hired professional tax preparers; an army of accountants and lawyers made their living from the tax code.
>
> Tax laws were unfair in treating various sources of income differently; the many exemptions, deductions, and special treatments were perceived as "loopholes" that allowed the privileged to escape fair taxation.

TABLE 10-1 Who Bears the Burden: Distribution of Federal Income Tax Payments, 1988

ADJUSTED GROSS INCOME CLASS	NUMBER OF TAXPAYERS	ADJUSTED GROSS INCOME B$	TAXABLE INCOME B$	EFFECTIVE TAX RATE ON ADJUSTED GROSS INCOME	TAXPAYERS AS PERCENT OF TOTAL TAXPAYERS	TAXES PAID AS PERCENT OF TOTAL TAX COLLECTED
Under $25,000	68,100,000	608.0	329.6	7.8%	62.0	11.4
$25,000–$50,000	27,700,000	988.1	659.2	10.8	25.2	25.7
$50,000–$100,000	11,400,000	747.1	543.6	14.7	10.4	26.5
$100,000–$500,000	2,400,000	401.2	322.4	21.9	2.2	21.1
$500,000–$1,000,000	119,231	80.7	70.7	24.8	0.1	4.8
over $1,000,000	65,303	172.5	155.6	25.4	0.06	10.5
All taxpayers	109,800,000	$2,997.6	$2,081.1	20.0%	100	100

Source: Tax Foundation computations from Statistics and Income, U.S. Internal Revenue Service.

Tax laws encouraged tax avoidance, directing investment away from productive uses and into inefficient tax shelters; whenever people make decisions about savings and investment based on tax laws instead of most productive use, the whole economy suffers.

Tax laws encouraged cheating and reduced trust in government; they encouraged the growth of an underground economy, transactions which were never reported on tax forms.

High marginal tax rates discouraged work and investment; economic growth was diminished when individuals faced tax rates of 50 percent or more on additional income they received from additional work, savings, or investment.

When the Reagan team arrived in Washington in 1981, its first priority was to reduce high marginal rates of taxation in the hope of stimulating economic growth. According to its supply-side economists, poor economic growth rates and high inflation were caused in large part by high tax rates. High tax rates were discouraging Americans from working and investing; the resulting lower production levels were causing inflation. If tax rates could be lowered, argued the supply siders, more Americans would work, save, and invest, and a larger supply of goods would be produced. This increased supply of goods would keep prices in check and reduce inflation.

The Laffer Curve. Do tax cuts create government deficits? Not necessarily, argue the supply siders. If tax rates are reduced, the paradoxical results may be to *increase* government revenue because more people will work harder and start new businesses knowing they can keep a larger share of their earnings. Tax cuts will stimulate increased economic activity, and this increased activity will produce more government revenue even though tax rates are lower.

Economist Arthur Laffer developed the diagram shown in Figure 10-1. If the government imposed a zero tax rate, of course, it would receive no

FIGURE 10-1. The Laffer Curve.

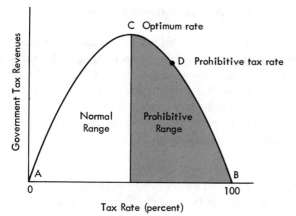

revenue (point *A*). Initially, government revenues rise with increases in the tax rate. However, when tax rates become too high (beyond point *C*), they discourage workers and businesses from producing and investing. When this discouragement occurs, the economy declines, and government revenues fall. Indeed, if the government imposed a 100-percent tax rate (if the government confiscated everything anyone produced), then everyone would quit working and government revenues would fall to zero (point *B*).

According to the "Laffer curve," modest increases in tax rates will result in increased government revenues up to an optional point (point *C*), after which further tax increases discourage work and investment. Laffer does not claim to know exactly what the optimum rate of taxation should be. But Laffer (and the Reagan administration) clearly believe that the United States had been in the "prohibitive range" throughout the 1970s.

Bracket creep is a term used to describe a particular contribution to the adverse economic effect of high personal income tax rates. Bracket creep occurs when individuals receive higher wages due to inflation, but because of that inflation these higher wages do not add to their buying power. However, higher wages cause higher tax rates. In this way inflation gradually pushes all wage earners into higher tax brackets and increases everyone's tax burden. These tax increases occur "automatically," without a need for Congress to enact higher taxes. According to supply-side economists, this bracket creep, by increasing tax burdens, further erodes incentives to work, save, invest, and produce.

The Economic Recovery Tax Cut Act.   The Economic Recovery Tax Cut Act of 1981, pushed through Congress by President Reagan, reduced personal income taxes by 25 percent over a three-year period. Marginal tax rates were reduced from a range of 14 to 70 percent to a range of 11 to 50 percent; this was only a minor reduction at the bottom end of the income brackets but a very significant reduction in the highest income brackets. In addition, the act granted many new investment incentives for business, and "indexed" taxes against inflation in future years in order to prevent bracket creep.

The Reagan administration hoped that the tax cuts would stimulate work, productivity, investment, and economic growth. According to Reagan's budget calculations, the federal tax bite out of the nation's GNP would be reduced to less than 20 percent. Without the tax cuts, the tax bite would have climbed to nearly 25 percent of the GNP. Moreover, the tax cuts and the indexing of taxes in future years would place the government on a reduced "allowance." Hopefully, this "allowance" would force Congress to limit the growth of federal spending.

The Impact of the Reagan Tax Cuts.   The recession of 1981–82 was the deepest since the Great Depression of the 1930s. For the first time since the

Depression, unemployment reached double-digit levels—exceeding 10 percent. Total output declined, steel and automobile plants operated at less than half of capacity, house building was brought to a standstill, and business bankruptcies reached new highs. Personal income grew very slowly and corporate profits declined, while government unemployment compensation payments soared. The result was the largest peacetime federal deficit in history.

Traditionally in American politics, the "in" party is blamed when the economy falters. Yet the recession of 1981–82 was already underway before the Economic Recovery Tax Cut Act of 1981 took effect. The recession can be traced to high interest rates which slowed capital investment, and high interest rates can be traced to runaway inflation in the 1970s. The Reagan administration claimed that the recession would have been *worse* without its tax cuts. Throughout the recession, the Reagan administration believed that its economic recovery program would eventually bring economic growth, more jobs, and stable prices, if Americans would "stay the course." The important early accomplishments of their program included a reduced rate of inflation and lower interest rates.

Critics of Reaganomics argued that: (1) the tax cuts failed to result in new investment or new employment—in other words, "trickle down" did not work; (2) the huge federal deficits created by the tax cuts (and increased military spending) kept interest rates high—in other words, government borrowing crowded out private borrowing and increased interest rates; and (3) budget constraints on social programs added to the hardship of the poor.

THE POLITICS OF TAX REFORM

For fifty years, politicians in Washington promised to make tax laws simple and fair. Almost every year Congress tinkered with the laws, but the results of these changes only made matters worse. Or, as President Reagan observed: "They made it more like Washington itself: complicated, unfair, cluttered with gobbledygook and loopholes designed for those with the power and influence to hire high-priced legal and tax advisors."[4]

It comes as no surprise that most Americans believed that the federal tax system was unfair. Interestingly, this evaluation did *not* differ much by income class; people at all income levels believed federal taxes were unfair (see Table 10-2).

Although tax reform is popular as a general theme, most Americans want to keep their own favorite deductions. Despite these general negative views of the federal tax system. Americans consider most of the major personal deductions to be a "perfectly reasonable deduction" and not a tax

[4]Text of Presidential Address on Tax Reform, 28 May 1985. *Congressional Quarterly Weekly Report*, 1 June 1985, p. 1074.

TABLE 10-2   Public Opinion on Federal Taxes

	PERCENT AGREE
The federal tax system is unfair.	59%
The present tax system benefits the rich and is unfair to the ordinary working man or woman.	75%
Corporations are undertaxed.	52%
The rich tend to get out of paying taxes by using accountants and lawyers.	92%
Cheating on taxes is becoming more common these days.	54%

Source: *Public Opinion* February–March 1985.

loophole (see Table 10–3). Obviously, the popularity of these deductions and exemptions made it difficult for the president and Congress to fashion true tax reform.

Public opinion generally supports a shift from individual income taxes to corporate taxes and "sin" taxes on liquor and cigarettes. Other types of federal revenue raising are generally unpopular, even "to reduce the deficit" (see Table 10–4).

More importantly, there are a host of special interest groups who want to keep special provisions in the tax laws that benefit themselves. These interest groups, representing manufacturers, oil and gas companies, farmers, accountants, real estate developers, bankers, charities and foundations, and even state and local government officials, all combine to place major obstacles in Washington to comprehensive tax reform.

Congress has always had a strong distaste for the medicine of tax reform. Instead it made only incremental changes in the tax laws over the years. In the early 1960s the Kennedy administration reduced the progressivity of the federal income taxes—from the previous 20–91 percent to rates of 14–70

TABLE 10-3   Public Opinion on Various Federal Tax Deductions and Exemptions

	PERCENT SAYING PERFECTLY REASONABLE
Property taxes	93%
Interest on home mortgages	92%
State and local income taxes	88%
Interest paid on loans	87%
Child care for working parents	84%
Contributions to charity	71%
Social Security income as nontaxable	92%
Municipal bond income as nontaxable	53%

Source: *Public Opinion*, February–March 1985

TABLE 10-4 Public Opinion on Various Deficit-Reducing Measures

	PERCENT AGREEING A STEP THAT SHOULD BE CONSIDERED VERY SERIOUSLY TO REDUCE THE DEFICIT
An increase in corporate income taxes	78%
Raising taxes on liquor and cigarettes	76%
A national lottery	66%
Raising user taxes—gasoline taxes for drivers, airport taxes for passengers, etc.	38%
A value-added or national sales tax	34%
An increase in personal income taxes	24%

Source: *Public Opinion*, February–March 1985.

percent—but retained all of the traditional exemptions and deductions. In 1968, the costs of the Vietnam War moved Congress to raise personal income taxes; but instead of tampering with basic tax laws, Congress chose to impose a "surtax"—a 10 percent increase over whatever the individual was already paying. President Reagan's Economic Recovery Tax Cut Act of 1981 was the largest tax cut in history, but it did not make any significant changes in the traditional exemptions and deductions. Its greatest change was a lowering of the top income tax bracket from 70 to 50 percent. None of these changes in tax laws could be called tax *reform*.

In 1985, President Reagan launched a campaign for sweeping tax reform:

> For the sake of fairness, simplicity, and growth, we must radically change the structure of a tax system that still treats our earnings as the personal property of the Internal Revenue Service, radically change a system that still treats similar incomes much differently. And yes, radically change a system that still causes some to invest their money, not to make a better mousetrap, but simply to avoid a tax trap.[5]

The major features of the Reagan tax reform package were:

Reduce marginal tax rates and number of brackets.

Index bracket amounts to protect taxpayers from inflation.

Increase the personal exemption to $2,000 (from $1,000) and index it in later years for inflation.

Raise the zero bracket amount so that the poor (families of four under $12,000) would pay no federal income tax.

[5]Text of presidential address on tax reform, 28 May 1985. *Congressional Quarterly Weekly Report*, 1 June 1985, p. 1074.

Eliminate interest deductions except for home mortgages.

Eliminate deductions for state and local taxes paid.

Retain deductions for charitable contributions and medical expenses over 5 percent of income.

End investment tax credits for business.

Tighten rules on estimating depreciation on building and machinery.

Reduce the number and size of many business deductions, including entertainment.

Reduce the corporate tax rate from 46 to 33 percent.

Impose a minimum tax of 20 percent for individuals and corporations who otherwise would pay no taxes because of depreciation and interest deductions.

Eliminate the depletion allowance for large oil and gas companies.

STRUGGLING WITH THE SPECIAL INTERESTS

Tax reform turned out to be the most heavily lobbied legislation in the history of the Congress of the United States. The task fell first to the House Ways and Means Committee to try to shape President Reagan's tax reform proposal into law. The committee was chaired by Chicago Democrat Dan Rostenkowski, a man of extraordinary stamina and political skill and a supporter of tax reform. Yet no one knew better than Rostenkowski that a host of deals would have to be made with the powerful special interests in order to pass any tax bill. Indeed, some would argue that Rostenkowski made so many deals over tax reform that the final version of the tax reform bill had little "reform" left in it. Nonetheless, without Rostenkowski's skill and dedication, there would have been no tax bill at all.

Industry.   Opponents of tax reform were led by the U.S. Chamber of Commerce, the National Association of Manufacturers, and the Business Roundtable. Heavy manufacturing businesses strongly opposed the elimination of the investment tax credit, accelerated depreciation and foreign tax credit provisions in existing tax laws. The lowering of the corporation tax rate from 46 to 33 percent did not really appeal to large manufacturers as few of them paid any taxes anyway because of the generous loopholes in the law.

Real Estate and Housing.   The National Association of Home Builders strongly opposed the elimination of interest deductions for second and vacation homes, as well as the elimination of real estate tax shelters which encouraged investors to put money into real estate projects that earned little or no income. The real estate industry also wanted to preserve deductions for property taxes.

Multinational Corporations.   Businesses involved in international trade opposed efforts to eliminate the foreign tax credit, which allows U.S. companies to use taxes paid to other countries to reduce their U.S. tax liability.

Timber.   Existing tax laws treat corporate income from timber sales as capital gains rather than ordinary income. The timber companies fought hard to retain their special treatment.

Oil and Gas.   The American Petroleum Institute, representing the United States' powerful oil companies, fought bitterly against any reductions in their "depletion allowance" or deductions for "intangible costs." Their familiar argument was that any change in their privileged status in the tax code would inhibit capital investment in energy and reduce production. But as an old Washington hand observed: "There are three reasons for keeping the oil depletion allowance—Texas, Oklahoma, and Louisiana."

Wall Street Investment Firms.   The Securities Industries Association, the American Council for Capital Formation, and the nation's large investment firms lobbied heavily to keep preferential treatment of capital gains—profits from the sales of stocks and bonds. And the investment firms joined with banks in arguing for the retention of tax-free Individual Retirement Accounts (IRAs).

Charities and Foundations.   Even before President Reagan sent his tax reform proposals to Congress, the nation's leading foundations had petitioned the president to retain deductions for charitable contributions.

Restaurants and Entertainment.   The president proposed to limit business deductions for meals to $25 per person per meal and to eliminate entertainment deductions—night clubs, concerts, sport tickets, and so forth. The National Restaurant Association, representing high-priced restaurants, convinced Congress that business would falter without $100 meals and three-martini lunches; even the restaurant workers union appeared to plead the same case. The National Football League, the National Basketball Association, and the National Hockey League all reported that businesses purchased most of their season tickets as tax deductions.

Labor Unions.   The AFL-CIO was unimpressed with the notion of reducing and simplifying tax rates. Instead, it focused its opposition on the proposal to tax fringe benefits, including employer-paid health insurance and group life insurance. Unions also tried to keep the deduction for union dues.

Banks.   Banking interests, led by the American Bankers Association, wished to continue unlimited deductions for all interest payments. This makes borrowing easier by shifting part of the costs of borrowing from the debtor to the government and the taxpayers who must make up the lost revenue. Interest deductions make more customers for banks.

Auto Industry.   The auto industry fought hard to keep deductions for interest paid on auto loans.

These special interests are powerful in Congress. An estimated one-third of all campaign contributions in congressional elections come from Political Action Committees, or PACs, which distribute these contributions on behalf of business, trade associations, and labor unions. Most of these contributions go to *incumbent* members of Congress. Seldom do PACs try to bargain on specific pieces of legislation, that is to "buy votes," because bribery is illegal. But every member of Congress knows who has contributed to his or her campaign costs in the past and who may do so in the future. When these same interests strongly urge him or her to vote with them on pending legislation, attention must at least be paid to their urgings.

NEGOTIATIONS AND COMPROMISES

Representative Dan Rostenkowski devoted two months of closed-door sessions of his Ways and Means Committee to writing a tax reform bill. Popular enthusiasm for tax reform appeared to waiver; even the President was unable to stir much popular interest, although he announced that tax reform was the top legislative priority of his second term. Rostenkowski hammered out innumerable compromises with the special interests, restoring many popular deductions. "We have not written a perfect law," he admitted, "but politics is an imperfect process." He argued that the House bill was nonetheless a "vast improvement over current law." It limited many tax deductions and credits (see Table 10–4), and shifted part of the burden of taxation away from individuals and toward corporations. All participants in tax reform agreed that the new law should be *revenue neutral*, that is, it should not raise or lower overall taxes. The Democratic-controlled House succeeded in passing the Rostenkowski tax reform bill. If tax reform failed in the Republican-controlled Senate, the Democrats could blame the failure on the Republicans.

In the Senate, the principal responsibility for tax reform fell on Senate Finance Committee Chairman Robert Packwood (R.–OR). Initially Packwood was lukewarm on tax reform: "I kind of like the present tax code,"[6] he said, defending special tax breaks as a way for government to shape society. He also announced that unless tax breaks for Oregon's timber industry were

---

[6]*Congressional Quarterly Weekly Report*, 10 May 1986, p. 101.

retained he would oppose tax reform. Lobbyists converged on Packwood's committee in droves. Packwood initially attempted to accommodate them, writing so many special preferences into the law that little revenue remained. The result was "an orgy of special interest trading." Packwood was leading his committee through tax writing in the traditional way—by trading breaks to the special interest groups for their support. Indeed, the special interest trading became an embarrassment to members of the committee. The bill accumulated more special preferences than the existing law; tax "reform" was dying. The President's "top" legislative priority appeared to be a lost cause, and Democrats were prepared to blame the GOP-controlled Senate for failure to reform the nation's tax laws. When it became clear that Packwood himself would bear most of the responsibility for the failure of reform, he became a "convert" to tax reform.

The key to overcoming the opposition of the special interests was to offer a tax rate low enough that most people would be willing to give up their deductions and preferences. Packwood decided to throw out the old bill and begin anew with a "clean" bill. The new bill had fewer deductions than the House bill and lower rates than either the President's plan or the House bill. To preserve low top rates—28 percent for individuals and 34 percent for corporations—and keep the bill "revenue neutral," senators had to reject amendments by the special interests. The strategy worked to the surprise of everyone. The Senate Finance Committee voted 20–0 to send the clean bill to the full Senate. In an atmosphere of nonpartisanship the full Senate passed the bill with a vote of 97–3. A political "miracle" had occurred: Democrats and Republicans, liberals and conservatives, had united against the special interests.

Nevertheless, the special interests succeeded in keeping many of their favorite exemptions, deductions, and special treatments (see column "Tax Reform Act" on Table 10–5). Business lost its battle to keep the investment tax credit, and depreciation schedules were generally lengthened to curtail "fast tax write-offs." The real estate industry—builders, developers, mortgage lenders—succeeded in restoring deductions for vacation homes. But depreciation of housing investments was lengthened and investors were prevented from using paper losses from real estate depreciation to "shelter" unrelated income. Indeed tax shelters of many kinds were eliminated; the Act prevented taxpayers from using "passive" losses generated from investments to be used to reduce other income for tax purposes. The oil and gas industry, however, succeeded in retaining most of their special preferences in the tax code, including "depletion allowances" and "intangible" drilling costs. But the banking and automotive industries lost their fight to retain interest deductions on auto and consumer loans. The AFL-CIO knocked out the proposal to tax employer-paid fringe benefits, but lost its fight to keep union dues deductible. The restaurant and entertainment industries restored 80 percent of their favorite deductions. State and local governments were successful in retaining the exemption from taxation of interest received from

TABLE 10-5   The Evolution of Tax Reform

PROVISIONS	PREVIOUS LAW	TAX REFORM ACT OF 1986
Individual Tax Rate	11–50% 14 brackets	15 and 28%; 2 brackets (a shadow rate of 33% for high-middle income taxpayers is created by the phase out of deductions)
Personal Exemption	$1,040	$2,000, but phased out for high income tax-payers.
Interest Payments	Unlimited deductions	Deductions for first and second residences; no consumer interest deductions
Charitable Deductions	Deductible	Deductible
Fringe Benefits	Not taxed	Not taxed
Depreciation	Short: 3–19 years; plus accelerated write-offs	Longer: 3–31½ years; fewer accelerated write-offs.
Capital gains	20%	Same as income: 15 and 28%
Corporate tax rate	46%	34%
Investment tax credit	10%	Repealed
Business entertainment	Unlimited deductions	Allow deductions of 80% of all meals and entertainment
Oil and gas depletion and "intangible" cost deduction	Allowed deductions	Allowed deductions
State and local taxes	Fully deductible	Full deductions for income and property taxes; no deduction for sales taxes
Individual Retirement Accounts (IRA)	$2000 deductible contribution each year; IRA earnings tax free	Deductible contributions eliminated except for low income families

state and local government bonds, and they also succeeded in keeping the deduction for most state and local government taxes. But on balance the special interests suffered their single greatest defeat in many decades.

Reversing Course.   George Bush campaigned for the presidency with an emphatic promise to veto any attempt to raise taxes—"Read my lips! No new taxes!" But the president's pledge did not last through his second year in office. In a budget "summit" with leaders of the Democratically-controlled Congress, President Bush announced his willingness to support a tax increase as part of a deficit-reduction agreement. Once the Democratic leaders in Congress detected the irresolution of the Republican president, they proceeded to enact their own taxing and spending program, while placing the political blame on George Bush. The resulting budget plan made deep cuts in defense spending, token cuts in Medicare, increases in other social spending programs, together with major tax increases.

Reversing the downward trend in top marginal tax rates, the 1990 budget package raised the highest income tax rate from 28 to 31 percent. The resulting rate structure is a three-tiered one—15, 28, and 31 percent. However, phaseouts of various exemptions for high income taxpayers raised their real marginal rates to 33 percent or more. The budget package also raised the federal gasoline taxes, as well as taxes on alcohol, tobacco, and airline tickets, and imposed a new federal "luxury" tax on expensive items.

GOVERNMENT AS A SPECIAL INTEREST

One of the more controversial debates for federal tax reform focused on the elimination of the tax deduction for state and local income, sales, and property taxes. This was the largest personal deduction (aside from the personal exemption), exceeding deductions for medical and dental expenses, home mortgage interest, other interest, and charitable contributions. President Reagan argued that this deduction should be dropped because it "actually provides a special subsidy for high-income individuals in a few high-tax states. Two-thirds of Americans don't even itemize so they receive no benefit from the state and local tax deduction. But they're being forced to subsidize the high tax policies of a handful of states."[7]

The effect of the federal deduction for state and local income, sales, and property taxes is to lighten the burden of state and local government financing. The burden of these deducted taxes is reduced by the marginal value of the federal tax against which it is deducted. For example, a 10 percent state income tax is reduced to 7.2 percent for taxpayers in the 28-percent bracket who deduct their state income tax payments from their federal taxable income.

Opposition to the elimination of deductibility came from high-income taxpayers in high-tax states. This opposition was informed, active, skilled, and well positioned to influence policy discussion. The deductibility question is the type of policy issue on which everyone loses something, but some lose more than others. The people who will lose most—the high-income taxpayers in high-tax states—have more reason to inform and activate themselves politically, and by so doing, weigh the outcome of the collective choice process in their own favor.

[7]President Ronald Reagan, Address to the Nation on Tax Reform, 28 May 1985.

These taxpayers were joined by state and local officials throughout the country who understood that federal deductibility would reduce the direct costs of their own taxing decisions. In other words, when these state and local officials vote for higher taxes in their states, they know that their higher income taxpayers can deduct these taxes from their federal income tax liability, in effect shifting the cost to the federal government.

So lobbyists from state, county, and city governments, particularly those with high taxes, convened in Washington to lobby against tax reform. The leading state and local government lobbying organizations were the National Governors' Association, the National League of Cities, the National Conference of State Legislatures, the U.S. Conference of Mayors, the Council of State Governments, the International City Managers Association, and the American Federation of State, County, and Municipal Employees. They were joined by labor unions representing public employees.

The governmental lobby triumphed over the president and tax reform. Deductions for state and local income and property taxes were retained by Congress. Only the deduction for sales taxes was eliminated.

CAPITAL GAINS: RETURN OF THE SPECIAL INTERESTS

A central reform in the Tax Reform Act of 1986 was the elimination of preferential treatment for income from capital gains. (A capital gain is the profit made from buying and selling any asset—real estate, bonds, stocks, and so forth.) Prior to 1986, income from capital gains had been taxed at a *lower* rate than income from wages and salaries. A lower capital gains rate was defended as an incentive for people to save and invest their money and a stimulus to capital accumulation and economic growth. It is true, of course, that lower tax rates encourage economic growth, but it is not clear why rates on income from capital gains should be lower than rates on income from work. More importantly, from a political perspective, lower rates on income from capital gains favor the wealthy who generally derive more of their income from this source than do middle-class wage earners. Taxing income made from profit lower than income made from work is widely perceived as unfair. Fairness requires that all income be taxed equally.

A major compromise in the Tax Reform Act of 1986 was that in return for cutting the top tax rate of the wealthiest Americans nearly in half, from 50 percent to 28 percent, capital gains would no longer be given preferential treatment but instead be taxed at the same rate as other income.

But George Bush was never an enthusiastic supporter of tax reform. As vice-president he pressed to retain tax breaks for the oil and gas industry. And since becoming president, he has pressed hard to restore preferential treatment for capital gains income.

The pressure to regain old tax breaks is strong from the special interest lobbies, notably oil and gas industries, timber and cattle industries, real estate and building interests, the banking industry, and so on. President Bush's campaign for a lower capital gains rate threatens to pull the thread that will unravel the whole fabric of tax reform. Special interests will be given encouragement to seek their own preferential treatment.

A reasonable argument can be made that the definition of a capital gain should exclude inflationary effects of price increases over time. That is, if the increase in the price of an asset at sale is attributable to inflation and not a true gain in value, there should be no capital "gain" tax. Capital gains should be indexed for inflation; the proportion of the capital gain that results from inflation should be deducted from the nominal capital gain. But the Tax Reform Act of 1986 did not provide for indexing of capital gains.

THE FEDERAL TAX SYSTEM TODAY

Federal taxes are derived from five major sources:

Individual Income Taxes.   The personal income tax is the federal government's largest source of revenue; it accounts for 43 percent of the federal government's income (see Figure 10–2).

Individual income is now taxed at three rates: 15, 28, and 31 percent. For married couples, the bracket changes occur at $32,450 (to 28 percent) and $78,400 (to 31 percent). These figures are indexed annually to reflect

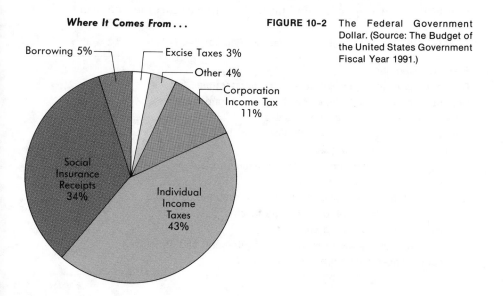

Where It Comes From . . .

FIGURE 10-2   The Federal Government Dollar. (Source: The Budget of the United States Government Fiscal Year 1991.)

Borrowing 5%

Excise Taxes 3%

Other 4%

Corporation Income Tax 11%

Social Insurance Receipts 34%

Individual Income Taxes 43%

inflation. A personal exemption of $2,000 for each taxpayer and dependent, together with a standard deduction of $5,000 for married couples, insures that poor working families will pay no income tax. (However, they still must pay social security taxes.) The personal exemption and standard deduction is also indexed to protect against inflation.

The income tax is automatically deducted from the paychecks of all employees except farm and domestic workers. This "withholding" system is the backbone of the individual income tax. There is no withholding of nonwage income, but taxpayers with such income must file a "Declaration of Estimated Taxes" and pay this estimate in quarterly installments. Before April 15th of each year, all income-earning Americans must report their taxable income to the Internal Revenue Service on its 1040 Form.

Americans are usually surprised to learn that half of all personal income is *not* taxed. To understand why, we must know how the tax laws distinguish between *adjusted gross income* (which is an individual's total money income minus expenses incurred in earning that income) and *taxable income* (that part of adjusted gross income subject to taxation). Federal tax rates apply only to *taxable* income. Federal tax laws allow many reductions in adjusted gross income in the calculation of taxable income.

"Tax expenditures" is a term meant to identify tax revenues that are lost to the federal government because of exemptions, deductions, and special treatments in tax laws. Table 10–6 lists the major "tax expenditures" in federal tax law. There is a continual struggle between proponents of special tax exemptions to achieve social goals, and those who believe the tax laws should be simplified and social goals met by direct expenditures.

Most Americans fail to itemize their deductions: Those who do are mostly middle- and upper-income taxpayers. Lower-income taxpayers seldom

TABLE 10–6   Major "Tax Expenditures" in Federal Tax Policy

Personal exemption
Deductibility of mortgage interest on owner-occupied homes
Deductibility of property taxes on first and second homes
Deferral of capital gains on home sales
Deductibility of charitable contributions
Credit for child care expenses
Exclusion of employer contributions to pension plans and medical insurance
Exclusion of Social Security benefits
Exclusion of interest on public-purpose state and local bonds
Deductibility of state and local income taxes
Exclusion of income earned abroad
Accelerated depreciation of machinery, equipment, and structures
Medical expenses over 7.5 percent of income

itemize their deductions, while upper-income taxpayers almost always do so. Itemizing deductions reduces the progressivity of the federal income tax.[8]

Corporate Income Tax.   The corporate income tax provides only 11 percent of the federal government's total income. The Tax Reform Act of 1986 reduced the top corporate income tax from 46 to 34 percent. However, prior to this Act, corporations had many ways of reducing their "taxable income," often to zero. The result was that many very large and profitable corporations paid little or no taxes. Some of the most notorious of these corporate tax breaks were modified or eliminated in the Tax Reform Act of 1986.

Tax reform succeeded in shifting some of the overall federal tax burden from individual to corporations. The corporate share of federal revenues (8 percent) has risen to 11 percent and the individual income tax share (49 percent) before reform has declined to 43 percent. These changes have reversed trends in the previous twenty years, which saw corporate taxes decline from 20 percent of total federal revenue to 8 percent.

Who pays the corporate income tax? Economists differ over whether this tax is "shifted" to consumers or whether corporations and their stockholders bear its burden. The evidence on the *incidence*—that is, who actually bears the burden—of the corporate income tax is inconclusive.[9]

Religious, charitable, and educational organizations, as well as labor unions, are exempt from corporate income taxes, except for income they may derive from "unrelated business activity."

Social Security Taxes.   The second largest and fastest growing source of federal revenue is the social security tax; it now provides 34 percent of the federal government's income. It is withheld from paychecks as the "FICA" deduction, an obscure acronym which helps to hide the true costs of social security from wage earners. To keep up with the rising number of beneficiaries and the higher levels of benefits voted by Congress, the social security tax has risen incrementally each year in two ways: (1) a gradual increase in the combined employer-employee tax rate (percent); and (2) a gradual increase in the taxable earnings base.

The taxes collected under social security are earmarked (by social security number) for the account of each taxpayer. Workers, therefore, feel they are receiving benefits as a right rather than as a gift of the government. However, benefits are only slightly related to the earnings record of the individual worker; there are both minimum and maximum benefit levels which prevent benefits from corresponding to payments. Indeed, for current re-

---

[8]Joseph A. Pechman, *Federal Tax Policy*, 5th ed. (Washington, D.C.: Brookings Institution, 1987).

[9]Pechman, *Federal Tax Policy*, ch. 5.

TABLE 10-7 Social Security Taxes

	COMBINED EMPLOYEE-EMPLOYER TAX RATE	MAXIMUM WAGE BASE	MAXIMUM INDIVIDUAL TAX
1937	2.0%	$ 3,000	$ 30
1950	3.0	3,000	45
1960	6.0	4,800	144
1970	9.6	7,800	374
1980	12.26	25,900	1,588
1985	14.10	39,600	2,792
1990	15.3	50,400	3,856

Source: *Statistical Abstract of the United States 1990.*

cipients of social security, less than 15 percent of the benefits can be attributed to their prior contributions. Current taxpayers are paying over 85 percent of the benefits being received by current retirees.

Because of the top limit on the amount of earnings subject to the social security tax ($50,400 in 1990), the tax is considered regressive in its treatment of incomes above that level. In other words, income above the top level is not subject to the social security tax; once the top payment is reached in any year, no social security taxes are levied on additional income. However, benefits are also capped. High-income earners cannot expect high social security benefits upon retirement. This is the traditional justification for the regressivity of the tax.

Today a majority of taxpayers pay more in social security taxes than income taxes. Indeed, combined employer and employee social security taxes now amount to nearly $8,000 at the top of the wage base. If we assume that the employer's share of the tax actually comes out of wages that would otherwise be paid to the employee, then over 75 percent of all taxpayers pay more in social security taxes than income taxes.

Estate and Gift Taxes.   Taxes on property left to heirs is one of the oldest forms of taxation in the world. Federal estate taxes begin on estates of $600,000 and levy a tax of 37 percent on accounts above this level. Because taxes at death could be easily avoided by simply giving estates to heirs while still alive, a federal gift tax is also levied. There is an annual exclusion of $10,000 in gifts per donee.

Excise Taxes and Custom Duties.   Federal taxes on liquor, tobacco, gasoline, telephones, air travel, and other so-called luxury items account for only about 1 to 2 percent of total federal revenue. Customs taxes on imports provide another 1 to 2 percent of total federal revenues.

SUMMARY

Modern pluralism praises the virtues of an interest group system in which public policy represents the equilibrium in the group struggle and the best approximation of the public interest. Yet it is clear that the interest group system disadvantages broad segments of the American public, especially individual taxpayers.

1. Tax reform to achieve fairness, simplicity, and economic growth is an elusive goal. The interest group system, designed to protect special privileges and treatments, especially in the tax code, frustrates efforts to achieve true tax reform.

2. Special interests can take advantage of the difficulties in defining fairness. Is fairness proportionality, with everyone paying the same percentage of income in taxes? Or is fairness progressivity, with the percentage of income paid in taxes increasing with increases in income?

3. Over half of the nation's total personal income escapes income taxation through exemptions, deductions, and special treatments. Most individual taxpayers fail to itemize their deductions. "Itemizers" are mostly middle- and upper-income taxpayers.

4. The corporate income tax is only 11 percent of total federal revenues. The individual income tax (43%) and the social security payroll tax (34%) provide most of the federal government's revenue.

5. Most federal tax revenues are derived from the middle classes—married taxpayers with incomes between $25,000 and $100,000. The nation's 65,000 taxpayers with $1 million incomes account for almost as much tax revenue as the nation's 68 million taxpayers with incomes under $25,000.

6. Supply-side economists are concerned about the impact of high marginal tax rates on economic behavior, including disincentives to work, save, and invest, and on inefficiencies created by tax avoidance activity. According to the Laffer curve, reducing high marginal tax rates will increase government revenues by encouraging productivity.

7. The Economic Recovery Tax Cut Act of 1981, lowered the top marginal rate from 70 to 50 percent, and the Tax Reform Act of 1986 lowered it again to 28 percent. But in 1990 Congress raised the top rate to 31 percent.

8. The Tax Reform Act of 1986 was the most heavily lobbied piece of legislation in the history of Congress. Powerful interests opposing significant tax reform included the nation's largest manufacturers, the real estate and housing industries, multinational corporations, timber, oil, and gas companies, labor unions, banks, the restaurants and entertainment industries, and even many state and local governments. While these special interests won some important battles, on balance they lost the war over tax reform.

BIBLIOGRAPHY

BIRNBAUM, JEFFREY H., and ALAN S. MURRAY. *Showdown at Gucci Gulch.* New York: Random House, 1987.

CONLON, TIMOTHY, MARGARET WRIGHTSON, and DAVID R. BEAM. *Taxing Choices: The Politics of Tax Reform.* Washington: CQ Press, 1989.

JOSEPH A. PECHMAN. *Federal Tax Policy.* 5th ed. Washington, D.C.: The Brookings Institution, 1987.

_____. *Who Paid the Taxes* 1966–85. Washington, D.C.: The Brookings Institution, 1985.

STOCKMAN, DAVID A. *The Triumph of Politics.* New York: Harper & Row, 1986.

WITTE, JOHN F. *The Politics and Development of the Federal Income Tax.* Madison: University of Wisconsin Press, 1985.

11

AMERICAN FEDERALISM
institutional arrangements
and public policy

The national government cannot address the needs of all states; moreover, state and local governments may be better suited to deal with specific state and local problems. (AP/Wide World Photos)

AMERICAN FEDERALISM

Virtually all nations of the world have some units of local government—states, "republics," provinces, regions, cities, counties, villages. Decentralization of policy making is required almost everywhere. But nations are not truly *federal* unless both national and subnational government exercise separate and autonomous authority, both elect their own officials, and both tax their own citizens for the provision of public services. Moreover, federalism requires that the powers of the national and subnational governments be guaranteed by a constitution that cannot be changed without the consent of both national and subnational populations.[1]

The United States, Canada, Australia, India, the German Federal Republic, and Switzerland are generally regarded as federal systems. But Great Britain, France, Italy, and Sweden are not. While these nations have local governments, they are dependent on the national government for their powers. They are considered *unitary* rather than federal systems, because their local governments can be altered or even abolished by the national government acting alone. In contrast, a system is said to be *confederal* if the power of the national government is dependent upon local units of government. While these terms—federal, unitary, and confederal—can be defined theoretically, in the real world of policy making it is not so easy to distinguish between governments that are truly federal and those that are not. Indeed, it is not clear whether government in the United States today retains its federal character.

There are over eighty-three thousand separate governments in the United States, over sixty thousand of which have the power to levy their own taxes. There are states, cities, counties, towns, boroughs, villages, special districts, school districts, and public authorities (see Table 11–1). However, only the national government and the states are recognized in the U.S. Constitution; all other governments are subdivisions of states. States may create, alter, or abolish these other governments by amending their laws or constitutions.

---

[1]Other definitions of federalism in American political science: "Federalism refers to a political system in which there are local (territorial, regional, provincial, state, or municipal) units of government as well as a national government, that can make final decisions with respect to at least some governmental authorities and whose existence is especially protected." James Q. Wilson, *American Government*, 4th ed. (Lexington: D.C. Heath, 1989), p. 47. "Federalism is the mode of political organization that unites smaller polities within an overarching political system by distributing power among general and constituent units in a manner designed to protect the existence and authority of both national and subnational systems enabling all to share in the overall system's decision making and executing processes." Daniel J. Elazar, *American Federalism: A View from the States* (New York: Thomas Y. Crowell, 1966), p. 2.

TABLE 11-1   Governments in the United States

U.S. government	1
State government	50
Counties	3,041
Municipalities	19,205
Townships	16,691
School district	14,741
Special districts	29,487
Total	83,217

Source: *Statistical Abstract of the United States 1990.*

WHY FEDERALISM?

Why have state and local governments anyway? Why not have a centralized political system with a single government accountable to national majorities in national elections—a government capable of implementing uniform policies throughout the country?

Protection Against Tyranny. The nation's Founders understood that "republican principles"—periodic elections, representative government, political equality—would not be sufficient in themselves to protect individual liberty. These principles may function to make governing elites more responsive to popular concerns, but they do not protect minorities or individuals, "the weaker party or an obnoxious individual," from government deprivations of liberty or property. Indeed, according to the Founders, "the great object" of constitution-writing was to both preserve popular government and at the same time to protect individuals from "unjust and interested" *majorities.* "A dependence on the people is, no doubt, the primary control of government, but experience has taught mankind the necessity of auxiliary precautions."[2]

Among the most important "auxiliary precautions" devised by the Founders to control government was federalism. Federalism was viewed by the Founders as a source of constraint on big government. Governments and government officials were seen as likely to act in their own self interest. Therefore constitutional arrangements had to be devised so that the personal interest of government officials coincided with the interest of society.

The solution to the problem of adjusting the self-interests of government officials to interests of the larger society was *competition.* Rather than

[2]James Madison, Alexander Hamilton, John Jay, *The Federalist,* Number 51 (New York: Modern Library, 1958).

rely on the "better motives" of statesmen, the Founders sought to construct a governmental system incorporating the notion of "opposite and rival interests." Governments and government officials could be constrained by competition with other governments and other government officials.[3]

Policy Diversity. Today, federalism continues to permit policy diversity. The entire nation is not "straitjacketed" with a uniform policy that every state and community must conform to. State and local governments may be better suited to deal with specific state and local problems. Washington bureaucrats do not always know best about what to do in Commerce, Texas.

Conflict Management. Federalism helps manage policy conflict. Permitting states and communities to pursue their own policies reduces the pressures that would build up in Washington if the national government had to decide everything. Federalism permits citizens to decide many things at the state and local levels of government and avoid battling over single national policies to be applied uniformly throughout the land.

Dispersal of Power. Federalism disperses power. The widespread distribution of power is generally regarded as an added protection against tyranny. To the extent that pluralism thrives in the United States, state and local governments have contributed to its success. State and local governments also provide a political base for the survival of the opposition party when it has lost national elections.

Increased Participation. Federalism increases political participation. It allows more people to run for and hold political office. Nearly a million people hold some kind of political office in counties, cities, townships, school districts, and special districts. These local leaders are often regarded as "closer to the people" than Washington officials. Public opinion polls show that Americans believe that their local governments are more manageable and responsive than the national government.

Improved Efficiency. Federalism improves efficiency. Even though we may think of having eighty-thousand governments as inefficient, governing the entire nation from Washington would be even worse. Imagine the bureaucracy, red tape, delays, and confusion if every government activity in every community in the nation—police, schools, roads, firefighting, garbage collection, sewage disposal, street lighting, and so on—were controlled by a central government in Washington.

---

[3]See Thomas R. Dye, *American Federalism: Competition Among Governments* (Lexington: Lexington Books, 1990).

Insuring Policy Responsiveness.   Federalism encourages policy responsiveness. Multiple, competing governments are more sensitive to citizen views than monopoly government. The existence of multiple government offering different packages of benefits and costs allows a better match between citizen preferences and public policy. People and businesses can "vote with their feet" by relocating themselves to those states and communities that most closely conform to their own policy preferences. Americans are very mobile. About four of every ten Americans move in just a five-year period. One in five Americans moves to a different county and one in ten to a different state. Businesses and industry are also increasingly mobile. Mobility not only facilitates a better match between citizens' preferences and public policy, it also encourages competition between states and communities to offer improved services at lower costs.

Encouraging Policy Innovation.   Federalism encourages policy experimentation and innovation. Federalism may be perceived today as a "conservative" idea, but it was once viewed as the instrument of "progressivism." A strong argument can be made that the groundwork for the New Deal was built in state policy experimentation during the Progressive Era. Federal programs as diverse as income tax, unemployment compensation, countercyclical public works, social security, wage and hour legislation, bank deposit insurance, and food stamps all had antecedents at the state level. Indeed, much of the current "neoliberal" policy agenda—mandatory health insurance for workers, child care programs, notification of plant closings, government support of industrial research and development—has been embraced by various states. Indeed, the compelling phrase "laboratories of democracies" is generally attributed to the great progressive jurist, Supreme Court Justice Louis D. Brandeis, who used it in defense of state experimentation with new solutions to social and economic problems.

WHY CENTRALIZATION?

Political conflict over federalism—over the division of responsibilities and finance between national and state/local governments—has tended to follow traditional liberal and conservative political cleavages. Generally, liberals seek to enhance the power of the *national* government. Liberals believe that people's lives can be changed by the exercise of governmental power to end discrimination, abolish poverty, eliminate slums, ensure employment, uplift the downtrodden, educate the masses, and cure the sick. The government in Washington has more power and resources than state and local governments have, and liberals have turned to it rather than to state and local governments to cure America's ills. State and local governments are regarded as too slow, cumbersome, weak, and unresponsive. The government in Washington is seen as the principal instrument for liberal social and economic reform. Thus, liberalism and centralization are closely related in American politics.

The liberal argument for national authority can be summarized as follows:

1. State and local governments have insufficient awareness of social problems. The federal government must take the lead in civil rights, equal employment opportunities, care for the poor and aged, the provision of adequate medical care for all Americans, and the elimination of urban poverty and blight.

2. It is difficult to achieve change when reform-minded citizens must deal with fifty state governments or eighty thousand local governments. Change is more likely to be accomplished by a strong government.

3. State and local governments contribute to inequality in society by setting different levels of services in education, welfare, health, and other public functions. A strong national government can ensure uniformity of standards throughout the nation.

4. A strong national government can unify the nation behind principles and ideas of social justice and economic progress. Extreme decentralization can foster local or regional special interests at the expense of the general public interests.

Generally, conservatives seek to return power to *state and local* governments. Conservatives are more skeptical about the good that government can do. Adding to the power of the national government is not an effective way of resolving society's problems. On the contrary, conservatives argue that "government is the problem, not the solution." Excessive governmental regulation, burdensome taxation, and inflationary government spending combine to restrict individual freedom, penalize work and savings, and destroy incentives for economic growth. Government should be kept small, controllable, and close to the people.

INSTITUTIONS AND INTERESTS

Debates about federalism are seldom constitutional debates; rather, they are debates about policy. People decide which level of government—national, state, or local—is most likely to enact the policy they prefer. Then they argue that level of government should have the responsibility for enacting the policy. Political scientist David Nice explains "the art of intergovernmental politics" as "trying to reduce, maintain, or increase the scope of conflict in order to produce the policy decisions you want." Abstract debates about federalism or other institutional arrangements, devoid of policy implications, hold little interest for most citizens or politicians. "Most people have little interest in abstract debates that argue which level of government should be responsible for a given task. What people care about is getting the policies they want."[4]

Thus, the case for centralizing policy decisions in Washington is almost always one of substituting the policy preferences of national elites for those of state and local officials. It is not seriously argued on constitutional grounds that national elites better reflect the policy preferences of the American people. Federal intervention is defended on policy grounds—the assertion that the goals and priorities that prevail in Washington should prevail throughout the nation.

Concentrating Benefits to Organized Interests

The national government is more likely to reflect the policy preference of the nation's strongest and best-organized interest groups than that of eighty-three thousand state and local governments. This is true, first, because the costs of "rent seeking"—lobbying government for special subsidies, privileges, and protections—are less in Washington in relation to the benefits available from national legislation than the combined costs of rent seeking at eighty-three thousand subnational centers. Organized interests, seeking concentrated benefits for themselves and dispersed costs to the rest of society, can concentrate their own resources in Washington. Even if state and local governments individually are more vulnerable to the lobbying efforts of wealthy, well-organized special interests, the prospect of influencing all fifty separate state governments, or worse, eighty-three thousand local governments, is discouraging to them. The costs of rent seeking at fifty state capitols, three thousand county courthouses, and tens of thousands of city halls, while not multiplicative by these members, are certainly greater than the costs of rent seeking in a single national capitol.

Moreover, the benefits of national legislation are comprehensive. A single act of Congress, or a federal executive regulation, or a federal appellate court ruling can achieve what would require the combined and coordinated action by hundreds, if not thousands, of state and local government agencies. Thus, the benefits of rent seeking in Washington are larger in relation to the costs. Lobbying in Washington is efficient.

Dispersing Costs to Unorganized Taxpayers

Finally, and perhaps most important, the size of the national constituency permits interest groups to disperse the costs of specialized, concentrated benefits over a very broad constituency. Cost dispersal is the key to interest group success. If costs are widely dispersed, it is irrational for individuals, each of whom bear only a tiny fraction of these costs, to expend

[4]David C. Nice, *Federalism: The Politics of Intergovernmental Relations* (New York: St. Martin's Press, 1987), p. 24.

time, energy, and money to counter the claims of the special interests. Dispersal of cost over the entire nation better accommodates the strategies of special interest groups than the smaller constituencies of state and local government.

In contrast, state and local government narrows the constituencies over which costs must be spread, thus increasing the burdens to individual taxpayers and increasing the likelihood that they will take notice of these burdens and resist their imposition. Economist Randall G. Holcombe explains:

> One way to counteract this [interest group] effect is to provide public goods and services at the smallest level of government possible. This concentrates the cost on the smallest group of taxpayers possible and thus provides more concentrated costs to accompany the concentrated benefits.[5]

He goes on to speculate whether the tobacco subsidies granted by Washington to North Carolina farmers would be voted by the residents of that state if they had to pay the full costs of these subsidies. Lobbying in Washington disperses costs.

The rent-seeking efficiencies of lobbying in Washington are well-known to the organized interests. As a result, the policies of the national government are more likely to reflect the preferences of the nation's strongest and best-organized interests.[6]

AMERICAN FEDERALISM: VARIATIONS ON THE THEME

American federalism has undergone many changes over the two hundred years since the Constitution of 1787. The original constitutional rules have stayed the same, but their use and interpretation over the years have changed dramatically.

Dual Federalism (1787–1913).   For the nation's first hundred years, the pattern of federal-state relations has been described as "dual federalism." Under this pattern, the states and the nation divided most governmental functions. The national government concentrated its attention on the "delegated" powers—national defense, foreign affairs, tariffs, commerce crossing state lines, coining money, establishing standard weights and measures, maintaining a post office and building post roads, and admitting new states. State governments decided the important domestic policy issues—slavery (until the Civil War), education, welfare, health, and criminal justice. This separa-

[5]Randall G. Holcombe, *An Economic Analysis of Democracy* (Carbondale: Illinois University Press, 1986), p. 174.

[6]This argument is derived from public choice theory (see Chapter 2), and is developed further in Thomas R. Dye, *American Federalism: Competition Among Governments* (Lexington, Mass.: Lexington Books, 1990).

tion of policy responsibilities was once compared to a "layer cake"[7] with local governments at the base, state governments in the middle, and the national government at the top. This view implied that state and local governments were "closer" to people than the national government, that the national government did not serve the people directly, and that governmental responsibility was parceled out to *either* states or localities, or to the national government.

The national government was not completely divorced from local concerns.[8] The national government financed state militias, which eventually became the National Guard. The U.S. Army Corps of Engineers helped build roads and canals. The national government appropriated money for various "internal improvements"—these expenditures for roads, rivers, and harbors were the forerunners of what we call pork-barrel legislation today. Nonetheless, most important policy decisions were made by the states.

The greatest crisis in American federalism occurred during this period—the struggle over slavery, the attempted secession of eleven Southern states, and the Civil War, 1861–1865. The national government intervened forcefully in what had been a state affair to end slavery. During the reconstruction period, 1865–1877, Congress and the national military-occupation governments in the Southern states also tried to guarantee black voting rights and end many forms of racial discrimination. But this national effort failed when "states' rights" were restored; the national government waited until the 1960s before reasserting its authority in civil rights.

Dual federalism came to an end in the twentieth century. With the emergence of a national industrial economy, Congress began to intervene in economic affairs—with the Interstate Commerce Commission in 1887 and the Sherman Anti-Trust Act in 1889. But it was the passage of the Sixteenth Amendment in 1913 giving the national government the power to levy the income tax that brought the era of dual federalism to an end. The income tax shifted the balance of financial power to the national government and paved the way for national intervention in many fields once "reserved" to the states.

Cooperative Federalism (1913–1964).   The Industrial Revolution and the development of a national economy, the shift in financial resources to the national government, and the challenges of two world wars and the Great Depression, all combined to end the distinction between national and state concerns. The new pattern of federal-state relations was labeled "cooperative federalism." Both the nation and the states exercised responsibilities for welfare, health, highways, education, and criminal justice. This merging of policy responsibilities was compared to a "marble cake." As the colors are

---

[7]Morton Grodzins, *The American System* (Chicago: Rand McNally, 1966), pp. 8–9.

[8]See Daniel Eldzar, *The American Partnership* (Chicago: University of Chicago Press, 1962).

mixed in a marble cake, so functions are mixed in the American federal system.[9]

The Great Depression of the 1930s forced states to ask for federal financial assistance in dealing with poverty, unemployment, and old age. Governors welcomed massive federal public works projects. In addition, the federal government intervened directly in economic affairs, labor relations, business practices, and agriculture. Through the grant-in-aid device, the national government cooperated with the states in public assistance, employment services, child welfare, public housing, urban renewal, highway building, and vocational education.

Yet even in this period of shared national-state responsibility, the national government emphasized cooperation in achieving common national and state goals. Congress generally acknowledged that it had no direct constitutional authority to regulate public health, safety, or welfare. Congress relied primarily on its powers to tax and spend for the general welfare to provide financial assistance to state and local governments to achieve shared goals. Congress did not usually legislate directly on local matters. For example, Congress did not require the teaching of vocational education in public high schools because public education was not an "enumerated power" of the national government in the U.S. constitution. But Congress could offer money to states and school districts to assist in teaching vocational education, and even threaten to withdraw the money if federal standards were not met. In this way the federal government involved itself in fields "reserved" to the states.

Centralized Federalism (1964 to the Present).   Over the years it became increasingly difficult to maintain the fiction that the national government was merely assisting the states in performing their domestic responsibility. By the time President Lyndon B. Johnson launched the "Great Society" in 1964, the federal government had clearly set forth its own "national" goals. Virtually all problems confronting American society—from solid waste disposal and water and air pollution, to consumer safety, home insulation, noise abatement, and even metric conversion—were declared to be national problems. Congress legislated directly on any matter it chose, without regard to its "enumerated powers" and without pretense to financial assistance. The Supreme Court no longer concerned itself with the "reserved" powers of the states; the Tenth Amendment lost most of its meaning. The pattern of national-state relations became centralized. As for the cake analogies, one commentator observed: "The frosting had moved to the top, something like a pineapple upside-down cake.[10]

[9]Grodzins, *The American System*, p. 265.
[10]Charles Press, *State and Community Governments in the Federal System* (New York: John Wiley, 1979), p. 78.

The states' role is now often one of carrying out federal mandates. The administrative role of the states remains important; states help to implement federal policies in welfare, Medicaid, environmental protection, employment training, public housing, and so on. But the states' role is determined not by the states themselves but by the national government.

Bureaucracies at the federal, state, and local levels are increasingly undistinguishable. Coalitions of professional bureaucrats—whether in education, public assistance, employment training, rehabilitation, natural resources, agriculture, or whatever—work together on behalf of shared goals, whether they are officially employed by the federal government, the state government, or a local authority. One commentator refers to this type of policy making as "functional federalism.[11] State and local officials in agencies receiving a large proportion of their funds from the federal government feel very little loyalty to their governor or state legislature.

The "New Federalism." Efforts to reverse the flow of power to Washington and return responsibilities to state and local government have been labeled the "New Federalism." The phrase originated in the administration of President Richard M. Nixon, who used it to describe General Revenue Sharing, that is, federal sharing of tax revenues with state and local governments, with few strings attached. Later the phrase "New Federalism" was used by President Ronald Reagan to describe a series of proposals designed to reduce federal involvement in domestic programs and encourage states and cities to undertake greater policy responsibilities themselves. These efforts included the consolidation of many categorical grant programs into fewer block grants; and an end to General Revenue Sharing.

THE GROWTH OF POWER IN WASHINGTON

Over time governmental power has been centralized in Washington. While the formal constitutional arrangements of federalism remain in place, power has flowed relentlessly toward the national government since the earliest days of the nation.

Government Centralization.   At the beginning of the twentieth century, most government activity in the United States was carried on at the local level. Table 11–2 shows that local governments once made about 59 percent of all government expenditures in the United States, compared to 35 percent for the federal government and 6 percent for state governments. But the Great Depression of the 1930s and World War II in the 1940s helped

---

[11]Michael D. Reagan, *The New Federalism* (New York: Oxford University Press, 1972).

TABLE 11-2   A Comparison of the Expenditures of Federal, State, and Local Governments over Eight Decades (percentages of total general expenditures of governments)

	FEDERAL[a]	STATE[b]	LOCAL
1902	35	6	59
1927	31	13	56
1936	50	14	36
1944	91	3	7
1950	60	16	24
1960	60	15	25
1970	62	18	20
1980	64	18	18
1985	65	18	18
1987	64	18	19

Sources: U.S. Department of Commerce, *Statistical Abstract of the United States 1988*, p. 257; and *Statistical Abstract of the United States 1990*, p. 273.

[a]Figures include social security and trust fund expenditures.

[b]State payments to local governments are shown as local government expenditures; federal grants-in-aid are shown as federal expenditures.

bring about centralization in the federal system. In recent decades, federal spending has amounted to 55 to 60 percent of all government spending in the United States.

The extent of centralization of government activity in the American federal system varies widely according to policy area (Table 11–3). In the fields of national defense, space research, and postal service, the federal government assumes almost exclusive responsibility. In all other fields, state and local governments share responsibility and costs with the federal government. State and local governments assume the major share of the costs of

TABLE 11-3   Federal and State-Local Shares of Expenditures by Policy Area, 1927–1985

	1927		1985	
	FEDERAL	STATE AND LOCAL	FEDERAL	STATE AND LOCAL
National defense	100%	0%	100%	0%
Education	1	99	14	86
Highways	1	99	27	73
Welfare	6	94	72	28
Health and hospitals	18	82	29	71
Police and fire	7	93	14	86
Natural resources	31	69	85	15
Housing and urban renewal	—	—	65	35

Source: U.S. Bureau of the Census, *Government Finance* 1984–85.
Note: Federal grants-in-aids are shown as federal expenditures.

education, highways, health and hospitals, sanitation, and fire and police protection. Welfare costs have gradually shifted to the federal government, and the federal government assumes the major share of the costs of natural resource development and housing and urban renewal.

Federal Grants-In-Aid. The federal grant-in-aid has been the principal instrument for the expansion of national power. As late as 1952, federal intergovernmental transfers amounted to about 10 percent of all state and local government revenue. Federal transfers creeped up slowly for a few years, leaped ahead after 1957 with the National Defense (Interstate) Highway Program and a series of post-Sputnik educational programs, and then surged in the welfare, health, housing and community development fields during the Great Society period (1965–1975). President Richard Nixon not only expanded these Great Society transfers but added his own general revenue-sharing program. Federal financial interventions continue to grow despite occasional rhetoric in Washington about state and local responsibility. By 1980, over 25 percent of all state-local-revenue came from the federal government. (See Table 11–4.) So dependent had state and local governments become on federal largess, that the most frequently voiced rationale for continuing federal grant programs was that states and communities had become accustomed to federal money and could not survive without it.

Reducing State Reliance on Federal Aid. Ronald Reagan challenged the nation's movement toward centralized government:

> Our citizens feel they have lost control of even the most basic decisions made about the essential services of government, such as schools, welfare, roads, and even garbage collection. They are right. A maze of interlocking jurisdictions and levels of government confronts the average citizen in trying to solve even

TABLE 11-4 Trends in Federal Grants-in-Aid

		FEDERAL GRANTS AS A PERCENTAGE OF:		
	TOTAL ($ billions)	TOTAL FEDERAL SPENDING	STATE AND LOCAL EXPENDITURES	GROSS NATIONAL PRODUCT
1950	2.3	5.3	10.4	0.8
1960	7.0	7.6	14.6	1.4
1970	24.1	12.3	19.2	2.4
1975	49.8	15.0	22.7	3.3
1980	91.5	15.5	25.8	3.4
1985	105.9	11.2	21.1	2.7
1990 (est.)	123.6	10.7	18.2	2.2

Source: U.S. Office of Management and Budget, *Special Analysis of the Budget 1988*, p. 11–22; and *Statistical Abstract of the United States 1990*, p. 276.

the simplest of problems. They do not know where to turn to for answers, who to hold accountable, who to praise, who to blame, who to vote for or against. The main reason for this is the overpowering growth of federal grants-in-aid programs during the past few decades.[12]

Washington had heard that kind of rhetoric from Republican presidents before, but Reagan actually proceeded to reverse the growing dependency of state and local governments on federal money. Federal intergovernmental transfers fell from a high of about 25 percent of total state-local revenue to a more modest 18 percent by 1990. Most of what Reagan accomplished in this area occurred in the first years of his presidency.

Ending General Revenue Sharing.   The Reagan administration did succeed in its efforts to eliminate general revenue sharing (GRS); to consolidate many categorical grant programs in larger block grants, allowing for greater local control over revenue allocation; and to reduce the rate of growth in federal intergovernmental transfer payments. Regarding GRS, the president argued that it was unreasonable to expect the federal government, which was running deep deficits, to turn over revenues to state and local governments, which had no deficits. Most GRS funds went for traditional services (police, fire, streets, sanitation, sewage, parks and recreation, and so forth) that local taxpayers should fund themselves. For several years, state and local government officials successfully lobbied Congress to restore GRS funds cut from the president's budget, but deficit pressures finally ended GRS in 1986.

Block Grants.   The Reagan administration also succeeded in consolidating many categorical grant programs into fewer larger block grant programs. A block grant is a payment to a state or local government for a general function, such as community development or education. State and local officials may use such funds for their stated purposes without seeking the approval of federal agencies for specific projects. Many categorical grant programs were merged, but many others remained independent.

Summary.   A critical summary of the Reagan accomplishments in federalism concludes:

> In sum, the administration has reversed the trend of growing financial dependence of lower levels of government on the national government, put in place a grant structure that is less restrictive and provides less encouragement to local spending, challenges the assumption that there should be uniform national standards for public services, and more fully engages the states as partners in the effort to contain domestic program costs.[13]

[12]President Ronald Reagan in his State of the Union Address, January 1982.

[13]John L. Palmer and Isabel V. Sawhill, eds. *The Reagan Record* (Cambridge MA: Ballinger, 1984).

INSTITUTIONS AND PUBLIC POLICY

In politics, constitutional decisions are never separated from policy outcomes. People know what the policy consequences of various institutional arrangements will be. Citizens as well as political leaders consistently subordinate constitutional questions to immediate policy concerns. History is replete with examples of the same political leaders arguing one notion of federalism at one point in time to achieve their immediate policy goal, and the turning around and supporting a contradictory notion of federalism at a later time when it fits a new policy goal. No American politician, from Thomas Jefferson onward, has ever so strongly supported a view of federalism that he or she ended up conceding a policy battle.

Types of Policy.   Let us consider the impact of intergovernmental competition for different types of policy decisions. Policies have been usefully classified as allocational, developmental, or redistributional.[14] *Allocational* policies produce and distribute public goods and services to consumer-taxpayers. These policies encompass the provision of a broad range of state and local government services, including education, health, welfare, streets and highways, police and fire protection, sewers, water and utilities, garbage disposal, parks and recreation, and so on. *Developmental* policies are those that directly enhance the economic well-being of the state or community. These policies are directed toward economic growth; they include attracting industry, building transportation facilities, providing utilities, renewing urban areas, training the labor force for work, and so on. *Redistributional* policies are designed to redirect wealth to benefit particular segments of society to satisfy equity concerns. These policies include traditional welfare services, health care for the poor, unemployment compensation, low-income housing, as well as progressive taxation. Note that these are analytical distinctions among types of policies; any specific government activity may have allocational, developmental, and redistributive elements within it.

Allocational Policy.   Federalism directly strengthens the allocative functions of government. Decentralization permits governments to match services with variations in demand. Greater overall citizen satisfaction can be achieved with multiple governments offering different packages of public services at different prices. Competition forces governments to become more efficient in their allocative activities, providing better services at lower costs. Competition forces government to be more responsive to citizen preferences than monopoly government. Paul E. Peterson, one of the few political scientists to incorporate the notion of competition into a coherent theory of federalism, appears to agree:

[14]Theodore J. Lowi, "American Business, Public Policy and Political Theory," *World Politics,* 16 (July 1964), 677–715.

Allocation is the function that local governments can perform more effectively than central governments, because decentralization allows for a closer match between the supply of public services and their variable demand. Citizens migrate to those communities where the allocation best matches their demand curve.[15]

Developmental Policy.   Federalism and intergovernmental competition inspires state and local governments to be concerned with the impact of their taxing and spending policies on economic growth and to become directly involved in economic development activities. The states' role in economic development has traditionally centered on the provision of *physical infrastructure,* especially transportation. Indeed for many years economic growth in the states correlated closely with state expenditures for transportation.[16] But it is likely that economic growth in the future will depend more upon state investment in *intellectual infrastructure.* Economic growth is always and everywhere a function of human creativity. In practical terms, investment in education at all levels—elementary and secondary schools, trade and vocational schools, community colleges and state universities, research institutions and parks—is likely to become the key to competitive advantage in the economy of the future. Fortunately for America's future, education is largely a function of competitive state and local governments, rather than of monopoly centralized government. Economic competition between the states can become the driving force behind improvements in education and research.

In addition to improvements in physical and intellectual infrastructure, competition can also drive states and communities to improve the *quality of life* in their locales. A skilled, educated, creative workforce can neither be recruited to a state nor retained there if the general quality of life is considered unattractive.

Thus, development policies are well served by federalism. Peterson argues convincingly that the federal government would be wise to leave economic development policy to state and local government:

> Since state and local governments are well equipped to pursue developmental objectives, most public efforts of this type should be left to them. By delegating responsibility for most developmental programs to state and local governments, the federal government would frankly admit its incapacity to use those programs to help populations with special needs.[17]

Redistributional Policy.   The most serious challenge to intergovernmental competition arises in redistributional policy. Can multiple, competing governments undertake redistributive policies without creating unbearable

[15]Paul E. Peterson, *City Limits* (Chicago: University of Chicago Press, 1981), p. 77.

[16]Thomas R. Dye, "Taxing, Spending, and Economic Growth in the American States," *Journal of Politics,* 42 (Nov. 1980), 1085–1107.

[17]Paul E. Peterson, *When Federalism Works* (Washington, D.C.: Brookings Institution, 1986), p. 230.

free rider problems for themselves? Will states and communities be restrained from providing the welfare services they would otherwise prefer because of the threat of an inundation of poor people from less beneficent "free riding" jurisdictions? Will each state and community wait for other states and communities to provide welfare services in the hope that their poor people will migrate to the more generous jurisdictions? Will tax burdens to support generous welfare services encourage the nonpoor—both households and businesses—to migrate to jurisdictions that impose lighter tax burdens because they provide frugal welfare services?

Federalism and Welfare Policy. The argument that intergovernmental competition disadvantages the poor rests on a version of the free rider problem: competing state and local governments will set welfare benefits below the true preferences of their citizens out of fear that poor people will migrate into generous jurisdictions. Governments consequently limit their welfare provision to levels at or below those of their neighbor states.

This argument assumes that welfare benefits influence the decisions of the poor about where to live—that generous welfare benefits attract inmigrating poor and discourage resident poor from out-migrating in search of a better life. The argument also assumes that affluent individuals, investors, and firms are repelled by the higher costs imposed by larger numbers of welfare recipients attracted by high benefits. By attracting "welfare seekers," states discourage productive labor and capital from coming to their states and may even encourage them to leave in search of lighter welfare burdens. Finally, the argument assumes that state and local policy makers act to avoid the free rider problem—providing less redistribution than preferred by their median voter. This means that policy makers are aware of the benefit levels provided by neighbor states and they use these levels as guidelines in their own decision making. Fearing an influx of poor, they deliberately restrict welfare benefits to levels provided by their neighbor states, or perhaps even more meanspiritedly, they deliberately set benefit levels below those of their neighbor states to encourage the poor to leave their own state.

However, the evidence to support these arguments is weak. Many studies indicate that the poor migrate for job opportunities and family reasons, not welfare benefits. While other studies suggest that benefit levels attract some "welfare seekers," there is no evidence that affluent individual or business firms avoid states with high benefit levels. In the 1970s when the oil industry boomed, it appeared that the Southwestern states, with their low welfare benefits, were attracting industry; but in the early 1980s the Northeastern states, with their hi-tech industries and high welfare benefits, were enjoying the highest economic growth rates. Finally there is little evidence to indicate that policy makers in the states may much attention to welfare benefits levels in their neighbor states in determining their own benefit levels. If they did so, we would expect welfare benefit levels in the states to converge over time, but they have not done so. (For example, average monthly AFDC payments in 1986 varied from highs of $532 in California and $507 in Minnesota to lows of $116 in Mississippi and $114 in Alabama, see Chapter 12.) Continuing wide variations on welfare benefit levels suggests that welfare policy in each state is made independently of other states.

Nonetheless, the possibility that interstate competition might drive down welfare benefits has inspired some political scientists to call for the "federalization" of welfare policy.[18]

SUMMARY

American federalism creates unique problems and opportunities in public policy. For nearly two hundred years, since the classic debates between Alexander Hamilton and Thomas Jefferson, Americans have argued the merits of centralized versus decentralized policy making. The debate continues today.

1. Eighty thousand separate governments—states, counties, cities, towns, boroughs, villages, special districts, school districts, and authorities—make public policy.

2. Proponents of federalism since Thomas Jefferson have argued that it permits policy diversity in a large nation, helps to reduce conflicts, disperses power, increases political participation, encourages policy innovation, and improves governmental efficiency.

3. Opponents of federalism argue that it allows special interests to protect positions of privilege, frustrates national policies, distributes the burdens of goverment unevenly, disadvantages poorer states and communities, and obstructs action toward national goals.

4. The growth of power in Washington is revealed in figures showing that the federal government collects nearly 60 percent of all governmental revenues. About one-fifth of all state and local government revenues comes from federal grants.

5. In recent years state and local governments have reduced their dependency on federal aid. Federal aid as a share of total state-local revenue has declined from a high of about 22 percent to about 18 percent today. "New Federalism" in the Reagan administration meant an end to General Revenue Sharing, consolidation of many individual grant programs into block grants, and a lower rate of growth in federal aid.

6. Policies may be broadly categorized as allocational (distributing public goods and services), developmental (enhancing economic growth),

[18]See Paul E. Peterson, *City Limits;* and Paul E. Peterson and Mark Rom, "American Federalism, Welfare Policy and Residential Choices," *American Political Science Review,* 83 (September 1989), 711–728.

or redistributional (transferring wealth or income among groups). Most analysts believe that state and local governments are better prepared institutionally to decide and implement allocational and developmental policies.

7. The federal government may be better positioned institutionally to undertake redistributional policy. Competition between states and communities may disadvantage the poor. Each state and community may wait for other states and communities to provide welfare benefits in the hope that their poor people will migrate to generous jurisdictions and relieve their own taxpayers of the burdens of welfare. However, data to support this thesis is weak: poor people migrate for jobs and economic opportunity not welfare benefits.

BIBLIOGRAPHY

Dye, Thomas R. *American Federalism: Competition Among Governments.* Lexington, Mass.: Lexington Press, 1990.
Elazar, Daniel J. *American Federalism: A View from the States.* New York: Harper & Row, 1966.
Nice, David C. *Federalism: The Politics of Intergovernmental Relations.* New York: St. Martin's Press, 1987.
Peterson, Paul E. *City Limits.* Chicago: University of Chicago Press, 1981.
_____. *When Federalism Works.* Washington, D.C.: Brookings Institution, 1986.
Reagan, Michael D. *The New Federalism.* New York: Oxford University Press. 1972.

12

INPUTS, OUTPUTS, AND BLACK BOXES
a systems analysis of state policies

Public policy is created *via* the political system, not as a result of it.

COMPARING PUBLIC POLICIES OF THE AMERICAN STATES

The American states provide an excellent setting for comparative analysis and the testing of hypotheses regarding the determinants of public policy. State policies in education, welfare, health, transportation, natural resources, and public safety, and many other areas vary a great deal from state to state. These differences are important in systems analysis because they enable us to search for relationships between different socioeconomic conditions, political system characteristics, and public policies.

"Nationalization" of the States. Economic differences among the states have been diminishing over time—a process that has been labeled the "nationalization" of the states. A graphic portrayal of diminishing *income* differences over the century among regions is presented in Figure 12–1. As industry, people, and money move from the Northeast and Midwest to the

FIGURE 12–1 Regional Economic Convergence. Source: *Public Opinion* (May–June 1986).

> (Note: Bureau of Economic Analysis regional groupings: *New England* = Maine, New Hampshire, Vermont, Massachusetts, Connecticut, Rhode Island. *Mideast* = New York, Pennsylvania, New Jersey, Delaware, Maryland, District of Columbia. *Southeast* = Virginia, West Virginia, North Carolina, South Carolina, Georgia, Florida, Kentucky, Tennessee, Alabama, Mississippi, Arkansas, Louisiana. *Southwest* = Oklahoma, Texas, Arizona, New Mexico. *Rocky Mountain* = Colorado, Wyoming, Montana, Idaho, Utah. *Far West* = Nevada, California, Oregon, Washington. *Plains* = Minnesota, Iowa, Missouri, North Dakota, South Dakota, Nebraska, Kansas. *Great Lakes* = Ohio, Michigan, Indiana, Wisconsin, Illinois. Not classified, Alaska, Hawaii.)

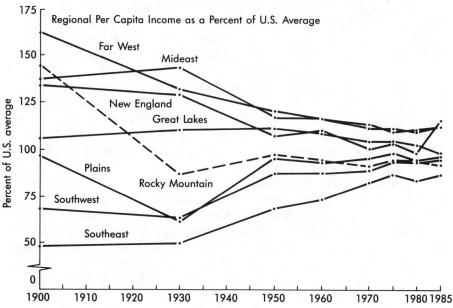

South, the historic disadvantage of the South gradually diminishes. As people move about the country, the distinct cultural and ethnic differences of the regions also diminish. Even regional accents become less pronounced. The impact of national television, motion pictures, and the record industries adds to the "homogenization" of state and regional cultures.

Continuing Policy Variations Among the States.   Nonetheless, even though the states are gradually becoming more similar over time in many respects, there is still enough variation to merit comparative analysis. Interestingly, *policy* variation among the states does *not* appear to be declining over time. There is no reliable evidence that the policy preferences of the states are becoming homogenized, or even that federal intervention is forcing uniform policies on the states. For example, Table 12–1 shows that variation among the states in spending for education and welfare are very large: some states spend almost three times as much for the education of a single pupil in public schools as other states; some states provide AFDC welfare families with monthly payments over four times higher than those provided by other states.

POLICY RESPONSIVENESS AND THE MEDIAN VOTER

An important criterion in evaluating democratic political systems—including the American states—is their responsiveness to citizen preferences. The test of responsiveness is whether state policies reflect the preferences of the "median voter" in the states.

Median voter models have provided economists and political scientists with simplified sets of assumptions about democratic political systems— assumptions that have expressly or implicitly formed the basis of a great deal of empirical research in state and local government. In the basic model, each individual voter tries to maximize the trade-off between various public goods and services and disposable private income. Each voter balances the "utilities" obtained from higher levels of public services against the "disutilities" of higher taxes, in order to choose an "optimal" benefit level. After each voter has made a choice based on his or her own preferences, tastes, needs, and so on, the choice of the median voter in any democratic political system should determine public policy.

A simple version of the median-voter model treats the political system itself as a neutral conversion mechanism that transforms the needs, demands, and preferences of the median voter into public policy. The model is similar to the early systems model in political science literature.[1] It was assumed that democratic political processes would produce public policies largely reflective of the preferences of voter-taxpayers. These preferences were usual-

---

[1]David Easton, *A Framework for Political Analysis* (Englewood Cliffs, N.J.: Prentice Hall, 1965).

TABLE 12-1   Policy Variation among the States

AFDC AVERAGE MONTHLY PAYMENT, 1986 (IN DOLLARS)		PER PUBLIC EXPENDITURES ELEMENTARY AND SECONDARY EDUCATION, 1988	
1. Alaska	$565	1. Alaska	$7,038
2. California	532	2. New Jersey	6,910
3. Minnesota	507	3. Wyoming	6,885
4. Wisconsin	496	4. New York	6,864
5. New York	483	5. Connecticut	6,141
6. Michigan	474	6. Rhode Island	5,456
7. Connecticut	466	7. Massachusetts	5,396
8. Massachusetts	449	8. Pennsylvania	5,063
9. Vermont	441	9. Delaware	4,994
10. Washington	431	10. Wisconsin	4,991
11. Rhode Island	412	11. Vermont	4,949
12. Hawaii	402	12. Maryland	4,871
13. Iowa	351	13. Oregon	4,574
Montana	351	14. Minnesota	4,513
15. New Jersey	349	15. Florida	4,389
16. Maine	348	16. Colorado	4,359
17. North Dakota	344	17. Maine	4,276
18. Utah	341	18. Kansas	4,262
19. Pennsylvania	339	19. Illinois	4,217
20. New Hampshire	329	20. Virginia	4,145
Oregon	329	21. Michigan	4,122
Wyoming	329	22. Washington	4,083
23. Kansas	328	23. Montana	4,061
24. Nebraska	316	24. Ohio	4,019
25. Colorado	309	25. California	3,994
26. Illinois	306	26. New Hampshire	3,990
27. Maryland	302	27. North Carolina	3,911
28. Ohio	296	28. West Virginia	3,895
29. Oklahoma	278	29. Hawaii	3,894
30. South Dakota	266	30. New Mexico	3,880
31. Arizona	264	31. Iowa	3,846
32. Missouri	262	32. Nevada	3,829
33. Virginia	255	33. Nebraska	3,641
34. Idaho	254	34. Indiana	3,616
35. Delaware	253	35. Missouri	3,566
36. West Virginia	247	36. Texas	3,462
37. Nevada	238	37. Kentucky	3,355
38. New Mexico	235	38. North Dakota	3,353
39. Georgia	228	39. Arizona	3,265
North Carolina	228	40. Louisiana	3,211
41. Florida	227	41. Tennessee	3,189
42. Indiana	220	42. South Dakota	3,159
43. Kentucky	193	43. South Carolina	3,075
44. South Carolina	186	44. Oklahoma	3,051
45. Arkansas	178	45. Georgia	2,939
46. Texas	171	46. Idaho	2,814
47. Louisiana	168	47. Mississippi	2,760
48. Tennessee	143	48. Alabama	2,752
49. Mississippi	116	49. Utah	2,658
50. Alabama	114	50. Arkansas	2,410

Source: *Statistical Abstract of the United States 1989.*

ly specified in state policy studies in terms of median or average characteristics of the population—for example, median family income, median school level completed, or percentage of the population aged, young, black, urban, and so on. This required an inferential leap that characteristics of the populations determined median voter preferences and, hence, community preferences. When variations in public policies among the states were shown to correlate with variations in population characteristics, this simple median-voter model gained empirical support. The traditional literature on the "determinants" of state and local government taxing and spending policies relied implicitly on this median-voter model.[2]

Thus, the median-voter model assumes that individual voter preferences in a democracy determine governmental decisions. Elected politicians reflect the preferences of their constituents because they wish to maximize community welfare and to get reelected. Politicians seek the package of public services and taxes desired by the median voter; the median voter's indifference curve is considered the state's indifference curve. Public spending will increase as long as the number of votes won by these increases exceeds the number of votes lost by the increasing costs of financing this spending. Politicians must estimate the numbers and preferences of voters in their separate roles as consumers and taxpayers. Their task is to balance votes won by each expenditure decision with votes lost by each revenue decision, and try to insure that the votes won will exceed the votes lost.

ECONOMIC RESOURCES AND PUBLIC POLICY

Economists have contributed a great deal to the systematic analysis of public policy. Economic research very early suggested that government activity was closely related to the level of economic resources in a society.[3] Economic development was broadly defined to include levels of wealth, industrialization, urbanization, and adult education.

We can picture the relationship between economic resources and public policy by viewing a "plot" of the relationship between per capita personal income and per pupil spending in public schools as shown in Figure 12–2. Per capita income is measured on the horizontal or X axis, while per pupil spending is measured on the vertical or Y axis. Each state is plotted in the graph according to its values on these two measures. The resulting

---

[2]Thomas R. Dye, *Politics, Economics, and the Public* (Chicago: Rand McNally, 1966); Roy W. Bahl, "Determinants of State and Local Government Expenditures," *National Tax Journal*, 18 (March 1965), 50–57; Glenn W. Fisher, "Interstate Variation in State and Local Government Expenditures," *National Tax Journal* 17 (March 1964) 57–74.

[3]See Solomon Fabricant, *Trend of Government Activity in the United States Since 1900* (New York: National Bureau of Economic Research, 1952); Seymour Sachs and Robert Harris, "The Determinants of State and Local Government Expenditures and Intergovernmental Flow of Funds," *National Tax Journal*, 17 (March 1964), 78–85; Glenn W. Fisher, *op. cit.*; Roy W. Bahl, *op. cit.*

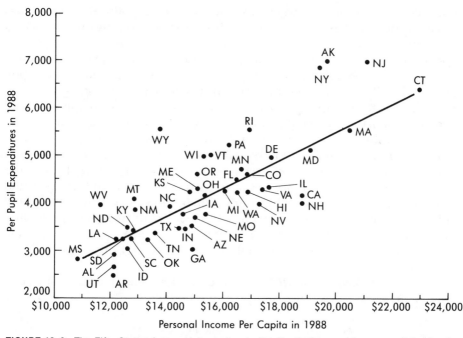

FIGURE 12-2   The Fifty States Arranged According to Per Capita Personal Income and Per Pupil Educational Expenditures

pattern—states arranged from the lower left to the upper right—shows that increases in income are associated with increases in educational spending. The diagonal line is a representation of the hypothesis that income determines educational spending. To the extent that states cluster around this line, they conform to the hypothesis. States that are above the line spend more for education than their income level predicts; states that are below the line spend less than their income predicts. In general, states tend to cluster around the line, indicating considerable support for the hypothesis.

POLITICS AND PUBLIC POLICY

The political system functions to transform demands generated in the environment into public policy. The traditional literature in American politics instructed students that characteristics of the political system, particularly two-party competition, voter participation, and apportionment had a direct bearing on public policy.[4] Because political scientists devoted most

[4]V. O. Key, Jr., *American State Politics: An Introduction* (New York: Knopf, 1956); also his *Southern Politics in State and Nation* (New York: Knopf, 1951); Duane Lockard, *The Politics of State and Local Government* (New York: Macmillan, 1963); John H. Fenton, *People and Parties in Politics* (Glenview, Ill.: Scott, Foresman, 1966).

of their time to studying what happened *within* the political system, it was easy for them to believe that the political processes and institutions which they studied were important determinants of public policies. Moreover, the belief that competition, participation, and equality in representation had important consequences for public policy squared with the value placed upon these variables in the prevailing pluralist ideology.

The assertion that political variables such as party competition and voter participation affected public policy rested more upon a priori reasoning than upon systematic research. It seemed reasonable to *believe* that an increase in party competition would increase educational spending, welfare benefits, numbers of welfare recipients, highway spending, health and hospital care, and so on, because competitive parties would try to outbid each other for public favor by offering such inducements, and the overall effect of such competition would be to raise levels of spending and service. It also seemed reasonable to believe that increased voter participation would influence public policy, presumably in a more liberal direction.

Political Competition Model.   The earliest systems model in the state policy field was a "political competition" model:

Economic Resources	$\longrightarrow$	Competition Participation	$\longrightarrow$	Public Policies

in which economic resources determined political competition and participation, and these political factors in turn determined public policies in welfare, education, health, highway, taxation, and spending. For many years there was no empirical evidence to contradict this model: poor, rural, agrarian states tended to have less competitive parties ("one-party" systems, in contrast to "two-party" systems), and these same states spent less per capita for education, welfare, health, and other social services.

However, in order to assess the *independent* effect of politics on public policy, it is important to control for the intervening effects of socioeconomic variables. For example, if it is shown that, in general, wealthy states have more party competition than poor states, it might be that differences in the level of welfare benefits of competitive and noncompetitive states are really a product of the fact that the former are wealthy and the latter are poor. If this is the case, policy differences between the states might be attributable to wealth rather than to party competition. In order to isolate the effect of party competition on education and welfare policies from the effect of economic resources, it is necessary to control for these variables.

Economic Resource Model.   Evidence that political variables might *not* be as influential in determining levels of public taxing, spending, and service as commonly supposed came in a comprehensive analysis of public policy in the American states published in 1965 by Thomas R. Dye.[5] Four of the most commonly described characteristics of political systems—(1) Democratic or Republican control of state government, (2) the degree of interparty competition, (3) the level of voter turnout, and (4) the extent of malapportionment—were found to have less effect on public policy than environmental variables reflecting the level of economic development— urbanization, industrialization, wealth, and education. The conclusion: "The evidence seems conclusive: economic development variables are more influential than political system characteristics in shaping public policy in the states." Most of the associations that occur between political variables and policy outcomes are really a product of the fact that economic development influences both political system characteristics and policy outcomes. When political factors are controlled, economic development continues to have a significant impact on public policy. But when the effects of economic development are controlled, political factors turn out to have little influence on policy outcomes.

The resulting "economic resources" model may be viewed as follows:

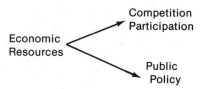

In this view, economic resources shape both the political system characteristics (competition and participation) and public policy, but characteristics of the political system have no direct causal effect on public policy.

The Politics-Versus-Economics Debate. These findings—regarded as commonplace by economists—were very disturbing to political scientists who were committed to a pluralist ideology which asserted the importance of competition and participation in politics. Now of course most of us would prefer to live in a political system in which there are high levels of competition and participation, since these conditions are highly valued in any democracy. But it remains a scientific question whether these political conditions produce different kinds of policies than noncompetitive, nonparticipating political systems. We cannot *assume* that competition and participation will produce "better" public policies simply because we prefer a competitive, participating political system.

Nonetheless, the challenge to political scientists to prove that "politics count" in shaping public policy inspired a new systematic reexamination

---

[5]Thomas R. Dye, *Politics, Economics, and the Public* (Chicago: Rand McNally, 1966).

of the determinants of public policy. A number of scholars were stimulated to reexamine systematically the traditional wisdom in the state politics field. New and more sophisticated methods were introduced;[6] additional political variables were tested for their policy impact;[7] some policy variables other than levels of public expenditures and sources were examined;[8] changes over time were described and analyzed;[9] some more sophisticated conceptual notions were explored;[10] and policy innovation became an important topic itself.[11] In short, a whole subfield grew to maturity in a short period of time.

Implicit in much of this literature, however, was a reluctance to accept the view that political system characteristics, particularly those reflecting the pluralist values of competition and participation, possessed less policy relevance than economic resources. Indeed, there seemed to be a great deal of scrambling about by political scientists ideologically committed to proving that party competition, voter participation, partisanship, and apportionment did indeed influence public policy.[12] Of course, there is nothing wrong with trying to find the policy relevance of differing governmental structures or political processes, but we should not insist that political variables *must* influence public policy simply because our traditional training in political science has told us that political variables should be important.

[6]Ira Sharkansky and Richard Hofferbert, "Dimensions of State Politics, Economics, and Public Policy," *American Political Science Review*, 63 (September 1969), 867–79; James C. Strouse and Oliver J. Williams, "A Non-Additive Model for State Policy Research," *Journal of Politics*, 35 (May 1972), 648–57.

[7]Ira Sharkansky, "Agency Requests, Gubernatorial Support, and Budget Success in State Legislatures," *American Political Science Review*, 62 (December 1968), 926–39; Thomas R. Dye, "Executive Power and Public Policy in the States," *Western Political Quarterly*, 22 (December 1969), 926–39.

[8]Bryan R. Fry and Richard Winters, "The Politics of Redistribution," *American Political Science Review*, 64 (June 1970), 508–22; Ronald E. Weber and William R. Schaffer, "Public Opinion and American State Policy-Making," *Midwest Journal of Political Science*, 16 (November 1972), 683–99; Anne H. Hopkins, "Public Opinion and Support for Public Policy in the American States," *American Journal of Political Science*, 18 (February 1974), 167–78.

[9]Virginia Gray, "Models of Comparative State Politics: A Comparison of Cross-Sectional and Time Series Analyses," *American Journal of Political Science*, XX, 2 (May 1976), 235–56; Richard Hofferbert, "Socioeconomic Dimensions of the American States, 1890–1960," *Midwest Journal of Political Science*, 2 (August 1968), 401–18; Richard Hofferbert, "Ecological Development and Policy Change," *Midwest Journal of Political Science*, 10 (November 1966), 464–83.

[10]Ira Sharkansky, "Environment, Policy, Output and Input: Problems of Theory and Method in the Analysis of Public Policy," in *Policy Analysis in Political Science*, Ira Sharkansky, ed. (Chicago: Markham, 1970); Strouse and Williams, "A Non-Additive Model for State Policy Research."

[11]Jack L. Walker, "The Diffusion of Innovation Among the American States," *American Political Science Review*, 63 (September 1969), 880–89; Virginia Gray, "Innovation in the States," *American Political Science Review*, 67 (December 1973), 1174–85.

[12]John Crittenden, "Dimensions of Modernization in the American States," *American Political Science Review*, 61 (December 1967), 982–1002; Alan G. Pulsipher and James L. Weatherby, "Malapportionment, Party Competition, and the Functional Distribution of Government Expenditures," *American Political Science Review*, 62 (December 1968), 1207–20; Guenther F. Schaefer and Stuart Rakoff, "Politics, Policy, and Political Science," *Politics and Society*, 1 (November 1970), 52.

The Hybrid Model. One interesting model of policy determination to emerge from this research was a "hybrid model" suggested by political scientists Charles F. Cnudde and Donald J. McCrone, illustrated in the following diagram:[13]

In this model, economic resources shape public policy both *directly* and *indirectly* by affecting competition and participation, which in turn affect public policy. This study focused on only one policy field—welfare—rather than on the broader array of policies in education, health, highways, spending, taxation, and so on. Welfare policy was thought to magnify the conflict between "haves" and "have-nots" and therefore to magnify the effect of competition and participation.

Cnudde and McCrone reported that both economic resources and political competition and participation independently affected welfare policies in the States. Similar findings were reported by political scientist Michael Lewis-Beck, using a statistical model based on the hybrid model just described.[14] Both studies acknowledged that economic resources were stronger determinants of welfare policies than party competition or voter turnout.

THE POLITICAL SYSTEM AS A CONVERSION PROCESS

The general failure of political variables to be influential determinants of public policy raises the question of whether we should view politics as a conversion system, rather than a direct cause of public policy. In other words, politics does not *cause* public policy, but rather, it *facilitates* the conversion of demands and resources into public policy.

If we accept this view, we would not really expect variations in political systems—variations in competition, participation, partisanship, and reformism—directly to cause public policy. Instead, we would expect variations in political systems to affect *relationships* between demands and resources and public policies. For example, we would not expect highly competitive political systems to produce policies different from noncompetitive systems, but instead we might inquire whether the relationships between population

[13]Charles F. Cnudde and Ronald J. McCrone, "Party Competition and Welfare Policies in the American States," *American Political Science Review*, 62 (December 1968), 1220–31.

[14]Michael Lewis-Beck, "The Relative Importance of Socioeconomic and Political Variables in Public Policy," *American Political Science Review*, 71 (June 1977), 559–66.

characteristics and public policy are closer in competitive than in non-competitive systems. Our focus would shift to the impact of political system variables on *relationships* between environmental conditions (measures of demands and socioeconomic resources) and public policies.

Party and Policy in the States.   Political scientists have long placed great faith in party government. E. E. Schattschneider expressed this faith when he wrote: "The rise of political parties is undoubtedly one of the principal distinguishing marks of modern government . . . political parties created modern democracy and modern democracy is unthinkable save in terms of parties."[15] Recently Sarah McCally Morehouse reaffirmed faith in the centrality of political parties in the American states: "The single most important factor in state politics is the political party. It is not possible to understand the differences in the way sovereign states carry out the process of government without understanding the type of party whose representatives are making decisions that affect the health, education, and welfare of its citizens.[16]

Yet other "spatial" theories of parties suggest that parties have little policy relevance given a normal unimodal distribution of opinion on most policy questions. Anthony Downs explained: "In the middle of the scale, where most voters are massed, each party scatters its policies on both sides of the midpoint. It attempts to make each voter in this area feel that it is centered right at his position. Naturally this causes an enormous overlapping of moderate positions." Downs acknowledged that a left or right party may "sprinkle these moderate policies with a few extreme stands in order to please its far-out voters," but overall, "both parties are trying to be as ambiguous as possible" about policy positions. "Political rationality leads parties in a two-party system to becloud their policies in a fog of ambiguity."[17]

For example, if most voters in a state were found in the middle of an opinion scale on a policy issue, the parties in that state would be encouraged to take moderate policy positions not very different from each other. Both parties would be competing for the many voters in the center. Since both parties took moderate positions on the issue, a change in party control of state government (the governor's office, the state legislature, or both) would *not* result in any significant shift in public policy (see top of Figure 12–3). Only if the voters were divided on a policy issue into a bimodal distribution would we expect the parties to take significantly different policy positions (see bottom of Figure 12–3). The parties would be constrained by the large number of voters on each side of the issue from moving toward the center.

[15]E.E. Schattschneider, *Party Government* (New York: Rinehart, 1942), p. 1.

[16]Sarah McCally Morehouse, *State Politics, Parties, and Policy* (New York: Holt, Rinehart, & Winston, 1981), p. 29.

[17]Anthony Downs, *An Economic Theory of Democracy* (New York: Harper & Row, 1957), pp. 135–36.

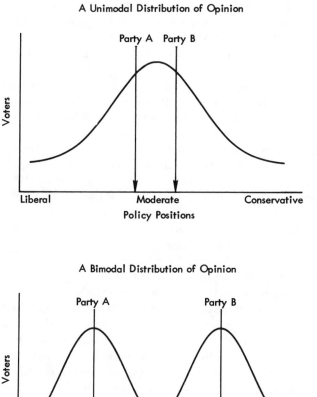

A Unimodal Distribution of Opinion

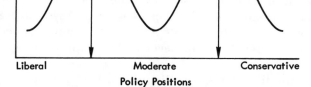

A Bimodal Distribution of Opinion

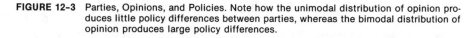

FIGURE 12-3   Parties, Opinions, and Policies. Note how the unimodal distribution of opinion produces little policy differences between parties, whereas the bimodal distribution of opinion produces large policy differences.

In this case, a change in party control of state government might result in a significant shift in public policy.

Searching for Policy-Relevant Parties.   A careful specification of the conditions under which party competition and Democratic or Republican control of state government would directly affect public policy was provided by Edward T. Jennings.[18] He correctly observed that the early assumption

---

[18]Edward T. Jennings, "Competition, Constituencies, and Welfare Policies in the American States," *American Political Science Review*, 73 (1979), 414–29.

that party competition would always assist the "have-nots" is not theoretically valid. He reasoned that party competition would increase policy benefits to "have-nots" only when: (1) parties in the states reflected class divisions; and (2) the party associated with the lower- or working-class gained control of government.

The distinction between competitive parties and policy-relevant parties is an important one. Competitive parties do not by themselves ensure that the "have-nots" will succeed in politics. Competition itself is not a cause of increased welfare spending. Nor is there any theoretical reason to believe competitive parties will necessarily offer alternative policies. Indeed if Downs is correct and if many state electorates cluster at the midpoints of their respective opinion distributions on policy issues, then competitive parties will have no incentive to offer significantly different policies. Only if the parties reflect different class constituencies, the party activists are concerned with policy issues, and the party of the "have-nots" gains control of state government, can we then expect party politics to influence public policy.

A classification of state political systems based on *both* the *competitiveness* of their parties and the *policy relevance* of their parties is shown in Table 12–2. The determination of whether their party systems are policy relevant or non–policy relevant is based upon observations of changes in welfare spending and changes in party control of state government over thirty years.[19] If welfare spending in a state increased more under Democratic administrations than under Republican administrations, then the party system is classified as policy relevant. But if there were no significant differences in welfare spending in Democratic or Republican state administrations, then the party system is classified as non–policy relevant. Some Southern states' party systems are also classified as non–policy relevant because Republicans have never gained control of state government and therefore never had the opportunity to change policy.

Note that thirty of the fifty states are adjudged to have non–policy-relevant party systems. Some of these states (for example, New York) have *competitive* party systems, but the election of Democratic or Republican governors or state legislatures does not significantly affect welfare spending in these states. (Welfare spending increased as rapidly in New York under Republican Governor Rockefeller as under Democratic Governor Carey). Hence, their party systems are adjudged to be non–policy relevant. Of course, most non–policy-relevant party systems are found in noncompetitive states, especially in the South. But even when one of these states elects a Republican governor, welfare spending is unaffected, that is, it rises no more slowly than under Democratic governors. Rhode Island, with its long history of Democratic party domination of state politics, is the only noncompetitive

---

[19]See Thomas R. Dye, "Party and Policy in the States," *Journal of Politics*, 46 (1984), 1097–1116.

TABLE 12-2   The Policy Relevance of the Parties in the States

FIFTY STATES CLASSIFIED BY PARTY COMPETITION
AND POLICY RELEVANCE OF THEIR PARTY SYSTEMS

	POLICY RELEVANT	NON-POLICY RELEVANT
Competitive Parties	CA, HI, IA, ME, MI, MN, NE, ND, OR, WI, WY, NJ, OH, PA	AK, CT, IL, IN, NY, SD
Less Competitive Parties	ID, MA, MT, NV, UT	CO, KS, NH, VT, WA
Noncompetitive Parties	RI	AL, AZ, AR, DE, FL, GA, KY, LA, MD, MS, MO, NM, NC, OK, SC, TN, TX, VA, WV

Source: Thomas R. Dye, "Party and Policy in the States," *Journal of Politics*, 46 (November 1984), 1097–1116.

state where the parties are clearly distinguished along liberal and conservative lines. The pluralist ideal—competitive parties offering clear policy alternatives to the voters—occurs in only fourteen states.

SUMMARY

We have employed a systems model, and variations based on this model, to describe linkages between economic resources, political system characteristics, and public policies in the American states. Some general propositions about public policy which are suggested by our systems model include:

1. Economic resources are an important determinant of overall levels of government taxing, spending, and service in the states. Economic differences among the states have narrowed somewhat over time, but significant policy differences remain.

2. Federal grants-in-aid, considered "outside" money to state and local governments, help to free these governments from their dependence upon economic conditions within their jurisdictions and permit them to spend at higher levels than they would otherwise be able to do. Federal grants reduce the impact of a state's own economic resources on its level of spending and service.

3. The traditional literature in American politics asserted that characteristics of political systems—particularly party competition and voter

participation—had an important impact on the content of public policy. But systematic research suggests that the characteristics of political systems are not as important as economic resources in shaping public policy. Most of the correlations between political system variables and public policy measures are a product of the fact that economic resources shape both the political system and public policy.

4. The testing of alternative causal models in policy determination leads us to reject the proposition that economic resources shape public policy only through changes which are made in the political system. We must also reject the idea that the character of the political system must be changed in order to change public policy. Economic resources can affect public policy directly regardless of the character of the political system. However, in some policy areas, especially welfare, economic resources shape public policy both directly and indirectly through political variables.

5. Rather than think of the political system as causing public policy, perhaps we should think of it as facilitating public policy. Competition and participation may not affect public policy itself, but these political variables may affect the relationship between socioeconomic demands and resources and public policies.

6. Competition and participation may increase the *responsiveness* of public policies to environmental conditions.

7. State political systems may be classified by both the competitiveness and the policy relevance of their parties. By observing whether welfare expenditures change significantly with changes in party control of state government, we can estimate the policy relevance of state party systems.

8. In twenty of the fifty states a change in party control of state government results in significant changes in welfare expenditures. Thus, in most states the party system is non–policy-relevant.

BIBLIOGRAPHY

DOWNS, ANTHONY. *An Economic Theory of Democracy.* New York: Harper & Row, 1957.

DYE, THOMAS R. *Politics, Economics, and the Public: Policy Outcomes in the American States.* Chicago: Rand McNally, 1966.

KEY, V.O., Jr. *American State Politics: An Introduction.* New York: Knopf, 1956.

_____. *Southern Politics in State and Nation.* New York: Knopf, 1951.

MOREHOUSE, SARAH MCCALLY. *State Politics, Parties and Policy.* New York: Holt Rinehart & Winston, 1981.

SHARKANSKY, IRA. *Spending in the American States.* Chicago: Rand McNally, 1968.

13

THE POLICY-MAKING PROCESS

getting inside the system

Most of the communications received by policy makers come from people who share the same views.
(Rick Bloom)

THE BLACK BOX PROBLEM

It is important that we understand what goes on in the little black box labeled "political system." The systems approach employed in the previous chapter deals with aggregate characteristics of *whole* political systems; this model does not say much about what goes on *within* political systems. Our comparative systems analysis focused attention on the linkages between economic resources, system characteristics, and public policy, and dealt with whole political systems. But we also want to know what happens *within* political systems. We want to know how public policy is generated within the political system, how institutions and processes function to handle demands generated in the environment, and how parties, interest groups, voters, governors, legislators, and other political actors behave in the policy-making process.

Let us try to illustrate the differences between a *comparative systems* approach and a *within-system* approach. Finding a high correlation between cigarette smoking and the incidence of cancer among human systems is important. But this correlation does not in itself reveal the functioning of cells within the human body: we still want to know *how* cancers are formed and how they behave. So also, finding a high correlation between urbanization and police protection does not in itself reveal the functioning of political systems; we still want to know *how* a political system goes about transforming demands arising from the socioeconomic environment into public policy.

The process model of public policy assists in identifying various processes occurring *within* the political system. They are:

the *identification* of policy problems through public demands for government action;

agenda-setting, or focusing the attention of the mass media and public officials on specific public problems deciding what will be decided;

the *formulation* of policy proposals through the initiation and development of policy proposals by policy-planning organizations, interest groups, government bureaucracies, and the president and Congress;

the *legitimation* of policies through political actions by parties, interest groups, the president, and Congress;

the *implementation* of policies through organized bureaucracies, public expenditures, and the activities of executive agencies;

the *evaluation* of policies by government agencies themselves, outside consultants, the press, and the public.

In describing these political processes, however, it is important to remember that the activities of the various political actors are greatly constrained by socioeconomic conditions. We have already described the great influence economic resources have on the character of the political system and the content of public policy. It is true that not *all* the variance in public policy can be explained by economic resources. However, the activities of parties, groups, and individuals *within* the political system are heavily influenced by socioeconomic conditions. So our systems model has warned us not to expect the activities of individuals, groups, parties, or decision makers to produce policies at variance with socioeconomic resources and constraints.

IDENTIFYING POLICY ISSUES: PUBLIC OPINION

The influence of public opinion over government policy has been the subject of great philosophical controversies in the classic literature on democracy. Edmund Burke believed democratic representatives should serve the *interest* of the people but not necessarily conform to their *will* in deciding questions of public policy. In contrast, some democratic theorists have evaluated the success of democratic institutions by whether or not they facilitate popular control over public policy.

The philosophical question of whether public opinion *should* be an important independent influence over public policy may never be resolved. But the empirical question of whether public opinion *does* constitute an important independent influence over public policy can be tackled by systematic research. However, even this empirical question has proved very difficult to answer.

Opinion-Policy Linkage.   The probem in assessing the independent effect of mass opinion on the actions of decision makers is that their actions help to mold mass opinion. Public policy may be in accord with mass opinion but we can never be sure whether mass opinion shaped public policy or public policy shaped mass opinion.

In V. O. Key's most important book, *Public Opinion and American Democracy,* he wrote: "Government, as we have seen, attempts to mold public opinion toward support of the programs and policies it espouses. Given that endeavor, perfect congruence between public policy and public opinion could be government *of* public opinion rather than government *by* public opinion."[1] Although Key himself was convinced that public opinion did have an independent effect on public policy, he was never able to demonstrate this in any systematic fashion. He lamented:

> Discussion of public opinion often loses persuasiveness as it deals with the critical question of how public opinion and governmental action are linked. The democratic theorists founds his doctrines on the assumption that an interplay occurs between mass opinion and government. When he seeks to delineate that interaction and to demonstrate the precise bearing of the opin-

[1]V. O. Key, Jr., *Public Opinion and American Democracy* (New York: Knopf, 1967), pp. 422–23.

ions of private citizens on official decision, he encounters almost insurmountable obstacles. In despair he may conclude that the supposition that public
opinion enjoys weight in public decision is a myth and nothing more, albeit
a myth that strengthens a regime so long as people believe it.[2]

Yet Key compiled a great deal of circumstantial evidence supporting
the notion that elections, parties, and interest groups do institutionalize channels of communication from citizens to decision makers. But there is very
little *direct* evidence in the existing research literature to support the notion
that public opinion has a significant *independent* influence over public policy.

Policy Shapes Opinion.   Public policy shapes public opinion more often
than opinion shapes policy. There are several reasons why policies are
relatively unconstrained by public opinion. First, few people have opinions
on the great bulk of policy questions confronting the nation's decision
makers. Second, public opinion is very unstable. It can change in a matter
of weeks in response to news events precipitated by leaders. Third, leaders
do not have a clear perception of mass opinion. Most communications received by decision makers are from other elites—newsmakers, interest group
leaders, and other influential persons—and not from ordinary citizens.

Media Effects.   We must not assume that the opinions expressed in the
news media are public opinion. Frequently, this is a source of confusion.
Newspersons believe *they* are the public, often confusing their own opinions
with public opinion. They even tell the mass public what its opinion is, thus
actually helping to mold it to conform to their own beliefs. Decision makers,
then, may act in response to news stories or to the opinions of influential
newsmakers in the mistaken belief that they are responding to "public opinion."

Opinion Polls.   Most people do not have opinions on most policy issues.
Public opinion polls frequently create opinions by askng questions that respondents never thought about until they were asked. Few respondents are
willing to admit they have no opinion; they believe they should provide some
sort of answer, even if their opinion is weakly held or was nonexistent before
the question was asked. Thus pollsters produce "doorstep" opinions. But
it is unlikely that many Americans have seriously thought about, or gathered
much information on, such specific issues as AFDC eligibility, Medicaid cost
containment, Gramm-Rudman deficit reduction ceilings, the B-1 bomber,
investment tax credits, and similar specific questions; nor do many Americans
have information on these topics.

[2]Ibid., p. 411.

Instability of Opinion. Public opinion is also very unstable. Mass opinion on a particular issue is often very weakly held. Asked the same question at a later date, many respondents fail to remember their earlier answers and give the pollster the opposite reply. These are not real changes in opinion, yet they register as such.

Wording of Questions. Opinions also vary according to the wording of questions. It is relatively easy to word almost any public policy question in such a way as to elicit mass approval or disapproval. Thus, differently worded questions on the same issue can produce contradictory results. Opinion polls that ask the exact same question over time are more reliable indicators of public opinion than one-shot polls. Respondents in a one-shot poll may be responding to the wording of the question. But if the same wording is used over time, the bias in the wording remains constant and changes in opinion may be observed. This is why only verbatim wording used continuously over time produces reasonably accurate information about the public mood.

Communicating to Policy Makers. Finally, decision makers can easily misinterpret public opinion because the communications they receive have an upper-class bias. Members of the masses seldom call or write their senators or representatives, much less converse with them at dinners, cocktail parties, or other social occasions. Most of the communications received by decision makers are *intra-elite* communications—communications from newspersons, organized group leaders, influential constituents, wealthy political contributors, and personal friends—people who, for the most part, share the same views. It is not surprising, therefore, that members of Congress say that most of their mail is in agreement with their own position; their world of public opinion is self-reinforcing. Moreover, persons who initiate communication with decision makers, by writing or calling or visiting their representatives, are decidedly more educated and affluent than the average citizen.

In a classic study of the relationship between mass opinion and congressional voting on policy issues, Warren E. Miller and Donald Stokes found very low correlations between the voting records of members of Congress and the attitudes of their constituents on social welfare issues, and even lower correlations on foreign policy issues.[3] Only in the area of civil rights did members of Congress appear to vote according to the views of a majority of their constituents. In general, "the representative has very imperfect information about the issue preferences of his constituency, and constituency's awareness of the policy stands of the representative is ordinarily slight." With

[3]Miller and Stokes, "Constituency Influence on Congress," *American Political Science Review*, 57 (March 1963), 55–65; see also Charles F. Cnudde and Donald J. McCrone, "The Linkage Between Constituency Attitudes and Congressional Voting Behavior," *American Political Science Review*, 60 (March 1966), 66–72.

the possible exception of civil rights questions, most members of Congress are free from the influence of popular preferences in their legislative voting.

IDENTIFYING POLICY ISSUES: ELITE OPINION

When V. O. Key wrestled with the same problem confronting us—namely, the determination of the impact of popular preferences on public policy— he concluded that "the missing piece of the puzzle" was "that thin stratum of persons referred to variously as the political elite, the political activists, the leadership echelons, or the influentials."

> The longer one frets with the puzzle of how democratic regimes manage to function, the more plausible it appears that a substantial part of the explana- tion is to be found in the motives that activate the *leadership echelon,* the values that it holds, the rules of the political game to which it adheres, in the expecta- tions which it entertains about its own status in society, and perhaps in some of the objective circumstances, both material and institutional, in which it functions.[4]

In view of the difficulty in finding direct links between public policy and popular preferences, it seems reasonable to ask whether the preferences of elites are more directly reflected in public policy than the preferences of masses. Do elite attitudes independently affect public policy? Or are elite attitudes so closely tied to socioeconomic conditions that elites have relatively little flexibility in policy making and therefore little independent influence over the content of public policy?

Elite preferences are more likely to be in accord with public policy than mass preferences. This finding is fairly well supported in the existing research literature. Of course this does not *prove* that policies are determined by elite preferences. It may be that government officials are acting rationally in response to events and conditions, and well-educated, informed elites under- stand the actions of government better than do the masses. Hence, it might be argued that elites support government policies because they have greater understanding of and confidence in government, and they are more likely to read about and comprehend the explanations of government officials. On the other hand, the correspondence between elite opinion and public policy may also indicate that it is really *elite* opinion that determines public policy.

Liberal and Conservative Opinion in the States.   Let us consider for ex- ample, the influence of mass and elite opinion on public policy in the American states. Liberal and conservative states can be defined in terms of

[4]Key, *Public Opinion and American Democracy,* p. 537.

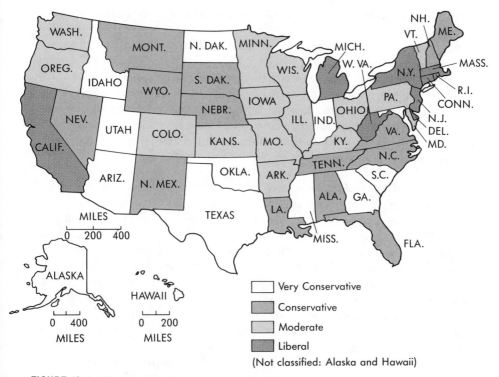

FIGURE 13-1 Liberalism and Conservatism in the States.

how their voters identify themselves in opinion surveys—as "liberal," "moderate," or "conservative." One study aggregated the results of national opinion polls over six years (1976–82) and then observed the responses of voters in each state.[5] During this period 32 percent of the respondents nationwide identified themselves as "conservative," while 40 percent said "moderate," and 21 percent said "liberal." Figure 13–1 shows the "conservative" responses in each state: the most conservative state in terms of self-identification of the voters was Utah (45% conservative, 37% moderate, and 13% liberal), followed by Indiana (42% conservative, 39% moderate, and 13% liberal). The most liberal states were Massachusetts (26% conservative, 42% moderate, and 25% liberal) New York (29% conservative, 39% moderate, and 25% liberal), and New Jersey (28% conservative, 40% moderate, and 26% liberal).

The ideological identification of the voters in the states correlates very closely with some measures of policy liberalism and conservatism. Liberal and conservative states can be distinguished by their policy enactments. For example, "policy liberalism" is reflected in the adoption of relaxed eligibility standards for receipt of welfare and medical benefits, decriminalization of marijuana possession, an absence of the death penalty, extensive regulation of business, state ratification of the Equal Rights Amendment, and the adoption of progressive state income taxes. "Policy conservatism" is reflected in the opposite of these enactments. Of course, socioeconomic conditions in the states—income and education levels, urbanization and industrialization, race and ethnicity—help to shape public opinion; and public opinion in turn influences public policy. But on many policy issues, public opinion appears to have a direct and independent effect on policy that is not explained by socioeconomic conditions.

Party Activists and Political Ideology.   While political parties are pushed toward the center on most policy issues in order to win elections, the activists in the parties tend to be strong ideologues—people who take consistently "liberal" or "conservative" positions on the issues. Republican party activists in most states are more conservative than Democratic party activists. Indeed, Republican party activists tend to be more conservative than the general public, and Democratic party activists tend to be more liberal than the general public. This is true even though activists in both parties will tend to be more conservative in a conservative state and more liberal in a liberal state. We might represent the ideological positions of party activists in the states in Figure 13–2.

In conservative states, both Democratic and Republican activists are more conservative than their counterparts in liberal states. But in each state Democratic party activists are more liberal than Republican party activists. In the most liberal states, the Republican activists are more liberal than the Democratic activists in the most conservative states. According to this theory, we expect the Republican party activists in New York and Connecticut (liberal states according to Figure 13–1) to be more liberal than Democratic party activists in Arizona, Utah, or Mississippi. Some evidence to support this theory has been gleaned from public opinion polls and surveys of party leaders in the states.[6]

In short, we know that party control of state government is not a good predictor of public policy. But this does not necessarily mean that there are no differences between the parties. *Party activists* may differ over the issues, yet the parties in the government may be obliged to respond to public opinion in the states.

AGENDA SETTING AND "NONDECISIONS"

Who decides what will be decided? Defining the problems of society, and suggesting alternative solutions, is the most important stage of the policy-

---

[6]Robert S. Erikson, Gerald C. Wright, and John P. McIver, "Political Parties, Public Opinion, and State Policy," *American Political Science Review,* 83 (September 1989), 729–750.

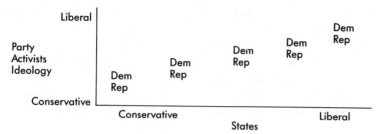

FIGURE 13-2

making process. We can refer to this stage as "agenda setting." Conditions in society which are not defined as a problem, and for which alternatives are never proposed, never became policy issues. They never get on the "agenda" of decision makers. Government does nothing and conditions remain the same. On the other hand, if certain conditions in society are defined as problems and alternative solutions put forward, the conditions become policy issues. Governments are forced to decide what to do.

Clearly then, the power to decide what will be a policy issue is crucial to the policy-making process. Deciding what will be the problems is even more important than deciding what will be the solutions. Political scientist E. E. Schattschneider once wrote:

> . . . As a matter of fact, the definition of the alternative is the supreme instrument of power; the antagonists can rarely agree on what the issues are because power is involved in the definition. He who determines what politics is about runs the country, because the definition of the alternatives is the choice of conflicts, and the choice of conflicts allocates power.[7]

Many civics textbooks imply that agenda setting just "happens." It is sometimes argued that in an open plural society such as ours, channels of access and communication to government are always open, so that any problem can be discussed and placed on the agenda of national decision making. Individuals and groups, it is said, can organize themselves to assume the tasks of defining problems and suggesting solutions. People can define their own interests, organize themselves, persuade others to support their cause, gain access to government officials, influence decision making, and watch over the implementation of government policies and programs. Indeed, it is sometimes argued that the absence of political activity such as this is an indicator of "satisfaction."

But, in reality, policy issues do not just "happen." Creating an issue, dramatizing it, calling attention to it, and pressuring government to do something about it are important political tactics. These tactics are employed by influential individuals, organized interest groups, policy planning organiza-

[7]E. E. Schattschneider, *The Semisovereign People* (New York: Holt, Rinehart & Winston, 1961), p. 68.

tions, political candidates and officeholders, and perhaps most importantly, the mass media. These are the tactics of "agenda setting."

On the other hand, *preventing* certain conditions in society from becoming policy issues is also an important political tactic. "Nondecision making" occurs when influential individuals or groups, or the political system
itself, operate to prevent the emergence of challenges to the dominant values
or interests in society. According to political scientists Peter Bachrach and
Morton Baratz:

> A nondecision, as we define it, is a decision that results in the suppression or
> thwarting of a latent or manifest challenge to the values and interests of the
> decision-maker. To be more clearly explicit, non-decision-making is a means
> by which demands for change in the existing allocation of benefits and privileges
> in the community can be suffocated before they are even voiced; or kept covert;
> or killed before they gain access to the relevant decision-making arena; or failing
> all these things, maimed or destroyed in the decision-implementing stage of
> the policy process.[8]

Nondecision making may occur when dominant elites act openly or
covertly to suppress an issue because they fear that if public attention is
focused on it something will be done and what is done will not be in their
interest.

Nondecision making may also occur when political candidates or officeholders or administrative officials anticipate that elites will not favor a particular idea and therefore these officeholders and officials drop the idea.
They do not want to "rock the boat." Elites do not have to *do* anything. Officials are acting in anticipation of what they *might* do.

Finally, and perhaps most importantly, nondecision making occurs because the political system itself is structured in such a way as to facilitate
the resolution of some kinds of issues and to obstruct the resolution of others.
There is a "mobilization of bias" within the political system itself, that is,
"a set of predominant values, beliefs, rituals, and institutional procedures ... that operate systematically and consistently to the benefit of
others."[9] For example, many scholars believe that the interest group system
is the key to understanding how issues are identified, solutions proposed,
and policies adopted. However, we know that the political system responds
well to large-scale, well-organized, wealthy, active interest groups with good
access to government officials. It responds less well to smaller, unorganized,
poorer, inactive interest groups with few available channels of communication to government officials. According to Schattschneider the interest group
system "has an upper-class bias":

---

[8]Peter Bachrach and Morton S. Baratz, *Power and Poverty* (New York: Oxford University
Press, 1979), p. 7.
[9]Ibid., p. 43.

The business or upper-class bias of the pressure system shows up everywhere.... The data raise a serious question about the validity of the proposition that special interest groups are a universal form of political organization reflecting all interests.[10]

The same observations might be made for the party system—that parties respond to well-organized, wealthy, skilled, active, and knowledgeable individuals and groups rather than to the disorganized, poor, unskilled, inactive, or unknowledgeable. Indeed, all governmental bodies—elected and appointed; legislative, executive, and judicial; federal, state, and local—contain this same bias.

Thus, it is difficult to maintain the fiction that anyone in a democracy can raise any policy issue anytime he or she wishes. Who, then, is responsible for "agenda setting"? Who decides what will be decided?

AGENDA SETTING AND MOBILIZING OPINION: THE MASS MEDIA

Television is the major source of information for the vast majority of Americans. Over two-thirds of Americans report that they receive all or most of their news from television. Television is really the first form of *mass* communication, that is, communication which reaches nearly everyone, including children. The television viewer *must* see the news or else turn off the set; the newspaper reader can turn quickly to the sports and comics without confronting the political news. More importantly, television presents a *visual* image, not merely a printed word. The visual quality of television—the emotional impact that is conveyed by pictures—enables the television networks to convey emotions as well as information.

Media Power.   Great power derives from control over a society's media of communication. The media are both players and referees in the game of politics. They not only report to the people on the struggles for power in society, but are participants in those struggles themselves. They are an elite group, competing for power alongside the more traditional leadership groups from business, labor, government, and other sectors of society. As political journalist Theodore White once observed, "The power of the press in America is a primordial one. It sets the agenda of public discussion; and this sweeping power is unrestrained by any law. It determines what people will talk about and think about—an authority that in other nations is reserved for tyrants, priests, parties, and mandarins."[11]

[10]Schattschneider, *The Semisovereign People,* p. 31.
[11]Theodore White, *The Making of the President, 1972* (New York: Bantam, 1973), p. 7.

Media power is concentrated in the hands of a relatively small number of people: the editors, producers, anchors, reporters, and columnists of the leading television networks (ABC, CBS, NBC, and CNN) and the prestigious press (*The New York Times, The Washington Post, The Wall Street Journal, Newsweek, Time,* and *U.S. News and World Report*). Producers and editors generally work behind the scenes, and many influential print journalists are known only by their bylines. But most Americans have come to recognize the faces of the television network anchors and leading reporters: Dan Rather, Tom Brokaw, Peter Jennings, Ed Bradley, Sam Donaldson, Mike Wallace, Dianne Sawyer, and others. These media people are courted by politicians, treated as celebrities, studied by scholars, and known to millions of Americans by their television images.

The television network people who decide which issues, events, and personalities will be covered interact daily with their counterparts in the national press—the executives and editors of *The New York Times, The Washington Post, Time, Newsweek,* and so on. Even at the working level, the television and newspaper reporters interact in the "Washington press corps." This interaction reinforces decisions about what the "news" should be. As a result, there is not much diversity in news reporting. All the networks, as well as the major newspapers and news magazines, will carry stories on the same topics at the same time.

Newsmaking.   Newsmaking involves all-important decisions about what is "news" and who is "newsworthy." Television executives and producers and newspaper and magazine editors must decide what people, organizations, and events will be given attention. This attention makes these topics matters of general public concern and political action. Without media coverage the general public would not "know" about these personalities, organizations, or events. They would not become objects of political discussion, nor would they be likely to be considered important by government officials.

Media attention can create issues and personalities. Media inattention can doom issues and personalities to obscurity. The television camera cannot be "a picture of the world," because the whole world cannot squeeze into the picture. News executives must sort through a tremendous surplus of information and decide what is "news."

In addition to deciding what is and what is not news, news executives provide cues to mass audiences about the importance of an issue, personality, or event. Some matters are covered prominently by the media, with early placement on a newscast and several minutes of time, or with front-page newspaper coverage including big headlines and pictures. The amount of coverage tells us what is important and what is not.

Of course, politicians, professional public relations people, interest group spokespersons, and various aspiring celebrities all *know* that the decisions of the media are vital to the success of their issue, their organization, and themselves. So they try to attract media attention by deliberately engaging in behavior or manufacturing situations that are likely to win media coverage. The result is the "media event"—an activity arranged primarily to stimulate media coverage and thereby attract public attention to an issue or individual. Generally, the more bizarre, dramatic, and sensational it is, the more likely it is to attract coverage. A media event may be a press conference to which reporters from the television stations and newspapers are invited by public figures—even when there is really no news to announce. Or it may be a staged debate, confrontation, or illustration of injustice. Political candidates may visit coal mines, ghetto neighborhoods, and sites of fires or other disasters. Sometimes protests, demonstrations, and even violence have been staged primarily as media events in order to dramatize and communicate grievances.

Media Bias. In exercising their judgement regarding which stories should be given television time or newspaper space, the media executives must rely on their own political values and economic interests as guidelines in determining what will be "news." In general, the media executives are more "liberal" in their views than other segments of the nation's leadership. Topics selected weeks in advance for coverage reflect, or often create, current liberal issues: concern for problems affecting the poor, blacks, and minorities; women's issues; opposition to defense spending; environmental concerns; and so forth. But liberalism is *not* the major source of bias in the news.

The principal source of distortion in the news is caused by the need for drama, action, and confrontation to hold audience attention. Television must entertain. To capture the attention of jaded audiences, news must be selected on the basis of emotional rhetoric, shocking incidents, dramatic conflict, overdrawn stereotypes. Race, sex, violence, and corruption in government are favorite topics because of popular interest. More complex problems such as inflation, government spending, and foreign policy must either be simplified and dramatized, or ignored. To dramatize an issue the news executives must find or create a dramatic incident; film it; transport, process, and edit the film; and write a script for the introduction, the "voice-over," and the "recapitulation." All this means that most "news" must be created well in advance of scheduled broadcasting.

Media Effects. Media effects can be categorized as: (1) identifying issues and setting the agenda for policy makers, (2) influencing attitudes and values toward policy issues, and (3) changing the behavior of voters and decision makers. These categories of effects are ranked by the degree of influence the media are likely to have over us. The power of television is not really in persuading viewers to take one side of an issue or another. Instead, *the power of television is in setting the agenda for decision making*—deciding what issues will be given attention and what issues will be ignored.

The media can create new opinions more easily than they can change existing ones. The media can often suggest how we feel about new events or issues—those for which we have no prior feelings or experiences. And the media can reinforce values and attitudes that we already hold. But there is very little evidence that the media can change existing values.

The viewer's psychological mechanism of *selective perception* helps to defend against bias in news and entertainment programming. Selective perception means mentally screening out information or images with which one disagrees. It causes people to tend to see and hear only what they want to see and hear. Selective perception reduces the impact of television bias on viewer attitudes and behavior.

The networks' concentration on scandal, abuse, and corruption in government has not always produced the desired liberal, reformist notions in the minds of the masses of viewers. Contrary to the expectations of network executives, their focus on governmental scandals—Watergate, illicit activities by government agencies, congressional sex scandals, and power struggles between Congress and the executive branch—has produced feelings of general political distrust and cynicism toward government and the system. These feelings have been labeled *television malaise*: a combination of social distrust, political cynicism, feelings of powerlessness, and disaffection from parties and politics, which seems to stem from television's emphasis on the negative aspects of American life.

Network executives do not intend to create "television malaise" among the masses. But scandal, sex, abuse of power, and corruption do attract large audiences and increase ratings.

FORMULATING POLICY

Policy formulation is the development of policy alternatives for dealing with problems on the public agenda. Policy formulations occur in government bureaucracies, interest group offices, legislative committee rooms, meetings of special commissions, and policy planning organizations, otherwise known as "think tanks." The details of policy proposals are usually formulated by staff members of these think tanks rather than by their bosses. But staff are guided by what they know their leaders want.

The Bureaucracy.   The President and the executive branch are generally expected to be the "initiators" of policy proposals, with Congress members in the role of "arbitors" of policy alternatives. The same division of labor is usually found at the state and local level, with governors, mayors, and even city managers expected to formulate policy proposals and state legislators and city councils to approve, amend, or reject them. The Constitution of the United States appears to endorse this arrangement in Art. II Section 3: "[The President] shall from time to time give to Congress information of the State of the Union, and recommend to their consideration such measures as he shall judge necessary and expedient." Each year the principal policy statements of the President come in the *State of the Union* message, and more importantly, in *The Budget of the United States Government,* prepared by Office of Management and Budget (see Chapter 9). Many other policy proposals are developed by executive departments in their specialized areas; these proposals are usually transmitted to the White House for the President's approval before being sent on to Congress.

Interest Groups.   Interest groups may formulate their own policy proposals, perhaps in association with members of Congress or their staffs who share the same interest. Interest-group staff often bring valuable technical knowledge to policy formation, as well as political information about their group's position on the issues. Because Congress members and their staffs value both kinds of information, interest groups can often provide the precise language they desire in proposed bills and amendments. Thus, interest-group staff often augment the work of congressional staff. Interest groups also provide testimony at congressional hearings as well as technical reports and analyses used by congressional staff.

Commissions.   Frequently the president or Congress will create special commissions to research issues and formulate policy proposals. The decision to create a special commission may be motivated by symbolic reasons— the president or Congress may wish to appear to be taking action on a problem of great public concern. For example, presidents have appointed a Commission on Civil Disorders (after urban riots in the 1960s), a Commission on Violence (after the assassinations of John F. Kennedy, Robert F. Kennedy, and Martin Luther King, Jr.), the Tower Commission (to revamp the National Security Council after the Iran-Contra affair), a Commission on Financial Markets (following the stock market collapse in 1987), a Commission on Pornography, a Commission on Privatization, and so on. While these symbolic commissions usually make a series of policy recommendations and win effusive praise from the president, the recommendations are often ignored. The commission reports are delivered long after public attention has shifted to other topics; the commission served its symbolic purpose by merely showing government concern about a problem.

The decision to create a commission may also be motivated by political reasons—the president or Congress may wish to shift blame for necessary but unpopular policy changes to a separate commission. The National Commission on Social Security Reform, divided evenly between Democrats and

Republicans, was appointed to justify social security tax increases in 1983; the president and Congress adopted its policy recommendations to "save" the social security system. However, a bipartisan Commission on Budget Deficits, appointed by President Bush to seek long term proposal for balancing the federal budget, collapsed in partisan bickering.

Legislative Staff.   Congressional staff, and the staff personnel in state legislatures, have grown rapidly in recent years, so that this new "legislative bureaucracy" is itself becoming an important source of policy formulation. Committee staff, staff personnel in the offices of the legislative leadership, and aides to individual legislators, are all political appointees; they generally reflect the political views of their legislator-bosses. Over time some "staffers" become so knowledgeable about specific policy areas, including budget complexities, that they keep their jobs even when their original sponsor leaves the capital. Staffs are expected to research issues, schedule legislative hearings, line up experts and interest groups to testify, keep up to date on the status of bills and appropriation measures as they move through the legislative branch, maintain contact with executive agencies, write and rewrite bills, and perform other assorted chores. As legislators come to rely on trusted staffers, the staffers themselves become powerful policy formulators. Their advice may kill a bill or appropriation item or their work may amend a bill or change an appropriation, without a legislator ever becoming directly involved. Serious staff of Congressional leaders and influential committees exercise a great deal of influence in policy making.

Think Tanks.   Policy-planning organizations are central coordinating points in the policy-making process. Certain policy-planning groups—for example, the Council on Foreign Relations, the American Enterprise Institute, Heritage Foundation, and the Brookings Institute—are influential in a wide range of key policy areas. Other policy-planning groups—the Urban Institute, Resources for the Future, the Population Council, for example—specialize in a particular policy field.

These organizations bring together the leadership of corporate and financial institutions, the foundations, the mass media, the leading intellectuals, and influential figures in the government. They review the relevant university and foundation-supported research on topics of interest, and more importantly, they try to reach a consensus about what action should be taken on national problems under study. Their goal is to develop action recommendations—explicit policies or programs designed to resolve national problems. These policy recommendations of the key policy-planning groups are distributed to the mass media, federal executive agencies, and the Congress. The purpose is to lay the groundwork for making policy into law.

The following are among the more influential think tanks in Washington:

THE BROOKINGS INSTITUTION

This organization has long been the dominant policy-planning group for American domestic policy, despite the growing influence of competing think tanks over the years. Brookings staffers dislike its reputation as a "liberal think tank," and they deny that Brookings tries to set national priorities. Yet the Brookings Institution has been very influential in planning the war on poverty, welfare reform, national defense, and taxing and spending policies. *The New York Times* columnist and Harvard historian writing team, Leonard and Mark Silk, describe Brookings as the central locus of the Washington "policy network," where it does "its communicating: over lunch, whether informally in the Brookings cafeteria or at the regular Friday lunch around a great oval table at which the staff and their guests keen over the events of the week like the chorus of an ancient Greek tragedy; through consulting, paid or unpaid, for government or business at conferences, in the advanced studies program; and, over time, by means of the revolving door of government employment."[12]

THE AMERICAN ENTERPRISE INSTITUTE

For many years Republicans dreamed of a "Brookings Institution for Republicans" that would help offset the liberal bias of Brookings itself. In the late 1970s, that role was assumed by the American Enterprise Institute (AEI). AEI appeals to both Democrats and Republicans who have doubts about big government. President William Baroody, Jr., distinguished the AEI from Brookings: "In confronting societal problems those who tend to gravitate to the AEI orbit would be inclined to look first for a market solution . . . while the other orbit people have a tendency to look for a government solution."[13]

THE HERITAGE FOUNDATION

Conservative ideologues have never been welcome in the Washington establishment. Yet influential conservative businesspersons gradually came to understand that without an institutional base in Washington they could never establish a strong and continuing influence in the policy network. So they set about the task of "building a solid institutional base" and "establishing a reputation for reliable scholarship and creative problem solving."[14] The result of their efforts was the Heritage Foundation.

[12]Leonard Silk and Mark Silk, *The American Establishment* (New York: Basic Books, 1980), p. 160.

[13]Silk and Silk, *The American Establishment*, p. 179.

[14]*Heritage Foundation Annual Report 1985,* Washington D.C.: Heritage Foundation.

THE COUNCIL ON FOREIGN RELATIONS

Political scientist Lester Milbraith observes that the influence of the CFR throughout government is so pervasive that it is difficult to distinguish the CFR from government programs: "The Council on Foreign Relations, while not financed by government, works so closely with it that it is difficult to distinguish Council actions stimulated by government from autonomous actions."[15] The CFR itself, of course, denies that it exercises any control over U.S. foreign policy. Indeed, its by-laws declare that "The Council shall not take any position on questions of foreign policy and no person is authorized to speak or purport to speak for the Council on such matters."[16] But policy initiation and consensus-building do not require the CFR to officially adopt policy positions.[17]

POLICY LEGITIMATION: THE "PROXIMATE POLICY MAKERS"

What is the role of the proximate policy makers?[18] The activities of the "proximate policy makers"—the president, Congress, federal agencies, congressional committees, White House staff, and interest groups—in the policy-making process have traditionally been the central focus of political science. Political scientists usually portray the activities of the proximate policy makers as the whole of the policy-making process. But our notion of public policy making views the activities of the proximate policy makers as only the *final phase* of a much more complex process. This final stage is the open, public stage of the policy-making process, and it attracts the attention of the mass media and most political scientists. The activities of the "proximate policy makers" are much easier to study than the private actions of corporations, foundations, the mass media, and the policy-planning organizations.

---

[15]Lester Milbraith, "Interest Groups in Foreign Policy," in *Domestic Sources of Foreign Policy,* ed. James Rosenau (New York: Free Press, 1967), p. 247.

[16]Council on Foreign Relations, *Annual Report,* 1988, p. 160.

[17]Serious students of public policy are advised to read the books and journals published by these leading policy planning organizations, especially *The Brookings Review* (published quarterly by the Brookings Institution, 1775 Massachusetts Avenue NW, Washington, D.C., 20036); *The American Enterprise* (published bimonthly by the American Enterprise Institute, 1150 17th St. NW, Washington, D.C., 20036); *Policy Review* (published quarterly by the Heritage Foundation, 214 Massachusetts Avenue NE, Washington, D.C., 20002); and *Foreign Affairs* (published five times annually by the Council on Foreign Relations, J8 East 68th Street, New York, NY 10021).

[18]The phrase "proximate policy maker" is derived from political scientist Charles E. Lindbloom, who uses the term to distinguish between citizens and elected officials: "Except in small political systems that can be run by something like a New England town meeting, not all citizens can be the immediate, or proximate, makers of policy. They yield the immediate (or proximate) task of decision to a small minority." See Charles E. Lindbloom, *The Policy-Making Process* (Englewood Cliffs, N.J.: Prentice Hall, 1968), p. 30.

Many scholars concentrate their attention on this final phase of public policy making and conclude that policy making is a process of bargaining, competition, persuasion, and compromise among interest groups and government officials. Undoubtedly, bargaining, competition, persuasion, and compromises over policy issues continue throughout this final "law-making" phase of the policy-making process. Conflict between the president and Congress, or between Democrats and Republicans, or liberals and conservatives, and so forth, may delay or alter somewhat the final actions of the "proximate policy makers."

But the agenda for policy consideration has been set before the "proximate policy makers" become actively involved in the policy-making process—the major directions of policy change have been determined, and the mass media have prepared the public for new policies and programs. The formal law-making process concerns itself with details of implementation: who gets the "political" credit; what agencies get control of the program; and exactly how much money will be spent. These are not unimportant questions, but they are raised and decided within the context of policy goals and directions which have already been determined. The decisions of the "proximate policy makers" tend to center around the *means* rather than the *ends* of public policy.

PARTY INFLUENCE ON PUBLIC POLICY

Parties are important institutions in the American political system, but it would be a mistake to overestimate their impact on public policy. It makes relatively little difference in the major direction of public policy whether Democrats or Republicans dominate the political scene. American parties are largely "brokerage" organizations, devoid of ideology and committed to winning public office rather than to advancing policy positions. Both the Democratic and Republican parties and their candidates tailor their policy positions to societal conditions. The result is that the parties do not have much independent impact on policy outcomes.

Both American parties subscribe to the same fundamental political ideology. Both share prevailing democratic consensus about the sanctity of private property, a free enterprise economy, individual liberty, limited government, majority rule, and due process of law. Moreover, since the 1930s both parties have supported the same major domestic programs—social security, unemployment compensation, a national highway program, a federally aided welfare system, and countercyclical fiscal and monetary policies. Finally, both parties have supported the basic outlines of American foreign and military policy since World War II—international involvement, anticommunism, the cold war, European recovery, NATO, military preparedness, and even the Korean and Vietnam wars. A change in party control of the presidency or Congress has not resulted in any significant shifts in the course of American foreign or domestic policy.

Yet there are nuances of differences between the parties that can be observed in the policy-making process. The social bases of the Democratic and Republican parties are slightly different. Both parties draw support from all social groups in America, but the Democrats draw disproportionately from labor, big-city residents, ethnic voters, blacks, Jews, and Catholics; while Republicans draw disproportionately from rural, small-town, and suburban Protestants, businessmen, and professionals. To the extent that the policy orientations of these two broad groups differ, the thrust of party ideology also differs. However, the magnitude of this difference is not very great.

Conflict between parties occurs most frequently over issues involving social welfare programs, housing and urban development, Medicare, anti-poverty programs, and the regulation of business and labor. On some issues, such as civil rights and appropriations, voting will follow party lines during roll calls on preliminary motions, amendments, and other preliminary matters, but swing to a bipartisan vote on passage of the final legislation. This means that the parties have disagreed on certain aspects of the bill, but compromised on its final passage.

What are the issues that cause conflict between the Democratic and Republican parties? In general, Democrats have favored federal action to assist low-income groups through public assistance, housing, and anti-poverty programs; and generally a larger role for the federal government in launching new projects to remedy domestic problems. Republicans, on the other hand, have favored less government involvement in domestic affairs, and greater reliance on private action (see Table 13-1).

POLICY INNOVATION

Policy innovation has been a central concern of students of the policy processes.[19] Policy innovation is simply the readiness of a government to adopt new programs and policies. Several years ago, political scientist Jack L. Walker constructed an "innovation score" for the American states based upon elapsed time between the first state adoption of a program and its later adoption by other states. Walker monitored eighty-eight different programs adopted by twenty or more states, and he averaged each state's score on each program adoption to produce an index of innovation for each state. The larger the innovation score, the faster the state has been on the average in

[19]Victor Thompson, *Bureaucracy and Innovation* (Tuscaloosa: University of Alabama Press, 1969); Lawrence B. Mohr, "Determinants of Innovation in Organizations," *American Political Science Review,* 63 (March 1969), 111–26; Michael Aiken and Robert R. Alford, "Community Structure and Innovation: The Case for Public Housing," *American Political Science Review,* 64 (September 1970), 843–64; Jack L. Walker, "The Diffusion of Innovations Among the American States," *American Political Science Review,* 63 (September 1969), 880–99.

TABLE 13-1   Party Division on Selected Votes in Congress

	HOUSE VOTES			
	REPUBLICANS		DEMOCRATS	
	YES	NO	YES	NO
Medicare (1965)	65	73	248	42
Establish Department of Housing and Urban Development (1965)	9	118	208	66
Make Martin Luther King Jr.'s birthday a holiday	39	101	213	32
Chrysler loan guarantee (1979)	62	88	209	48
No abortion funds under Medicaid (1979)	119	23	116	132
Implement Panama Canal Treaty (1979)	19	125	173	78
Reagan domestic program budget cuts (1981)	191	0	62	182
Reagan income tax cuts (1981)	189	1	48	196
MX missile production (1985)	158	24	61	189
Federal aid for child care (1990)	47	119	218	26
Constitutional amendment to prohibit flag desecration (1990)	159	17	95	160

	SENATE VOTES			
	REPUBLICANS		DEMOCRATS	
	YES	NO	YES	NO
Medicare (1965)	13	14	55	7
Antiballistic missile (ABM) system (1970)	29	14	21	36
Increase food stamps (1976)	13	18	39	4
Delay production of B-1 bomber (1976)	7	22	37	15
Establish new cabinet-level Department of Education (1979)	18	17	51	5
Reagan income tax cuts (1981)	51	0	20	26
Reduce "Star Wars" funding (1985)	6	45	32	12
Capital gains tax cut (1989)	45	0	6	47
Constitutional amendment to prohibit flag desecration (1989)	33	11	18	37

Source: *Congressional Quarterly,* "Key votes" in various issues, 1965–1990.

responding to new ideas or policies.[20] Walker proceeded to explore relationships between innovation scores in the fifty states and socioeconomic, political, and regional variables. It turned out that innovation was more readily accepted in urban, industrialized, wealthy states.

However, in a subsequent study of policy innovation in the American states, Virginia Gray argued persuasively that no general tendency toward "innovativeness" really exists—that states which are innovative in one policy area are not necessarily the same states which are innovative in other policy areas. She examined the adoption of twelve specific innovations in civil rights,

[20]Walker, "Diffusion of Innovations Among the American States," p. 883.

welfare, and education, including the adoption of state public accommodations, fair housing and fair employment laws, and merit systems and compulsory school attendance. States that were innovative in education were not necessarily innovative in civil rights or welfare. Nonetheless, she discovered that "first adopters" of most innovations tended to be wealthier states.[21]

Let us try to explain why wealth, urbanization, and education are associated with policy innovation. First of all, *income* enables a state to afford the luxury of experimentation. Low incomes place constraints on the ability of policy makers to raise revenues to pay for new programs or policies; high incomes provide the *tax resources* necessary to begin new undertakings. We can also imagine that *urbanization* would be conducive to policy innovation. Urbanization involves social change and creates demands for new programs and policies, and urbanization implies the concentration of creative resources in large cosmopolitan centers. Rural societies change less rapidly and are considered less adaptive and sympathetic to innovation. Finally, it is not unreasonable to expect that *education* should facilitate innovation. An educated population should be more receptive toward innovation in public policy, and perhaps even more demanding of innovation in its appraisal of political candidates. In summary, wealth, urbanization, and education, considered together, should provide a socioeconomic environment conducive to policy innovation.

We might also expect both party competition and voter participation to affect policy innovation. Closely contested elections should encourage parties and candidates to put forward innovative programs and ideas to capture the imagination and support of the voter. Competitive states are more likely to experience turnover in party control of state government. Innovations in policy are more likely when a new administration takes office. An increase in political participation should also encourage policy innovation.

The decision-making milieu itself—characteristics of the legislative and executive branches of state government—can also be expected to influence policy innovation. Specifically, we expect that the ethic of "professionalism" among legislators and bureaucrats is a powerful stimulus to policy innovation. Professionalism involves, among other things, acceptance of professional reference groups as sources of information, standards, and norms. The professional bureaucrat attends national conferences, reads national journals, and perhaps even aspires to build a professional reputation that extends beyond the boundaries of a home state. Thus, he or she constantly encounters new ideas, and he or she is motivated to pursue innovation for the purpose of distinction in a chosen field. Moreover, one might argue that professional bureaucrats are also moved to propose innovative programs in order to expand their authority within the bureaucracy—"empire building."

[21]Virginia Gray, "Innovation in the States," *American Political Science Review*, 67 (December 1973), 1174–85.

TABLE 13-2 Correlates of Policy Innovation in the American States

FIGURES ARE SIMPLE CORRELATION COEFFICIENTS FOR RELATIONSHIPS WITH THE INNOVATION INDEX			
Income	.56	Party Competition	.34
Urbanization	.54	Voter Participation	.28
Education	.32	Civil Service Coverage	.53
Tax Revenue	.28	Legislative Professionalism	.62

All these factors—income, urbanization, education, tax revenue, party competition, voter participation, civil service coverage, and legislative professionalism—are *related* to policy innovation. Table 13-2 shows the simple correlation coefficients between each of these explanatory variables and the policy innovation scores.

Further causal analysis reveals that "professionalism" in the legislative and executive branches of state government appears to be the most direct source of policy innovation. We might speculate that professionalism among both legislators and bureaucrats encourages the development of national standards for governmental administration. Professionals know about programmatic developments elsewhere through professional meetings, journals, newsletters, etc. More importantly, they view themselves as professional administrators and governmental leaders and they seek to adopt the newest reforms and innovations for their own states. As Jack Walker comments, "They are likely to adopt a more cosmopolitan perspective and to cultivate their reputations within a national professional community rather than merely within their own state or agency.[22] Even if individual legislators themselves do not think in professional terms, legislatures with professional staffs may be influenced by these values.

Education, participation, and innovation appear to be linked in a causal fashion. This lends some limited support to the pluralist contention that an educated and active political constituency can have an impact on public policy—at least to the extent that such a constituency seems to promote novelty and experimentation in programs and policies. In summary, the explanation of policy innovation turns out to be one that emphasizes professionalism in legislature and bureaucracies, and an educated and politically active population.

SUMMARY

Systems theory helps us to conceptualize the linkages between the socioeconomic environment, the political system, and public policy, but it does not really describe what goes on inside the "black box" labeled "political

[22]Walker, "Diffusion of Innovations Among the American States."

system." The *process model* identifies a variety of activities which occur *within* the political system, including identification of problems and "agenda setting," formulating policies proposals, legitimating policies, implementing policies, and evaluating their effectiveness. Although political science has traditionally concerned itself with describing political institutions and processes, seldom has it systematically examined the impact of political processes on the *content* of public policy. Let us try to set forth some general propositions about the impact of political processes on policy content.

1. It is difficult to assess the independent effect of public opinion on public policy. Public policy may accord with mass opinion but we can never be certain whether mass opinion shaped public policy or public policy shaped mass opinion. The "public" does not have opinions on many major policy questions; public opinion is unstable; and decision makers can easily misinterpret as well as manipulate public opinion.

2. Public policy is more likely to conform to elite opinion than mass opinion. Elite opinion has been particularly influential in the determination of foreign policy. However, it is unlikely that elites can operate independently of socioeconomic resources and demands for very long.

3. Deciding what will be decided—agenda setting—is a crucial stage in the policy process. Policy issues do not just "happen." Preventing certain conditions in society from becoming policy issues—"nondecision making"—is an important political tactic of dominant interests.

4. The mass media, particularly the three television networks, play a major role in agenda setting. By deciding what will be "news," the media set the agenda for political discussion, whether or not the media can persuade voters to support one candidate or another. The continuing focus on the dramatic, violent, and negative aspects of American life may unintentionally create apathy and alienation—"television malaise."

5. A great deal of policy formulation occurs outside the formal governmental process. Prestigious, private, policy-planning organizations—such as the Council on Foreign Relations—explore policy alternatives, advise governments, develop policy consensus, and even supply top governmental leaders. The policy-planning organizations bring together the leadership of the corporate and financial worlds, the mass media, the foundations, the leading intellectuals, and top government officials.

6. The activities of the "proximate policy makers"—the president, Congress, executive agencies, and so forth—attract the attention of most commentators and political scientists. But nongovernmental leaders, in business and finance, foundations, policy-planning organizations, the mass media, and other interest groups, may have already set the policy agenda and selected major policy goals. The activities of the "proximate policy makers" tend to center around the *means,* rather than the *ends,* of public policy.

7. The Democratic and Republican parties have agreed on the basic outlines of American foreign and domestic policy since World War II. Thus,

partisanship has not been a central influence on public policy. However, there have been some policy differences between the parties. Differences have occurred most frequently over questions of welfare, housing and urban development, antipoverty efforts, health care, and the regulations of business and labor.

8. Most votes in Congress and state legislatures show the Democratic and Republican party majorities to be in agreement. However, when conflict occurs it is more likely to occur along party lines than any other kind of division.

9. Policy innovation—the readiness of a government to adopt new programs and policies—is linked to urbanization, education, and wealth, as well as competition, participation, and professionalism. Specifically, policy innovation appears to be a product of professionalism in legislatures and bureaucracies, and an educated and politically active population.

BIBLIOGRAPHY

DYE, THOMAS R. *Who's Running America: The Bush Era.* Englewood Cliffs, N.J.: Prentice-Hall, 1990.
EDELMAN, MURRAY. *The Symbolic Uses of Politics.* Urbana: University of Illinois Press, 1964.
ERIKSON, ROBERT S., NORMAN R. LUTTBEG, and KENT L. TEDIN. *American Public Opinion,* 3rd ed. New York: Macmillan, 1988.
EYESTONE, ROBERT. *From Social Issues to Public Policy.* New York: John Wiley, 1978.
KEY, V. O., JR., *Public Opinion and American Democracy.* New York: Knopf, 1967.
KINGDOM, JOHN W. *Agendas, Alternatives, and Public Policies.* Boston: Little, Brown, 1984.
SCHATTSCHNEIDER, E. E. *The Semisovereign People.* New York: Holt, Rinehart & Winston, 1960.

14

POLICY EVALUATION
finding out what happens
after a law is passed

To assess the impact of public policy, one must find changes in society that are associated with government activity. (David Valdez/The White House)

DOES THE GOVERNMENT KNOW WHAT IT IS DOING?

Americans generally assume that once we pass a law, create a bureaucracy, and spend money, the purpose of the law, the bureaucracy, and the expenditure should be achieved. We assume that when Congress adopts a policy and appropriates money for it, and when the executive branch organizes a program, hires people, spends money, and carries out activities designed to implement the policy, the effects of the policy will be felt by society and will be those intended by the policy. Unfortunately, these assumptions are not always warranted. The national experiences with many public programs indicate the need for careful appraisal of the real impact of public policy. America's problems cannot always be resolved by passing a law, creating a new bureaucracy, and throwing a few billion dollars in the general direction of the problem in the hope that it will go away.

Does the government really know what it is doing? Generally speaking, no. Governments usually know how much money they spend, how many persons ("clients") are given various services, how much these services cost, how their programs are organized, managed, and operated, and perhaps how influential interest groups regard their programs and services. But even if programs and policies are well organized, efficiently operated, widely utilized, adequately financed, and generally supported by major interest groups, we may still want to ask: "So what?"; "Do they work?"; "Do these programs have any beneficial effects on society?"; "Are the effects immediate or long-range? positive or negative?"; "What about persons *not* receiving these services?"; "What is the relationship between the costs of the program and the benefits to society?"; "Could we be doing something else with more benefit to society with the money and workforce devoted to these programs?" Unfortunately, governments have done very little to answer these more basic questions.

A candid report on federal evaluation effort is worth quoting at length:

> The most impressive finding about the evaluation of social programs in the federal government is that substantial work in this field has been almost nonexistent.
>
> Few significant studies have been undertaken. Most of those carried out have been poorly conceived. Many small studies around the country have been carried out with such lack of uniformity of design and objective that the results rarely are comparable or responsive to the questions facing policy makers.
>
> There is nothing akin to a comprehensive federal evaluation system. Even within agencies, orderly and integrated evaluation operations have not been established. . . .
>
> The impact of activities that cost the public millions, sometimes billions, of dollars has not been measured. One cannot point with confidence to the difference, if any, that most social programs cause in the lives of Americans.[1]

[1]Joseph S. Wholey et al., *Federal Evaluation Policy* (Washington, D.C.: Urban Institute, 1970), p. 15.

This is a damning appraisal. It is just as true today as it was twenty years ago. The government does not know how to tell whether or not most of the things it does are worth doing at all.

POLICY EVALUATION:
ASSESSING THE IMPACT OF PUBLIC POLICY

Policy evaluation is learning about the consequences of public policy. Other, more complex definitions have been offered: "Policy evaluation is the assessment of the overall effectiveness of a national program in meeting its objectives, or assessment of the relative effectiveness of two or more programs in meeting common objectives."[2] "We should reserve the name 'program evaluation' for when we are referring to a comprehensive evaluation of the entire system under consideration, and call it 'problem or procedure evaluation' when we refer to some segment within that system."[3] "Policy evaluation research is the objective, systematic, empirical examination of the effects ongoing policies and public programs have on their targets in terms of the goals they are meant to achieve."[4]

Note that some of these definitions tie evaluation to the stated "goals" of a program or policy. But since we do not always know what the "goals" of a program or policy really are, and because we know that some programs and policies pursue conflicting "goals," we will not limit our notion of policy evaluation to the achievement of goals. Instead, we will concern ourselves with *all* of the consequences of public policy, that is, with "policy impact."

The impact of a policy is all its *effects on real-world conditions*. The impact of a policy includes its:

1. impact on the target situation or group
2. impact on situations or groups other than the target ("spillover effects")
3. impact on future as well as immediate conditions
4. direct costs, in terms of resources devoted to the program
5. indirect costs, including loss of opportunities to do other things.

All the benefits and costs, both immediate and future, must be measured in terms of both *symbolic* and *tangible* effects.

Measuring Impact, Not Output.   "Policy impact" is not the same as "policy output." In assessing policy impact, we cannot be content simply to measure government activity. For example, the number of dollars spent per member

---

[2]Ibid., p. 25.

[3]Paul R. Binner, cited in Jack L. Franklin and Jean H. Thrasser, *An Introduction to Program Evaluation* (New York: John Wiley, 1976), p. 22.

[4]David Nachmias, *Public Policy Evaluation* (New York: St. Martin's Press, 1979), p. 4.

of a target group (per pupil educational expenditures, per capita welfare expenditures, per capita health expenditures) is not really a measure of the *impact* of a policy on the group. It is merely a measure of government activity—that is to say, a measure of *policy output*. Unfortunately many government agencies produce reams of statistics measuring outputs—such as welfare benefits paid, criminal arrests and prosecutions, Medicare payments, and school enrollments. But this "bean counting" tells us little about poverty, crime, health, or educational achievement. We cannot be satisfied with measuring how many times a bird flaps its wings, we must know how far the bird has flown. In *describing* public policy, or even in *explaining* its determinants, measures of policy output are important. But in assessing the *impact* of policy, we must find changes in society that are associated with measures of government activity.

Target Groups.   Identifying the *target groups* means defining the part of the population for whom the program is intended—such as the poor, the sick, the ill-housed. Then the desired effect of the program on the target group must be determined. Is it to change their physical or economic circumstances—for example, the percentage of blacks or women employed in professional or managerial jobs, the income of the poor, the housing conditions of ghetto residents? Or is it to change their knowledge, attitudes, awareness, interests, or behavior? If multiple effects are intended, what are the priorities among different effects—for example, is a high payoff in terms of positive attitudes toward the political system more valuable than tangible progress toward the elimination of black-white income differences? What are the possible unintended effects (side effects) on target groups—for example, does public housing achieve better physical environments for many urban blacks at the cost of increasing their segregation and alienation from the white community? What is the impact of a policy on the target group in proportion to that group's total need? Accurate data describing the unmet needs of the nation are not generally available, but it is important to estimate the denominator of total need so that we know how adequate our programs are. Moreover, such an estimate may also help in estimating symbolic benefits or costs; a program that promises to meet a national need but actually meets only a small proportion of it may generate great praise at first but bitterness and frustration later when it becomes known how small its impact is relative to the need.

Nontarget Groups.   All programs and policies have differential effects on various segments of the population. Identifying important *nontarget groups* for a policy is a difficult process. For example, what is the impact of the welfare reform on groups other than the poor—government bureaucrats, social workers, local political figures, working-class families who are not on welfare, taxpayers, and others? Nontarget effects may be expressed as benefits as well as costs, such as the benefits to the construction industry of public housing projects. And these effects may be symbolic as well as tangible—for example, wealthy liberals enjoy a good feeling from supporting antipoverty programs, whether the programs help the poor or not.

Short-Term and Long-Term Effects. When will the benefits or costs be felt? Is the program designed for short-term, emergency situations? Or is it a long-term, developmental effort? If it is short-term, what will prevent the processes of incrementalism and bureaucratization from turning it into a long-term program, even after immediate need is met? Many impact studies show that new or innovative programs have short-term positive effects—for example, Operation Head Start and other educational programs. However, the positive effects frequently disappear as the novelty and enthusiasm of new programs wear off. Other programs experience difficulties at first, as in the early days of social security and Medicare, but turn out to have "sleeper" effects, as in the widespread acceptance of social security today. Not all programs aim at the same degree of permanent or transient change.

Indirect and Symbolic Costs and Benefits. Programs are frequently measured in terms of their direct costs. We generally know how many dollars go into program areas, and we can even calculate (as in Chapter 9) the proportion of total governmental dollars devoted to various programs. Government agencies have developed various forms of cost-benefit analysis, such as Program, Planning, and Budgeting Systems (PPBS) and operations research, to identify the direct costs (usually, but not always, in dollars) of government programs. But it is very difficult to identify the indirect and symbolic costs of public programs. Rarely can all these cost factors be included in a formal decision-making model. Often political intuition is the best guide available to the policy maker in these matters. What are the symbolic costs for the working poor of large numbers of welfare recipients? What were the costs of the Vietnam War in terms of American morale and internal division and strife? Moreover, it is very difficult to measure benefits in terms of general social well-being. Cost accounting techniques developed in business were designed around units of production—automobiles, airplanes, tons of steel, etc. But how do we identify and measure units of social well-being?

Calculating Net Benefits and Costs. All these aspects of public policy are very difficult to identify, describe, and measure. Moreover, the task of calculating *net* impact of a public policy is truly awesome. The *net* impact would be all the symbolic and tangible benefits, both immediate and long range, minus all the symbolic and tangible costs, both immediate and future (see Table 14–1). Even if all the immediate and future and symbolic and tangible costs and benefits are *known* (and everyone *agrees* on what is a "benefit" and

TABLE 14-1 Assessing Policy Impact

	BENEFITS			COSTS	
	PRESENT	FUTURE		PRESENT	FUTURE
Target Groups and Situations	Symbolic Tangible	Symbolic Tangible		Symbolic Tangible	Symbolic Tangible
Nontarget Groups and Situations (Spillover)	Symbolic Tangible	Symbolic Tangible		Symbolic Tangible	Symbolic Tangible
	Sum Present Benefits	Sum Future Benefits		Sum Present Costs	Sum Future Costs
	Sum All Benefits		minus	Sum All Costs	
			Net Policy Impact		

what is a "cost"), it is still very difficult to come up with a net balance. Many of the items on both sides of the balance would defy comparison—for example, how do you subtract a tangible cost in terms of dollars from a symbolic reward in terms of the sense of well-being felt by individuals or groups?

THE SYMBOLIC IMPACT OF POLICY

The impact of a policy includes both its *symbolic* and *tangible* effects. Its symbolic impact deals with the perceptions that individuals have of government action and their attitudes toward it. Even if government policies do not succeed in reducing dependency, or eliminating poverty, or preventing crime, and so on, this may be a rather minor objection to them if the failure of government to *try* to do these things would lead to the view that society is "not worth saving." Individuals, groups, and whole societies frequently judge public policy in terms of its good intentions rather than its tangible accomplishments. The general popularity and public appraisal of a program may be unrelated to the real impact of a program in terms of desired results. The implication is that very popular programs may have little positive impact, and vice versa.

The policies of government may tell us more about the aspirations of a society and its leadership than about actual conditions. Policies do more than effect change in societal conditions; they also help hold people together and maintain an orderly state. For example, a government "war on poverty" may not have any significant impact on the poor, but it reassures moral persons, the affluent as well as the poor, that government "cares" about poverty. Whatever the failures of the antipoverty programs in tangible respects, their symbolic value may be more than redeeming. For example, whether the fair housing provisions of the Civil Rights Act of 1968 can be enforced or not, the fact that it is national policy to forbid discrimination in the sale or rental of housing reassures people of all races that their government does not condone such acts. There are many more examples of public policy serving as a symbol of what society aspires to be.

The subjective condition of the nation is clearly as important as the objective condition. For example, white prejudices about blacks in schools, in public accommodations, or in housing may be declining over time. But this may not reduce racial tension if blacks *believe* that racism is as prevalent as it ever was.

Once upon a time "politics" was described as "who gets what, when, and how." Today it seems that politics centers about "who *feels* what, when, and how." The smoke-filled room where patronage and pork were dispensed has been replaced with the talk-filled room where rhetoric and image are dispensed. What governments *say* is as important as what governments *do*. Television has made the image of public policy as important as the policy itself. Systematic policy analysis concentrates on what governments *do*, why they do it, and what difference it makes. It devotes less attention to what governments *say*. Perhaps this is a weakness in policy analysis. Our focus has been primarily upon activities of governments rather than the rhetoric of governments.

PROGRAM EVALUATION: WHAT GOVERNMENTS USUALLY DO

Most government agencies make some effort to review the effectiveness of their own programs. These reviews usually take one or another of the following forms:

Hearings and Reports.   This is the most common type of program review. Government administrators are asked by chief executives or legislators to give testimony (formally or informally) regarding the accomplishments of their own programs. Frequently, written "annual reports" are provided by program administrators. But testimonials and reports of administrators are not very objective means of program evaluation. They frequently magnify the benefits and minimize the costs of programs.

Site Visits.   Occasionally teams of high-ranking administrators, or expert consultants, or legislators, or some combination of these people, will decide to visit agencies or conduct inspections in the field. These teams can pick up impressionistic data about how programs are being run, whether programs are following specific guidelines, whether they have competent staffs, and sometimes whether or not the "clients" (target groups) are pleased with the services.

Program Measures. The data developed by government agencies themselves generally cover policy *output* measures: the number of recipients in various welfare programs; the number of persons in workforce training programs; the number of public hospital beds available; the tons of garbage collected; or the number of pupils enrolled. But these program measures rarely indicate what *impact* these numbers have on society: the conditions of life confronting the poor; the success of workforce trainees in finding and holding skilled jobs; the health of the nation's poor; the cleanliness of cities; and the ability of graduates to read and write and function in society.

Comparison with Professional Standards. In some areas of government activity, professional associations have developed standards of excellence. These standards are usually expressed as a desirable level of output: for example, the number of pupils per teacher, the number of hospital beds per 1,000 people, the number of cases for each welfare worker. Actual governmental outputs can be compared with "ideal" outputs. While such an exercise can be helpful, it still focuses on government outputs and not the *impact* of governmental activities on the conditions of target or nontarget groups. Moreover, the standards themselves are usually developed by professionals who are really guessing at what ideal levels of benefits and services should be. There is rarely any hard evidence that ideal levels of governmental output have any significant impact on society.

Evaluation of Citizen Complaints. Another common approach to program evaluation is the analysis of citizen complaints. But not all citizens voluntarily submit complaints or remarks regarding governmental programs. Critics of governmental programs are self-selected and they are rarely representative of the general public or even of the target groups of government programs. There is no way to judge whether the complaints of a vocal few are shared by the many more who have not spoken up. Occasionally, administrators develop questionnaires to give to participants in their program in order to learn what their complaints may be and whether they are satisfied or not. But these questionnaires really test *public opinion* toward the program and not its real impact on the lives of participants.

PROGRAM EVALUATION: WHAT GOVERNMENTS CAN DO

None of the common evaluative methods mentioned above really attempts to weigh *costs* against *benefits*. Indeed, administrators seldom calculate the ratio of costs to services—the dollars required to train one worker, to provide one hospital bed, to collect and dispose of one ton of garbage. It is even more difficult to calculate the costs of making specific changes in society— the dollars required to raise student reading levels by one grade, to lower the infant death rate by one point, to reduce the crime rate by one percent. To learn about the real *impact* of governmental programs on society, more complex and costly methods of program evaluation are required.

Systematic program evaluation involves *comparisons*—comparisons designed to estimate what changes in society can be attributed to the program rather than nonprogram factors. Ideally, this means comparing what "actually happened" to "what would have happened if the program had never been implemented." It is not difficult to measure what happened; unfortunately too much program evaluation stops here. The real problem is to measure what would have happened without a program, and then compare the two conditions of society. The difference must be attributable to the program itself and not to other changes which are occurring in society at the same time.

Before versus After Comparisons.   There are several common research designs in program evaluation.[5] The most common is the "before-and-after" study, which compares results in a jurisdiction at two points in time—one before the program was implemented and the other some time after implementation. Usually it is only target groups that are examined. These before and after comparisons are designed to show program impacts, but it is very difficult to know whether the changes observed, if any, came about as a result of the program or as a result of other changes which were occurring in society at the same time (see Design 1, Figure 14–1).

Projected-Trend-Line versus Postprogram Comparisons.   A better estimate of what would have happened without the program can be made by projecting past (preprogram) trends into the postprogram time period. Then these projections can be compared with what actually happened in society after the program was implemented. The difference between the projections based on preprogram trends and the actual postprogram data can be attributed to the program itself. Note that data on target groups or conditions must be obtained for several time periods before the program was initiated, so that a trend line can be established (see Design 2, Figure 14–1). This design is better than the before-and-after design, but it requires more effort on the part of program evaluators.

Comparisons Between Jurisdictions With and Without Programs.   Another common program evaluation design is to compare individuals who have par-

---

[5]The following discussion draws on Harry P. Hatry, Richard E. Winnie, and Donald M. Fisk, *Practical Program Evaluation* (Washington, D.C.: Urban Institute, 1973).

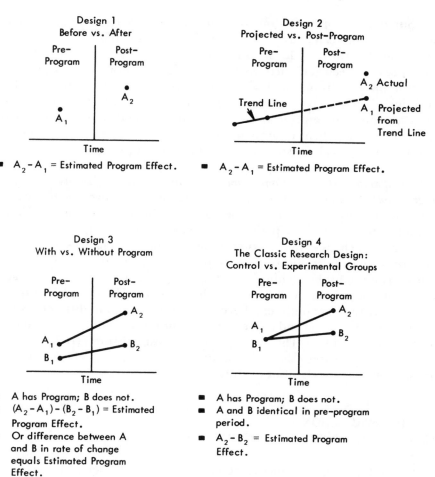

FIGURE 14-1   Policy Evaluation Research Designs.

ticipated in programs with those who have not; or to compare cities, states, or nations which have programs with those which do not. Comparisons are sometimes made in the postprogram period only; for exmaple, comparisons of the job records of those who have participated in workforce training programs with those who have not, or comparisons of homicide rates in states which have the death penalty with the homicide rates in states without the death penalty. But there are so many other differences between individuals or jurisdictions, that it is difficult to attribute differences in their conditions to differences in government programs. For example, persons who voluntarily enter a workforce training program may have greater motivation to find a job or different personal characteristics from those who do not. States with the death penalty may tend to be rural states which have lower homicide rates than urban states which may or may not have the death penalty.

Some of the problems involved in comparing jurisdictions with and without programs can be resolved if we observe both kinds of jurisdictions before and after the introduction of the program. This enables us to estimate differences between jurisdictions before program efforts are considered. After the program is initiated, we can observe whether the differences between jurisdictions have widened or not (see Design 3, Figure 14–1). This design provides some protection against attributing differences to a particular program when underlying socioeconomic differences between jurisdictions are really responsible for different outcomes.

Comparisons Between Control and Experimental Groups Before and After Program Implementation. The "classic" research design involves the careful selection of control and experimental groups which are identical in every way, the application of the policy to the experimental group only, and the comparison of changes in the experimental group with changes in the control group after the application of the policy. Initially, control and experimental groups must be identical, and the preprogram performance of each group must be measured and found to be the same. The program must be applied only to the experimental group. The postprogram differences between the experimental and control groups must be carefully measured (see Design 4, Figure 14–1). This classic research design is preferred by scientists because it provides the best opportunity of estimating changes which can be from the effects of other forces affecting society.

FEDERAL EVALUATION:
THE GENERAL ACCOUNTING OFFICE

The General Accounting Office (GAO) is an arm of the Congress. It has broad authority to audit the operations and finances of federal agencies, to evaluate their programs, and to report its findings to Congress. For most of its history, the GAO confined itself to financial auditing and management and administrative studies. In recent years, however, the GAO has increasingly undertaken *evaluative* research on government programs.

The GAO was established by Congress as an independent agency in 1921, in the same Budget and Accounting Act that created the first executive budget; its authority to undertake evaluation studies was expanded in the Congressional Budget and Impoundment Control Act of 1974, the same act that established the House and Senate Budget Committees and the Congressional Budget Office (see Chapter 9). The GAO is headed by the Comptroller General of the United States. Most GAO reports are requested by Congress, although the office can undertake studies on its own initiative.

According to the GAO, "Program evaluation—when it is available and of high quality—provides sound information about what programs are actually delivering, how they are being managed, and the extent to which they are cost-effective."[6] The GAO believes that evaluation efforts by federal agencies fall woefully short of what is required for rational decision making. The GAO has been especially critical of the Defense Department for failing to test weapons systems adequately, or to monitor defense contractors and their charges, or to adjust its future plans to expected reductions in defense spending (see Chapter 8). The GAO has criticized the Environmental Protection Agency for measuring its own success in terms of "input measures"—numbers of inspections performed and enforcement actions undertaken—rather than actual improvements in environmental conditions, such as in water quality or air quality (see Chapter 7). The GAO has also reported on the social security trust fund and the dangers of spending trust fund money on current governmental operations (see Chapter 5). It has reported on the high and growing cost of medical care in the United States, especially Medicaid and Medicare, and noted the lack of correlation between medical spending and measures of the nation's health (see Chapter 5). The GAO has strongly urged Congress and the president to reduce annual deficits, and has provided information on both official budget deficits and additional "off-budget" debts (see Chapter 9). It has undertaken to assess the overall impact of drug control policies (see Chapter 4), and it has studied the default rate on student loans and recommended collection of overdue loans by the Internal Revenue Service's withholding of tax refunds (see Chapter 3). In short, the GAO has been involved in virtually every major policy question confronting the nation.[7]

EXPERIMENTAL POLICY RESEARCH:
THE GUARANTEED INCOME EXPERIMENTS

Many policy analysts argue that "policy experimentation" offers the best opportunity to determine the impact of public policies. This opportunity rests upon the main characteristics of experimental research: the systematic selection of experimental and control groups, the application of the policy under study to the experimental group only, and the careful comparison of differences between the experimental and the control groups after the application of the policy.

Evaluating the Effects of a Guaranteed Income.   Some interesting examples of government policy experimentation occurred in research on the effects of a government-guaranteed family income. Debates over welfare reform

---

[6]General Accounting Office, *Federal Evaluation Issues* (Washington, D.C.: General Accounting Office, 1989).

[7]See General Accounting Office, *Annual Index of Reports Issued* (Washington, D.C.: General Accounting Office, annual).

have long generated certain questions that social science presumably could answer with careful, controlled experimentation. Would a guaranteed family income reduce the incentive to work? If payments were made to poor families with employable male heads, would the men drop out of the labor force? Would the level of the income guarantee or the steepness of the reductions of payments with increases in earnings make any difference in working behavior? Because welfare programs did not provide a guaranteed minimum family income, make payments to families with employable males, or graduate payments in relation to earnings, these questions could only be answered through *policy experimentation.*

The New Jersey Guaranteed Income Experiment. During President Lyndon Johnson's "war on poverty" the Office of Economic Opportunity (OEO) undertook one of the first large scale experimental studies of public policy ever attempted by the federal government. The New Jersey Graduated Work Incentive Experiment was designed to resolve some serious questions about the impact of welfare payments on the incentives for poor people to work. In order to learn more about the potential effects of a guaranteed family incomes, the Office of Economic Opportunity funded a three-year social experiment involving 1,350 families in New Jersey and Pennsylvania, beginning in 1968. The research was conducted by the Institute for Research on Poverty at the University of Wisconsin.[8] To ascertain the effects of different levels of guaranteed income, four guarantee levels were established. Some families were chosen to receive 50 percent of the Social Security Administration's poverty level income, others 75 percent, others 100 percent, and still others 125 percent. In order to ascertain the effects of graduated payments in relation to earnings, some families had their payments reduced by 30 percent of their outside earnings, others 50 percent, and still others 70 percent. Finally, a control sample was observed—low-income families who received no payments at all.

Enter Politics. But political events moved swiftly and soon engulfed the study. In 1969 President Nixon proposed the Family Assistance Plan (FAP) to Congress, which promised all families a minimum income of 50 percent of the poverty level and a payment reduction of 50 percent of outside earnings. The Nixon administration had not waited to learn the results of the OEO experiment before introducing FAP. Nixon wanted welfare reform to be his priority domestic legislation and the bill was symbolically numbered HR 1 (House of Representatives Bill 1).

After the FAP bill had been introduced, the Nixon administration pressured OEO to produce favorable supporting evidence on behalf of the guaranteed income—specifically, evidence that a guaranteed income at the

[8]See Harold M. Watts, "Graduated Work Incentives: An Experiment in Negative Taxation," *American Economic Review*, 59 (May 1969), 463–72.

levels proposed in FAP would *not* reduce incentives to work among the poor. The OEO obliged by hastily publishing a short report, "Preliminary Results of the New Jersey Graduated Work Incentive Experiment," which purported to show that there were no differences in the outside earnings of families receiving guaranteed incomes (experimental group) and those who were not (control group).[9]

The director of the research, economics professor Harold Watts of the University of Wisconsin, warned that "the evidence from this preliminary and crude analysis of the earliest results is less than ideal." But he concluded that "no evidence has been found in the urban experiment to support the belief that negative-tax type income-maintenance programs will produce large disincentives and consequent reductions in earnings." Moreover, the early results indicated that families in all the separate experimental groups, with different guaranteed minimums and different graduated payment schedules, behaved in a fashion similar to each other and to the control group receiving no payments at all. Predictably, later results confirmed the preliminary results, which were produced to assist the FAP bill in Congress.[10]

Reanalyzing the Data. However, when the results of the Graduated Work Incentive Experiment later were *reanalyzed* by the Rand Corporation (which was not responsible for the design of the original study), markedly different results were produced.[11] The Rand Corporation reports that the Wisconsin researchers working for OEO originally chose New Jersey because it had no state welfare programs for "intact" families—families headed by an able-bodied, working-age male. The guaranteed incomes were offered to these families to compare their work behavior with control group families. *But* six months after the experiment began, New Jersey changed its state law and offered *all* families (experimental *and* control group families) very generous welfare benefits—benefits equal to those offered participants in the experiment. This meant that for most of the period of the experiment, the "control" group was being given benefits which were equivalent to the "experimental" groups—an obvious violation of the experimental research design. The OEO-funded University of Wisconsin researchers failed to consider this factor in their research. Thus, they concluded that there were no significant differences between the work behaviors of experimental and control groups, and they implied that a national guaranteed income would not be a disincentive to work. The Rand Corporation researchers, on the other

[9]U.S. Office of Economic Opportunity, "Preliminary Results of the New Jersey Graduated Work Incentive Experiment," 18 February 1970. Also cited in Alice M. Rivlin, *Systematic Thinking for Social Action* (Washington, D.C.: Brookings Institution, 1971).

[10]David Kershaw and Jerelyn Fair, eds. *Final Report of the New Jersey Graduated Work Incentive Experiment* (University of Wisconsin, Institute for Research on Poverty, 1974).

[11]John F. Cogan, *Negative Income Taxation and Labor Supply: New Evidence from the New Jersey-Pennsylvania Experiment* (Santa Monica, Calif.: Rand Corporation, 1978).

hand, considered the New Jersey state welfare program in their estimates of work behavior. Rand concluded that recipients of a guaranteed annual income will work 6.5 fewer hours per week than they otherwise would work in the absence of such a program. In short, Rand study suggests that a guaranteed annual income will produce a very substantial disincentive to work.

The Rand study was published in 1978 after enthusiasm in Washington for a guaranteed annual income program had already cooled. The Rand study conflicted with the earlier OEO study and confirmed the intuition of many members of Congress that guaranteed annual income would reduce willingness to work. The Rand study also suggested that a *national* program might be very costly and involve some payments to nearly half the nation's families. Finally, the Rand study noted that its own estimates of high costs and work disincentives may "seriously understate the expected cost of an economy-wide ... program."

A New Study.   The controversy surrounding the flawed New Jersey study prompted a new effort to assess the effects of a guaranteed annual income on work incentives. The states of Washington and Colorado contracted with two independent research firms, SRI International and Mathematica Policy Research, for a guaranteed income experiment that was much larger (almost 5000 families) and lasted longer (five years) than previous experiments.[12] The study was launched in Seattle and Denver and earned the label SIME/DIME (for Seattle/Denver Income Maintenance Experiment) study. Like the New Jersey study, this experiment included a control group of families receiving no cash payments and several experimental groups receiving smaller and larger cash payments and subject to different rates of payment reductions with increases in earned income. But SIME/DIME also introduced job counseling and training to some groups to test whether income payments combined with counseling and training would increase the likelihood of persons joining the workforce. Some families were guaranteed income for only three years while others received a five-year guarantee. The families selected were representative of the likely population to be included in any national guaranteed income program. The working behavior of both husbands and wives in intact families and single women in female headed families was examined.

Different Results.   The SIME/DIME study produced a series of important findings that contrasted sharply with the early report on the New Jersey experiment and that severely undermined the future prospects for enacting a national guaranteed family income. The following were among the most notable findings:

[12]SRI International, *Final Report of the Seattle-Denver Income Maintenance Experiment* (Washington, D.C.: Washington Government Printing Office, 1983).

1. Job counseling and training had *no* effect on persons' earnings or hours of work over five years.

2. A guaranteed income significantly lowered earnings and hours of work for husbands (a decline of 13.6 percent), wives (a decline of 27.1 percent), and female heads of households (a decline of 31.8). However the size of the cash payment did not affect the decline in work, and the response to various rates of reductions in payments with earnings was minimal.

3. Persons in families selected for a five-year guarantee worked significantly less than those selected for only a three-year guarantee.

4. Husband-wife families selected for income guarantees suffered significantly more marital dissolutions than the control group receiving no income payments.

PROBLEMS IN POLICY EXPERIMENTATION

The whole excursion into government-sponsored policy experimentation raises a series of important questions. First of all, are government-sponsored research projects predisposed to produce results supportive of popular reform proposals? Are social scientists, whose personal political values are generally liberal and reformist, inclined to produce findings in support of liberal reform measures? Would the OEO have rushed to produce "preliminary findings" in the New Jersey experiment *if* they had shown that the guarantees did in fact reduce the incentive to work? Or would such early results be set aside as "too preliminary" to publish? Because the participants in the experiment knew that they were singled out for experimentation, did they behave differently than they would have if the program had been applied universally? Would the work ethic be impaired if *all* American families were guaranteed a minimum income for life rather than a few selected families for a temporary period of time? Thus, the questions raised by this experiment affect not only the issues of welfare policy but also the validity of policy experimentation itself.

Experimental strategies in policy impact research raise still other problems. Do government researchers have the right to withhold public services from individuals simply to provide a control group for experimentation? In the medical area, where the giving or withholding of treatment can result in death or injury, the problem is obvious and many attempts have been made to formulate a code of ethics. But in the area of social experimentation, what are we to say to control groups who are chosen to be similar to experimental groups but denied benefits in order to serve as a base for comparison? Setting aside the legal and moral issues, it will be politically difficult to provide services for some people and not others. Perhaps only the fact that relatively few Americans knew about the New Jersey experiment kept it from becoming a controversial topic.

Another reservation about policy-impact research centers on the bias of social scientists and their government sponsors. "Successful" experiments—where the proposed policy achieves positive results—will receive more acclaim and produce greater opportunities for advancement for social scientists and administrators than will "unsuccessful" experiments. Liberal, reform-oriented social scientists *expect* liberal reforms to produce positive results. When reforms appear to do so, the research results are immediately accepted and published; but when results are unsupportive or negative, social scientists may be inclined to go back and recode their data, or redesign their research, or reevaluate their results because they believe a "mistake" must have been made. The temptation to "fudge the data," "reinterpret" the results, coach participants on what to say or do, and so forth, will be very great. In the physical and biological sciences the temptation to "cheat" in research is reduced by the fact that research can be replicated and the danger of being caught and disgraced is very great. But social experiments can seldom be replicated perfectly, and replication seldom brings the same distinction to a social scientist as does the original research.

People behave differently when they know they are being watched. Students, for example, generally perform at a higher level when something— anything—new and different is introduced into the classroom routine. This "Hawthorne effect"[13] may cause a new program or reform to appear more successful than the old, but it is the newness itself that produces improvement rather than the program or reform.

Another problem in policy impact research is that results obtained with small-scale experiments may differ substantially from what would occur if a large-scale nationwide program were adopted. For example, a guaranteed annual income for a small number of families in New Jersey and Pennsylvania—a guarantee that lasted only three years—may not trigger as much change in attitudes toward work as a *nationwide* program guaranteed to last *indefinitely*. In the New Jersey experiment, participants may have continued to behave as their neighbors did. But if everyone had been guaranteed a minimum income, community standards might have changed and affected the behavior of all recipient families.

Finally, we must acknowledge that the political milieu shapes policy research. Politics helps decide what policies and policy alternatives will be studied. Certainly the decision to study the effects of a guaranteed annual income arose from the interest of reformers in proving that such a program would not reduce incentives to work, as charged by some opponents. Politics can also affect findings themselves, and certainly the interpretations and uses of policy research are politically motivated. Can it be merely coincidental that the guaranteed annual income was found to have no adverse effects when it was widely supported in the early 1970s, but it was later found to have

[13]The term is taken from early experiments at the Hawthorne plant of Western Electric Company in Chicago in 1927. It was found that worker output increased with any change in routine, even decreasing the lighting in the plant. See David L. Sills, ed., *International Encyclopedia of the Social Sciences*, 7 (New York: Free Press, 1968), 241.

major adverse effects on working behavior in the late 1970s after support for the program had declined?

Despite these problems, the advantages of policy experimentation are substantial. It is exceedingly costly for society to commit itself to large-scale programs and policies in education, welfare, housing, health, and so on, without any real idea about what works. Increasingly, we can expect the federal government to strive to test newly proposed policies and reforms before committing the nation to massive new programs.

PROGRAM EVALUATION: WHY IT USUALLY FAILS

Occasionally government agencies attempt their own policy evaluations. Government analysts and administrators report on the conditions of target groups before and after their participation in a new program and some effort is made to attribute observed changes to the new program itself. Policy experimentation is less frequent; seldom do governments systematically select experimental and control groups of the population, introduce a new program to the experimental group only, and then carefully compare changes in the conditions of the experimental group with a control group that has not benefited from the program. Let us turn first to some of the problems confronting policy evaluation studies.

1. The first problem confronting anyone who wants to evaluate a public program is to determine what the goals of the program are. What are the target groups and what are the desired effects? But governments often pursue incompatible goals to satisfy very diverse groups. Overall policy planning and evaluation may reveal inconsistencies of public policy and force reconsideration of fundamental societal goals. Where there is little agreement on the goals of a public program, evaluation studies may engender a great deal of political conflict. Government agencies generally prefer to avoid conflict, and hence to avoid studies that would raise such questions.

2. Many programs and policies have primarily symbolic value. They do not actually change the conditions of target groups but merely make these groups feel that the government "cares." A government agency does not welcome a study that reveals that its efforts have no tangible effects; such a revelation itself might reduce the symbolic value of the program by informing target groups of its uselessness.

3. Government agencies have a strong vested interest in "proving" that their programs have a positive impact. Administrators frequently view attempts to evaluate the impact of their programs as attempts to limit or destroy their programs, or to question the competence of the administrators.

4. Government agencies usually have a heavy investment—organizational, financial, physical, psychological—in current programs and policies. They are predisposed against finding that these policies do not work.

5. Any serious study of policy impact undertaken by a government agency would involve some interference with ongoing program activities. The press of day-to-day business generally takes priority over study and evaluation in a governmental agency. More importantly, the conduct of an experiment may necessitate depriving individuals or groups (control groups) of services to which they are entitled under law; this may be difficult, if not impossible, to do.

6. Program evaluation requires funds, facilities, time, and personnel, which government agencies do not like to sacrifice from ongoing programs. Policy-impact studies, like any research, cost money. They cannot be done well as extracurricular or part-time activities. Devoting resources to study may mean a sacrifice in program resources that administrators are unwilling to make.

HOW BUREAUCRATS EXPLAIN NEGATIVE FINDINGS

Government administrators and program supporters are ingenious in devising reasons why negative findings about policy impact should be rejected. Even in the face of clear evidence that their favorite programs are useless or even counterproductive, they will argue that:

1. The effects of the program are long range and cannot be measured at the present time.

2. The effects of the program are diffuse and general in nature; no single criterion or index adequately measures what is being accomplished.

3. The effects of the program are subtle and cannot be identified by crude measures or statistics.

4. Experimental research cannot be carried out effectively because to withhold services from some persons to observe the impact of such withholding would be unfair to them.

5. The fact that no difference was found between persons receiving the services and those not receiving them means that the program is not sufficiently intensive and indicates the need to spend *more* resources on the program.

6. The failure to identify any positive effects of a program is attributable to inadequacy or bias in the research itself, not in the program.

Harvard professor James Q. Wilson formulated two general laws to cover all cases of social science research on policy impact:

Wilson's First Law: All policy interventions in social problems produce the intended effect—if the research is carried out by those implementing the policy or by their friends.

Wilson's Second Law: No policy intervention in social problems produces the intended effect—if the research is carried out by independent third parties, especially those skeptical of the policy.

Wilson denies that his laws are cynical. Instead he reasons that

> Studies that conform to the First Law will accept an agency's own data about what it is doing and with what effect; adopt a time frame (long or short) that maximizes the probability of observing the desired effect; and minimize the search for other variables that might account for the effect observed. Studies that conform to the Second Law will gather data independently of the agency; adopt a short time frame that either minimizes the chance for the desired effect to appear or, if it does appear, permits one to argue that the results are "temporary" and probably due to the operation of the "Hawthorne Effect" (i.e., the reaction of the subjects to the fact that they are part of an experiment); and maximize the search for other variables that might explain the effects observed.[14]

WHY GOVERNMENT PROGRAMS ARE SELDOM TERMINATED

Government programs are rarely terminated. Even when evaluative studies produce negative findings; even when policy-makers themselves are fully aware of fraud, waste, and inefficiency in programs; even when highly negative benefit-cost ratios are reported; government programs manage to survive. Once policy is institutionalized within government, it is extraordinarily difficult to terminate.

Why is it so difficult for governments to terminate failed programs and policies? The answer to this question varies from one program to another, but a few generalizations are possible.

Concentrated Benefits, Dispersed Costs. Perhaps the most common reason for the continuation of inefficient government programs and policies is that their limited benefits are concentrated in a small, well-organized constituency, while their greater costs are dispersed over a large, unorganized, uninformed public. Although few in number, the beneficiaries of a program are strongly committed to it; they are concerned, well-informed, and active in their support of it. If the costs of the program are spread widely among all taxpayers, no one has a strong incentive to become informed, organized, or active in opposition to it. Although the costs of a failed program may be enormous, if these costs are dispersed widely enough so that no one individual or group bears a significant burden, there will be little incentive to organize an effective opposition. (Consider the case of a government subsidy program for tobacco growers. If $250 million per year were distributed to 5,000 growers, each would average $50,000 in subsidy income. If each grower would contribute 10 percent of this subsidy to a political fund to reward friendly legislators, the fund could distribute $25 million in cam-

---

[14]James Q. Wilson, "On Pettigrew and Armor," *The Public Interest,* 31 (Spring 1973), 132–34.

paign contributions. If the costs of the program could be dispersed evenly among 250 million Americans, each would pay only one dollar. No one would have a sufficient incentive to become informed, organized, or active in opposition to the subsidy program. So it would continue, regardless of its limited benefits and extensive costs to society.) When program costs are widely dispersed, it is irrational for individuals, each of which bears only a tiny fraction of these costs, to expand the time, energy, and money to counter the support of the program's beneficiaries.

Legislative and Bureaucratic Interests.   Among the beneficiaries of any government program are those who administer and supervise it. Bureaucratic jobs depend on a program's continuation. Government positions, with all of their benefits, pay, prerequisites, and prestige, are at stake. There are strong incentives for bureaucrats to resist or undermine negative evaluations of their programs, to respond to public criticism by making only marginal changes in their programs or even by claiming that their programs are failing because *not enough* is being spent on them.

Legislative systems, both in Congress and in state capitals, are structured so that legislators with the most direct control over programs are usually the most friendly to them. The committee system, with its fragmentation of power and invitation to log-rolling ("You support my committee's report and I'll support yours.") favors retention of existing programs and policies. Legislators on committees with jurisdiction over programs are usually the largest recipients of campaign contributions from the organized beneficiaries of the programs. These legislators can use their committee positions to protect failed programs, to minimize reform, and to block termination. Even without the incentives of bureaucratic position and legislative power, no public official wants publicly to acknowledge failure.

Incrementalism at Work.   Governments seldom undertake to consider any program as a whole in any given year. Active consideration of programs is made at the margin—that is, attention is focused on proposed changes in existing programs rather than on the value of programs in their entirety. Usually this attention comes in the budgetary process (see Chapter 9), when proposed increases or decreases in funding are under discussion in the bureaucracy and the legislature. Negative evaluative studies can play a role in the budgetary process—limiting increases for failed programs or perhaps even identifying programs ripe for budget-cutting. But attention is almost always focused on changes or reforms, increases or decreases, rather than on the complete termination of programs. Even mandating "sunset" legislation used in many states (requiring legislatures periodically to reconsider and reauthorize whole programs), seldom results in program termination.

Failed programs can also be "repackaged"—given new names and agency titles, while maintaining essentially the same goals, the same bureaucracy, and the same policy prescriptions. Many of the programs of Lyndon Johnson's "War on Poverty" of the 1960s were repackaged and placed in different federal departments following the official termination of the Office of Economic Opportunity. After much adverse publicity, the failed CETA job program (Comprehensive Employment and Training Act) was repackaged by Senators Edward Kennedy and Dan Quayle as the JTPS (Job Training and Placement Service program) with only modest reforms.

Complete program terminations in Washington are very rare. Among the precious few major program terminations have been: airline regulation of interstate routes and fares in 1978 and the abolishment of the Civil Aeronautics Board; general revenue sharing (federal sharing of general tax revenues with state and local governments) in 1986; oil price controls in 1980. Each of these terminations generated a great deal of controversy and each involved very special circumstances. Marginal policy changes are much easier to accomplish than program terminations.

THE LIMITS OF PUBLIC POLICY

Never have Americans expected so much of their government. Our confidence in what governments can do seems boundless. We have come to believe that governments can eliminate poverty, end racism, ensure peace, prevent crime, restore cities, provide energy, clean the air and water, and so on, if only they will adopt the right policies.

Perhaps confidence in the potential effectiveness of public policy is desirable, particularly if it inspires us to continue to search for ways to resolve societal problems. But any serious study of public policy must also recognize the limitations of policy in affecting societal conditions. Let us summarize these limitations:

1. Some societal problems are incapable of solution because of the way in which they are defined. If problems are defined in *relative* rather than *absolute* terms, they may never be resolved by public policy. For example, if the poverty line is defined as the line which places one-fifth of the population below it, then poverty will always be with us regardless of how well off the "poor" may become. Relative disparities in society may never be eliminated. Even if income differences among classes were tiny, then tiny differences may come to have great symbolic importance, and the problem or inequality may remain.

2. Expectations may always outrace the capabilities of governments. Progress in any policy area may simply result in an upward movement in expectations about what policy should accomplish. Public education never faced a "dropout" problem until the 1960s, when, for the first time, a majority of boys and girls were graduating from high school. At the turn of the century, when high school graduation was rare, there was no mention

of a dropout problem. Graduate rates have been increasing every year, as has concern for the dropout problem.

3. Policies that solve the problems of one group in society may create problems for other groups. In a plural society one person's solution may be another person's problem. For example, solving the problem of inequality in society may mean redistributive tax and spending policies which take from persons of above-average wealth to give to persons with below-average wealth. The latter may view this as a solution, but the former may view this as creating serious problems. There are *no* policies which can simultaneously attain mutually exclusive ends.

4. It is quite possible that some societal forces cannot be harnessed by governments, even if it is desirable to do so. It may turn out that government cannot stop urban migration patterns of whites and blacks, even if it tries to do so. Whites and blacks may separate themselves regardless of government policies in support of integration. Some children may not be able to learn much in public schools no matter what is done. Governments may be unable to forcibly remove children from disadvantaged environments because of family objections, even if this proves to be the only way to ensure equality of opportunity, and so on. Governments may not be *able* to bring about some societal changes.

5. Frequently people adapt themselves to public policies in ways that render the policies useless. For example, we may solve the problem of poverty by government guarantees of a high annual income, but by so doing we may reduce incentives to work and thus swell the number of dependent families beyond the fiscal capacities of government to provide guarantees. Of course, we do not really *know* the impact of income guarantees on the work behavior of the poor, but the possibility exists that adaptive behavior may frustrate policy.

6. Societal problems may have multiple causes, and a specific policy may not be able to eradicate the problem. For example, job training may not affect the hardcore unemployed if their employability is also affected by chronic poor health.

7. The solution to some problems may require policies that are more costly than the problem. For example, it may turn out that certain levels of public disorder—including riots, civil disturbances, and occasional violence—cannot be eradicated without the adoption of very repressive policies—the forceable break-up of revolutionary parties, restrictions on the public, appearances of demagogues, the suppression of hate literature, the addition of large numbers of security forces, and so on. But these repressive policies would prove too costly in terms of democratic values—freedom of speech and press, rights of assembly, freedom to form opposition parties. Thus, a certain level of disorder may be the price we pay for democracy. Doubtless there are other examples of societal problems that are simply too costly to solve.

8. The political system is not structured for completely rational decision making. The solution of societal problems generally implies a rational model, but government may not be capable of formulating policy in a rational fashion. Instead the political system may reflect group interests, elite preferences, environmental forces, or incremental change, more than rationalism. Presumably, a democratic system is structured to reflect mass influences, whether these are rational or not. Elected officials respond to the demands of their constituents, and this may inhibit completely rational approaches to public policy. Social science information does not exist to find policy solutions even if there are solutions. Moreover even where such information exists, it may not find its way into the political arena.

BIBLIOGRAPHY

BINGHAM, RICHARD D., and CLAIRE L. FELBINGER. *Evaluation in Practice.* New York: Longman, 1989.
HATRY, HARRY P., RICHARD E. WINNIE and DONALD M. FISK. *Practical Program Evaluation.* Washington, D.C.: Urban Institute, 1973.
HATRY, HARRY P., LOUIS BLAIR, DONALD FISK, and WAYNE KIMMEL. *Program Analysis for State and Local Governments.* Washington, D.C.: The Urban Institute, 1987.
MANHEIM, CAROL B., and RICHARD C. RICH. *Empirical Political Analysis.* 2nd ed. New York: Longman, 1986.
NACHMIAS, DAVID. *Public Policy Evaluation.* New York: St. Martin's, 1979.
PRESSMAN, JEFFREY L., and AARON WILDAVSKY. *Implementation.* Berkeley: University of California Press, 1974.
RIVLIN, ALICE M. *Systematic Thinking for Social Action.* Washington, D.C.: Brookings Institution, 1971.
WHOLEY, JOSEPH S., et al. *Federal Evaluation Policy.* Washington, D.C.: Urban Institute, 1970.
WILDAVSKY, AARON. *Speaking Truth to Power.* New York: John Wiley, 1979.

INDEX